The Writer on Film

The Writer on Film

Screening Literary Authorship

Edited by

Judith Buchanan

First published 2013 by
PALGRAVE MACMILLAN

Palgrave Macmillan in the UK is an imprint of Macmillan Publishers Limited, registered in England, company number 785998, of Houndmills, Basingstoke, Hampshire RG21 6XS.

Palgrave Macmillan in the US is a division of St Martin's Press LLC, 175 Fifth Avenue, New York, NY 10010.

Palgrave Macmillan is the global academic imprint of the above companies and has companies and representatives throughout the world.

Palgrave® and Macmillan® are registered trademarks in the United States, the United Kingdom, Europe and other countries.

ISBN 978–0–230–31384–2

This book is printed on paper suitable for recycling and made from fully managed and sustained forest sources. Logging, pulping and manufacturing processes are expected to conform to the environmental regulations of the country of origin.

A catalogue record for this book is available from the British Library.

A catalog record for this book is available from the Library of Congress.

Typeset by MPS Limited, Chennai, India.

for M and D,
with love

Contents

List of Figures ix

Notes on Contributors xi

Acknowledgements xiv

Introduction 3
Image, story, desire: the writer on film
Judith Buchanan

Part I   Cinema's Versions and Uses of Literary Lives

1   The writer in film: authorship and imagination 35
Laura Marcus

Gendered Authorship I
2   'Here is the story of my career…': the woman writer on film 50
Sonia Haiduc

Gendered Authorship II
3   'Mad, bad and dangerous to know': the male poet in
Sylvia (2003) and *The Edge of Love* (2008) 64
Siân Harris

Romantic Authorship
4   Romantic genius on screen: Jane Campion's *Bright Star* (2009)
and Julien Temple's *Pandaemonium* (2000) 77
Julian North

Authorship Iconized, Metonymized, Debunked
5   The 'tables of memory': Shakespeare, cinema and
the writing desk 92
Megan Murray-Pepper

Authorship Commercialized
6   Brit-lit biopics, 1990–2010 106
Andrew Higson

7   Literary biopics: a literary biographer's perspective 121
Geoffrey Wall

Part II Cinema's Authorial Proxies and Fictional Authors

Authorial Proxies I
8 Hemingway adapted: screening the star author 137
R. Barton Palmer

Authorial Proxies II
9 Becoming Jane in screen adaptations of Austen's fiction 151
Deborah Cartmell

Authorial Proxies III
10 Duplicated and duplicitous self-configurings in
Kaufman's *Adaptation* (2002) 164
Gennelle Smith

Architectures of Accreditation
11 Writing the endings of cinema: saving film authorship in the
cinematic paratexts of *Prospero's Books*, Taymor's
The Tempest and *The Secret of Kells* 178
Richard Burt

Fictional Writers on Screen I: Letters
12 Deliveries of absence: epistolary structures in classical cinema 193
Clara Rowland

Fictional Writers on Screen II: Diaries
13 'Far from literature': writing as bare act in Robert Bresson's
Journal d'un curé de campagne (1951) 206
Erica Sheen

Fictional Writers on Screen III: Plays and Factual Reports
14 Documentary li(v)es: writing falsehoods, righting wrongs in
von Donnersmarck's *The Lives of Others* (2006) 218
Judith Buchanan

Select Filmography 236

Bibliography 246

Index 259

List of Figures

Figures

I.1 Stills from: (a) *A Tale of Two Cities* (dir. Frank Lloyd, 1917); (b) *Julia* (dir. Fred Zinnemann, 1977); (c) *Prospero's Books* (dir. Peter Greenaway, 1991); (d) *The Lives of Others* (dir. Florian Henckel von Donnersmarck, 2006); (e) *Becoming Jane* (dir. Julian Jarrold, 2007); (f) *Howl* (dirs Rob Epstein and Jeffrey Friedman, 2010) 2

I.2 Copyright deposit still from Georges Méliès' *Shakespeare Writing Julius Caesar* (1907). Courtesy of the Motion Picture, Broadcasting and Recorded Sound Division of the Library of Congress 8

I.3 Still from *Shakespeare Writing Julius Caesar* (1907). Courtesy of the Museum of Modern Art Film Library, New York 8

I.4a–f Stills from *Enid* (2009) 11

I.5a–d Stills from *Howl* (2010) 13

I.6 Still from *Anonymous* (2011) 20

I.7 The Ben Jonson dedicatory poem and Droeshout engraving on facing pages in the frontismatter to the 1623 Shakespeare First Folio 21

2.1 Still from *Julia* (1977) 54

3.1 Stills from *Sylvia* (2003) 68

4.1 Stills from *Bright Star* (2009) 83

5.1 Still from *Prospero's Books* (1991) 99

6.1 Still from *Mansfield Park* (1999) 116

6.2 Still from *Becoming Jane* (2007) 116

8.1 Stills from *The Snows of Kilimanjaro* (1952) 145

9.1 Still from *Becoming Jane* (2007) 155

9.2 Still from *Shakespeare in Love* (1998) 156

10.1–10.2 Stills from *Adaptation* (2002) 169

11.1a–d Stills from *Sleeping Beauty* (1959) 181

11.2 Still from *The Tempest* (dir. Julie Taymor, 2010) 183

11.3a–d	Stills from *Prospero's Books* (1991)	186
11.4a–d	Stills from *Prospero's Books* (1991)	187
11.5a–d	Stills from *The Secret of Kells* (2009)	188
11.6a–d	Stills from *The Secret of Kells* (2009)	189
14.1–14.2	Stills from *The Lives of Others* (2006)	219
14.3–14.6	Stills from *The Lives of Others* (2006)	225
14.7–14.10	Stills from *The Lives of Others* (2006)	228
14.11a–f	Stills from *A Tale of Two Cities* (1917)	229

Notes on Contributors

Judith Buchanan is Professor of Film and Literature in the Department of English and Related Literature and Director of the Humanities Research Centre at the University of York. Publications include the monographs *Shakespeare on Film* (2005) and *Shakespeare on Silent Film: An Excellent Dumb Discourse* (2009) and numerous articles on silent cinema and its relations to the other arts. Current projects include work on *The Tempest* in performance, on the body and silent cinema and on cinema and the machine.

Richard Burt is Professor of English and Film and Media Studies at the University of Florida. He has published on Shakespeare, Renaissance drama, literary theory, film adaptation, telepolitics, cinematic paratexts and censorship. He is the author of *Medieval and Early Modern Film and Media* (2008, 2011); *Unspeakable ShaXXXspeares: Queer Theory and American Kiddie Culture* (1998); and *Licensed by Authority: Ben Jonson and the Discourses of Censorship* (1993).

Deborah Cartmell is Professor of English at De Montfort University and co-editor and founder of the journals *Adaptation* (2008) and *Shakespeare* (2005). She was a founding member of the British Shakespeare Association and the first Chair of the Association of Adaptation Studies. Her recent work includes *Screen Adaptation: Impure Cinema* (with Imelda Whelehan, 2010), *Screen Adaptations: Jane Austen's 'Pride and Prejudice'* (2010) and an edited collection, *A Companion to Literature, Film and Adaptation* (2012). She is currently working on adaptations in the sound era.

Sonia Haiduc lectures in English Literature at the University of Barcelona, where she is also the recipient of a research scholarship to complete her PhD on authorship, feminism and film adaptation. Beyond adaptation studies, her other research interests lie in late-Victorian Gothic and the intersections of literary and scientific discourses.

Siân Harris is an Education and Scholarship Lecturer in English at the University of Exeter. Her research focuses on the female *künstlerroman* narrative in twentieth-century Canadian fiction with a particular concentration on gender, genre and creative identities. Her interest in charting the ways in which writers engage with cultural preconceptions of authorship is pursued in her recent chapter contributions to *The Female Figure in Contemporary Historical Fiction* (Catherine Cooper and Emma Short, eds, 2012) and *J.K. Rowling: Harry Potter* (Cynthia J. Hallett and Peggy J. Huey, eds, 2012).

Andrew Higson is Greg Dyke Professor of Film and Television and Head of the Department of Theatre, Film and Television at the University of York, UK. He has published widely on British cinema from the silent period to the present, and has contributed to debates about heritage film, relations between literature and cinema, and national and transnational cinema. His most recent book is *Film England: Culturally English Filmmaking since the 1990s* (2011). His current research explores the ways in which Europeans come to know each other through film and television representations, and the contexts of production, distribution and reception that make this possible.

Laura Marcus is the Goldsmiths' Professor of English Literature at the University of Oxford and Professorial Fellow of New College Oxford. Her research and teaching interests are predominantly in nineteenth- and twentieth-century literature and culture, including life-writing, modernism, Virginia Woolf and Bloomsbury culture, contemporary fiction, and literature and film. Her book publications include *Auto/biographical Discourses: Theory, Criticism, Practice* (1994), *Virginia Woolf: Writers and their Work* (1997), *The Tenth Muse: Writing about Cinema in the Modernist Period* (2007) and, as co-editor, *The Cambridge History of Twentieth-Century English Literature* (2005). She is currently completing a book on writers and the cinema, from the beginnings to the present.

Megan Murray-Pepper is a doctoral student at King's College London, where she is completing an AHRC-funded PhD on Shakespearean appropriations in New Zealand. Other research interests include literature/film adaptation, heritage tourism and cultural representations of the writer at work.

Julian North is a senior lecturer at the University of Leicester. Her main research interests are in nineteenth-century literature, especially biography and autobiography. She has also published essays on Jane Austen adaptations and biopics. She is the author of *The Domestication of Genius: Biography and the Romantic Poet* (2009), and one of the editors of the *Works of Thomas De Quincey* (2000–2003).

R. Barton Palmer is Calhoun Lemon Professor of Literature at Clemson University, where he also directs the Global Cultural Studies and the Cinema and Cultural Studies programmes. Palmer is the author, editor, or general editor of more than forty volumes on various film and literary subjects. Among his works in the area of adaptation studies are: *Hollywood's Tennessee: The Williams Films and Postwar America* (with Robert Bray, 2009); *To Kill a Mockingbird: The Relationship Between the Text and the Film* (2008), as well as the edited collections *Nineteenth-Century American Fiction on Screen* and *Twentieth-Century American Fiction on Screen* (2007) and the upcoming *Modern British Drama on Screen* and *Modern American Drama on Screen* (both with Robert Bray).

Clara Rowland is Assistant Professor in the Romance Literatures Department and Researcher in the Centre for Comparative Studies at the University of

Lisbon. She is the co-ordinator of the three-year research project *False Movement – Studies on Writing and Film*. She works primarily in Comparative Studies, focusing on issues of representation and materiality in film and literature. Her monograph examining the book as a material object in the fiction of Brazilian writer João Guimarães Rosa, *A Forma do Meio: Livro e Narração na Obra de João Guimarães Rosa*, was published by UNICAMP in 2011.

Erica Sheen is Senior Lecturer in Film and Literature in the Department of English and Related Literature at the University of York. She is author of *Shakespeare and the Institution of Theatre: The Best in this Kind* (2009), and co-editor of *The Cinema of David Lynch: American Dreams, Nightmare Visions* (2004), *Literature, Politics and Law in Renaissance England* (2004) and *The Classic Novel from Page to Screen* (2000). She is currently completing studies of *Cold War Shakespeare* and *An Art of Possibility: International Cinema in Cold War Europe*.

Gennelle Smith previously worked for the Canadian Film Centre and now writes creative content for children's interactive media. Her academic interests include post-modern film, contemporary British cinema and cinematic representations of Canadian culture. She holds a Masters degree in Film and Literature from the University of York.

Geoffrey Wall is a literary biographer. He is currently writing a biography of Flaubert's father. His *Gustave Flaubert: A Life* (2001) was shortlisted for the Whitbread Prize and for the James Tait Black Memorial Prize. His four translations of Flaubert are published as Penguin Classics. His next project is a biography of George Sand and her circle. Geoffrey Wall teaches in the Department of English at the University of York, UK.

Acknowledgements

In March 2010, the Film and Literature programme at the University of York hosted an international conference entitled 'The Writer on Film'. This edited collection grew out of that conference. The York Film and Literature postgraduates who helped to run it and the broader conference community who participated in it are to be warmly thanked for a terrific event.

As the resulting volume has evolved, exchanges with contributors have proved the occasion for many entertaining and illuminating discussions, both on- and (better yet) off-subject. I thank them for their graciousness, patience and good humour about the process as well as for their stimulating contributions to the end product.

The editing of this volume has, in the way of these things, needed to be fitted in around the day job. The acute professionalism and keen sense of team endeavour of the University of York's excellent Humanities Research Centre staff – Helen Jacobs, Sarah Burton and Philip Morris – have made more things possible than ought to have been the case and I thank them all for a communal professional life that always combines the productive with the cheering. The University of York's Department of English and Related Literature remains not only an intensely stimulating environment in which to work, but also a significantly supportive one. It is a privilege to be part of both communities.

Epigraph quotations on p. xv are taken from Carol Rollyson, *Reading Biography* (Lincoln, NE: iUniverse, 2004), p. 51; John Worthen, 'The Necessary Ignorance of a Biographer' in John Batchelor (ed.), *The Art of Literary Biography* (Oxford: Clarendon Press, 1995), pp. 227–44 (231); and Richard Ellmann, *James Joyce* (Oxford: Oxford University Press, 1959), p. 114. The cover image shows Helena Bonham Carter in *Enid* (Carnival Film: dir. James Hawes, 2009). All appear with permission.

Hugh Haughton generously read, and gave discerning feedback on, the Introduction for which I am very grateful. Felicity Plester at Palgrave-Macmillan has been a model of supportive patience and Catherine Oakley an editorial assistant *extraordinaire* through the latter stages of this project. I am indebted to her for her discernment, clarity and company – excellent in each respect. I could not have wished for better: thank you Cat.

And I thank Kostja, Dougie and Freddie – bringers of delight and, as ever, more generously understanding than they should need to be – for cutting me sufficient slack to see this one through, and for much more besides.

Who first propounded the preposterous notion that writers' lives do not make for good biography? … That is like saying the life of the imagination has no story to tell.

Carl Rollyson

[B]iographies suggest that things as difficult as human lives can – for all their obvious complexity – be summed up, known, comprehended: they reassure us …

John Worthen

When a young man came up to him in Zurich and said, 'May I kiss the hand that wrote Ulysses?' Joyce replied, somewhat like King Lear, 'No, it did lots of other things too.'

Richard Ellmann

Figure I.1   A century of cinematic images of writers: (a) *A Tale of Two Cities* (dir. Frank Lloyd, 1917); (b) *Julia* (dir. Fred Zinnemann, 1977); (c) *Prospero's Books* (dir. Peter Greenaway, 1991); (d) *The Lives of Others* (dir. Florian Henckel von Donnersmarck, 2006); (e) *Becoming Jane* (dir. Julian Jarrold, 2007); (f) *Howl* (dirs Rob Epstein and Jeffrey Friedman, 2010).

Introduction

Image, story, desire: the writer on film

Judith Buchanan

A writer might seem unpromising subject matter for a film. A life of reflection, observation, composition and self-abstracting *literariness* does not self-evidently offer the sort of cinematic dynamism and narrative pulse usually considered the staple fare of the movies. 'If Mr Keats and I are strolling in the meadow, lounging on the sofa or staring into the wall, do not presume we are not working', announces Keats' friend, Charles Brown, in the literary biopic *Bright Star* (dir. Jane Campion, 2009). 'Doing nothing,' he continues loftily, 'is the musing of the poet'. The trailed, even celebrated 'nothing' being 'done' by Keats and Brown in the outer world is directly on offer here as a badge of poetic legitimacy. And it is clearly implied that these vaunted nothings mask a depth of enticing, but unseen, 'somethings' of a richly reflective and creative character.

For all their self-aggrandizing pomposity, Brown's words speak acutely to his off-screen as well as his on-screen audience. Through them, *Bright Star* explicitly draws attention to the significance of the unseen and inaccessible realms of a literary imagination, where the film's central (in)action is located. And in doing so, it illustrates the potentially self-thwarting nature of the project to make a literary biopic at all. Certainly acts of literary composition viewed purely from the perspective of an observing and non-intrusive camera would be hard pressed to yield momentum, trajectory and visual drama. '[W]e cannot know completely the intricacies with which any mind negotiates with its surroundings to produce literature', writes Richard Ellmann: 'The controlled seething out of which great works come is not likely to yield all its secrets.'[1] Since a dramatically fraught seething in the inner world may be made manifest in the outer only minimally (if at all), locating the dramatic action for a film about literary process can prove a challenge.

There are, however, few contexts in which an inability to 'know completely' has inhibited a desire to know in part. Moreover, at the point in mapping the emergence of a literary work where knowledge runs out, the curious, the creative and the commercially minded among filmmakers have rarely fought shy of reaching for conjecture as an appealing (and saleable) substitute for certainty.[2] So it has been, through imaginative projections of various sorts, that the nature of 'the intricacies with which [a] mind negotiates with its surroundings to produce literature', and the character of the 'controlled seething' from which great works might come has, with striking frequency across the history of the film industry, become the site of both earnest and impish speculative on-screen enquiry.

In the past twenty years, there has been a marked surge in the popularity of the literary biopic. Historical writers whose lives have been dramatized in recent films include Shakespeare, Jane Austen, Virginia Woolf, Iris Murdoch, Dylan Thomas, T.S. Eliot, Dorothy Parker, Sylvia Plath, Beatrix Potter, Anne Frank, F. Scott Fitzgerald, C.S. Lewis, Gertrude Stein, Edward de Vere, Dashiell Hammett, Lillian Hellman, Ayn Rand, the Earl of Rochester, Allen Ginsberg, J.M. Barrie, Truman Capote, Kafka, Keats, Kaufman and many more. To these we might add a host of fictional writers – playwrights, poets, novelists, diarists, journalists, screenwriters – who have been made the subject of contemporary releases. This phenomenon prompts a re-examination of the long and varied history of cinematic engagements with authorial creativity. This volume examines films about writers, real and fictional, and considers acts of writing as a filmed subject. It asks how filmmakers have configured writers' lives and acts of writing, and how they have reflected upon the material, imaginative and commercial operations of literary processes. What appeal do literary figures and literary process hold as a subject for screen presentation? What elements of a writing process have become cinematically iconized and even iconically conventionalized? And in response to such subjects, how do filmmakers attempt to catch the teasingly inaccessible processes of a literary imagination at work? Are the mechanisms by which thought takes shape and finds articulation in written form amenable to on-screen interpretation? What views of inspiration, muses, redrafting and publication have films taken? To what theoretical (and affective) versions of literary authorship, of reading and of literary interpretation has cinema subscribed in different national industries, in different periods and at the hands of different filmmakers? How has cinema chosen to configure the tools and symbols of writing – quills, pens, ink pots, desks, studies, paper, typewriters, keyboards? What cultural and commercial agendas are evidenced through cinema's compulsive return not just to literary material (whose story is well logged in adaptation studies) but, specifically, to literary process (whose story is significantly less so)? And – a question that literary biographer Geoffrey Wall specifically asks in his chapter for this collection – might acts of literary composition even help cinema to define itself by proving profoundly *uncinematic* as a subject of cinematographic attention, a subject that thwarts an enlightening cinematic account even as its surface aesthetics might seem warmly to invite it?

Cinema's repeated (and currently modish) return to the writer and acts of writing is partly explained by the subject's broad appeal to the industry's key personnel base. For screenwriters, there can be few stories more potentially attractive than that of a writer. The empty page awaiting inscription as both tempting invitation and oppressive tyranny; the world of the desk, the pen, the typewriter, the computer; the impediments and the facilitators to literary inspiration and productivity; and the writer's sense of both privileging and tormenting *apartness*: for the screenwriter, these present a story of flatteringly familiar elements. Furthermore, the subject frequently holds a cultural allure for directors and actors through its kudos-courting association with a literary history; constitutes a sound market proposition for producers through the pre-sold character of certain sorts of cultural story for a defined market; and exercises a keen aesthetic draw for designers and cinematographers through the visual appeal of the space of the study and of the rich imaginary worlds that can be conjured in it.

Literary biopics make a feature of shots that lovingly fête the writing process. We are familiar with aestheticized views of desk, quill, parchment, inkpot, typewriter, the writer in a moment of meditative pause, the evocatively personal oddities that adorn the space of writing, the view from the window as a reflective space that feeds the imaginative process. Will Shakespeare (Joseph Fiennes) sucking the end of his quill in *Shakespeare in Love* (dir. John Madden, 1998); Beatrix Potter (Renée Zellweger) sharpening her pencil, selecting her paintbrush and urging her imaginative creations on the page to 'sit still' in *Miss Potter* (dir. Chris Noonan, 2006); Jane Austen (Anne Hathaway) hugging her shawl around her and obsessively snipping out excess adjectives in *Becoming Jane* (dir. Julian Jarrold, 2007); John Keats (Ben Whishaw) sitting, eyes closed, under a tree as we hear 'Ode to a Nightingale' spoken in voice-over as if new-arrived fully formed in his mind in *Bright Star* (dir. Jane Campion, 2009); Shakespeare/Prospero (Sir John Gielgud) melodiously voicing all the parts as he is shown entering the beautiful, hand-written script of *The Tempest* onto the parchment page in *Prospero's Books* (dir. Peter Greenaway, 1991); Georg Dreyman (Sebastian Koch) surreptitiously tapping out his 'seditious' piece about the German Democratic Republic on his illicit typewriter in *The Lives of Others* (dir. Florian Henckel von Donnersmarck, 2006); Maurice Bendrix (Ralph Fiennes) downing whisky at the opening of *The End of the Affair* (Neil Jordan, 1999) and typing the arresting words 'This is a diary of hate' for an as-yet undisclosed addressee; Marcel Proust (André Engel) dictating breathlessly from his death bed while an amanuensis scratches it down beside him in *Time Regained* (dir. Raoul Ruiz, 1999); Allen Ginsberg (James Franco) smoking incessantly and punching his typewriter keys with percussive emphasis in *Howl* (dirs. Rob Epstein and Jeffrey Friedman, 2010). There is often a near-liturgical quality in the adherence to the detail in these writing sequences. In her chapter for this collection, Erica Sheen discusses the 'non-significant variation' in the sequences of writing that punctuate and anchor Robert Bresson's *Diary of a Country Priest* (1951): many of the films examined here have such sequences that serve as visual refrain, returning us to the scene of writing with only minor variations. It is, typically, the cumulative effect of these recurring shots rather than the particular character of any one that seasons the film. And, by extension, it is the cumulative effect of these recurring shots *across films* that generates a sense of consoling familiarity and of a visual terrain reassuringly easy to navigate for the generically attuned spectator.

The opportunity to conventionalize some aspects in the presentation of a subject depends both on a considerable body of work and upon some longevity in the approach. Both are securely in place for writer films. And cinema's long-standing and significant interest in literary process provides a useful filter through which the film industry has been able to reflect upon the processes and cultural cachet of a precursor, rival and sister medium. One of the things to emerge from a consideration of writer films is, therefore, a reinvigorated sense of the set of attitudes that cinema as a cultural institution has adopted, through a cumulative set of aggregated instances, towards literature as another. Moreover, in implicitly casting literary production as both foil and mirror for itself, the film industry has found a conveniently displaced means of reflecting upon its own identity and processes. This volume's focus on the gaze of one medium at another not only, therefore, provides a mediated perspective on literary production but can also illuminate cinema's remediated *self*-configurings as both artistic medium and market force. How does cinema's gaze at literary process – compulsive, admiring, competitive, idealizing, reductive, interrogative, suspicious, romanticized, yearning, condescending and self-metaphorizing as it is – reflect upon the ontology, reputation and perpetual remakings of cinema itself in its cultural circulations, practices and aspirations? This question, explicit in some of the analyses in prospect, has resonance for them all.

In any Western consideration of authorship, Shakespeare's influence is never far from view. In acknowledgement of the bearing Shakespeare's case has had on how authorship has been packaged for public consumption more generally, I bookend this introductory chapter with Shakespeare: at its start, a tale of the 1907 Shakespearean biopic that launched the genre of writer films; at its close, a reflection on the forms of authorial interest being courted (and deflected) in the opening double spread of the 1623 Shakespeare ('First') Folio frontispages. In between these Shakespearean endmarkers, I consider ways of representing literary process on screen through a discussion of *Enid* (dir. James Hawes, 2009) and *Howl* (dirs. Rob Epstein and Jeffrey Friedman, 2010); reflect on the myths of elevation we visit upon our authors through a consideration of *Bright Star* and William Edward West's portrait of Lord Byron; and interrogate the cultural desire to *know* the personalized source of works read that prompts the frequent return to the story of our writers. In the final section, I provide descriptive alerts to the individual chapters that follow.

Material and imaginary worlds

Pioneering an interest that would become considerably more pronounced later in cinema's history, the 1907 film *Shakespeare Writing Julius Caesar* (*Shakespeare Écrivant La Mort de Jules César*), from zany, experimental French filmmaker Georges Méliès, was the first film to be made specifically about literary process.[3] Sadly, the film, like so many from the era, is now believed lost. Nevertheless, a detailed catalogue entry furnishes us with a clear indication of its action. In addition, two stills from the film survive, archived in the Library of Congress (Washington DC) and the Museum of Modern Art (New York) respectively. Placed together for the first time here (Figures I.2 and I.3),[4] to help us re-imagine the lost work, they provide an insight into the film's design, its engaging taste for spatial transformation and the mechanism by which its central structuring transition (from playwright's mindworld to realized dramatic scene) was innovatively negotiated.

The film's action was clearly both visually and narratively energetic. It opened on a temporarily uninspired Shakespeare (played by Méliès himself) sitting at his desk trying, but failing, to write the assassination scene for *Julius Caesar*. In blocked frustration, he leaves his desk and papers and paces the room trying to catch and conjure the dramatic scene currently eluding him. 'At his wits' end,' as the catalogue entry expresses it, 'he sits down in an armchair, crosses his legs, and leaning on his hand prepares for a good, long think.' Both the desk which he has abandoned and the armchair (in right of frame) in which he then sits to think are clearly visible in the surviving copyright still of the set (Figure I.2). The action of the film continues: 'Suddenly his thoughts take life, and right before him appears an old Roman forum. Shakespeare is still seated in his armchair and now watches all that occurs.' With the stop-motion transformative magic characteristic of so many Méliès films, the study, including his writing desk, has vanished and, without having moved, Shakespeare has been directly transplanted into the scene of Caesar's assassination, converted in the instant from frustrated writer to rapt spectator (Figure I.3). Thus it is that the spectacular action of the Roman drama plays out for his (and the audience's) delight in the protean space of his erstwhile study – a space now magically reconstituted as the cinematic incarnation of Shakespeare's graphically imaginative mindworld. Indeed, the scene seems to have arrived in Shakespeare's mindworld fully formed, allowing him to enjoy it, as the catalogue explains, as himself 'an interested spectator – it seems to be just what he had been striving for.'

However, the Roman forum that Méliès' Shakespeare sees, and that we see through the agency of his creating mind and observing eyes, is not the forum of Julius Caesar's day – imperial, architecturally impressive, entire. Rather it is the forum of both the early modern (Shakespeare's) and modern (Méliès') world – crumbling, ruined, architecturally scarred.

Figure I.2 Shakespeare's study: the set for the opening scene of Georges Méliès' *Shakespeare Writing Julius Caesar* (1907). Copyright deposit still, courtesy of the Motion Picture, Broadcasting and Recorded Sound Division of the Library of Congress.

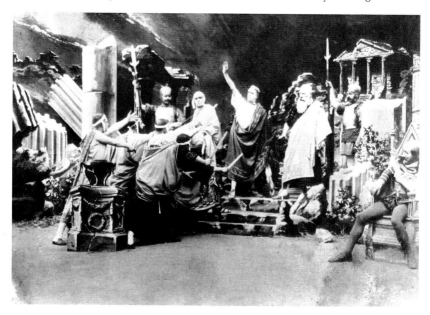

Figure I.3 Shakespeare (Méliès), and the armchair in which he sits (extreme right of frame), are the only points of continuity between the study (Figure I.2) and the Roman assassination scene conjured by the playwright's dramatic imagination. Film still courtesy of the Museum of Modern Art Film Library, New York.

The assassination scene therefore takes on prophetic resonances as here configured, as an act that – in a speeded-up version of history – brings down not just Caesar, but, by implied association, the stones of the Roman Republic also. Moreover, its depiction of turbulent skies showcases the scene's pathetic fallacy in the terms in which this Shakespeare imagines it, matched as the weather clearly is to the cataclysmic character of the scene's human action.

Beyond the figure of Shakespeare himself, the only other point of continuity between the writer's study space (Figure I.2) and this Roman scene of human, architectural and meteorological disturbance (Figure I.3) is the distinctive wooden armchair in which Shakespeare sits. The sustained presence of this identifiable armchair across magically con-verted planes of action serves, symbolically, to remember Shakespeare's actual continuing placement within his own study – even as his potent imagination transports him to other dramatic realms. Once the climac-tic Roman action is completed, Shakespeare and his armchair are then reabsorbed back into the prosaic surrounds of his study, leaving him joy-ously inspired about the scene he can now commit to paper. The film's final dissolve leads into a coda symbolically celebrating Shakespeare's universal genius: 'a bust of William Shakespeare, around which all the nations wave flags and garlands.'[5] It is the fluidity and reach of his own sympathies as a writer – demonstrably, in this short film, enabling him to escape from the singularity and containment of his modest study – that ushers in and legitimizes the breadth of this subsequent international recognition.

Even the still showing the film's bare set before the action begins (Figure I.2) can, therefore, speak to us about how the writerly process is being cinematically configured in this film. The desk on show here proves to be a place of stultification for Shakespeare, fettering the playwright's imagi-nation: the literary impediments blocking his imagination are materially represented by the books and papers that occupy his writing space. It is a telling launch for a long run of films about writers that these papers and books must be abandoned in order to 'release' the drama of the highly cinematic images that illustrate the liberated muse at work: it is the very act of leaving his papers that will in due course equip Méliès' Shakespeare to return to them to record the fruits of the muse's visitation, betokening a view of creativity that favours a romantic abstraction from conspicuous forms of literary erudition. It was Byron who (reportedly) insisted that no books or pens should appear in his portraits since they suggested a hum-drum dependence on books as opposed to the visitation of the inspiring muse.[6] Méliès' Shakespeare is in this sense Byronic: it is only by leaving his desk and freeing himself from literary clutter and bookish distraction that his inspiration can then flow unfettered and his natural genius find expression.[7] Across the hundred years since Méliès' inventive Shakespearean film sketch, the transitions from the writer to the written – away from, or through, the writing page (mere material repository of ink marks acting as conduit to a story actually happening in an imaginative domain elsewhere) – has become the trigger for much inventive cinematic play, as documented in many of the chapters that follow.

Paul Arthur suggests that, as a film subject, writing presents a challenge not only because it tends to be solitary and static, but also because it is 'performed in dull locations over excruciating stretches of time'.[8] Nonetheless, the *spaces* of writing are not, of necessity, dull – not even aesthetically so. Or, in the case of beautifully bookish studies, *especially* not aesthetically so. The point about the potential tedium in depicting the writing *process*, however, holds. The question therefore bears asking: beyond Méliès' realm-slipping armchair as a vehicle for negotiating the transitions between material and imaginary worlds, what other resources and strategies do film-makers employ to catch and animate literary process?

The self-interrogating interest of *Enid* (dir. James Hawes, 2009) in the construction and representation of authorial process provides a short sequence of illustrative interest here. A strikingly composed shot sequence of the writer Enid Blyton (Helena Bonham Carter) at a mid-point in the film effectively anthologizes a range of strategies available to filmmakers with which to represent the processes of literary composition. By this point, the film has educated us into a familiarity with the aesthetics of Enid at work.

She is regularly viewed in long shot as the happily absorbed, domestically abstracted writer, ensconced in her writing room, with dramatic shafts of light streaming appealingly into the room (book cover image). In this particular sequence, a succession of brief shots economically summons a sense of busy productivity: a close-up of her eyes as synecdochic suggestion of the imagination at work; a close-up of fingers on typewriter keys; a close-up of the busily active typewriter ribbon and carriage arm; a shot of the window framing the hills and cliff beyond, the long window latch lightly evoking a visual rhyme with the carriage return of the previous shot (Figure I.4a–e). The window shot (Figure I.4c) earns its place in the sequence as the space of inspiration that is giving birth to the story. It is a space, what's more, that is indwelt by the presence of the author, her image symbolically retained in it as a reflection on the glass pane. When the window shot is then reprised (Figure I.4f), not only is the reflection of the writer retained as a crucially determining part of the visual field, but now, additionally, the words she is producing on the page appear superimposed as overlay upon the view of the cliffs, acoustically matched by the character's voice heard speaking them. The final visual addition to this richly composite space is, inevitably, the gradual materializing into the landscape of the Famous Five themselves (Julian, George, Dick, Anne and Timmy the dog). They are seen scampering towards the cliffs, apparently conjured by the eyes, fingers, keys, ribbon, shafts of

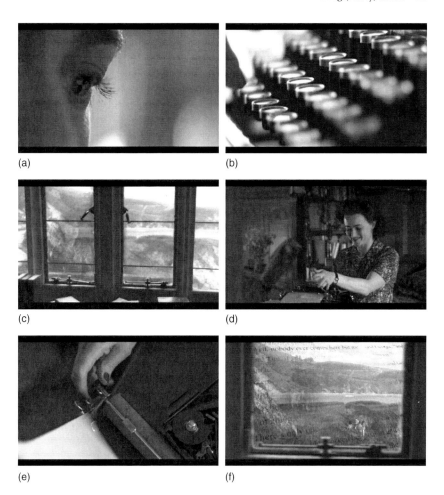

Figure I.4a–f A romantic montage summons the fictional characters of the Famous Five into the inviting landscape viewed through the window pane in *Enid* (2009). The final shot of the sequence anthologizes the component elements of the writing process as previously itemized: the writer (her image reflected in window); the type-writer (its carriage arm visually remembered in the window latch); the page (its text superimposed on the scenery); and the natural space viewed through the window collectively prompting in (f) the evocation of the fictional narrative of the Famous Five.

light, voice, printed words and inviting landscape-awaiting-occupation that have been claiming our attention across the succession of previous shots. This inclusive final shot of the sequence also, however, allows for an eloquent equivocation about what it is that has conjured this last overlay of the fictional characters. The symbolic accumulation of iconic elements conventionally associated with the cinematic scene of writing gently licenses the possibility that the four fictional children and one fictional dog seen on the cliffs outside the writer's window might even have been brought into being through the viewer's learnt processes of aggregation. We recognize the anatomized elements of inspiration (poetic shafts of light, gazing into the middle distance), perspiration (clickety-clackety typewriter keys, busy fingers) and production (the words appearing on the page, the voice reading these) to which we have just been made privy and, drawing upon our foreknowledge both of Enid Blyton's literary output and, significantly, of how such film sequences *work*, we infer what this rich assembly of satisfyingly conventionalized visual elements *should* collectively now generate. As if to seal the reflexive quality of the all-encompassing shot (the sum of view through window *plus* shadowy writer seen in reflection *plus* typescript on the page *producing* sight of the fictional scene), this panoptic vision of literary production is framed by the screen-imitative window. This visually gestures towards the project of this film itself, and, by extension, of other films in the genre. As the 1907 *Shakespeare Writing Julius Caesar* and many subsequent films also illustrate, such films take pleasure in creating the cinematically elided space in which the inner and outer worlds of the author may meet.

By contrast, the typewriter ribbon in *Howl* (a film discussed by Laura Marcus in Chapter 1) starts, conventionally enough, by producing words on the pages (Figure I.5b), but scuttles off quickly and imagistically into producing musical notes (Figure I.5c), cityscapes and then animated scenes of varying degrees of urban freneticism and torment. The filmmakers here (specifically writer-directors Rob Epstein and Jeffrey Friedman, production designer Thérèse DePrez, art director Russell Barnes and illustrator/animation designer Eric Drooker) have presumed to enter the poem and, drawing directly on Eric Drooker's illustrations previously commissioned by Ginsberg,[9] to work energetically *with* it by producing animated cartoon images in lurid colours, as both illustration and counterpoint to the work read. This is, therefore, a film that dares to intrude on, participate in, and collaborate with the poetic operations of the poem 'Howl' and with its subsequently commissioned illustrations. It captures and suggests the heightened aesthetics of an evocative trip of morphing shapes and shifting associations, using words as tools towards images and felt responses. Consequently, the modest materiality of the clickety-clack of the typewriter's alphabetic repertoire is shown to produce much more than unevenly inked letters on the page: instead it becomes the mechanism for releasing a series of wild and disturbing animated sequences. Moreover in giving an abrasively dynamic account of the relationship of the life of the writing (Ginsberg at his typewriter) to the life of the thing written (graphically suggested through phantasmagoric animated sequences), it also itself poetically metaphorizes the processes by which words become films.

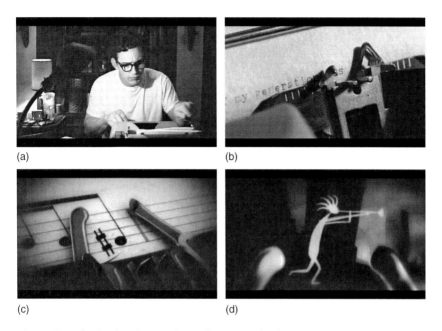

(a) (b)

(c) (d)

Figures I.5a–d Ginsberg's typed words in *Howl* (dirs. Rob Epstein and Jeffrey Friedman, 2010) transmute into musical notation and then on into free-wheeling patterns of imagery.

Imagining the Author

'You're not at all how I imagined an author to be you know. I thought authors were all vague and wiffly with muses and all that sort of thing', says Kenneth Waters (Denis Lawson) to Enid Blyton (Bonham Carter) during their first meeting in *Enid*. How we might 'imagine an author to be' is central to the dramatic interest of that film and to the psychology of its central character. Bonham Carter's Enid wants her readers to find her a wholesome match for the uplifting tenor of her books; she believes the tonal character of her children's stories should be recognizably refracted in the person she is. And so, at some cost to those around her, she duly fashions herself to seem feasibly the writer of her own fiction. While 'performing' a winning version of authorial identity for her public, however, her private life in *Enid* is seen to be of a decidedly different hue.[10]

This desire to find a satisfying synergy between the life and the work becomes central to many literary biopics and biographically inflected adaptations. Upon meeting the established novelist Mrs Radcliffe (Helen McCrory), the young Jane Austen (Anne Hathaway) of the 2007 film *Becoming Jane* expresses some surprise at the disjuncture she detects between the novelist's life and the spirit of her novels: 'You live so quietly, and yet your novels are filled with romance, danger, terror.' 'Everything my life is not', replies Mrs Radcliffe, correctly inferring Jane's near-disappointment at the life-art divergence she discerns. Equally struck by his own inability, as he perceives it, to act true to what he feels and writes, in *Bright Star* John Keats (Ben Whishaw) tells Fanny Brawne (Abbie Cornish), in true Keatsian fashion: 'A poet is not at all poetical. He is the most unpoetical thing in existence.'[11] Just as *Shakespeare in Love*, *Becoming Jane* and *Howl* show their gifted young writers, Will Shakespeare, Jane Austen and Allen Ginsberg respectively, stepping out from these more tepid models of artistry to live the feelings each then commits to the page, so Whishaw's Keats' own sensitive beauties, passionate outbursts, attentive gazing, self-denying mindset and social gaucheries conspicuously give the lie to his theorizing about the 'not at all poetical' life of a poet. Whishaw's Keats' attempt to debunk the perceived poeticism of the poet is, in fact, trumped by the counter-strategy of the aesthetically heightened film through which his story is being told – a film that glories in showing a sympathetic match between the delicate tenor of Keats' poetry and of the 'Keatsian' life from which it emanates.

This portrait of Keats identifies *Bright Star*, as Julian North discusses later in this volume, as a film wedded to a High Romanticism in its reading of an authorial life and of authorial process. The prevalence of such readings of authorship stems from a cultural – even, in its more extreme expressions, a quasi-mystical – compulsion to invest in heightened terms in what an author-artist *is*. What are his/her authorial modes of relating to the more mundane world of common interests around him/her, a world less touched, and less burdened, by the transfiguring imperative to create? Through riffing variously on this question, and trailing its will to find an abstracted otherness in the artists whom we revere, *Bright Star* proves conspicuously well-attuned to the market-driven imperatives of its genre.

If the project of *Bright Star* is partly to validate the sense of privileged election that accompanies a romantic version of the poetic life, other literary biopics make it their project to demystify or even banalize the writerly life. In *Sylvia* (dir. Christine Jeffs, 2003), Ted Hughes (Daniel Craig) refuses any mystification not just of his person but of the writing process also: 'There's no secret to it', he announces unsparingly: 'You've just got to pick a subject and stick your head into it.' By this account, writing a poem is almost artisanal, a question of starting and of keeping going, like building a wall or cooking a meal. Such deliberate debunking of the high-minded rhetoric of 'inspiration' that can threaten to refine the process beyond the realm of the intelligible implicitly returns us to the Greek roots of the word 'poem' (*poiēma*), meaning simply – prosaically even – *thing made*. The will to strip away the cant and 'render ordinary' in this way is also felt in the striking predilection for first names in recent film titles of the genre: *Tom and Viv* (1994), *Dash and Lily* (1999), *Iris* (2001), *Sylvia* (2003), *Becoming Jane* (2007), *Enid* (2009). This suggests a desire to be on familiar terms with the life in ways that self-consciously reject a 'lit crit' approach with its well-established convention for discussing authors by last name (more disciplinary brand than person perhaps). The chummy, even presumptuous, intimacy of dropping the last name for these film titles has, of course, infused the titles of some recent literary biographies and biographical novels also: Emma Tennant's *Ted and Sylvia* (2001), Stephen Greenblatt's *Will in the World* (2005), Claire Harman's *Jane's Fame* (2009), Duncan Mclaren's *Looking for Enid* (2007). The movie *Becoming Jane*, however, was inspired by Jon Spence's interpretive biography *Becoming Jane Austen* (2003). The interventionist decision to excise 'Austen' for the film title emblematizes this desire to recuperate the personal from behind the established literary badge and to find ways of mapping the life onto the works, or of holding the two in creative tension. This has been part of the inspiration for the recent flurry of cinematic and televisual engagements with authors and authorial process. The 'Meet Bill' section that featured on the website for Baz Luhrmann's 1995 release *William Shakespeare's Romeo + Juliet* may be taken as symptomatic of the impetus to bring the writerly life within reach and render it commonplace, composed of the same stuff as us and, in expression of this, even comfortably amenable to pally nicknames. This volume documents and interrogates these conflicting impulses: to declare special and to render ordinary; to endorse, even sometimes to sanctify the received readings of a writer's professional life and personal aura on the one hand and, on the other, to puncture these things systematically, unsparingly and/or humorously.

The myths of elevation and abstraction we might wish to project on to, dimensions to ascribe to, and individual attributes to visit upon, our authors are aptly illustrated in the American painter William Edward West's personal account of his meeting with Lord Byron in 1822.[12] Byron was due to sit for a portrait with West and, writing up the encounter subsequently, the artist remembers having been nervous ahead of time about meeting a man of such celebrated 'genius and talent'. He then weighs the specifics of his anticipation against the man Byron turned out to be:

> I expected to see a person somewhat thin and swarthy with a high forehead and black curly hair with a countenance severe and stern and manners reserved and lofty. I fancied him in a black mantle with a diamond hilted dagger in his bosom and that to hear the common ideas of conversation attended with the purest eloquence if not in poetry. I was mistaken and much surprised to see almost the reverse of what I had imagined. He received us with somewhat of embarassment (sic) in his manner, but not the least ceremony. Altogether he was a larger man than I had fancied, rather fat and apparently effeminate – a delicate complexion light blue or grey eyes – dark hair rather long and combed over his forehead with a few curls down about his neck which he cut shortly after. He had on a sky-blue camelot frock coat with a cape or lapell (sic) falling over his shoulders – boots light rust and pantaloons, and rather the cut of a dandy in his own way …

[After some acquaintance] ... I now felt nothing like awe or embarrassment in the company of this great man – he was so perfectly simple in his manners – so free and easy and even familiar and friendly that I parted with him quite delighted. The day after I returned and had another sitting of an hour.

[...]

Asked me what I thought of him before I saw him – when I told him as I have described him above he laughed very much and said 'well and you find me like other people don't you?' At other times he would often laugh and say 'well and so you thought me a princely fellow didn't you?'[13]

West's anticipatory ideas about Byron (his romantic appearance, behaviour, dress, manner of speech and general drama of presentational style) were, presumably, generated by an acquaintance with his poetry and/or his broader reputation. These romantic ideas are, however, dispelled by an encounter with the real man. Nevertheless, the portrait of Byron that West then painted (now in the National Portrait Gallery of Scotland) is serious, dreamy and fully romantic in *timbre*, apparently uninflected by, and even resistant to, the low-key air of friendly jocularity that characterized the real Byron of West's actual acquaintance. The poet's reputation was, for West, too established, and perhaps too artistically appealing also, to be worth disrupting by an inconvenient evocation of the spirit of the real man sitting before him. Some writers' reputations, and some myths of authorship, it seems, are too culturally satisfying to be relinquished, even in the face of evidence that could potentially take the authorial story in another direction. And so it has been that on the screen, John Keats is shown perfectly dramatizing, point by point, the romantic ideal and Jane Austen is configured as the ur-Elizabeth Bennet in both circumstance and sensibility; while in portraiture, Lord Byron remains the moody, abstracted, high-minded melancholic, dreamily disengaged from the immediacy of his surroundings.

In telling a biographical story about writers visually, objects frequently assume a heightened symbolic value within the narrative. Having available economically encoded signifiers of a more expansive emotional landscape is, of course, particularly helpful in the compressed time-frame of a movie. In her essay 'Great Men's Houses' (1931), Virginia Woolf claimed for writers a special capacity for imprinting themselves upon things: 'it would seem to be a fact that writers stamp themselves upon their possessions more indelibly than other people ... making the table, the chair, the curtain, the carpet into their own image.'[14] This beguiling, if extravagant, position suggests that those able to create literary works of distinction are correspondingly gifted with a capacity for personal imprimatur onto their material environment in ways that remain legible to later generations. Without needing to ascribe a metaphysics to this, there is no doubting that for observers invested in a literary history, the 'pulse' of an object, as Edmund de Waal terms it, is likely to resonate more when 'emitted' by an artefact linked to a literary life of significance.[15]

The belief, even the experiential *sense*, that a little human specialness can be imparted to objects so that their substance retains the trace memory of their erstwhile owners is also an intuitively felt item of faith for many of us in our familial lives, springing from a desire to resist, or at least temper, the separation of the grave. As applied to the lives of artists, however, this cultural and emotional craving takes on an additional commercial dimension. In a paper given at the 2010 'Writer on Film' international conference at the University of York, Megan Murray-Pepper pointed out that Charlotte Brontë's writing desk sold at Sotheby's in December 2009 for £20,000 – considerably in excess of its pre-sale valuation. The Woolfian belief in the writer's lasting and legible imprint upon possessions can, it seems, produce more than merely a tingle of excited recognition in the observer: it can also – as the Sotheby's sale demonstrates – translate directly into considerable commodifiable market value.[16]

Given the level of emotional and capital investment in the things writers once touched and treasured, it is little wonder, perhaps, that literary biopics should reach gratefully for totemic objects as place holders for, and communicators about, their writer subjects – as they frequently do. Jane Austen's shawl, Freud's miniature statues of Greek and Egyptian deities, Shakespeare's desk, Flaubert's green leather couch, even the back scratcher that takes on freighted significance in *The Lives of Others*: all are invited to assume symbolic weight and thereby help compensate for the purely partial and necessarily circumscribed nature of the mere slice of a life that a biopic is confined to offering.

Desiring the Author

Chafing against the convention that 'the explanation of a work' should always be 'sought in the man or woman who produced it', in his seminal 1967 essay 'The Death of the Author', Roland Barthes argued that the author's effective erasure from the present-tense operations of the book is part of what publication means and achieves. 'The Death of the Author' influentially redefined how we conceive meaning to be constructed from a work. No longer was a written text understood as simply a transmission vehicle for a settled and stable meaning determined by an author and awaiting decoding in those terms; now it had become 'a multi-dimensional space in which a variety of writings, none of them original, blend and clash' – a place, in fact, 'where all identity is lost, starting with the very identity of the body writing'.[17] The necessary accompaniment to these processes of semantic multiplicity and authorial loss, Barthes further argued, is that the publication process empowers readers, formally licensing them to derive and construct meaning from (and with) a work according to their own sensitivities, circumstances and predispositions.

Barthes did not, of course, fundamentally change how a text works; he simply changed the terms in which its operations are described, by making conspicuous what was already the case. A process of professional severance, author from work and work from author, is, and always has been, the necessary psychological, emotional, symbolic and material corollary to publication. Whatever level of authorial self-inscription there may be in a work, however intimately that work may be seen to express a writer's sensibility, and however frequently he or she may subsequently choose to speak about it, upon publication it becomes a thing apart and beyond authorial governance. Consciously or otherwise, that is the transaction authors make, and have always made, with their work.

While the work's disengagement from its author is true in formal terms, however, experientially it is rarely so simple. In making sense of the work, readers crave, and seek, origins. However potentially empowering for readers, a work's proffered autonomy – part of the received critical landscape of a post-Barthesian world – does not entirely satisfy. Since cultural works do not emerge from vacuums, they cannot be received as entities without prior attachments. A contextualizing origin is therefore sought, and the most potently desired expression of artistic origin is always personal. In part-accommodation of this, Barthes conceded:

> As institution, the author is dead: his civil status, his biographical person have disappeared; dispossessed, they no longer exercise over his work the formidable paternity whose account literary history, teaching, and public opinion had the responsibility of establishing and renewing; but in the text, in a way, I desire the author: I need his figure (which is neither his representation nor his projection), as he needs mine...[18]

This 'desire' for, and 'need' of, the 'figure' of the author as, what Michel Foucault referred to as, a 'function' of the reading process[19] gives rise to the psycho-social impulse to reconstruct the line of transmission backwards from readers to writers – a reconstituting process that is intuitively pursued. Thus the real-world sequential process by which:

 i an author writes a book;
 ii the book is published;
iii a reader buys and reads it

is effectively inverted in the reading process so that:

 i a reader reads a book;
 ii the reader ponders how the book came to be, and specifically how it came to be *like this*; and

iii the reader (or body of readers) constructs a 'version' of the work's origins, seeking images and narratives to feed, supplement and refine an impression of knowledgeable intimacy with the work's source.

In this way a mental map of artistic production and reception emerges partly from the interstices of the reading experience, fed by a greater or lesser degree of extra-textual information, intuition and fantasy. And in fact the 'desire' for the figure of the author is often not comprehensively slaked through the construction of an author-function, crucial though that is in the interpretive process. Indeed, the 'representation' or 'projection' of an author that Barthes specifically declares irrelevant as a product of 'author-desire' – what he earlier referred to as the 'identity of the body writing' – can often be the very thing the reader *does* seek as the completion of the circle of connectedness that the encounter with the literary work has provoked.

A more commonly expressed desire for the author – and, inevitably, for some authors in particular – is sufficiently recognizable as an impulse to have become suitable material for popular satirical treatment. This temptation is most conspicuous in relation to Shakespeare. In the Doctor Who episode 'The Shakespeare Code' (first broadcast BBC One, April 2007), an anachronistic desire to see the playwright is self-consciously introduced to the assembled audience at the Globe in 1599 by Martha Jones (Freema Agyeman), new assistant of the time-travelling doctor (David Tennant). From her standing position among the groundlings in the yard at the Globe, at the end of a performance of *Love's Labours Lost*, Martha takes it upon herself to shout 'Author' and – without recorded precedent on the Early Modern stage – the call is taken up by the Globe audience resulting eventually in a gratifying on-stage personal appearance by Shakespeare himself.[20] As it played out as a dramatic moment, it was too delicious an anachronism, and too good an on-screen joke, not to be emulated subsequently. In the skittish children's feature film, *Gnomeo and Juliet* (dir. Kelly Asbury, 2011), for example, the talking statue of William Shakespeare (voiced by Patrick Stewart) fondly remembers the end of early performances of *Romeo and Juliet* concluding with a 'standing ovation' and cries of 'author, author'. And amidst an unabashed host of conspicuous departures not just from the historical record but also from the realm of the feasible, the effect is directly replayed in *Anonymous* (dir. Roland Emmerich, 2011). Here, though, the joke reappears without the self-evident advertisement of its own anachronistic impishness – a self-awareness that had formed part of its joyous flavour in 'The Shakespeare Code'. In *Anonymous*, at the end of a performance of *Henry V* (a play on offer here as a work secretly written by the Earl of Oxford), with one voice the audience at the Rose (sic) takes up the chant 'Playwright, playwright, playwright' as if this were standard practice for well-received plays on the late sixteenth-century London stage. It is this appreciative – if resoundingly

Figure I.6   Will Shakespeare (Rafe Spall) carries quill and manuscript onto the stage in a fraudulent masquerade of authorship in *Anonymous* (2011).

anachronistic – clamour to see, know, commend and collectively own the desired author that persuades Will Shakespeare (Rafe Spall), the charlatan non-playwright of this film, to step forward and fraudulently claim the work as his own (Figure I.6).

Though late sixteenth-century audiences at the Globe or the Rose almost certainly did not call for an on-stage appearance by a playwright at the end of a production (personal authorship not yet having become the defining identity of dramatic works), for the publication of the 1623 ('First') Shakespeare Folio, by contrast, the desire for a personalized authorial connection to wrap into the reading experience of Shakespeare's plays was, by then, emphatically determining how the edition should be presented and marketed. With a predictably canny eye on the anticipated preferences of their market in this respect, for the prefatory pages for the 1623 Shakespeare Folio, John Heminge and Henrie Condell, producers of the volume, inserted a directly configured image of Shakespeare himself in the form of the famous high-foreheaded Droeshout engraving. No codified allegorical engravings saturated in erudite references here of the sort that had, for example, graced the frontispiece of Ben Jonson's 1616 *Workes*: just a directly appreciable portrait of a man – the very authorial 'representation', in fact, of Barthes' dismissive aside. The unrivalled positioning of this simple engraving at the front of the First Folio's prefatory pages seems to invite and validate the reader's attention to it as both relevant to, and potentially enriching of, the experience of reading the work that will follow. The direct invitation to readers both to gaze upon, and draw interpretive currency from, the image, is, moreover, consolidated by the opening lines of the First Folio's poetic address 'To the Reader', commissioned from Ben Jonson, published on the facing page opposite the Droeshout engraving (Figure I.7) and explicitly tasked to comment upon it:

> This Figure, that thou here seest put,
> It was for gentle Shakespeare cut,

Not content merely to *point* to the 'figure' in this way, however, Ben Jonson (who had himself known Shakespeare) feels it encumbent upon him also to address its inadequacies as a representation:

> Wherein the Graver had a strife
> With Nature, to out-doo the life:
> O, could he but have drawne his wit
> As well in brasse, as he hath hit
> His face; the Print would then surpasse
> All, that was ever writ in brasse.
> But, since he cannot, Reader, looke
> Not on his Picture, but his Booke.

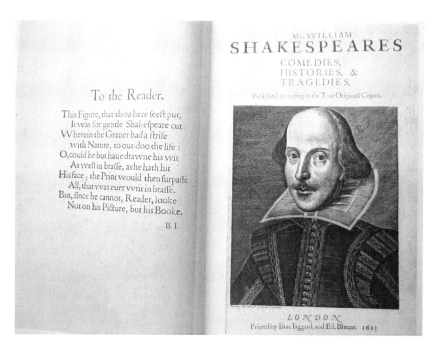

Figure I.7 The Ben Jonson dedicatory poem and Droeshout engraving on facing pages in the frontismatter to the 1623 Shakespeare First Folio.

Laura Cumming has suggested that in this poem Ben Jonson 'worryingly endorsed' the Droeshout image.[21] But endorsement is not the project of this dedicatory poem. Indeed, by its close, Jonson has become so persuaded of the futility of the (en)graver's 'strife' to capture the man, and so of the inability of this image, or perhaps of any image, adequately to represent Shakespeare's 'wit', that he ends the dedicatory verse with the now celebrated imprecation (ll.9-10): 'Reader, looke/Not on his picture, but his Booke.' And so it is that, in urging us to look *away from* the picture and *towards* the works, the poem commissioned to accompany the authorial engraving acts partly to deflect the reader's gaze from the very image it had apparently sought to promote. In effect, it shows us an authorial image to demonstrate its diversionary character as an aid to the reading experience.

Though literary portraiture abounds (even now prominently part of the Kindle e-reader's basic provision),[22] writers themselves have often fought shy of compromising the potential profile of their work through what might be perceived as a distracting concentration on their person. Famously, Charles Dickens was clear about where *he* thought the public's attention should be directed in relation to authors' physical selves and their works. In line with his principles in this respect, he both outright refused to contribute to the funding of a proposed statue of Shakespeare,[23] and, in his own will, conjured his friends 'on no account to make me the subject of any monument, memorial or testimonial whatever.'[24] Despite having some sympathy for the view that visual configurations of an author serve principally to distract from the work, for the Shakespeare First Folio, Jonson finds himself more awkwardly caught than Dickens would subsequently be: Jonson both wants the reader to have the pleasure of seeing the writer accessibly (if unsubtly) configured, *and* wants to advertise the broader insufficiency of such configurations as contributors to more subtle, and more lasting, authorial *truths*.

While the scruples of Jonson and Dickens – seeking to resist fuelling interest in an author's person – constitute an honourable and appealing side note to this enquiry, the reality of the literary market-place in the twentieth and twenty-first centuries speaks back emphatically, and profitably, to these nice scruples: the number of new editions of key literary works by an author that follow, or are timed to coincide with, the release of a literary biopic demonstrate that far from diverting attention from the literary output, screening a version of the author's story for a mass audience at the very least re-energizes sales of the works. Moreover, in temporarily claiming the column inches and determining the terms of the debate in relation to that author, the release of a literary biopic invariably also inspires renewed critical interest in the works. In the contemporary world's fluidly inter-referential cultural field, it is therefore neither possible nor desirable to protect the purity of the *literary* monument as separate from the personal one in quite the high-minded terms in which Dickens engagingly (though, even then, impossibly) envisaged it.

Georges Méliès' 1907 film *Shakespeare Writing Julius Caesar* exhibited no anxieties about the worth of personal monuments. The bust of Shakespeare into which the action dissolves at its end stills the freneticism of the preceding scenes into a tableau iconizing the ongoing, international reputation of the dramatist. In this moment, the (historically contested) details about the place and mode of Shakespeare's writing fall away and we are left instead with the enduring, and apparently unifying, bust 'around which all the nations wave flags and garlands'.[25] It is apt that more than a century of movies about writers and writing should have been launched by a film that so clearly showcased a triangulated interest in literary process (Shakespeare writing), literary product (the play) and authorial legacy (the bust). Although few writer films since have been so explicit in their flag-waving as a celebration of the universal greatness of their central character, the movies themselves now form part of the evolving cultural monuments we collectively erect, and variously rewhittle, to the writers whose stories we want to tell and retell.

The Volume's Organization

The book is divided into two sections of seven chapters each. Those in Part I examine cinema's versions and uses of real-world literary lives. Those in Part II consider: (i) cinema's constructions of on-screen authorial proxies, including both authorially inscribed characters and the semantics of the labelling of authorship in bookending credit sequences; and (ii) a sample range of films that illustrate cinema's taste for telling stories with, and about, fictional authors.

Part I: Cinema's versions and uses of literary lives

In Chapter 1, Laura Marcus attends to a series of illustrative moments of cinematic transition between acts of literary authoring on the one hand and the fictional world created through those acts on the other. She cites several Dickens film adaptations to demonstrate a range of ways in which both on-screen text in the process of coming into being, and text already produced, can cede to, and become, the on-screen Dickensian action. In each case the transitional process retrospectively advertises the authoring act, and, by implication, the authorial presence that lies behind the adapted work then enacted. These transitional moments between text and action are pressed into interpretive service as usefully illustrative of on-screen (and novelistic) word–image relations more generally. Marcus then moves discussion of authoring agents from the implicitly to the explicitly configured in, for example, Spike Jonze's *Adaptation* (2002), Marc Forster's *Stranger than Fiction* (2006), Joe Wright's *Atonement* (2007) and Epstein and Friedman's *Howl* (2010). In these films, authorial presences at their typewriters specifically drive the narrative in self-reflexive ways, prompting discussion of the meanings of a typewriter for writers and how these meanings have been cinematically rendered across films. Marcus argues that under the film industry's old celluloid order, in which a material film print needed to be materially manipulated, the mechanisms of the typewriter as the front-line medium for literary production were intermedially aligned with those of film production. Moreover, she maintains, the aptness of the analogy between literary and film production holds even after the digital turn, since a further suggestive rhyme across media is now discernible between the manipulability of text in digital word processing and the fluency of the edit possible in digital filmmaking.

In Chapters 2 and 3, Sonia Haiduc and Siân Harris take on questions of male and female gendered authorship respectively. In Chapter 2, Sonia Haiduc examines the 'unremitting drive to place female literary icons under the lens'. She considers how authorial acts by women writers have been differently configured across films, as, for example, 'an act of self-affirmation in *My Brilliant Career* (dir. Gillian Armstrong, 1979); a life-saving strategy in *An Angel at My Table* (dir. Jane Campion, 1990); a self-authorizing strategy in a male-dominated culture in *Mansfield Park* (dir. Patricia Rozema, 1999); an integral part of personal identity in *Iris* (dir. Richard Eyre, 2001); a vehicle for the promotion of heritage tourism in the case of *Miss Potter* (dir. Chris Noonan, 2006); and an emotional reaction to romantic turmoil in *Becoming Jane* (dir. Julian Jarrold, 2007).' From *Julia* (1977) to *Miss Austen Regrets* (2008), and taking in a series of other films in its generous sweep, this chapter asks trenchant questions about the place of women writers in our culture and the variant effects of their culturally revealing on-screen configurations.

In Chapter 3, Siân Harris examines the underpinnings and constructions of poetic masculinity through the depiction of Ted Hughes in *Sylvia* (2003) and of Dylan Thomas in *The Edge of Love* (2008). She considers the potency of the Byronic myth and asks how competing images of the male poet (the uber-masculinity of the Byronic bad-boy versus the image of the emasculated, sensitive and sickly poet in the Keatsian mould) have been treated in the cinema. As part of this discussion, she considers the determining and licensing significance of the female characters in both biopics and their role in permitting and defining the attitudes and behaviours here associated with male 'poeticism'.

In Chapter 4, Julian North extends the examination of the myth of the lone Romantic genius, its specific processes of construction and promotion in the nineteenth century and its levels of remove from the often more practically engaged, earthed, connected and commercially astute tendencies of the Romantic writers themselves. Turning to cinema, North maps the problematic emergence of *auteurism* in film criticism. In a series of nimbly executed trans-temporal and trans-medial comparisons, North places Keats's ideas of creative presence alongside those espoused by *auteurism*, and Keats's own creative presence as both self-configured within his own writing and as dramatized within *Bright Star* alongside Jane Campion's directorial presence as the name-above-the-title artist-author behind that film. The vision of authorship on offer in *Bright Star* – that of a man divorced from a broader social engagement but irresistibly enmeshed in a particular domestic world – is then pitted against Julien Temple's *Pandaemonium* (2000). This film, with its dramatized account of the relationship between Wordsworth and Coleridge, sites artistic creativity – in line with Temple's own oft-demonstrated interests – firmly in the context of other significant social and cultural forces. It is a film that not only serves as illuminating counterpoint to *Bright Star* but also usefully offers a response to some of the concerns about the genre of the literary biopic *per se* articulated in Chapter 7 by Geoffrey Wall.

In Chapter 5, Megan Murray-Pepper considers films about Shakespeare. Where Laura Marcus's concentration was in part on the operations and meanings of the typewriter, Murray-Pepper's is on the geometry and meanings of the dramatist's study space, with a particular focus on the writing desk at its metonymic centre. The desk at which Shakespeare works is on offer as the site of inspiration, labour and subsequent retrospective fantasy about authorial process, mythicized gifting and reassuringly comic banalizing. Into her readings of both the materiality, and the symbolic loading, of cinematically configured desks, Murray-Pepper works a variety of Early Modern uses of the word 'table'. The on-screen versions of Shakespeare's writing desk that she analyses are also used to consider the culturally charged quality of the spectatorial gaze that its variously cinematically configured forms teasingly invite. *How* do we gaze at Shakespeare's writing space, and when we do, what is it that we see there and want to see there? From the enclosed scholarship of Sir John Gielgud's Shakespeare in Peter Greenaway's *Prospero's Books* (1991) to Joseph Fiennes' 'enlarged' boy-about-town in John Madden's *Shakespeare in Love* (1998), and taking in many lesser-known works of cinema along the way, Murray-Pepper examines the shifting semantics of tables and the differing levels of abstraction and worldly integration of cinematic Shakespeares. In the process she shows both how very *placed* and, simultaneously, how very *unplaced* we want our writers to be.

With a more firmly industrial and market focus than other chapters in the volume, in Chapter 6 Andrew Higson discusses literary biopics produced by the British film industry between 1990 and 2010. He asks how these films identify and frame their appeal to a market through plotting, titling, casting, publicity strategies and patterns of distribution roll-out. He considers the variety of potential audiences for British literary biopics (the 'Brit-lit biopic') and the finely differentiated target markets into which the films are typically promoted. For some of these audiences, as Higson shows, it is crucially relevant that these are 'quality' films about the lives of writers. For others, the protagonists of these films just happen to be authors: what is of real interest is their romantic lives, or the pleasing aesthetics (sartorial, architectural, natural) of their settings. In common with Haiduc, Murray-Pepper, Wall and Cartmell (though each in a tonally distinct register), Higson draws attention to the frequency with which romance is made the driver for a film narrative about creativity. He takes as his principal case-study in this the Jane Austen franchise, showing in a variety of ways how its cultural capital has been identified, commercially developed and profitably deployed by the British film industry.

In Chapter 7, Geoffrey Wall asks what, from the range of contradictory desires we have of writers, might motivate an interest in seeing their lives dramatized on screen. Conceived emphatically from the perspective of a literary biographer, Wall's chapter is punctuated throughout by a comparison between literary biopics and literary biographies and underpinned by an implied medium essentialism as he considers what a literary biography can achieve (in particular in its exploration of what he terms the 'deep time' of a life) that, he suggests, a literary biopic cannot. In comparison with the taste for detail, the capacity for sympathy and the commitment to truth-telling to which Thomas Carlyle, for example, thought all biographers should subscribe,[26] Wall rues the generic restrictiveness of the literary biopic in its most conventional expression. Being required to see the life of the writer so frequently through the defining prism of a love story, makes him crave something more, or something different. He challenges himself to try to imagine a different sort of cinema; one that would allow literary biopics to be stories of dissent, or satire, or the scourge of injustice, without needing to embrace the conveniently easy sell of a framing love story as a necessary sop to the perceived tyrannies of the market.

Part II: Cinema's authorial proxies and fictional authors

Savvily recognising the satisfaction to be had in believing fiction to be only lightly codified autobiography, the film industry has frequently harnessed and extended that interpretive habit to generate a symbiotic process of exchange between writers and their work. Thus it is that film adaptations of a work may be invited to resonate discernibly with the life of its author; and, reciprocally, fictionalized film versions of the writer's life to mimic one of a writer's most celebrated or prominent works (what Paul Arthur calls a writer's 'signature creation').[27]

Such courted continuities and symbiotic exchanges between life and work are the focus of the opening three chapters of Part II. R. Barton Palmer's, Deborah Cartmell's and Gennelle Smith's case studies on Ernest Hemingway, Jane Austen and Charlie Kaufman respectively examine works of cinematic literary adaptation that, in more or less self-advertising ways, encode elements of authorial biography within the fabric of their adaptational approach. In the light of a part-fictionalized authorial visibility often drawn to the fore within cinematic adaptations, their chapters show how elements of the writer's life and/or metaphorical presence are suggestively conjured in each case through the filter of cinematic adaptations.

In Chapter 8, R. Barton Palmer argues that Hemingway's public (and publicly performed) self acts as the authorial master text against which, and through which, his works may be judged. This self-narrating Hemingway, Palmer argues, consistently conjured for himself an analogue presence (mimetic and/or counterfactual) in his fiction. Through his analysis of the films *The Snows of Kilimanjaro* (dir. Henry King, 1952), *Hemingway's Adventures of a Young Man* (dir. Martin Ritt, 1962) and *Islands in the Stream* (dir. Franklin J. Schaffner, 1977), Palmer shows how the reflective and refractive properties of the authorial presence to be found in the literary works are rendered yet more conspicuous in their film adaptations – given, in effect, a public airing to correspond to the very public airing of this particular writer's life as performatively lived.

In Chapter 9, Deborah Cartmell considers the ways in which Austen's characters, as represented on screen since 1940, have frequently been invested with Austenian overtones. Reciprocally, she explores how the compliment has been returned in on-screen portrayals of Austen, invited to reverberate, as these often are, with her own fictional characters. The Jane of *Becoming Jane*, for example, argues Cartmell, 'begins the film as Elizabeth Bennet and ends it as Anne Elliot', thereby offering, condensed within her own authorial person, a thumbnail summative tour of Austen's entire fictional oeuvre. Screen adaptations of Jane Austen's fiction and screen versions of Jane Austen's life are thus seen as mutually validating in Cartmell's chapter, each seen through the 'authorizing' filter of the other.

In Chapter 10, Gennelle Smith considers the duplicitous and duplicatory reflections on screenwriting and authorship on offer in Charlie Kaufman's *Adaptation* (dir. Spike Jonze, 2002). She examines Kaufman's own insistent (though literally absent) 'presence' in that film through the variety of entertaining, and neurotically configured, on-screen proxies written into it. Smith uses a consideration of the institutional status of the Hollywood screenwriter, and the necessary collaborations with other institutional players that form part of the screenwriter's trade, to highlight the collaborative processes of writing *per se*, occluded though these more typically are in other, more autonomous-seeming, forms of writing. Within such institutional norms, Smith considers the particularity of Kaufman's own unusual position as a screenwriter with a profile higher than that of most directors. And in relation to *Adaptation* specifically, she interrogates the duplicitous post-modern wrapping of the film, peeling that away to reveal a singular search for truth lurking anxiously within.

In Chapter 11, Richard Burt takes a more oblique approach to the writer on film. He traces the processes of textual *becoming* and the subtle dialects of authorial presence and absence in the production of Medieval and Early Modern manuscripts as dramatized on-screen in *Prospero's Books* (dir. Peter

Greenaway, 1991), *The Tempest* (dir. Julie Taymor, 2010) and *The Secret of Kells* (dir. Tomm Moore, 2009). Burt's interest here centres on the role of opening title sequences and end credit sequences and specifically in the frequency with which the architecture of a book is invited to serve as the framing referent for the 'bookending' packaging of a film. In relation to all three films, and to a range of other animations besides, he considers the ways in which films invite spectators to 'read their way out of the film'. Burt analyses some of the complexities that the resulting book-film homology presents, focusing this analysis on the vexed question of film authorship, and its credited, peritextual and epitextual advertisements, in comparison with literary authorship and its related but distinct formal systems of authorial badging.

The final three chapters of the book take as their subject cinematic configurations of fictional writers: letter writers, diarists, playwrights and writers of non-fiction.

In Chapter 12, through a study of Max Ophüls' *Letter from an Unknown Woman* (1948) and Joseph L. Mankiewicz's *A Letter to Three Wives* (1949), Clara Rowland discusses the evocation of authorial presence and the advertisement of authorial displacement in on-screen letters. She cites one would-be letter-writer in François Truffaut's *Stolen Kisses* (1968) who steps out from behind pen and ink to present herself in person as, fully deliberately, both the message she would otherwise have committed to paper, and, simultaneously, its now-embodied mechanism of delivery. This rendering redundant of the expected letter and insertion in its place of an arrestingly incarnated writer-and-message-in-one inevitably serves as a foil to highlight the defining quality of authorial absence that more conventionally attends the arrival and reception of a letter. Rowland pits this sequence against a later one in *Stolen Kisses* in which two lovers sit at a kitchen table together, and – as if to distance themselves from the full co-presence that their shared breakfasting otherwise constitutes – mimetically exchange love notes. Throughout the chapter, Rowland uses the letter as a charged metaphor for authorial process and authorial absence, and also – in part through its illuminating alignment and distinctive comparison with the telephone – as a metonym for cinema itself, which comparably advertises the absence of both author and actor-agent through a form of partial, substitutory presence.

In Chapter 13, Erica Sheen discusses Robert Bresson's *Journal d'un curé de campagne/Diary of a Country Priest* (1951), arguing that the film presents, in terms drawn from the seventeenth-century writer and thinker Zachary Mayne, a 'bare act' of writing. This is on offer as an act of writing that advertises itself, in the context of its on-screen presentation, *as an act*, in the process speaking back to 'the parasitically literary values of the adaptive process to reveal a radically non-literary understanding of the role of writing in the making of film'. Sheen examines how written text, voice and performance have been variously theorized in complex relation to each other, and how in the midst of such theoretical positions, Bresson manages in *Journal d'un curé de campagne* to negotiate their integrated co-ordination with 'supreme clarity'. In setting the priest's daily process of diary-writing in the context of other forms of reading and writing in the film, she shows how acutely Bresson sensitizes the film's audience to respond to on-screen writing as much in relation to its graphic qualities as to its specific contents (which are, in any case, frequently withheld from view). This preference for textual aesthetics over literary semantics contributes to one strand of Sheen's argument as she argues for the release from the literary that Bresson's cinema potently constitutes.

In Chapter 14, I draw attention to the starkly distinguished versions of (fictional) authorship dramatized in Florian Henckel von Donnersmarck's *Das Leben der Anderen/The Lives of Others* (2006). As the film tracks the incremental erosion of an established dialectic between two politically and aesthetically opposed authoring acts, the suspicions that attach to authorship in the literarily censorious German Democratic Republic before the fall of the Wall come under direct scrutiny. The self-preserving imperative to anonymize a dissenting piece of work is shown to be more than matched by the institutional imperative to *de*anonymize such a work. And the matched quests to discover and know the author of a work – the Stasi operative's desire to know the playwright, the state's desire to know the dissident writer, the playwright's desire to know the author of his own surveillance report – illustrate, in politically hyperbolized form, a psycho-social 'desire' for the author that arguably informs every act of reading.

The draw for the film industry of the lives of authors and of an attentive engagement with authorial process has always been invested with complexity. As one influential cultural institution (cinema) has looked at the processes of another (literature), its trans-medial gaze has been torn between admiring envy and condescension, between an impulse to idealize and the temptation to debunk.[28] Behind both impulses often lurks a suggestively competitive *frisson* as one creative medium appraises, narrates and iconizes the form and functioning of another. But, more than this, in cinema's compulsive return to stories about writing and writers, it is possible to discern a desire to find intimately and intricately analogue tales of creativity through which to metaphorize and cross-examine its own medium ontology, aspirations and competitive position within artistic hierarchies. Looking, as this volume does, at films about writers and about acts of writing can therefore serve, by synecdoche, as an unexpected route into a consideration of the two media of film and literature *per se*.

Notes

1. Richard Ellmann, *Golden Codgers: Biographical Speculations* (London, New York, Toronto: Oxford University Press, 1973), p. 16.

2. The taste for conjecture is not unknown in literary biographies either. Writing in 2007 in *The Chronicle of Higher Education*, American writer and literary commentator Edward Champion wrote: 'Two things can be said about the ever-popular genre of literary biography: Trade and university presses show no reticence in chipping and pulping the forests on behalf of almost any conceivable figure. And both increasingly prize conjecture over scholarship, with biographers salivating over half-baked thoughts frosted with significance and treating minor foibles as if they were as important as an author's work.' Champion, 'The Perils of Literary Biography', *The Chronicle of Higher Education*, 'The Chronicle *Review*' (21 Dec 2007). At: http://chronicle.com/article/The-Perils-of-Literary/10084/ (accessed 10 December 2012).

3. There are earlier films in which people write by hand and write at typewriters, but none that I have (yet) found in which an act of writing is the central engine of the action, or the life of the writer the central subject. If, however, others know of earlier films that do this, I would be grateful to hear from them.

4. The second still (Figure I.3), held at the Museum of Modern Art in New York, formed part of Robert Hamilton Ball's impressively ranging research findings. The first still (Figure I.2) was deposited for copyright purposes at the Library of Congress on 25 October 1907 but escaped Ball's notice (who at that time found 'nothing now on deposit'). See Robert Hamilton Ball, *Shakespeare on Silent Film: A Strange Eventful History* (New York: Theatre Arts Books, 1968), p. 308.

5. The entry from the Star Catalogue is quoted in full in Ball, *Shakespeare on Silent Film* (1968), pp. 35–6. This lost film is further discussed in both Laura Marcus's and Megan Murray-Pepper's chapters in this volume.

6. On Byron's image, see: Christine Kenyon-Jones, *Byron: The Image of a Poet* (Newark: University of Delaware Press, 2008); Robert Beevers, *The Byronic Image: The Poet Portrayed* (Abingdon: Olivia Press, 2005); Annette Peach, *Portraits of Byron* (London: The Walpole Society, 2000). For counter examples – portraits of Byron with a book or pen – see Beevers (2005), pp. 62, 96 and Peach (2000), p. 80, Figure 48. I am grateful to Spiz Demetriou for an illuminating exchange about Byron's image.

7. The Shakespearean figure in Peter Greenaway's much later film *Prospero's Books* (1991) – discussed in both Megan Murray-Pepper's and Richard Burt's chapters in this volume – is, by contrast, anti-Byronic: ostentatiously learned, immersed in a culture of excessive literariness and occupying a Renaissance scholar's writing cell that sits at the iconic and thematic centre of the film. The meanings and effects of the scholarly character rhyme explicitly signalled between Greenaway's Prospero and the learned St. Jerome are discussed in Buchanan, *Shakespeare on Film* (Harlow: Longman-Pearson, 2005), pp. 225–30. In Chapter 7 of this volume, Geoffrey Wall laments that the temporal restrictions on biopictorial form so often mean that the literariness of the writing process, and a writer's imbibing of literary precedents, tend to be omitted from writer films (see p. 130).

8. Paul Arthur 'The Written Scene: Writers as Figures of Cinematic Redemption', in Robert Stam and Alessandra Raengo (eds) *Literature and Film: A Guide to the Theory and Practice of Film Adaptation* (Oxford: Blackwell, 2005), p. 331.

9. In 1996, to mark forty years since the first publication of Ginsberg's 'Howl', Ginsberg published *Illuminated Poems* as a close collaboration with graphic artist Eric Drooker. For the 2010 film *Howl*, Drooker then animated his own illustrations from the 1996 volume, and also published *Howl: A Graphic Novel* (Penguin) as an analogue text to the film. This latter volume includes not only Ginsberg's poem but also stills from the film showing Drooker's own animated illustrations. The circularity of this transmedial sequential publication process is striking.

10. In the extent to which it is an iconoclastic *exposé*, the film follows Enid Blyton's younger daughter's own reminiscences. See Imogen Smallwood, *A Childhood at Green Hedges: A Fragment of Autobiography by Enid Blyton's Daughter* (London: Methuen, 1989). The film's secondary source is Barbara Stoney's biography, *Enid Blyton* (London: Hodder and Stoughton, 1974), commissioned by Blyton's elder daughter, Gillian Baverstock. *Enid*'s director, James Hawes, is known for biographical films of controversial female characters and for exhibiting a taste for puncturing the moral and/or social dimensions of a legend (*The Chatterley Affair, Fanny Hill, Miss Marie Lloyd*).

11. Keats originally expressed this thought in a letter to Richard Woodhouse (27 October 1818). See Hyder Edward Rollins (ed.) *The Letters of John Keats, 1814–21*, 2 vols (Cambridge, MA: Harvard University Press, 1958), vol. 1, p. 387.

12. These sittings took place at the Villa Rossa, Leghorn, near Pisa.

13. West's account is published as appendix to William Edward West and Estill Curtis Pennington, 'Painting Lord Byron: An Account by William Edward West', *Archives of American Art Journal* v.24, n. 2 (1984), pp. 16–21 (19–20). West's 1822 dreamy portrait of Byron in oils (30 x 25 ins) is on exhibition at the National Portrait Gallery of Scotland.

14. Virginia Woolf, 'Great Men's Houses', in *The London Scene* (first pub. 1931) (London: Snowbooks, 1975), pp. 37–47 (37–8).

15. Edmund de Waal, *The Hare with Amber Eyes* (London: Chatto and Windus, 2010), p. 16.

16. By anonymous donation, the desk has now been gifted to the Brontë Parsonage Museum in Haworth, to help assert authentic and materially coherent 'Brontë-ness' to the thousands of visitors who visit the Parsonage each year.

17. See Roland Barthes, 'The Death of the Author' (first pub. 1967), *Image-Music-Text* trans. Stephen Heath (New York: Hill and Wang, 1978), pp. 142–8 (143, 142).

18. Roland Barthes, *The Pleasure of the Text*, translated by Richard Miller (New York: Hill and Wang, 1975), p. 27.

19. Michel Foucault, 'What is an Author' (a 1969 lecture), in Paul Rabinow (ed.) *The Foucault Reader: An Introduction to Foucault's Thought* (London: Penguin, 1991), pp. 101–20.

20. This moment from Doctor Who was entertainingly discussed by Peter Holland in his talk 'Shakespeare, Humanity Indicators and the Seven Deadly Sins', part of the 'What Public Value the Arts and Humanities?' Jane Moody Memorial Debate in the Humanities Research Centre of the University of York (9 March 2012).

21. Laura Cumming, *A Face to the World: On Self-Portraits* (London: HarperPress, 2009), p. 4.

22. The Kindle responds to the 'power off' instruction by automatically switching to the image of a literary writer, selected at random from a hidden, and inaccessible, archival bank of authorial images. Virginia Woolf, Charles Dickens, Mark Twain, Jules Verne, James Ellison, Charlotte Bronte, John Steinbeck, Alexandre Dumas, St. Jerome, Agatha Christie, Erasmus. Though nowhere detailed in Kindle's advertising materials, nor as yet commented upon in mainstream user reviews, this serial ambush of literary portraiture is an untrumpeted bonus the Kindle offers its readers.

23. 'I must candidly express my opinion that Shakespeare's last monument is in his works, and that it would be but a poor act of homage to his memory and genius to set up a memorial to him among the London statues.' Graham Storey (ed.) *The Letters of Charles Dickens 1820–1870*, v.10 1862–1864, Preface p. ix (quoting from Letter to John Bainbridge (6 September 1864)).

24. Graham Storey (ed.) *The Letters of Charles Dickens 1820–1870*, v.12 1868–1870, Last Will (12 May 1869), p. 732.

25. The entry from the Star Catalogue is quoted in full in Ball, *Shakespeare on Silent Film* (1968), pp. 35–6.

26. For a discussion of Carlyle's principles of biographical writing see Hermione Lee, *Body Parts: Essays on Life Writing* (London: Chatto and Windus, 2005), p. 1.

27. Paul Arthur 'The Written Scene' (2005), p. 332.

28. This closely mimics the processes of 'homage and rivalry' by which Jay David Bolter and Richard Grussin characterize acts of appropriative *intra*-medial refashioning. Bolter and Grusin, *Remediation: Understanding New Media* (Cambridge, MA: MIT Press, 2000), p. 49. Both homage and rivalry are clearly discernible in the acts of both *remediation* and of medium *incorporation* under consideration in this volume.

Part I
Cinema's Versions and Uses of Literary Lives

1
The writer in film: authorship and imagination

Laura Marcus

The relationship between the visual and the verbal, image and word, has been the ground of longstanding aesthetic debate. The representation of literary authorship in film bears on this in close and complex ways. This chapter considers a number of films and texts in which the transition between book and film, word and image, is foregrounded both thematically and through formal strategies. The focus of the chapter will be on recent film and literature, though there will also be some discussion of the ways in which authorship is represented in earlier cinema. One significant contrast to which this discussion will point is early film's use of the dissolve, or similar modes of signalling transition, to represent the move from the authorial mind/hand to his or her created world, actualized in film. In recent cinema, by contrast, there has been a tendency to break down the distinction between 'real' and 'imagined' worlds, so that 'the author' becomes part of, and subject to, the dimensions of the fictional world.

In early cinema we find the representation of the figure of the author in the act of creation or composition, and the production of his characters as emanations of the self. George Méliès' 1907 film (now lost), *Shakespeare writing Julius Caesar*, was described by 'The Star' film catalogue as:

> show[ing] the bard of Avon seated in his study, trying to devise the scene in which Caesar is murdered by the conspirators ... [A]t his wit's end, he sits down in an armchair, crosses his legs, and leaning on his hand prepares for a good long think. Suddenly, his thoughts take life, and right before him appears an old Roman forum. Shakespeare is still seated in his armchair and now watches all that occurs.[1]

Shakespeare thus becomes a spectator, as the assassination unfolds in front of him. The film returns to Shakespeare in his study:

> Alone he goes through the whole scene and winds up by raising a knife and plunging it furiously into the loaf of bread which was on the table.

Realizing the humour of the situation he now joins in a hearty laugh with his servant, but is unable to eat from enthusiasm. When the servant leaves the room he steps back and folds his arms, and the scene dissolves into a bust of Shakespeare around which all the nations wave flags and garlands'.[2]

In the 1924 film *Dickens' London* (dirs. Frank Miller and Harry B. Parkinson), the representation of 'thoughts taking life' is inaugurated through images of the writing hand. We see Dickens writing at his desk, representing the composition of characters who then 'come to life' on the page/screen.[3] There is thus a construction of an identity between the page and screen, word and image. The image of a character emerging from the novelist's birthplace, a further trope in this film, also becomes emblematic of authorship, understood as a form of generation or birthing. We should also note, however, the continuities between the strategies of this film and those of early films, most notably of British filmmaker Thomas Bentley, which presented 'life-like' recreations of Dickens' and of Dickens' characters against the 'real background' of their geographical settings.[4] The performances were theatrical presentations of 'character', which in turn drew for their detail on the illustrations to the novels: the cinema added the dimension unavailable to the stage, in the photographic representation of place. Literature was both the origin of incident and re-entered the filmic space as inter-title. The translation that took place from page to screen thus passed through, or brought in its train, many different forms of representation – graphic, verbal, visual and aural. *Dickens' London*, in its movement from the act of authorial creation to the author's created world, anticipated the devices employed in numerous later Dickens' adaptations, which marked authorial origin and the book as origin of its cinematic interpretation, at the same time as the author's words (in the era of sound) 'meld', in Guerric DeBona's words, 'with those of the first person narrator, and finally with the dramatized action [of the film].'[5]

On the one hand, such sequences might be seen to secure authorial origin and the primacy of the book/literature. On the other, they suggest the singular power of film to bring words to life and to vision, even implying that cinematic/visual imaging may be closer to the dreams and imaginings of authors than writing/language could ever be. Among the most significant examples here are David Lean's adaptation of *Great Expectations* (1946) and George Cukor and David O. Selznick's *David Copperfield* (1935). At the start of Lean's film, we see a hand opening a book, and (bypassing the title page) the voice-over begins to read the lines of the first page: 'My father's family name being Pirrip, and my Christian name Philip, my infant tongue could make of both names nothing longer or more explicit than Pip. So, I called myself Pip, and came to be called Pip.' As the camera moves in, the words become legible, so that the spectator can read the words as the voice-over speaks them. The pages of the book begin to be ruffled as by the wind, and we move from the book and voice-over to the image of a boy (Tony Wager) running on a path through marshes, with the sound of the wind that the image of the turning pages had first released. Once the boy has run past a gibbet and into a graveyard, some new text, this time diegetically integrated into the fabric of the scene, appears in shot in the names of Philip Pirrip and 'also Georgiana, wife of the above' engraved upon a tombstone.

The opening of Cukor and Selznick's *David Copperfield* similarly works to connect page and screen, word and image. Here the credits appear as a form of title page, which resembles an illustrated book. The film's first shot is of an open volume: written on the page is the epigraph from the revised preface of the 1869 edition of *David Copperfield* – 'Like many fond parents I have in my heart of hearts a favourite child. And his name is DAVID COPPERFIELD' – with the signature of Charles Dickens underneath. As DeBona has argued: 'This particular film presents us with a "Charles Dickens" who seems to endorse the visual project with his very signature ... [I]t invites the audience to think of "Charles Dickens" as the ultimate creator of the cinematic space.'[6] A hand then turns the page to the opening lines of the novel (without voice-over). In the sequence that follows, the figure of a woman (David's aunt, Betsey Trotwood (Edna May Oliver)), battling her way through the wind to knock on the window of a cottage, emerges as if it were an animated illustration: these first images of the novel's characters thus appear to connect writing, illustration and film. As in Lean's *Great Expectations*, the hero's father's tombstone becomes a central image, its inscriptions (naming father and mother, or father alone) a form of writing which transcribes a life as origin and end. In the case of Cukor's *David Copperfield*, the gravestone is also the inscribed surface (like a page) over which shots of the changing seasons mark the passing of time, coming between the image of the newborn David and his appearance as a boy by his father's grave.

In mapping and dramatizing the transitions between novel and film, as both films do, the use of voice-over at the opening of *Great Expectations* is a way of importing, in only minimally transmediated form, the novel's first-person narrative into the film medium. By contrast, Lean's *Oliver Twist* (1948) opens voicelessly with a lengthy Expressionist-influenced sequence. We see a young pregnant woman, outlined against the sky, held back by a fierce storm as she struggles towards the workhouse, the wind bending both the tree to which she clings and her body. There appears less concern than in *Great Expectations* with the process of moving from book to film, and fuller engagement with the question of film language itself. The opening sequence represents both the hostile environment and the body in pain, while both body and tree become hieroglyphics of the kind that silent cinema had so fully developed. The *Oliver Twist* sequence seems indeed to echo films such as D.W. Griffith's *Way Down East* (1920) and *Orphans of the Storm* (1921), as well as F.W. Murnau's *Faust* (1926), in which Gretchen (Camilla Horn) is cast into a blizzard with her new-born child.

Despite their differences (including the dominance of voice at the start of Lean's *Great Expectations* and of the silent image in his *Oliver Twist*), the opening sections of all three of the Dickens' adaptations discussed are connected by their use of wind or storm as energies that drive the transition from one medium into another (book to film, word to image), rather as the tornado in Victor Fleming's *The Wizard of Oz* (1939) transports Dorothy, and the spectator, both from one world to another, and, in the process, from sepia-tone to Technicolor.

In these films, as in film adaptations more broadly, issues of visual/verbal relationships as well as those of film history and film technology, including the silent/sound transition, become central. Fiction, as well as film, of the past few decades has seen a widespread engagement with relationships and transitions between the written or printed word and the cinematic image. The intense focus on the materiality of film, which marks much recent film theory, has produced a renewed engagement with the represented word on the screen. This acts as a recapitulation of cinema's original encounter with written language, which turned upon the use of intertitles, as well as on the 'film hieroglyphics' that defined, for many of the film's early commentators, the pictorial language of silent cinema. For the early film theorist Vachel Lindsay, the hieroglyphic language of film was perceived as a 'picture writing', a 'new universal alphabet' and 'a moving picture Esperanto'.[7] It was at one, for Lindsay, with the intensely 'pictorial psychology' of modern American life and with the graphic dimensions of urban modernity, figured in media such as advertisements, billboards and newspapers.

Much recent fiction has taken up anew the charged and complex relationship between the visual and the verbal, with film often entering the novelistic framework as a distinct but parallel mode of representation and narration. In Paul Auster's 2002 novel, *The Book of Illusions*, to take one prominent example, the central protagonist and first person narrator, David Zimmer, desolated by the death of his wife and sons in a plane crash, becomes fascinated, in his grief, by the films of a silent screen actor, Hector Mann, and finds that he is sustained by his research and writing on them. The silent film comedians had, Zimmer asserts:

> understood the language they were speaking. They had invented a syntax of the eye, a grammar of pure kinesis ... We watched them across a great chasm of forgetfulness, and the very things that separated them from us were in fact what made them so arresting; their muteness, their absence of color, their fitful, speeded-up rhythms.[8]

Most interesting here is the alliance or allegiance that is being forged between the contemporary novel and the silent film. There is a suggestion that cinema, having given up on these early manifestations of its medium, having allowed this silent art to die, has in some sense released it for re-animation by the writer, even though it is, Auster insists, a wholly visual language. Describing the processes of putting his film-book together, Zimmer tells a friend: 'I was writing about things I couldn't see anymore and I had to present them in purely visual terms. The whole experience was like a hallucination'.[9]

Auster has his narrative move through the films he has invented for Mann in precise sequential detail, so that we are asked, as readers, to visualize his words as linear film-images. The film that is recounted in the fullest detail was Mann's last silent film, and its story is that of a man who is rendered invisible by a jealous employer. For Auster, the thematic and the process of 'becoming invisible' are at one with the novel's preoccupations with cinema as a presence of absence; with annihilation and 'the anguish of selfhood';[10] with the destruction of films in the desert landscape. As always in Auster's work, however, the question of authorship, of the role of the writer and of writing, are the most fundamental preoccupations.

The silent film in *The Book of Illusions* is represented as a co-creation of the actor's face and the camera lens: the close-up of the face is pure interiority, 'a reflection of what we all are when we're alone inside ourselves'.[11] When these close-up sequences occur:

> everything else stops. We can read the content of Hector's mind as though it were spelled out in letters across the screen, and before those letters vanish, they are no less visible than a building, a piano, or a pie in the face.[12]

Auster would appear to be calling here on the concept of 'inner speech', central to early film theory, and, in particular, to early Soviet writings on film. The Formalist theorist Boris Eikhenbaum, in his 'Problems of Film Stylistics', published in 1927, argued that it is 'inner speech' that allows the spectator to make the connections between separate shots, verbal discourse being the ground upon which the filmic is figured.[13] Other contemporary thinkers, including linguist Lev Vygotsky, emphasized the differentially discursive aspects of 'inner speech': 'Inner speech is to a large extent thinking in pure meanings. It is a dynamic, shifting, unstable thing, fluttering between word and image'.[14] In Auster's novel, 'inner speech' is represented as a relationship between the actor and the camera, rather than as an inner property of the spectator, but there is nonetheless an understanding, similar to that of the Soviet theorists and their later commentators in film theory, of a film-mind embodied, or projected forth, as a mode of writing on the screen.

This image of screen-writing or inscription is illuminated by Garrett Stewart's discussions of the *photogram* of the film (defined as 'the image track's smallest sequenced unit of eventual screen manifestation … the individuated photographic unit on the transparent strip that conduces in motion to screen movement'),[15] and the *phonogram* of literary language.

While Stewart refers only in passing to Auster's novels, he attends in more detail to the 1995 film *Smoke*, written and co-directed by Auster (with Wayne Wang). The sequence in *Smoke* in which Auggie Wren, the cigar-shop proprietor, shows the writer Paul Benjamin his albums of photographs – taken each day on the same spot at the same time – points up significant questions of repetition and difference, and of the arrest by the photographic image of time and movement. As in virtually all Auster's fictions, his central writer-protagonist is in mourning – in this case, for his wife, who was caught up, and killed, in a shooting on the corner outside the cigar shop. As Paul turns the pages of the albums, he sees the image of his living wife, caught by the camera lens: 'Oh Jesus – look, it's Ellen – It's Ellen. Look at her.' It's an arrest that takes us back to that very early story of cinema, Rudyard Kipling's 'Mrs Bathurst', and its resonant line, as the narrator watches the film of the train coming into the station and the passengers moving along the platform: 'Christ! There's Mrs B!'[16]

For Stewart, *Smoke* is 'a kind of summa: namely, of photography's relation to diurnal reality, to temporality, to narrativity, to death, and ultimately to filmic visuality – and hence to the revealed imaginary of film's mechanized textuality'.[17] At the close of the film sequence discussed above, we see Auggie outside his shop taking his daily picture, and then cut to Paul Benjamin at his typewriter. An explicit correspondence is being drawn here between the acts of taking a photograph and of typing a line of text. This correspondence is reinvoked at the film's close, with a radical splitting between words (the recounting of a story whose factuality is in doubt) and images (the visual representation of the same story in silence and in black and white). This final sequence represents pure vision, one of its ironies being that its story is that of Auggie's masquerade, on Christmas Day, as the grandson of an old blind woman, who, unable to see him, chooses to pretend to believe his fictions. However, the sequence follows a shot of Paul Benjamin's typewriter and the words of his title page: 'Auggie Wren's Christmas Story by Paul Benjamin'. The two sequences thus pose questions about the relative authority of word and image: the visual seems to have primacy, but it is also represented as emerging from the writer's act of textual inscription. The typed story is in turn a transcription of Auggie's spoken words, recounted to Paul by Auggie in a sequence that focuses obsessively on the talking mouth of Auggie the narrator. In a further twist, the camera (originally stolen, we are led to assume, by the real grandson), picked up by Auggie as he leaves the old woman's house, appears to be the apparatus that has taken his diurnal photographs. These have punctuated the film and created their own form of storytelling.

Authorship and narration in *Smoke* are charged in ways relevant to contemporary cinema more broadly. First, the name of the author, Paul Auster, is partially contained within his character Paul Benjamin, in a form of part-doubling that encodes the relationship between the writer and his/her fictional creations. Second, the act of writing in *Smoke* is mediated through, or represented alongside, different forms of inscription: photography (whose etymology is 'light-writing'), typing and dictation. Auggie's monologue is first spoken and then represented visually (behind the lettering of the credits), but it is also understood to have passed through (or, more reflexively yet, to have been created by) the medium of Paul Benjamin's typed words. The complexities in concepts of authorship and of visual–verbal relationships that this posits contravene both a one-way transmission model from literary text to its filmic 'adaptation' and an authority attendant upon the primacy of the book.

The troubling of authority (of author over text, word over image, literature over film) occurs in a significant number of recent films in which the writer, and often the screenwriter, becomes a central figure – creating, or created by, his or her verbal/textual imaginings. These issues are at the heart of Spike Jonze's *Adaptation* (2002). In this radically self-reflexive film, the screenwriter Charlie Kaufman (Nicholas Cage) is working, with much difficulty, on an adaptation of *The Orchid Thief*, a (real) non-fictional work written by (real) *New Yorker* journalist, Susan Orlean (Meryl Streep). The film originated when the real Hollywood screenwriter Kaufman was in fact trying to adapt Orlean's book for a film: his struggles with the material led him to write his own predicament into the screenplay. He doubles his own fictionalized character by inventing a twin brother, Donald Kaufman, an aspirant, and ultimately more successful, scriptwriter who is more than willing to play the sensationalist and sentimental Hollywood game which Charlie repudiates. In the course of the film, Donald takes over the story that Charlie had been attempting to adapt. In Donald's hands, its more reflective narrative (about a man with a passion for orchids) becomes a highly charged plot whose narrative engine is both sex and violence. In this new, high-octane version of the story, the love-affair between Susan Orlean and the orchid-thief, John Laroche (whose story she is telling), ends in the murder of Donald and the death of Laroche, in the orchid-nurturing Florida swamp.

The film's self-reflexivity turns not only on metafictional modes of narration, reflecting on its own constructions of character and story, but on the very term 'adaptation'. Darwin's *The Origin of Species* (first published 1859) and the representation of Darwin writing his text, are brought into the film frame in relation to the biological meanings of 'adaptation' and mutation. 'Adaptation is a profound process,' Laroche claims, as he describes the specimens which he collects. Susan Orlean is more resistant to the concept: 'Adapting's almost shameful ... Change is not a choice.' Her comments bear, in ironic ways, on the act of adaptation of her own *The Orchid Thief*, initially an essay for the *New Yorker* and subsequently extended and transmuted from essay into book, and then, painfully and obliquely, into film.

At the film's conclusion, Charlie takes back his screenplay and his story. The film closes with his typing and with a voice-over, the very narrative device condemned in the strongest terms earlier in the film by screenwriter Robert McKee, whose weekend course on scriptwriting both Donald (successfully) and Charlie (in desperation) had attended. The voice-over, with which the film also opens, is ultimately reclaimed as a way of representing thought and interiority. It is also intimately linked to the act of typing: the opening credit sequence gives us small typewritten letters at the bottom of a black screen, and a voice-over narration. The manual typewriter is Charlie's writing instrument, whereas Susan Orlean uses a word-processor, the glow from which becomes part of the nocturnal milieu of her New York apartment. As Charlie types, the voice-over speaks the words as they emerge onto the page: writing/typing, voice, imagination and the visual image come together in a form of composite resolution.

Stranger than Fiction (dir. Marc Forster, 2006) shares this preoccupation with the act of writing/typing, narration, the voice in the head and the uncanny relationship between author and character. The film's central protagonist, Harold Crick (Will Ferrell), a tax inspector whose life runs like clockwork, one day begins to hear a voice narrating his actions as he performs them. Professor Jules Hilbert (Dustin Hoffman), the literary theorist he consults, has his attention caught when Crick repeats the narrated phrase 'little did he know', the third-person omniscient voice on which Hilbert has written extensively. He runs through the various possibilities of narrative, genre and plot in which Crick is living, revolving in particular around the question of whether his will be a comic or a tragic resolution. Crick discovers that his 'author' is a woman writer, Karen Eiffel (Emma Thompson), suffering from a long period of writer's block, whose previous novels have always ended with the violent deaths of their protagonists, a fate she also intends for the fictional creation with whom Crick shares an identity. He is able to meet her, and to read the manuscript of her novel. As the film moves towards its close, we see Karen Eiffel typing, on her manual typewriter, the words that seem to signal Crick's fate. She finds herself, however, unable to deliver the final narrative blow, instead allowing him to survive an accident that has been the result of his own good actions.

The film's popular metaphysics are by no means exceptional: they raise familiar issues of the symbiotic relationship between author and character, and of the author as God and the nature of free will and determinism in the plot of our lives. These concerns, as expressed in recent films such as *Adaptation, Stranger than Fiction* and *Barton Fink* (dirs. Joel and Ethan Coen, 1991), are also, however, part of a more particular contemporary preoccupation in cinema with issues of writing, narration and the visual. In *Stranger than Fiction*, there is an ambiguity over whether Crick's actions follow Karen Eiffel's words or, as Professor Hilbert suggests, whether her words are in fact led by his actions. The conundrum bears not only on who is 'authoring' whom, but on the question of the relative primacy of word or image in cinema, and on the relationship between the word and the filmic world.

The insistent representation of the manually typed word in these contemporary films is also striking. Ian McEwan's novel *Atonement* makes much of the danger of typed word on white page, while Joe Wright's 2007 film adaptation (scripted by playwright Christopher Hampton) begins with the sound of a typewriter, alerting us to the complex layerings of storytelling, authorship and temporality that make up the novel. The film's opening sequence tracks from a doll's house (a miniaturized version, or simulacrum, of the real house) across the bedroom to Briony Tallis (Saoirse Ronan) as a young girl typing her play on a manual typewriter to focus on the typed words 'THE END'. The noise of the typewriter is further incorporated into the film's soundtrack, becoming central to its emotive register. It also underscores other rhythmic or machine-like sounds in the film, some of which (the rhythm of a tram, the tapping of nurses' shoes as they walk along a hospital corridor) come to represent the inexorable march of time. Typing and the typewriter become inextricably linked in the film to passion, danger, betrayal and atonement (as the adult Briony types her confessional and consolatory fictions). Robbie Turner's (James McAvoy) sexually explicit note ('the wrong version' he tells Cecilia Tallis (Keira Knightley), 'it was never meant to be read') is typed: the safe, 'more formal', version he had intended to send was handwritten. The typed note is subsequently linked, in part by the soundtrack, to the false witness statements and the legal deposition: typewriting comes to embody fixity – that which cannot be undone. The representation of typing is thus ambiguous. The later love-letters between Cecilia and Robbie are handwritten, but it is the typed word and the sound of the typewriter that become the motor of the narrative, aligning typing, desire and even the mechanisms of the film itself.

Authorship, as in a number of the films discussed in this chapter, is frequently perceived to be at its most authentic with the use of the manual typewriter which, by contrast with the word-processor, fixes words and their sequence and renders their erasure an imperfect one. Paul Auster's *The Story of My Typewriter* is a vehicle not merely for Sam Messer's art work but also for Auster's own love song to his 'Olympia' manual typewriter. The West Germany from which the 'Olympia' came no longer exists as a country, Auster writes, but since the day in 1974 on which he bought the typewriter, 'every word I have written has been typed out on that machine.'[18] His statement echoes those of an earlier generation of writers. For William S. Burroughs, as Darren Wersher-Henry notes in his 'fragmented history of typewriting', writing *is* typing.[19] In Burroughs' words: 'Sinclair Lewis said: "If you want to be a writer, learn to type." This advice is hardly necessary now. So then sit at your typewriter and write.'[20]

The identity of typing takes on new resonances, however, in the age of the personal computer and word-processor. The typewriter gains auratic status in the face of the technology that has succeeded it: the typewritten word now represents a mode of composition from a moment when the writer's body was still intimately bound up with the production of the word. The insistent image of the typing writer in contemporary films also bears on another, more directly cinematic developmental shift: from analogue to digital technologies, and on the attendant sense of loss (as in concepts of 'the death of cinema') that has also accompanied the supersession of the typewriter. It could be argued that the very basis of cinema – its editing and re-ordering of material – has affinities with the computer and word-processing. Nonetheless, the 'materiality' of the manually typed word – its impressing, spacing, sequencing and rhythm – would seem to have become closely identified with the 'photogrammic' basis of the celluloid film, now being replaced by digital film.

An equation between typewriting and authentic authorship is central to the 2010 film *Howl* (dirs. Rob Epstein and Jeffrey Friedman). Using documentary re-enactment, as well as archival photography/film footage, the film cuts between the Allen Ginsberg figure (James Franco) writing/typing the poem 'Howl', his reading of the poem in San Francisco's Six Gallery in 1955, a 1957 re-enacted interview with Ginsberg and a re-enactment of the 1957 obscenity trial in San Francisco, in which the poet and City Light's publisher Lawrence Ferlinghetti was on trial, but at which Ginsberg was not himself present. The film also contains lengthy animation sequences, in which the poem is represented or realized through a visual imagery which references the form of the graphic novel. The animated sequences draw directly on Eric Drooker's art work, long admired by Ginsberg. Drooker had been commissioned to illustrate Ginsberg's *Illuminated Poems* (1996), and it is these illustrations that are animated in *Howl*. The relationship between the visual and the verbal is opened up in these images in ways inflected by the hallucinatory imagery of the drug experiences which are central to the poem's imaginative world.

The film's credit sequence opens in the Six Gallery, with Ginsberg reading the opening of 'Howl' from a manuscript. The film uses the words 'contemplating jazz' (line four of the poem) as the trigger to move into the rest of the credit sequence, with a shot of a typewriter and the on-screen words: 'In 1955, an unpublished 29 year-old poet presented his vision of the world as a poem in four parts. He called it ... HOWL. His name was Allen Ginsberg.' The film cuts to the (reconstructed) interview in 1957, and then back to 'Two Years Earlier'. The typewriter appears again and we see Franco's Ginsberg typing the first line of the poem: 'I saw the best minds of my generation destroyed.' The letters on the keys turn into musical notation and then animation. The animated sequence, beginning with a crawling, naked male figure, takes on its own life, accompanied and inspired now by the words heard in the Ginsberg-Franco performative voice-over: 'I saw the best minds of my generation destroyed.' A figure is seen typing within the animated sequence, and we return to live-action Ginsberg typing.

'The typewriter is holy', Ginsberg wrote in 'Howl'. He later told fellow Beat writer William Burroughs, in a discussion about the creation of 'Howl': 'The typewriter imagination tells the writer what to write.'[21] In a further retrospective account of the poem's composition, Ginsberg remembers how 'the whole first section' was:

> typed out madly in one afternoon, a tragic custard-pie of wild phrasing, meaningless images for the beauty of abstract poetry of mind running along making awkward combinations like Charlie Chaplin's walk, long saxophone-like chorus lines.[22]

The typewriter becomes a mediator between writing and film: typed composition is represented as at once spontaneous flow and as a mental mechanism analogous to Chaplin's mechanical, jerky walk. Ginsberg shared this understanding with other Beat writers, including his friend Jack Kerouac, whose novel *On the Road* (1957) was, famously, written on a typewriter using a continuous roll of paper, which both removed the interruption of the page break and rendered the act of writing, and the writing produced, akin to a continuous reel of film. As Ginsberg wrote:

> *On the Road* [was] an attempt to trap the prose of truth mind by means of a highly scientific attack on new prose method. The result was a magnificent single paragraph several blocks long, rolling, like the road itself, the length of an entire onionskin teletype roll. The sadness was that this was never published in its most exciting form – its original discovery – but hacked and punctuated and broken ... by presumptuous literary critics in publishing houses.[23]

Al Leslie (co-director, with Robert Frank, of the avant-garde film *Pull My Daisy* (1959), starring Beat writers including Ginsberg and Kerouac) told critic Daniel Kane in interview:

> *Pull My Daisy* was made in response to Jack's language. Jack used the typewriter as an instrument. He would sit down, he would get into his state, whether he was high or not, the idea was to get himself free enough to unleash all of those ideas and thoughts, but since he was a speed typist, he was able to pull that stuff out as fast as he could get it all down, and then by having his so-called roll of paper he was able to do it without any interruption, the way [saxophonist John] Coltrane would.'[24]

As Kane notes of this discussion in his book *We Saw the Light*, which explores the relationship between the New American poets and film-makers of the 1960s, there is 'a blurring of the boundaries between the various mechanisms of typewriter, film projector and saxophone.'[25] These connections find their way not only into the film *Howl* but also into other films which have explored or adapted Beat writing, notably David Cronenberg's *Naked Lunch* (1991). In this film, which intertwines, in surreal and hallucinatory fashion, an adaptation of William Burroughs' novel of that title with elements of Burroughs' own biography, the typewriter is a central 'character', morphing at various points into one of the grotesque talking insect-bodies that haunt the film. For Jack Kerouac, writing in the mid-1950s, 'Bookmovie is the movie in words, the visual American form.'[26] The various modes of Epstein and Friedman's *Howl* – archive photographs, constructed photographs, animation, documentary re-enactment, reconstructed court-room scenes – become multiple ways of interpreting the 'bookmovie' that is Ginsberg's poem. The depiction of the process of creation (the typing hand/body), which is then translated into the colour and moving forms of the animated poetic imagery, is an attempt (if perhaps only a partially successful one) to represent the relationship between word/text and visual/mental picturing. The film also moves repeatedly between the act of writing/typing the poem and its reading/performance by Ginsberg, to an audience that included Kerouac and Neal Cassady: the reading of the poem indeed frames the film, providing its narrative line and temporal progression, though there is also a continual return to the lines of verse. This use of repetition is closely connected to the question of adaptation which is, as Linda Hutcheon has argued, a form of 'repetition without replication' or 'repetition with variation'.[27] The different sites and contexts represented in the film are also the various reception sites of the poem 'Howl' (Ginsberg's own 'reception' of his typed words, the reading in the Six Gallery, the dissection of the poem in the court-room). These in turn bear on different modes of mediation in and between writing and film.

Ginsberg's reading is brought into ironic relationship with the reading of its lines in the court-room scenes, by the prosecuting lawyer in particular. As Stanley Fish noted in a review of *Howl*, this is film as literary criticism.[28] The actual trial process brought in a large number of expert witnesses, of which the film selects a representative few. New critical tenets were played out in the courtroom discussion of the poem: these included both the restrictive formalisms of some of the 'expert witnesses' (placed in ironic contrast to the Ginsberg character's insistence, in the dramatized interviews, on the spontaneity of poetic creation) and critic and literature professor Mark Schorer's invocation of 'the heresy of paraphrase', as a way of defending poetry against both crude literalism and the charges of obscenity.[29] One of the central aspects of the trial highlighted in the film is the discussion of influence and originality that formed part of the evidence of the expert witnesses and was taken up by both the prosecution and the defence. For the prosecution, Ginsberg's indebtedness to Walt Whitman in particular, renders 'Howl' less than literature, and hence unprotected from the charge of obscenity. The defence counters with the suggestion that Whitman (and by extension all writers) was himself writing out of a tradition and that no writer is ever entirely *fons et origo*. The film's focus on this aspect of the trial – the issue of 'Howl' as a derivative work – again brings in its train the question of adaptation, and the issues it raises about originality, influence and derivation.

One of the most interesting aspects of the film *Howl* is that it is not a biopic of Allen Ginsberg but, in substantial part, an exploration of the relationship and transmutation between visual and verbal images that the common title of poem and film suggests. Earlier twentieth-century writers commenting on film, including Virginia Woolf and W.H. Auden, defined poetry through the complexity and multisensory dimensions of its images.[30] Visual images, by contrast, were seen to be more limited in their resonances and sensory aspects, making their appeal to the eye alone. *Howl*, like other cine-poems, refuses the implied containment of such a division, intertwining, in particular, the visual and the verbal, the graphic and the aural. As with the other films cited here, we are indeed seeing new ways of representing the encounters between literature and film, including a radical reformulation of the concept of 'adaptation' as a mode of 'remediation', in which works of art are refashioned in other media forms.[31] In the field of fiction, the incorporation of film into literature seems to depart from earlier manifestations of 'the cinematic novel', newly engaging with the materiality of film and attempting to reproduce, along the track of the sentence, both the image and sequence. In turn, contemporary films are revealing a fascination with that track of the sentence, as it appears, for example, on the screen in the form of a line of type. The transformations of this moment in media history are thus not only those of media forms but of the ways in which literature and film encounter, and inhabit, each other.

Notes

1. See Robert Hamilton Ball, *Shakespeare on Silent Film: A Strange Eventful History* (New York: Theatre Arts Books, 1968), pp. 36–7.
2. Hamilton Ball, pp. 36–7. The presentation of authorship in this scene is discussed in the Introduction to this volume and the flag-waving in Judith Buchanan, *Shakespeare on Silent Film: An Excellent Dumb Discourse* (Cambridge: Cambridge University Press, 2009), p. 119.
3. *Dickens' London* (Miller and Parkinson, UK, 1924, for Graham-Wilcox productions, the 'Wonderful London' series), in the DVD compilation *Dickens Before Sound* (British Film Institute). It should be noted that for this film, as for many Dickens adaptations, the illustrations to the novels played a crucial role in determining subjects and design choices for the production.
4. A notice on 'Dickens on the Cinematograph' in *The Dickensian* 8 (1912): 48 referred to the journal's 'occasional references to the various stories of Dickens which the cinematograph has recently presented at the picture halls':

The most novel we have yet seen is entitled 'Leaves from the Books of Charles Dickens,' in which Mr. Thomas Bentley appears in certain characters from the novels in incidents enacted in the real background of their setting in their respective books. Mr. Bentley first appears made up to represent Dickens himself walking about the lawn of Gads Hill, and then in turn as Mr. Micawber emerging from the birthplace of the novelist at Portsmouth, as Mark Tapley at the Blue Lion, Amesbury, as Dick Swiveller outside the Red Lion, Bevis Marks, as Mr. Pickwick at the Leather Bottle, Cobham, as Mr. Jingle at the Bull Inn, Rochester, as Uriah Heep and David Copperfield outside Agnes' Wickfield's House at Canterbury, and as other notable characters. In each of these an incident connected with the association of character and place is acted, which, with the aid of a short, descriptive sentence preceding the picture, brings it home to all who witness it. Mr. Bentley cleverly and faithfully presents each character, making the whole of the series wonderfully life-like. There is little doubt that the performance will be a favourite during the next few weeks.

5. Guerric DeBona, 'Dickens, the Depression, and MGM's *David Copperfield*', in James Naremore (ed.) *Film Adaptation* (NJ: Rutgers University Press, 2000), pp. 106–128 (117).
6. DeBona (2000), p. 115. It even perhaps, in Grahame Smith's terms, gestures at Dickens as the dreamer of cinema. G. Smith, *Dickens and the Dream of Cinema* (Manchester and New York: Manchester University Press, 2003).
7. Vachel Lindsay, *The Art of the Moving Picture* (1915/1922), (New York: Random House, 2000), pp. 118–9.
8. Paul Auster, *The Book of Illusions* (London: Faber, 2002), p. 15.
9. Auster (2002), p. 64.
10. Auster (2002), p. 53.
11. Auster (2002), p. 30.
12. Auster (2002), p. 30.
13. Boris Eikhenbaum, 'Problems of Film Stylistics' (1927), *Screen* 15.3 (1974): 7–34.
14. Lev Vygotsky, *Thought and Language* (1936) (Cambridge, MA: MIT Press, 1962), p. 2.
15. Garrett Stewart, *Between Film and Screen: Modernism's Photo Synthesis* (Chicago: University of Chicago Press, 1999), pp. 4–5.
16. Rudyard Kipling, 'Mrs Bathurst' (1904), *Collected Stories* (London: Everyman, 1994), pp. 577–597 (591).
17. Stewart (1999), p. 98.
18. Paul Auster/Sam Messer, *The Story of My Typewriter* (New York: Distributed Art Publishers, 2002), p. 10.
19. Darren Wershler-Henry, *The Iron Whim: A Fragmented History of Typewriting* (Ithaca: Cornell University Press, 2005), p. 110.
20. William S. Burroughs, 'Technology of Writing', in *The Adding Machine: Collected Essays* (London: John Calder, 1985), p. 37. Quoted in D. Werschler-Henry, *The Iron Whim: A Fragmented History of Typewriting* (Toronto: McClelland and Stewart, 2005), p. 110.
21. Quoted in Jonah Raskin, *American Screen: Allen Ginsberg's 'Howl' and the Making of the Beat Generation* (Los Angeles and Berkeley: University of California Press, 2005), p. 167.
22. 'Notes Written on Finally Recording *Howl*', in Bill Morgan (ed.) *Deliberate Prose: Selected Essays 1952–1995* (New York: HarperCollins, 2000), p. 229.
23. Morgan (ed.) (2000), p. 342.
24. Daniel Kane, *We Saw the Light: Conversations between the New American Cinema and Poetry* (Iowa City: University of Iowa Press, 2009), p. 20.

25. Kane (2009), p. 20.
26. Quoted in Raskin (2005), p. 129.
27. Linda Hutcheon, *A Theory of Adaptation* (London: Routledge, 2006), p. xvi.
28. Stanley Fish, 'Literary Criticism Goes to the Movies', *The New York Times*, 'Opinionator', (4 October 2010). At: http://opinionator.blogs.nytimes.com/2010/10/04/literary-criticism-comes-to-the-movies/ (accessed 11 December 2012).
29. 'Sir, you can't translate poetry into prose; that's why it is poetry'. The line is taken *verbatim* from the trial transcript. See Bill Morgan and Nancy Peters (eds.), *'Howl' on Trial: The Battle for Free Expression* (San Francisco: City Lights Books, 2006), pp. 125–199 (138).
30. See Virginia Woolf, 'The Cinema' (1926): 'But obviously the poet's images are not to be cast in bronze or traced with pencil and paint. They are compact of a thousand suggestions, of which the visual is only the most obvious or the uppermost … All this, which is accessible to words and to words alone, the cinema must avoid'. *Collected Essays*, vol. 4, Andrew McNeillie (ed.) (London: The Hogarth Press, 1994), pp. 348–354 (351). See also W.H. Auden's essay 'Poetry and Film' (1936).
31. For a discussion of this process, see Jay David Bolter and Richard Grusin, *Remediation: Understanding New Media* (Cambridge, MA: MIT Press, 1999).

2

'Here is the story of my career...': the woman writer on film

Sonia Haiduc

From Virginia Woolf's entreaty to women writers to embrace the androgynous mind[1] to the recent controversies surrounding the justification for the Orange Prize,[2] the convenience and usefulness of appending the word 'woman' before 'writer' when considering female authorship and female writers' place in the canon remains contentious. The conclusion of Mary Eagleton's 2005 study of the female writer in contemporary fiction is that 'it is inevitable that the figure of the woman author should feature so often in fiction as problem or irritant, as focus for struggles, as an expression of desire, as loss or as a harbinger of change'.[3] Writer Margaret Atwood's *Negotiating with the Dead* – a book she tentatively suggests is 'about the position the writer finds himself in; or herself, which is always a little different'[4] – provides a series of poignant insights into the grand subject of 'Writing, or Being a Writer'[5] by recalling her own first forays into the field in the 1950s:

> A man playing the role of Great Artist was expected to Live Life – this chore was part of his consecration to his art – and Living Life meant, among other things wine, women, and song. But if a female writer tried the wine and the men, she was likely to be considered a slut and a drunk, so she was stuck with the song; and better still if it was a swan song.[6]

She goes on to caution the blithe against taking for granted the freedoms of our contemporary age: 'the mythology still has power, because such mythologies about women still have power'.[7] Sensible to these cultural myths, adaptations of women writers' lives to film from the 1970s to the present day have constructed their characters in keeping with evolving cultural images of female autonomy and authority from the revolutionary period of second-wave feminism to our anxiety-ridden post-feminist times. An examination of the competing forces at play in a host of post-1970s literary biopics ranging from art-house to mainstream Hollywood, yields interesting results, most notably in the encounters between the filmmakers' attempts to convey in cinematic terms the processes of artistic creation on the one hand and, on the other, the generic conventions in part determined by the commercial demands of the industry.

One of the obvious problems of bringing a writer's life to the screen is that the act of writing itself can be dishearteningly unexciting to watch; however, it is precisely the work this act produces that legitimizes the cultural importance of the writer-subject and so generates a substantial part of the audience's interest in the screened life. In transferring literary figures from the school syllabus to the screen, biopics offer audiences skilfully constructed slices of intimacy, thus laying bare the humanity of canonical figures. Moreover, the high cultural status of the subject often tempts film-makers to make their story a neat one about a 'successful' life. These stories typically offer a point of cinematic closure by cathartically restoring the author to the realm of cultural history.

For women writers, the act of writing has been constructed cinemati-cally in a variety of ways across films: as an act of self-affirmation in *My Brilliant Career* (dir. Gillian Armstrong, 1979); a life-saving strategy in *An Angel at My Table* (dir. Jane Campion, 1990); a self-authorizing strategy in a male-dominated culture in *Mansfield Park* (dir. Patricia Rozema, 1999); an integral part of personal identity in *Iris* (dir. Richard Eyre, 2001); a vehicle for the promotion of heritage tourism in the case of *Miss Potter* (dir. Chris Noonan, 2006); an emotional reaction to romantic turmoil in *Becoming Jane* (dir. Julian Jarrold, 2007). What is particularly notable about the majority of films, in which the woman writer becomes the central character, is the way filmmakers frame her in ways that work as both affirmation and subversion of the assumptions of romance to which the majority of female biopics sub-scribe. The word 'frame' is used precisely because these scenes reach across media to another popular cultural icon: the woman reader in portraits of the nineteenth and early twentieth century.[8] In the film adaptations under scrutiny here, these iconized images of women in passive and receptive communion with the world of the imagination (through the act of reading) are replaced with images of active communication with the world of the imagination (through the act of writing). Both, though, suggest an engage-ment with the romance of the soul and with the imaginative creativity of solitude in ways that carry a specifically gendered charge.

As André Bazin noted in his 1948 essay 'Adaptation or the Cinema as Digest', in relation to myth-making, the public impact of films is greater than that of novels.[9] Cinematic images fuel our collective fantasies of divine creativity in which the writer is often constructed as a figure with access to mysterious areas of human experience. The attraction of the figure of the female writer for the cinema has a considerable history. As early as 1934 Robert Browning (Frederic March) saves his sickly future wife Elizabeth Barrett (Norma Shearer) from the clutches of her potentially incestuous father in the MGM classic *The Barretts of Wimpole Street* (dir. Sidney Franklin) as the tagline announced their special status: 'When poets love, Heaven and Earth fall back to watch!' In 1946 the Brontë sisters 'dare' to love stormily in the Warner Bros production *Devotion* (dir. Curtis Bernhardt). The 1970s witnessed a burst of biographical adaptations featuring strong female writer characters, including *Julia* (dir. Fred Zinnemann, 1977)[10] and *My Brilliant Career*. In the 1980s, the biopic *Cross Creek* (dir. Martin Ritt, 1983) about the Florida-based novelist Marjorie Kinnon Rawlings receives four Oscar nominations; in 1985 Meryl Streep incarnates Isak Dinesen in Sydney Pollack's *Out of Africa*. Ken Russell's surreal *Gothic* of 1986 features Mary Shelley and the Romantic poets Byron and Shelley at the Vila Diodati conjuring into life their darkest fears with the help of copious amounts of laudanum. In the past two decades the number of literary biopics featuring women writers has increased, both on the big screen and on TV, with such examples as *An Angel at my Table* (1990), *Shadowlands* (dir. Richard Attenborough, 1993), *Dash and Lilly* (dir. Kathy Bates, 1999), *The Passion of Ayn Rand* (dir. Christopher Menaul, 1999), *Iris* (dir. Richard Eyre, 2001), *Sylvia* (dir. Christine Jeffs, 2003), *The Hours* (dir. Stephen Daldry, 2002), *Miss Potter* (dir. Chris Noonan, 2006), the Jane Austen biopics *Becoming Jane* (dir. Julian Jarrold, 2007) and *Miss Austen Regrets* (dir. Jeremy Lovering, 2008), as well as *Enid* (dir. James Hawes, 2009) based on the scathing memoir of Enid Blyton written by her younger daughter. Judging by the recent multiplication of such films, there seems to be an unremitting drive to place female literary icons under the lens – a development in tune with the current voracious consumption of female celebrity across a variety of media.

In his analysis of the biopic genre *Whose Lives Are They Anyway?* Dennis Bingham separates male and female biopics and calls them 'essentially different genres' based on the assertion that:

> Films about men have gone from celebratory to warts-and-all to investigatory to postmodern and parodic. Biopics of women, on the other hand, are weighed down by myths of suffering, victimization, and failure perpetuated by a culture whose films reveal an acute fear of women in the public realm. Feminist biopics can be made empowering only by a conscious and deliberate application of a feminist point of view.[11]

Such a radical genre separation along gender lines is debatable. What is not in doubt, however, is that the construction of the woman writer on the screen feeds on often contradictory cultural readings of female autonomy, as her quest for self-definition is predominantly set against the background of romance and the love interest tends to overshadow all other concerns. However, in a few productions such as *Mansfield Park* (1999) or *Miss Austen Regrets* the discourses around the demands of romantic fulfilment adopt a more or less explicitly ironic tone, critiquing the audience's assumptions as consumers of women's stories filled with sentimental affliction. The titles of biopics show an interesting penchant for familiarity in connection with women writers, in an attempt to convey the intimate, personal relationship (female?) readers develop with their work, and, indirectly, with their persona. It is an effective marketing strategy since women represent the majority of their target audience. The Jane Austen cult is a case in point, reflected in the title *Becoming Jane*. Would *Becoming Jane Austen* have sounded too discouragingly literary for the average film spectator? It is indeed a common strategy specifically in relation to biopics of women writers – a strategy not pursued in relation to male biopics. To name just a few, one finds *Julia* (1977), *Stevie* (dir. Robert Enders 1978), *Nora* (dir. Pat Murphy, 2000), *Iris*, *Sylvia*, *Miss Potter*, the aforementioned *Becoming Jane*, *Miss Austen Regrets* and *Enid*. On the other side of the gender divide there is *Wilde* (dir. Brian Gilbert, 1997), *Shakespeare in Love* (dir. John Madden, 1998), *Byron* (dir. Julian Farino, 2003), *Capote* (dir. Bennett Miller, 2007), *Shadowlands* (1993), *Quills* (dir. Philip Kaufman, 2000), *Pandaemonium* (dir. Julien Temple, 2000), *Finding Neverland* (dir. Marc Forster, 2004), *The Libertine* (dir. Laurence Dunmore, 2004) and *Bright Star* (dir. Jane Campion, 2009). In choosing familiarity over distance the films may reflect the tension between the private and the public realms Bingham points to, with female experience more firmly tied to the private and intimate. The evidence begs the question whether these title choices ultimately work to undermine the cultural authority of the films' subjects. After all, as Seán Burke points out 'it would scarcely be an exaggeration to say that the struggles of feminism have been primarily a struggle for authorship – understood in the widest sense as the arena in which culture attempts to define itself.'[12] These biopics purport to celebrate female literary achievement in the public sphere (while selling tickets); their titles, on the other hand, temper that engagement with the public sphere and betray a sort of familiarity with their subjects that may be too close for comfort. In fact, the woman writer sometimes seems to be defined more by her (ordinary) first name than by her (extraordinary) place in literary history.

The figure of the woman writer in the 1970s was constructed in keeping with the militant feminism of the age. In the 20th Century Fox drama *Julia* (1977), based on playwright Lillian Hellman's controversial 1973 memoir *Pentimento*, the main character risks life and limb to help a female childhood friend smuggle money to Nazi Germany. The name of the friend becomes the title of the film, rendering central the question of female friendship and solidarity, and echoing contemporary discourses on feminine liberation. Afflicted with writer's block, the female author's violent physical reactions in relation to her work – growling, smoking furiously, raging and throwing her typewriter out of the window – evoke the confrontational spirit of 1970s feminism (see Figure 2.1). The choice of cast works to enlarge the contextual layer even further – Jane Fonda, a known feminist and political activist, is cast as Lillian, while Julia is played by Vanessa Redgrave, an actress openly engaged in political activities. Nine years earlier Redgrave had received another

Figure 2.1   Jane Fonda as playwright Lillian Hellman in *Julia* (1977).

Oscar nomination for her role in a biopic based on the life and loves of bisexual dancer Isadora Duncan, a role partly recapitulated in *Julia*'s ambiguous treatment of female friendship. The illuminating network of associations generated by the highly charged political or professional profiles of Fonda and Redgrave confirms the confrontational edge of the film's aspirations.

Two years later, in Gillian Armstrong's 1979 feminist period drama *My Brilliant Career*, aspiring artist Sybilla (Judy Davis) declares her all-consuming desire to become a writer:

> Dear fellow countrymen, just a few words to let you know that this story is going to be all about me. So, in answer to many requests, here is the story of my career ... I make no apologies for sounding egotistical because I am!

Her words point to the future insofar as they mark her initial enthusiastic scribblings as the fictional autobiography of an already established writer. On the other hand, they also function retrospectively in the context of the adaptation, positioning the story as a cinematic celebration of a canonical woman writer from the turn of the nineteenth century. The film is based on Australian writer Miles Franklin's homonymous book published in Scotland in 1901 to widespread acclaim. In spite of her rebellious and outspoken character, the author recoiled from the attention of the public, denying any connection between the book and her own life and turning her back on her native Australia for most of her life. According to her biography, marriage as a social imperative was a matter of relative inconsequence to her,[13] while maternity was pronounced 'rabbit work'.[14] Gillian Armstrong's adaptation augments the feminist tone of the story by casting newcomer Judy Davis, an unconventional beauty, as the boisterous, opinionated heroine struggling to leave behind her rural background in pursuit of a more elevated, artistic life.

In addition to an unruly mass of hair, the film is not afraid to endow its protagonist with an unruly spirit to match. This being a period romance, the director trades upon the aesthetic appeal of the clothes and comfortable homes of the middle classes at the end of the nineteenth century. Equally, she pays loving attention to the landscape of rural Australia. The lens, however, does not shy away from the harsher aspects of life in the bush – the mud, the draught and the dreary surroundings – rendering yet more dramatic the protagonist's yearning to escape. The heroine's looks and manners become more polished once she takes up with her wealthy aunt who urges her to look for a husband. 'Loneliness is a terrible price to pay for independence,' another aunt warns, as Sybilla resists giving in to her romantic feelings for the dashing Harry and her family's expectations. However, the price for security seems equally undesirable as an overhead shot of the heroine and her aunt inside a closed bird sanctuary makes visible the symbolic entrapment of genteel women. In the book's introduction, the narrator sternly warns the reader against misinterpreting the heroine's romantic troubles: 'This is not a romance – I have too often faced the music of life to the tune of hardship to waste time in snivelling and gushing over fancies and dreams ....'[15] The filmmakers transfer this rather neatly into the adaptation by giving the heroine the opportunity to make a speech about her life choices to her thwarted admirer. This choice is presented as a realistic comment on the consequences of marrying and the power of her own desires for self-fulfilment:

> The last thing I want is to be a wife out in the bush ... having a baby every year ... maybe I'm ambitious, selfish, but I can't lose myself in somebody else's life when I haven't lived my own yet. I want to be a writer. At least I'm going to try. But I want to do it now. And I want to do it alone.

These last lines, sealed with a tender kiss against the background of the blue sky, ultimately subvert the conventions of the period romance the adaptation had, until this point, apparently been following. Interestingly, the film's corporate producers and distributors pressured the filmmakers to change the ending, worried that the blatantly feminist ending might disturb the assumed conservatism of the standard audience for period dramas.[16]

A compromise was reached by having Sybilla tell Harry, 'I'm so near loving you.' The upbeat ending condenses the film's ideas in images full of lyricism, with the prospective author carrying her manuscript addressed to the publishers cradled in her arms and kissing it tenderly before placing it inside a post box. The voice-over of the narrator informs audiences that 'hope is whispering in my ear', signalling the film's ending as the moment when the 'real' story of the writer's 'brilliant career' truly begins. Fiction, autobiography and literary history come together in this film, iconicizing a tradition of feminist heroines who have managed to make their voices heard: the writer Miles Franklin, the filmmakers (a great number of whom in this case were women) and the female audience at the height of second-wave feminism.

In a now classic work of collected Jane Austen scholarship, *Jane Austen in Hollywood* (2001), contributors examine the ambiguities that the numerous Austen adaptations under scrutiny might be remediating from society at large, describing, for example, the cinematic adaptations of Austen's characters as echoes of the 'ambiguous position of women in the 1990s.' This, Linda Troost and Sayre Greenfield maintained, was 'feminist, traditionalist, or sometimes both, depending on whom one asks. Each screenwriter, director, and viewer sees the characters as reflecting his or her ideas of womanhood, and that may be the secret of Austen and the film adaptations....'[17] According to Deborah Kaplan, Jane Austen's novels have been subjected to 'harlequinisation'.[18] That is to say that the focus of the story stays firmly and almost exclusively on the main courtship plot, at the expense of other characters or experiences. The complaint rings true for the twenty-first century films *Miss Potter* and *Becoming Jane*, two broadly saccharine productions situated at the intersection of popular romance and post-feminist discourse, the plot structure of both of which undermines the supposedly feminist opinions voiced by the protagonists at strategic moments in the narrative. The two productions share strikingly similar marketing DVD cover designs: the heroine in each case is placed on the right side looking directly at the viewer with a smile, while the hero nuzzles up to her from the left. The taglines are similarly aligned, both making reference to a 'Greatest Love': 'One of the Greatest Love Stories Never Told' for *Miss Potter*; 'Jane Austen's Greatest Love Story was Her Own' for *Becoming Jane*. Even the presentation of the personal passion satisfyingly discovered to be at the centre of a woman writer's own story needs to fit predetermined marketing codes.

Miss Potter, a bland addition to the period romance genre, directed by Chris Noonan (who also directed *Babe*, 1995), turns the children's book writer of slightly unsettling stories into a cute eccentric. 'My dear Miss Potter, you are an author,' the publisher and future fiancé Norman beams over a freshly printed book to a pouty 'Bridget Jones' in period dress (Beatrix Potter, played by Renée Zellweger). Her professional ambitions give the filmmakers the occasion to fly the flag of female liberation tokenistically for a while as they include sound bites from second-wave feminist discourse as an anachronistic import into the script. Milly Warne (Emily Watson), the suffragist female character who is impressively vocal about the pressure of societal rules on the lives of women, first warns Beatrix that the price of marriage for women is 'enslavement'. However, even a liberationist rhetoric proves unable to resist the charms of romance for long. As she urges Beatrix to marry her brother Norman, Milly reveals her own true desires obscured by her liberated posturing when she confesses that if she were able to find someone to love and be loved by, she would trample her own mother. She is, in fact, the stereotype of everything the anti-suffragists meanly liked to suggest about campaigning women – that their militancy was merely an attempt to compensate for a lack of love in their lives. Confused about her friend's change of heart, Beatrix asks: 'What about all the talk about the blessings of being alone?' The answer given chimes with the contradictory message of popular post-feminist icons like Bridget Jones or *Sex and the City*'s Carrie Bradshaw: 'Hogwash! What else is a woman my age supposed to say?' This particular scene clearly echoes the contemporary cultural debates surrounding feminism and post-feminism, with accusations of betrayal of women's pursuits in favour of pre-feminist domestic values and consumerism on one side, and claims of feminism's failure to recognize women's real needs on the other.

Through both the associations of casting and the film's specific narrative treatment of its central character, the heroine of Miramax's *Becoming Jane* is, in effect, turned into the mother of chick lit (though with the enhanced polish of cultural respectability bestowed by Austen's canonical position). *Becoming Jane* could, in fact, legitimately be read as an expository prequel to the rash of Austen screen adaptations of the 1990s and 2000s. Based on Jon Spence's literary biography *Becoming Jane Austen: A Life* (2003), *Becoming Jane* investigates how a woman who never married and lived a quiet life was nevertheless able to write such convincing novels about love and marriage. Tania Modleski's observation about the decisive contribution of *Pride and Prejudice* to the formula of the romance novel[19] can be equally applied to the genre of the romantic comedy; initial disdain turning into love is an extensively used and immediately recognizable plotline. In Jarrold's *Becoming Jane* of 2007, as in the adaptations from the 1990s, emotions quickly become irrepressible for all parties involved,[20] culminating in a kiss against the backdrop of romantically lit gardens. The plucky heroine Jane (Anne Hathaway) defiantly ignores her rich admirer's stately house: 'His small fortune will not buy me.' In answer to her cousin's enquiry as to what would buy her, the film's next shot offers us Tom Lefroy's (James McAvoy) bare chest, thus obviating the need for any explicit answer from Jane. This Jane Austen may be a young wit, but she is equally in sore need of some literary recommendations on sexual matters from 'bad boy' Lefroy, a study task to which she applies herself studiously. A feminist avant-la-lettre, she repeatedly voices her discontent at the boundaries that prevent her from experiencing life the way a man does. Instead of Cassandra, her favoured female companion is now her flirty French cousin Madame de Feuillide, signalling her willingness to break certain social conventions, a willingness confirmed in her playing of cricket, her gazing at naked male bodies and finally in her eloping with the object of her infatuation.

However, it is not just the unconventional woman, but also the writer-in-the-making that the film's cinematography and editing seek to capture. The film opens with alternating shots of quiet countryside and the writer's hand holding the quill, tapping with it while thinking, dipping it into the ink bottle, holding it poised above the page and finally tracing the letters, a visual sign of reflective pause frequently used in literary biopics to make visible the intellectual engagement of the character with the solitary art of fiction. The similarities with the main character in *Shakespeare in Love* (dir. John Madden, 1998) are evident, down to the ink-stained fingers and the brutal disfigurement of the paper when the results are unsatisfying. In the case of *Becoming Jane*, however, the signs are introduced in relation to a variety of other symbols that specifically encourage a gendered reading: a shot of a sow suckling her piglets, for example, suggests both abundance and self-consuming maternity in stark contrast to the solitude and non-maternity of the woman writer configured. The film manifests throughout the 'ideological splitting' Madeleine Dobie identified in heritage films, which are seen to be 'gesturing towards the social and political concerns of feminism, but also firmly positioned in the well-charted territory of the romantic comedy'.[21] By combining plot elements of *Pride and Prejudice* with excerpts from the real Jane Austen's letters, together with some of Emma Thompson's social commentary from *Sense and Sensibility* (dir. Ang Lee, 1995) and a helping of the cult of sensibility (the object of much of Jane Austen's satire), *Becoming Jane* 'becomes' a successful film for audiences that loved Anne Hathaway in the romantic comedies *The Princess Diaries* (dir. Garry Marshall, 2001 and 2004) and *The Devil Wears Prada* (dir. David Frankel, 2006) and who are well-placed to enjoy a light dose of retroactive social criticism served up with their love story.

If *Becoming Jane* is made into an Elizabeth Bennet story, a story about a woman whose romantic fulfilment is thwarted by a Darcy figure who is in this case financially challenged, Patricia Rozema's earlier *Mansfield Park* (1999) is constructed as a political adaptation-cum-Austen-biopic in which the self-effacing Fanny Price's character (Frances O'Connor) is rewritten as an outspoken author to make her appealing to a clearly targeted feminist audience with a working knowledge of post-colonial discourse. The credits acknowledge Jane Austen's letters and early journals as a direct source, yet Rozema's auteurist approach is made visually clear from the beginning – the credits reading 'written and directed by Patricia Rozema' appear strategically across the entrance gate to the grounds of Mansfield Park in a gesture of authorial conquest. The writer, Fanny, is made to quote from Austen's parodic juvenilia and, upsetting the narrative status quo, to break the fourth wall by addressing the camera to indicate that the fictional world around her is but a construct and she is the master puppeteer. To strengthen the connections with Jane Austen's life yet further, the writer-director's visual cues emphasize the relationship between Fanny and her sister – more than glancing at Austen's own relationship with her sister Cassandra. In the opening credits, the visual signs associated with writing are fragmented and magnified, building a figurative landscape of the imagination: ink becomes a rippling lake, paper and quills turn into golden desert dunes and gently sloping fields. The body of the child fabulator emerges from the written text, while the voice accompanies the writing of the grown-up novelist and 'ignorant historian' in a blurring of temporal boundaries. Equipped with a 'tongue sharper than a guillotine', Fanny the writer is offered full command of 'herstory', as well as the pleasures of rewriting history and toying with the language and conventions of romance in a self-conscious exercise of genre critique. In the closing scene of her reunion with Edmund, the camera's gaze and Fanny's ambiguous smile once again subvert the pleasures of romantic fulfilment by implying the presence of a third character, the writer (Austen/Rozema) who acknowledges the artificiality of her fictional construct. Rozema's woman writer in *Mansfield Park* is thus constructed as the creator of her own story in the manner of Armstrong's Sybilla in *My Brilliant Career*. Unfortunately, the empowering message was lost on post-feminist audiences at the end of the twentieth century. As an adaptation, it 'fell between audiences'[22] due to its radical departure from the conventions of the period romance, failing to appeal either to the traditional heritage or the multiplex audience in spite of its playful tagline inviting them to enjoy 'Jane Austen's Wicked Comedy'. The film's fate with critics retrospectively adds piquancy to the conversation between Fanny and Mary Crawford: 'We all need an audience, wouldn't you say, Fanny?' asks Mary. 'To be truthful, I live in dread of audiences,' is the reply.

The made-for-television drama *Miss Austen Regrets* (dir. Jeremy Lovering, 2008), apparently marketed at the slightly more mature 'Janeite' audience, offers another take on the author's life. As a woman in her early forties, what does this Miss Austen (Olivia Williams) regret? Without offering a definitive answer, the film suggests an array of possible candidates for her regret, from sexual passion to authorial fulfilment. It reclaims Austen for a contemporary female audience that is able to identify with her conflicts between the professional and the domestic. In a moment that could legitimately have been received as a summative intertextual reference to *Becoming Jane*, the character Jane Austen answers her niece's enquiries (and the audience's expectations) about her love life as a young woman: 'I loved and lost and pined and yearned. And then swore myself to solitude and the consolations of writing about it instead.' The romantic illusion is shattered shortly afterwards when, addressing both her niece, and, through her, her off-screen female audience to boot, she quips: 'you have read too many novels.'

The film oscillates between Jane the woman and Jane the writer, between her flirty outspoken personality in society and her solitary self engaged in the act of writing. Her sisterly communion with Cassandra ends where her writing begins. In a revealing scene in which she is shown at work on her last novel, as her sister enters the room, she stops writing and remains perfectly still, in slight impatience to be left alone. For the imagination to take shape and find form, it is suggested, it is solitude not companionship that is required: there must be a free space, a Woolfian 'room of one's own', that the writer can claim, removed from the demands of domestic life, family love and other distracting connections to the world.

This private space of creative solitude is at the heart of the award-wining 1990 adaptation *An Angel at My Table*, directed by Jane Campion. A nuanced explorer of female subjectivity, Campion based her film on a three-part autobiography by New Zealand writer Janet Frame. Misdiagnosed with schizophrenia and almost lobotomized in the hospital where she spent eight years, she is literally saved by her collection of stories, awarded a national literary prize just days before the scheduled lobotomy. The adaptation portrays a highly sensitive, solitary being at odds with her surroundings, whose moments of personal fulfilment are connected with reading and writing. The camera follows Janet (Kerry Fox) from childhood to adolescence to adulthood, depicting her struggles against crippling shyness and the misconceptions of the medical establishment. Literature is shown to be her passion from a tender age; exposure to the influence of inspiring teachers keep her imagination afire until, finally, she is ready to give up her sensible plans in favour of her calling: 'I've made up my mind not to be a teacher, I'm going to be a poet.'

The film is composed of three parts, each one beginning with a literary quotation to signal the close interrelationship between Frame's life and her imaginary inner world. The adaptation repeatedly foregrounds the liberating quality of literature and writing. Confined inside a bare room awaiting a brain operation, Janet desperately scribbles lines from Shakespeare on the wall to keep herself sane. Even though, as a young woman in the midst of sexual awakening, she craves a human touch, her choice in favour of the pleasures of solitary creation is represented as natural and liberating. Her face is transformed when she is engaged in the act of writing, from pain to quiet exhilaration. Speaking of the occasion when she visited Janet Frame to discuss the adaptation of her books, director Jane Campion remembers:

> I see now that she was not, as I sometimes thought, lonely, but lived in a rare state of freedom, removed from the demands and conventions of a husband, children and a narrow social world. Near the end of her life in 2003, when she was diagnosed with acute leukaemia, she was reported to have said that her death was an adventure, 'and (quoting Frame) I've always enjoyed adventures.[23]

In contrast to earlier figures struggling against societal rules, the depiction of women writers from the twentieth century suggests that they fall prey to their inner demons of self-destruction and the shackles of mental illness. Madness and suicide plague the characters in *The Hours* (2002), the film adaptation of Michael Cunningham's loose homonymous rewriting of Virginia Woolf's *Mrs Dalloway*. Woolf herself (Nicole Kidman) looms large over the story, pen in hand, indicating her status as narrative origin and dispenser of life: 'Someone has to die, so the rest of us value life more.' The chronically depressed Sylvia Plath's relationship with Ted Hughes makes the 2003 BBC production *Sylvia* a relentlessly gloomy take on the consequences of unhealthy obsessions and trauma. And mental degeneration haunts the award-winning BBC adaptation *Iris* (2001), based on the two memoirs by Iris Murdoch's husband John Bayley.

Iris is structured around the contrast between the lively free-spirited Iris (Kate Winslet) at the beginning of their relationship and the old, fragile Iris (Judi Dench) whose intellectual and emotional capacity has been ravaged by Alzheimer's disease. As her formidable self is gradually eroded to a caricature, the biggest losses are shown to be her autonomy and her language. 'I wrote', she seems to remember, as Bayley (Jim Broadbent) reads to her from *Pride and Prejudice*, thus signalling that Iris and Jane belong to the same privileged category of the woman author and linking them through time via the act of reading the work of one to the other, as the privileged producers of words capable of touching others. The adaptation dwells painfully on the ravages of Alzheimer's – it is not so much a film about the writer Iris, in spite of the title, as one about loss of self and the value of domestic love. The passage from Jane Austen's novel that Bayley chooses to read to her is the one where Darcy notices Elizabeth's charms, thus poignantly highlighting the character, past and present, of their own long-term relationship. As the film unfolds, the carefree young Iris is incrementally confined to a house full of clutter and a husband who is slightly unsettling in his obsession with possessing her entirely. Relying on allusions to the fleeting quality of words and the fragility of the mind, however, writer-director Richard Eyre reaches repeatedly for rather heavy-handed symbolism through which to narrate her decline. Scenes dedicated to eloquent speeches on love and freedom contrast with the repetitive babbling outpouring of Iris's decaying mind; stones on the beach are placed on papers to signal her losing battle with the disease; glass panes distort the character's figure; and the songs of the Teletubbies replace the sparkling conversation of her Oxonian friends. Remaining true to his own words in interview that 'All drama is about extremes',[24] the director dwells as obsessively as Iris' husband on the humiliating aspects of a disease that displaces and eventually replaces the bright and clever Iris almost entirely. Furthermore, the film is marketed with a specifically consciousness-raising and educational agenda: the DVD extras contain a message about Alzheimer's with information and advice for viewers if affected. The vulnerability of the creative mind so painfully depicted on-screen is therefore explicitly invited to speak to comparable vulnerabilities off-screen.[25]

If we are to set any store by André Bazin's assertion of the superior myth-making powers of cinema over books in the contemporary world,[26] we need to take note of the contradictory discourses about female authorship and autonomy that film adaptations of literary lives peddle. And we need to take note of these specifically because cinematic myths not only mirror but also influence the real world. Now that female authorship is a publically configured part of the cultural arena, we should care how it is being configured in our mass media.

There is no doubt that literary biopics find a market and give pleasure. To exploit the commercial possibilities that attach to this pleasure, publishing houses typically ensure that a batch of new editions reaches its prospective readership after each cinema release. More often than not, for large swathes of the readership – especially younger audiences – the packaged cinematic images will precede those generated through reading the source texts. As a result, Jane's secret 'love story' will inevitably superimpose itself on the reading experience, the culturally prevalent tropes of romance and the easy-to-swallow post-feminist messages thereby potentially supplanting other literary and contextual aspects of the work. The cultural impact of these allegories that reflect complex literary and ideological discourses clashing with popular media clichés must not be underestimated. However, it is also essential to be able to acknowledge the 'sense of play' and 'the connected interplay of expectation and surprise'[27] that Julie Sanders finds at the heart of our experience of adaptations; it is indeed this sense of play that has kept part of our interest in literary adaptations and biopics very much alive. As these representations of women writers suggest, the word 'woman' appended to the word 'writer', in books as in film adaptations, still carries with it 'a lot of unfinished business'.[28]

Notes

1. Virginia Woolf, *A Room of One's Own* (London: Penguin Books, 2000; originally published 1928), p. 102.
2. The Orange Prize has been dismissed by A.S. Byatt as 'sexist'. C. Higgins and C. Davies, 'AS Byatt says women who write intellectual books seen as unnatural', *The Guardian*, 10 August 2010. At: http://www.guardian.co.uk/books/2010/aug/20/as-byatt-intellectual-women-strange (accessed 11 December 2012).
3. M. Eagleton, *Figuring the Woman Author in Contemporary Fiction* (New York: Palgrave Macmillan, 2005), p. 155.
4. Margaret Atwood, *Negotiating with the Dead. A Writer on Writing* (Cambridge: Cambridge University Press, 2002), p. xvii.
5. Atwood (2002), p. xvi.
6. Atwood (2002), p. 90.
7. Atwood (2002), p. 90.

8. See, for example, J. Phegley and J. Badia, 'Introduction: Women Readers as Literary Figures and Cultural Icons', in J. Badia and J. Phegler (eds.) *Reading Women: Literary Figures and Cultural Icons from the Victorian Age to the Present* (Toronto: TUP, 2005), pp. 3–26 (5).

9. A. Bazin. 'Adaptation, or the Cinema as Digest', in J. Naremore (ed.) *Film Adaptation* (London: The Athlone Press, 2000; originally published in French in 1948), pp. 19–27 (26).

10. *Julia*, dir. Fred Zinnemann, prod. Richard Roth, script. Alvin Sargent, Twentieth Century Fox Film Corporation, USA, 1977.

11. D. Bingham, *Whose Lives Are They Anyway? The Biopic as Contemporary Film Genre* (New Jersey: Rutgers UP, 2010), p. 10.

12. S. Burke, *Authorship: From Plato to the Postmodern* (Edinburgh: Edinburgh University Press, 1995), p. 145.

13. J. Roe, *Her Brilliant Career: The Life of Stella Miles Franklin* (Sydney: HarperCollins Publishers, 2008), p. 100.

14. J. I. Roe, 'Franklin, Stella Maria Sarah Miles (1879–1954)', *Australian Dictionary of Biography*, online edition, 2006. At: http://www.adb.online.anu.edu.au/biogs/A080591b.htm (accessed 11 December 2012).

15. M. Franklin, *My Brilliant Career* (London: Virago Press, 1980), no page given.

16. H. Carter, 'Gillian Armstrong', *Senses of Cinema* 22 (2002), online issue.

17. L. Troost and S. Greenfield, 'Watching Ourselves Watching', in L. Troost and S. Greenfield (eds.) *Jane Austen in Hollywood* (Lexington, Kentucky: University Press of Kentucky, 2001), pp. 1–12 (8).

18. D. Kaplan, 'Mass Marketing Jane Austen: Men, Women and Courtship in Two Film Adaptations', Troost and Greenfield (2001), pp. 177–187 (178).

19. T. Modleski, *Loving With a Vengeance* (London: Routledge, 1990), p. 36.

20. Male characters are also rewritten to conform to a 'model of masculinity far removed from Austen's in its emphasis on physicality and emotional expression'. M. Aragay and Gemma López, 'Inf(l)ecting Pride and Prejudice: Dialogism, Intertextuality, and Adaptation', in M. Aragay (ed.) *Books in Motion* (Amsterdam: Rodopi, 2005), pp. 201–219 (211).

21. M. Dobie, 'Gender and the Heritage Genre', in Suzanne R. Pucci and James Thompson (eds.) *Jane Austen & Co: Remaking the Past in Contemporary Culture* (Albany: University of New York Press, 2003), pp. 247–259 (251).

22. A. Higson, 'English Heritage, English Literature, English Cinema: Selling Jane Austen to Movie Audiences in the 1990s', in Eckhart Voigts-Virchow (ed.) *Janespotting and Beyond. British Heritage Retrovisions since the mid-1990s* (Tübingen: Gunter Narr Verlag, 2004), pp. 35–50 (48).

23. J. Campion, 'In Search of Janet Frame', *The Guardian*, 19 January 2008, online version. At: http://www.guardian.co.uk/books/2008/jan/19/fiction5 (accessed 11 December 2012).

24. The DVD commercialized by Buena Vista Home Entertainment contains the bonus material 'A Special Message from David Hyde Pierce' in which the speaker offers his family story, a PowerPoint-type presentation of the symptoms and a link to the Alzheimer's Disease International's website.

25. The music for *Iris* was composed by James Horner, who, in the same year, also composed the soundtrack for *A Beautiful Mind* (dir. Ron Howard, 2001), a biographical thriller about a genius's descent into madness.

26. Bazin in Naremore (2000), p. 24.

27. J. Sanders, *Adaptation and Appropriation* (London: Routledge, 2006), p. 25.

28. Eagleton (2005), p. 4.

3

'Mad, bad and dangerous to know': the male poet in *Sylvia* (2003) and *The Edge of Love* (2008)

Siân Harris

If one man can be held responsible for the vast majority of the clichés surrounding the male poet's masculine identity, that man is George Gordon Byron, 6th Baron Byron and subject of an international cult of literary celebrity. Byron's projected persona has become the basis for one of the most persistent and popular mythologies about the figure of the male poet. His name now stands as a byword for brooding charisma and saturnine sexual allure, suitably epitomized in Thomas Macaulay's description of him as 'a man proud, moody, cynical, with defiance on his brow, and misery in his heart, a scorner of his kind, implacable in revenge yet capable of deep and strong affection.'[1] Indeed, the infamous, reputation-defining epithet 'Mad, bad and dangerous to know', bestowed upon him by his rejected lover, Lady Caroline Lamb, has been received by subsequent generations less as insult than badge of honour.

The Byronic myth was not slow to take shape. Within just five years of his death in 1824, Byron was the subject of over thirty biographies, memoirs and critiques. Nor has the interest abated since. As Michael Benton notes: 'the Byronic myth mutated rapidly,' adapting itself and being adapted by the demands of the *zeitgeist*, but consistently promoting a recognizable and popular brand of troubled masculinity.[2] The legacy has proved pervasive across media. Atara Stein has identified Byron's spiritual progeny appearing across cultural forms ranging from Anne Rice's novel *Interview with the Vampire* to the character Q in the televised series *Star Trek: The Next Generation*.[3] The ubiquity and mutability of this legacy has been identified more recently by biographer, Benita Eisler, who observes the many ways in which;

> competing voices have invoked the poet as an idol in their own image: hero and martyr of revolutionary struggle, aristocratic aesthete and dandy, transgressive rebel of polymorphous sexuality fuelled by forbidden substances and with sulphurous whiffs of the Prince of Darkness swirling about him.[4]

The heady appeal of this myth is inextricably bound up with the portrayal of the male poet in popular culture, reincarnated across registers from the sublime to the ridiculous and frequently spawning characters that confuse petulance with charisma, promiscuity with prowess and affectation with talent. Notwithstanding such banalizing interventions, the myth retains its allure, assuming, if anything, an enhanced appeal when combined with the trope of the poet as tragic hero: a process through which 'myths carry meanings beyond mere narrative.'[5]

The resilience of the Byronic legend of masculine poetic potency can perhaps be partly accounted for as a necessary social counter to the inverse reputation for the male poet that has an equally tenacious cultural hold: 'the anxiety', as Alan Sinfield describes it, 'that actually poetry is effeminate'[6] and therefore that being a poet is somehow incompatible with being a 'real' man. The reputation of male poets as delicate, tortured souls, or socially awkward failures, incapable of any physical labour or practical reasoning, has enduring cultural currency. Irving Babbitt remarked at the turn of the twentieth century: 'The man who took literature too seriously would be suspected of effeminacy. The really virile thing is to be an electrical engineer.'[7] It is a view that has retained a profile in popular culture, establishing a counterpoint to the Byronic fantasy of dangerous potency.

This competitive conjunction of clichés in the reputation of the male poet provides the framework for my reading of two twenty-first century literary biopics, *Sylvia* (dir. Christine Jeffs, 2003) and *The Edge of Love* (dir. John Maybury, 2008). These films offer contrasting representations of the male poet's frequently aggressive, anti-social or addictive behaviour, which is offered as evidence of virility rather than instability, thus bolstering the conventional hetero-normative masculinity of a man engaged in an unconventionally masculine profession. *Sylvia* charts the relationship between Sylvia Plath (Gwyneth Paltrow) and Ted Hughes (Daniel Craig), from their first encounter in 1956 to Plath's suicide in 1963. The title signals the film's primary focus, but it is as much the biography of a relationship as of an individual. The film's working title was actually *Ted and Sylvia* – perhaps edited to distance the film from a perceived kinship with Emma Tennant's novel *The Ballad of Sylvia and Ted* (2001). *The Edge of Love* is equally concerned with relationships, focusing on a complex, wartime *ménage à trois* between Dylan Thomas (Matthew Rhys), his wife Caitlin (Sienna Miller), and his old flame Vera Phillips (Keira Knightley). The film portrays a fraught intimacy that culminates in violence when Vera's soldier husband William (Cillian Murphy) opens fire on the Thomas' house. This incident is based upon real events that occurred in 1945, but my concern for present purposes is not with the accuracy or otherwise of the depiction of either incidents or people in the films, but simply with the nature of the depiction itself and what this can tell us about reputation, contradiction and desire.[8]

The two male poets of my case study films have little self-evident kinship with each other: Ted is terse, Dylan grandiloquent; Ted powerful, Dylan petulant. However, throughout their respective films, the two poets are engaged in the same central struggle to define and distinguish their individual masculinities, without compromising their creative talents. This chapter charts the characters' initial exclusion from conventional streams of masculinity by virtue of their artistic identity, before revealing the strategies they use to overcome this exclusion and to challenge cultural assumptions about what it means to be a male poet. It is also crucial here to take account of female involvement and complicity in this identity, both in terms of individual relationships and cultural expectations. This consideration focuses the question whether the tropes of the Byronic myth might be deployed at the behest of male self-defensiveness or in the pursuit of female fantasy.

R.W. Connell has pointed out how 'Mass culture generally assumes there is a fixed, true masculinity beneath the ebb and flow of daily life. We hear of "real men", "natural man", the "deep masculine."'[9] This conventional notion of 'real' masculinity informs and infiltrates social preconceptions, fixing the terms of the debate and associating masculinity with factors such as physical strength, fiscal success, (hetero-)sexual prowess and virility. A strikingly stable cultural code of this sort traditionally isolates those who cannot fulfil its requirements. From the outset of *Sylvia*, Ted Hughes is established as a social outsider. The flat timbre of his rough Yorkshire accent jars against the cut-glass consonants of his fellow academics in the Cambridge scenes, and his working-class background is worlds apart from Sylvia's genteel family circle in America. Sylvia's mother, Aurelia, is particularly anxious about Ted's ability to provide financially, and less than reassured by Sylvia's plan to support the couple with her teaching salary. The doubt surrounding Ted's capacity as breadwinner seriously destabilizes his perceived masculinity. In a key scene early in the film, Aurelia throws a gala party for the newlywed couple. The guests comprise elegant middle-aged women dressed in delicate pastels, and distinguished middle-aged men dressed in dapper linen suits. They chatter politely in the sun-dappled garden, and accept dainty refreshments from the servants (the only black characters to appear in the film). Throughout this scene, Ted appears supremely uncomfortable. Clad in a sweltering dark suit, he lurches through the party, horribly conspicuous at all points. An apparently oblivious Sylvia thanks her mother, exclaiming that 'You've made us feel so at home,' to which Ted replies through gritted teeth, 'Oh yes, if I closed my eyes I could be back in Mytholmroyd.' The event serves to disenfranchise Ted both socially and financially, any potential masculine authority undermined in this social setting by his emasculating identity as poet.

In *The Edge of Love*, Dylan Thomas occupies a similarly precarious position. The film is set during World War II, at the height of the London Blitz. Dylan's self-inflicted health problems have kept him out of the armed forces, his lungs, as he boasts to Vera, being 'raddled like a Sunday whore'. Instead of fighting, he has found a cushy role within the propaganda department of the BBC. At one point, he is beaten up by a furious sailor, who informs him between kicks that his brother 'died for the likes of you'. Dylan's defiantly flippant response that he 'didn't bloody ask him to' is met with further kicks and an order from the sailor to 'Lick my boot, conchie, lick my bleeding boot.' Dylan is eventually ignominiously rescued by his love-rival, Captain William Killick. The image of the poet bleeding in the urine-drenched gutter while the 'real men' solve their dispute with the threat of increased violence offers an arresting image of masculine hierarchies, and of Dylan's place at the bottom of them – despite, or perhaps because of, his wit. His problems are compounded by his terminal financial insecurity – Dylan and his wife Caitlin are constantly on the verge of crisis, and forced to seek lodging first with Caitlin's sister, and later with Vera, the three of them sharing her single room. Dylan's inability to provide a home for his family and successive dependence on the indulgence of friends and relatives is, as for Ted, presented as a direct consequence of his identity as a poet. However, the responses of others to this perceived failure differ significantly. A research study in 1993 conducted by Thomas Gerschick and Adam Miller questioned a number of men who felt excluded from traditional masculine privilege – in their case, due to physical disability rather than professional status – and identified three main responses to this sense of social alienation.[10] These responses can be summarized as follows:

> One is to redouble efforts to meet the hegemonic standards, overcoming the physical difficulty – for instance, finding proof of continued sexual potency … Another is to reformulate the definition of masculinity, bringing it closer to what is now possible, though still pursuing masculine themes … The third is to reject hegemonic masculinity as a package.[11]

While an exploration of the third posited response here lies beyond the remit of this chapter, the first two responses provide a strikingly apt template for reading the differing behaviours respectively exhibited by Ted and Dylan.

In *Sylvia*, Ted is quick to challenge and overcome any misconceptions about his status and masculinity. Within his circle of friends at Cambridge, he is clearly the 'Alpha Male', and his fellow male poets all defer to his superior talent. This sense of Ted as a man among boys is, perhaps inadvertently, emphasized visually by Daniel Craig's rugged appearance (Figure 3.1); Craig was thirty-five when *Sylvia* was released, and several reviewers agreed that he 'played with verve and dash … but seems a bit old for these scenes.'[12] Nevertheless, he is presented as irresistible to women, thus reinforcing his heterosexual potency. Ted rarely appears to exert himself, but women are fascinated by him, and his appeal can be read as epitomizing that of the

Figure 3.1   The casting of Daniel Craig as Ted Hughes lends conspicuous masculinity to his on-screen presence in *Sylvia* (2003).

brooding outsider. Though pursued, he retains the upper hand, exuding an air of dominance and authority. Aurelia not only acknowledges this ascendancy, but suggests that it is the basis of Sylvia's infatuation for him: 'There were a lot of other boys, they didn't frighten her – I rather think she frightened them. But you frightened her, and that's why she likes you.' This combative take on the politics of attraction serves to reinforce the strength of Ted's personality and to confirm his superiority over the 'lot of boys' once his rivals.

Last, and most importantly, Ted is presented as an increasingly successful poet – successful financially as well as artistically. He is published, his work wins prizes, and he gives a series of lectures to suitably besotted audiences of attractive female students. In one such scene, as he stands confidently at the lectern, wearing what appears to be a suggestively brown-hued shirt and with a steely glint in his eye, he seems to completely embody the nickname Aurelia first bestowed upon him as a joke: he *is* the 'Übermensch'. Central to this reclamation of not just masculine but *hyper-masculine* identity is the presentation of Ted's attitude to poetry itself. He asserts that 'A fucking good poem, it's like a weapon and not just a little pop gun or something; it's like a bomb, a bloody big bomb.' This speech, littered as it is with violent imagery, indicates his determination to be taken seriously as a poet, as he endows his chosen metier with a specifically militarized and destructive charge. Rand Richards Cooper observes that 'these scenes capture the era's belief in poetry as dangerous and subversive. And erotic.'[13] And this assertion of poetry as both a physically and sexually dangerous occupation reconnects Ted to the hyperbole of the Byronic legend.

This aggressive course of action is never an option for Dylan, who is invariably more likely to transform into an 'Über-drunk' than an 'Übermensch'. Instead, he is presented as skilfully manipulating conventional notions of poetry and masculinity to serve his own advantage. In the London pub scenes, he may be the only man not enrolled and therefore not in uniform, but he manages nonetheless to have a beautiful woman on each arm and a drink in each hand. From this position of security, instead of feeling emasculated at his inability to pay for the drinks he holds, he is instead happy to borrow money from Vera: 'You pay lovey – support a starving poet.' Rather than impersonate the conventional masculinity of the soldiers, Dylan flouts the rules while still excelling at the game. In this sense, he can be read as embodying the rebellious nature of the Byronic hero in his refusal to conform, and his contentious dismissal of the soldiers as 'a bunch of buggering yes men' encapsulates his disdain for the norm. There is, understandably, a constant sense of antagonism between Dylan and his more conventional male peers, and the poet evidently delights in scoring points at their expense – sometimes literally, as Vera uses William's pay to help support the Thomases. Later on, he justifies his adultery to Vera with the grandiloquent proclamation that 'I sleep with other women because I'm a poet, and a poet feeds off life.' In attributing the excesses of his drinking and sexual behaviour to his creative identity, Dylan has created the perfect loophole for himself: he drinks and cheats because he is a man; he gets away with it because he is a poet, and so cannot be held to the same standards as other men. He is still, to reclaim Gerschick and Miller's terms, 'pursuing masculine themes' – in this case, drinking and womanizing – but his approach is adapted to suit his abilities. Indeed, if the root of Ted's attractiveness lies in the impression he gives of being a man among boys, Dylan's pose is that of a boy among men, vulnerable and in constant need of female affection. Caitlin responds with a quasi-maternal aura of longsuffering tolerance, while Vera welcomes the opportunity to revert to adolescence through the resumed relationship with her teenage sweetheart. Ty Burr has criticized the film for its characterization of Dylan as a 'goatish satyr, manipulating lesser mortals', a criticism that itself invokes the myth of Byronic superiority, and reaffirms the idea that the poet is fundamentally different from other, ordinary people.[14]

In both films, the masculinity of the poet-protagonist is further confirmed by the most basic of indicators – his virility is proven by his ability to father a child. As Connell notes, the most basic view of sexual difference is driven by biological determinism, and from this perspective 'masculinity, it would follow, is the social elaboration of the biological function of fatherhood.'[15] However reductive this line of argument might be, it is nevertheless crucial to appreciating the primal connection between masculinity and fatherhood that underlines the presentation of paternity in these films. In *Sylvia*, Ted and Sylvia have two children in quick succession, reflecting the real-life births of Frieda in 1960, and Nicholas in 1962. Ted is not, however, a hands-on father. The contrast between his readiness to write for children (a removed engagement mediated by the literary) and his relief at the opportunity to escape from his own child (a disquietingly proximous and unmediated engagement) is telling, as is the difference between the alacrity with which he answers the telephone and his reluctance to respond to the crying baby. Beyond his potency-asserting contribution to conception, he does not wish to assume further responsible for raising the resulting children. This is underscored in a later scene in which Sylvia attempts a last-ditch seduction of her errant husband. As they lie together in a gently lit moment of post-coital peace, Sylvia begins to outline her plans for their future together, but is interrupted by Ted's announcement that his new lover is already pregnant. The shock declaration serves to reassert Ted's potency and prowess as conventionally understood, and simultaneously reinforces the idea that his role is to beget rather than raise children: his sense of duty towards the unborn child he has conceived with Assia apparently trumps that which he feels for the two young children he shares with Sylvia. It is an account of fatherhood reduced to basic biological essentialism.

Meantime, *The Edge of Love* includes Dylan and Caitlin's son Llewellyn (b.1939) but erases their daughter Aeronwy (b.1943) from the biographical account. While the decision to reduce two real-world children to just one on-screen child makes editorial sense in terms of simplicity and focus, it is difficult to see the elimination of the daughter as a neutral choice. Indeed, the historically inscribed prioritising of male children remains a prevalent cultural signifier. Connell observes that among young men surveyed in the 1990s, 'Fatherhood is feared, because it means commitment, but also desired, especially if the child is a boy.'[16] The inclusion of Dylan's son rather than his daughter in the on-screen dramatization appears to be a matter of symbolic importance as well as narrative convenience. There is also the suggestion, never completely resolved, that Dylan may be the father of Vera's son Rowatt. Vera insists that the baby is William's, but the local gossips maintain otherwise, culminating in a distressing scene in which William refuses to hold the baby. Dylan's triumph over his soldier rival is completed by the suggestion that he has infiltrated William's family with his own gene pool, and passed off his biological son as William's responsibility. Caitlin's own infidelities slightly temper the impression of Dylan's roguishness. Nevertheless, she continues to shelter Dylan from the consequences of her own affairs: pregnant, and unsure whether the father is her lover or her husband, she enlists Vera's help to pay for an illegal abortion, and keeps Dylan in blissful ignorance.

Caitlin's protective attitude towards Dylan leads on to the second thread of my argument in this chapter. If the characters of Ted and Dylan are presented as well aware of how they can utilize cultural misconceptions about poetry and masculinity for their own purposes, it is equally important to address how they are aided and abetted in this process, and to ask if this is an issue of female fantasy as much as one of masculine identity crisis. Both films were co-created by women. *Sylvia* was written by John Brownlow and directed by Christine Jeffs; *The Edge of Love* written by Sharman MacDonald and directed by John Maybury. The films were also targeted at a primarily female audience. *Sylvia* was marketed as the story of a turbulent, tragic romance, while *The Edge of Love* was used as inspiration for high-profile 1940s-style fashion shoots in women's magazines, including *Vogue* and *ELLE*.[17] It is also worth taking into account the star status of the actors involved, at the time when each film was released. In 2003, Gwyneth Paltrow was the Hollywood golden girl, compared endlessly in the media to Grace Kelly. She had won an Oscar for *Shakespeare in Love* in 1998, and consolidated her reputation as a marketable star with films such as *The Talented Mr. Ripley* (dir. Anthony Minghella, 1999) and *The Royal Tenenbaums* (dir. Wes Anderson, 2001). On the other hand, Daniel Craig, if not quite a 'jobbing actor', was only just starting to progress from limited film roles such as that of the love interest in *Lara Croft: Tomb Raider* (dir. Simon West, 2001) to more high-profile parts in *Road to Perdition* (dir. Sam Mendes, 2002) and *The Mother* (dir. Roger Mitchell, 2003). Craig might now, that is, be synonymous with the hyper-masculinity of James Bond, but in 2003 he was still a long way from establishing himself as a bankable leading man. A similar imbalance can be found when considering the cast of *The Edge of Love*. Matthew Rhys's most recognizable role prior to the film was his part on the ensemble television series *Brothers and Sisters* (ABC, 2006–2011), while Cillian Murphy, despite his parts in *28 Days Later* (dir. Danny Boyle, 2002) and *Batman Begins* (dir. Christopher Nolan, 2005), was still completely overshadowed by the profiles of his female co-stars. Sienna Miller's fashionista status and tumultuous personal relationships compensated, in terms of media attention, for the less-than-stellar reception of films like *Layer Cake* (dir. Matthew Vaughn, 2004) and *Factory Girl* (dir. George Hickenlooper, 2006), while Keira Knightley joined *The Edge of Love* having starred in the phenomenally successful *Pirates of the Caribbean* franchise, as well as a critically acclaimed adaptation of *Pride and Prejudice* (dir. Joe Wright, 2005). Therefore, the films were marketed not only at a female audience, but on the strength of their female stars. The film poster for *Sylvia* shows a close-up of Paltrow's flawlessly composed face, lipsticked mouth curved in an enigmatic smile. Ted Hughes does not feature in the marketing. Lipstick also figures heavily in the promotional material for *The Edge of Love*, the poster featuring an image of Miller and Knightley taken from above. They lie prone, smiling seductively up at the camera. Dylan Thomas – the central pivot, and the point, of the story according to all synopses – is strikingly absent from the picture. How, then, do these foregrounded women help to shape a view of the male poet? Why might it be thought advantageous for a figure so narratively crucial to be so emphatically erased from the marketing? And how might the nature of his strategic absence and potent presence in these films reflect upon the inherited Byronic myth of the male poet?

The film suggests that Sylvia's configurations of Ted are influential in making him the man he is. Their first encounter is combative – she bites his cheek, he steals her jewellery – but she insistently and wilfully interprets aggression as ardour and conflates violence with grand passion. At the same time, she displays a startling naivety in love, chanting Ted's name to herself and trying out the sound of 'Mrs. Edward Hughes'. This unsettling combination of antagonistic sexuality and schoolgirl bravado is united in her poetry, although her more pragmatic flatmate is unimpressed:

Doreen (reading Sylvia's poem): "One day I'll have my death of him." Bit morbid isn't it?
Sylvia: He's my black marauder.
Doreen: Well, don't get your hopes up.

Sylvia's ecstatic proclamation disturbs: the suggestion is that from the earliest days of the relationship, she is, if not quite 'half in love with easeful death', then at least happy to embark upon a heavy flirtation with it. She is presented as craving drama, instigating violent arguments and hurling crockery, then compensating by performing the role of perfect housewife. Her jealous anger is subsumed by her desire to please – she is shown in a neat apron, cooking a sumptuous breakfast, then serving it to the husband who has spent the night sleeping drunk on the couch.

Her pattern of behaviour seems designed simultaneously to provoke and to license Ted's own. Jeffs also suggests a causal connection between Sylvia's insecurity and Ted's infidelity, as Joe Queenan points out:

Resorting to a series of Ted the swordsman scenes which may merely be the lurid fantasies of the heroine, [Jeffs] never makes it clear whether Hughes was a rampaging philanderer ... or a man driven into other women's arms by his wife's chronic melancholy.[18]

In refusing to clarify the extent of Ted's adulterous relationships prior to his affair with Assia, Jeffs implicates Sylvia as potentially culpable in creating a self-fulfilling prophecy: she expects Ted to be unfaithful, accuses him of being unfaithful, and so eventually, he *is* unfaithful and leaves her for another woman. Sylvia herself subscribes to this interpretation, telling her neighbour: 'All I could think about was what would happen if someone took him away from me … that woman, I invented her.' This perspective goes unchallenged within the film, effectively exonerating Ted, while severely compromising Sylvia. Rand Richards Cooper unfavourably compares *Sylvia* to Jeffs' 2001 film, *Rain*, which also deals with the aftermath of infidelity, but from the perspective of a child:

> To a child, parental marital deceit comes as a revelation … But Plath was already an adult when Hughes cheated on her. Jeffs doesn't quite seem to recognise this, and as a result, Sylvia flirts with what would seem to be an oddly antifeminist interpretation – Plath as the little girl who never grew up, whose rage at the husband-father is the rage of a child.[19]

Certainly, the film posits something disturbingly childlike in Sylvia's suscep-tibility to the myth that she has helped to perpetuate. She is so enveloped in, and enamoured of, her fantasies about Ted that she has come to believe not only that they are objectively true, but that they are equally appealing to others also.

If Ted's absence from the marketing for *Sylvia* configures Sylvia to some extent as his creator, so the presence of the two women in Dylan's life in the marketing for *The Edge of Love*, displacing Dylan himself from visibility, emphatically asserts their relationship as the most important in that film. The two women in Dylan's life enjoy a close, quasi-sexual bond that is independent of the poet. They are shown sleeping in the same bed and washing in the same bath; they take their children to the beach and go drinking together in the local pub. That the men are, at root, superfluous to their relationship is neatly illustrated in an early scene when Dylan invites both women to lie down with him. They respond to his suggestive remarks with raucous laugh-ter, until the affronted poet leaves the bed – and leaves the women together in it. Despite some significant tensions between them, however, both women prioritize Dylan's peace of mind above their own, and they repeatedly con-spire to protect him. As Burr notes:

> *The Edge of Love* isn't really about poetry, though, or even Dylan Thomas, but about the two women who love him … it peddles the time-honoured myth that poets make a lovely, worthwhile mess of everything they touch, and women are just there to marvel and clean up afterward.[20]

This being the case, why are they presented as bothering? Caitlin is clearly well aware of the limiting nature of the relationship, protesting that 'He thinks I'm put on this earth to nurture his bloody talent', and yet she con-tinues to accept this as a necessary sacrifice within marriage. She is, perhaps, as attached to the poetry as she is to the poet: she is willing to care for the body as long as she continues to inspire the mind. Vera, on the other hand, ultimately rejects Dylan in favour of her husband, explaining that 'You don't even see me, do you? Dylan! All you've got is stories in your head. Words. And I have to feel real. William makes me real.' While Sylvia sacrifices herself on the altar of warped hero-worship, and Caitlin is resigned to a life of domestic drudgery with a philandering spouse, Vera is one woman at least who proves less than enamoured of the self-serving mythology which supports the male poet's persona.

Despite Sylvia's admiration for Ted's talent and Caitlin's defensive attitude to her role as Dylan's muse, a sense of the poetry itself remains absent. In the case of *Sylvia*, this was partly enforced by legal restrictions, as Plath and Hughes's daughter objected strongly to the film and refused to license the use of her parents' poetry. In order, therefore, to convey the characters' intellectual and literary sensibilities, the filmmakers had to resort to scenes in which Ted and Sylvia quote the work of other poets, including Shakespeare, Chaucer and W.B. Yeats. But this enforced periphrasis may have been a blessing since the act of writing itself can struggle to maintain cinematic interest. Paul Arthur summarizes the challenge thus:

> On the surface, it is hard to imagine an activity less given to cinematic representation than a writer's struggle to transform observations or ideas into a finished manuscript. Writing is mostly solitary, static labour performed in dull locations over excruciating stretches of time.[21]

Ted is sometimes shown writing, and reveals a very pragmatic attitude to his work in conversation with Sylvia: 'There's no secret to it. You've just got to pick a subject and stick your head into it.' In comparison with this determinedly unpretentious attitude to his craft, in *The Edge of Love* Dylan is presented as a more instinctive poet, writing in a rush of inspiration. Burr complains that the effect is overworked: 'the words stream out of his inner consciousness directly onto the soundtrack, the musical score surging orgasmically, the writing issuing forth complete, each dactyl tucked neatly into place,' and the presentation of writing is clichéd.[22] More problematically still, the repeated use of the poetry in voiceovers separates Dylan from his work – it becomes increasingly difficult to associate the raffish, petulant man with the sonorous readings. This is especially incongruous when a sequence shows William, who is clearly traumatized by his wartime experience, walking on the beach to the strains of 'In My Craft or Sullen Art'. The effect is jarring, suggesting a spiritual sympathy between the men that is never delivered in person. The Byronic myth itself is perpetuated in these films through a personal rather than a critical reputation. It is, therefore, perhaps fitting that the focus of both films should be fixed so insistently upon the private lives rather than the public literature. This is compounded in that both films ultimately emphasize the success of the poetry and the failure of the men.

The Ted and Dylan of these films each manage the balancing act of dissociating themselves from the more undesirable clichés about male poets as weak, effete, incompetent, while simultaneously emulating the most attractive elements of the same stereotypes. Ted embodies the ideals of a traditional masculine identity, which are also then mapped onto his robust – and, by direct implication, male – definition of poetry. Dylan intuits and exploits the allowances made for creative talent, instinctively surrounding himself with people who will nurture and indulge him. However, in the final analysis, these suggestions of male strength in its various expressions are countered by the forlorn endings of the films. Ted must face up to the aftermath of Sylvia's suicide; the final shot frames him behind a gridded window, the panels of which are strongly suggestive of prison bars. Dylan is shown as similarly bereft, as, having destroyed his relationship with Vera, he faces an uncertain future with Caitlin. The final image of the male poet in each film is that of a broken man. In both cases, a degree of retribution is suggested. *Sylvia* does not blame Ted for the extent of Sylvia's final break-down, but neither is he completely exonerated. Rand Cooper summarizes *Sylvia* as the story of a 'very jealous woman whose very selfish husband has a very sloppy affair',[23] while Queenan's verdict is that Ted is 'luckless and perhaps in some ways wicked'.[24] The portrayal of Dylan tends to generate a more robust critical reaction: he is a 'wastrel poet'[25] and a 'boozy, boastful womanis[er]',[26] and his unhappiness at the close of the film is presented as a fitting punishment for his actions throughout it. While the male characters are, to varying extents, revealed to carry the responsibility of the narrative events, both films also confirm the extent of female complicity in the waywardness of the male characters. Sylvia's intensely idealized passion for Ted is presented as unhealthy, while Caitlin both shares and condones Dylan's main vices. In fact, it is their abjection that adds interest to Vera's final actions: she chooses the soldier over the poet. If Sylvia's relationship with Ted verges on a re-enactment of 'Daddy',[27] Vera's final actions owe more to the weary realism of Wendy Cope's 'Triolet'.[28] By the close of *Sylvia* and *The Edge of Love*, the male protagonists' poetic personae and the female protagonists' indulgence of the same are both revealed to be destructive tendencies that sabotage relationships. The bravado of the Byronic mantra finally rings hollow when confronted with a reality that is at once too tragic and too prosaic to be transformed by poetic licence and hyperbole. The image of the male poet as eternally 'mad, bad and dangerous to know' has an undeniable charm, but for these films, it is neither madness nor badness but rather sadness which lingers.

Notes

1. T.B. Macaulay, 'Review of Moore's *Life of Byron*', Edinburgh Review 53 (June 1831): 544–72.

2. M. Benton, *Literary Biography: An Introduction* (Chichester: John Wiley & Sons, 2009), p. 54.
3. A. Stein, *The Byronic Hero in Film, Fiction and Television* (Carbondale, IL: Southern Illinois University Press, 2004).
4. B. Eisler, *Byron: Child of Passion, Fool of Fame* (London: Vintage, 2000), p. 752.
5. Benton (2009), p. 167.
6. A. Sinfield, *Faultlines: Cultural Materialism and the Politics of Dissident Reading* (Berkeley, CA: University of California Press, 1992), p. 274.
7. I. Babbitt, *Literature and the American College* (Boston, MA: Houghton Mifflin, 1908), p. 172.
8. All references to 'Ted' or 'Dylan' therefore refer exclusively to the characters portrayed within the films, rather than to the individuals upon whom they are based.
9. R.W. Connell, *Masculinities* (Cambridge: Polity Press, 1996), p. 45.
10. T. Gershick and A. Miller, 'Coming to Terms: Masculinity and Physical Disability', *American Sociological Association Annual Meeting*, Miami 1993.
11. Connell (1996), p. 55.
12. J. Queenan, 'Without Rhyme or Reason' *The Guardian*, London, 31 January 2004.
13. R.R. Cooper, 'Daddy's Girl?' *Commonweal* 130(20) (2003): 17.
14. T. Burr, 'Review: *The Edge of Love*' *The Boston Globe*, Boston, 3 April 2009. At: http://www.boston.com/ae/movies/articles/2009/04/03/the_edge_of_love/ (accessed 11 December 2012).
15. Connell (1996), p. 52.
16. Connell (1996), p. 108.
17. *Vogue* September 2007 at: http://www.vogue.co.uk/magazine/archive/issue/2007/September/Page/1; *Elle* December 2008 at: http://www.elleuk.com/elle-tv/red-carpet/parties-events/elle-in-association-with-the-edge-of-love (both accessed 11 December 2012).
18. Queenan (2004).
19. Richards Cooper (2003), p. 17.
20. Burr (2009).
21. P. Arthur, 'The Written Scene: Writers as Figures of Cinematic Redemption', in R. Stam and A. Raengo (eds.) *Literature and Film: A Guide to the Theory and Practice of Film Adaptation* (Oxford: Blackwell, 2005), p. 331.
22. Burr (2009).
23. Richards Cooper (2003).
24. Queenan (2004).
25. P. Bradshaw, 'Review: *The Edge of Love*' *The Guardian*, London, 20 June 2008.
26. P. French, 'Review: *The Edge of Love*' *The Observer*, London, 22 June 2008.
27. Sylvia Plath 'Daddy', in *Ariel* (Harper Collins, 1999).
28. W. Cope, 'Triolet', in A. Goldrick-Jones and H. Rosengarten (eds.) *Broadview Anthology of Poetry*, 2nd edn (Broadview Press, 2008), p. 887.

4

Romantic genius on screen: Jane Campion's *Bright Star* (2009) and Julien Temple's *Pandaemonium* (2000)

Julian North

One of the most seductive and enduring models of literary authorship is that of Romantic genius. A complex and composite mythology, with its origins in late eighteenth-century European culture, it has traditionally been associated, in British literature, with the lives and writings of six male poets: Blake, Wordsworth, Coleridge, Shelley, Byron and Keats. Their self-mythologizing works, together with their popular and critical afterlives, have left us with an image of the Romantic poet as an inspired originator, a visionary prophet, a solitary figure, simultaneously authoring himself and his art; a man who is heroically but also tragically alienated from his society.

The Romantic poets themselves questioned, as they promoted, the idea of the solitary creator, divorced from the social world, and their Victorian biographers also mixed reverence with scepticism – focusing their attention especially on the apparent incompatibility of genius with ordinary, domestic life.[1] In academic studies of British Romanticism in the past thirty years, the myth of the poet as a lone, alienated male has been thoroughly exposed, through evidence of these writers' engagement with the literary market place and with the social and political movements of their times, as well as by the recovery of the extensive contribution of women poets to the literature of the period. Correspondingly, there has been an increasing emphasis on the collectivity of Romantic production – on the extent to which Romantic-period writers, male and female, created their work in collaboration with their domestic and intellectual communities, of family, friends and fellow writers, rather than in a state of solitary inspiration.[2]

The polarities of solitary versus collective creativity have proved peculiarly tenacious in contemporary discussions of authorship, including the theorization of authorship in film-making and the representation of the author on screen. Unsurprisingly, the debate gains a particular relevance and complexity when filmmakers attempt to represent Romantic genius. This chapter looks at two such films: Jane Campion's *Bright Star* (2009) and its portrayal of

Keats (played by Ben Whishaw); Julien Temple's *Pandaemonium* (2000) and its portrayals of Wordsworth (John Hannah) and Coleridge (Linus Roache). Both films are homages to Romantic genius that show the continuing relevance of this mythology of authorship for the twenty-first century, but both also, in different measures, open up to question the relationship between gender and creativity and the possibility of an autonomous, originating power. This tension between fascination with the mystery of Romantic genius and resistance to the idea of the author as a lone, male originator is not just a theme within these films. It is also central to the ways in which Campion and Temple present themselves as directors. In view of this, I start with a brief discussion of the contested figure of the Romantic auteur, and of the degree to which each director conforms to this model of authorship, before considering how their self-projections as filmmakers relate to their representations of Romantic genius in *Bright Star* and *Pandaemonium*.

The Auteur as Romantic Genius

As it developed in essays in *Cahiers du Cinema*, *Movie* and the work of Andrew Sarris, from the 1950s to the 1970s, auteur criticism had strongly Romantic affiliations. The director who merited the title 'auteur' was the presiding genius of a film, working in defiance of commercial and other constraints to articulate a personal vision, traceable in style and theme across the whole body of his work. The film rose to the status of a work of art by virtue of being an individual director's act of self-expression. As Jean-Luc Goddard wrote in 1958, suggesting an analogy between the filmmaker and the Romantic writer: 'The cinema is not a craft. It is an art. It does not mean teamwork. One is always alone; on the set as before a blank page'.[3] The links between post-war auteurism and early nineteenth-century Romantic conceptions of genius have not been lost on film theorists. John Caughie placed an extract from M.H. Abrams's seminal study of the emergence of an expressive aesthetic in Romantic literature, *The Mirror and the Lamp*, at the beginning of his influential 1981 anthology of key texts in the history of authorship in film, and Edward Buscombe compared Truffaut's, Bazin's and Rivette's approaches to the auteur with Coleridge's thinking on original genius.[4] Yet, like the figure of 'the Romantic poet', the film auteur has survived in our culture as a persistently demystified myth, a conception in a perpetual cycle of death and return.

Although Caughie argued that auteur criticism had opened up important new directions in film criticism and theory, he described the return to a Romantic conception of the author as 'a regressive step'.[5] The essays in his collection charted the structuralist and post-structuralist critique of Romantic auteurism that took place from the late 1960s, shifting the critical emphasis from the originating author to 'the process of reading or spectating'; and included Edward Buscombe's call in 1973 for a sociology of cinema that would relocate filmmaking in relation to history, genre, ideology and the industry – contexts that Romantic auteurism had occluded.[6] The figure of the director as a solitary, Romantic genius has continued to be variously rejected, problematized and reconfigured as film theorists have addressed the paradox of the auteurist approach to a medium that is, manifestly, a collective and collaborative enterprise, involving scriptwriters, producers, actors, cinematographers and many others, each of whom might claim a role in the authoring process. Thus, Thomas Schatz, rejecting the 'adolescent romanticism' of auteurism, wrote of the 'genius of the system', rather than that of the individual director.[7] Timothy Corrigan argued that the auteur should be understood as, itself, a collective construct, a '*commercial* strategy for organising audience reception … a critical concept bound to distribution and marketing aims'.[8] In 2001 Robert Carringer, who believed that auteur criticism 'as a methodology … was untenable from the outset', identified the current critical responses to the auteur as 'multiple authorship studies'; 'collective authorship studies', and 'collaboration analysis', all of them, in different ways and to different degrees, running counter to a Romantic focus on the film as an act of individual expression.[9] Critical interest in women filmmakers and in collective filmmaking within women's cinema, has also played a role in this debate. On the one hand, it has been suggested that 'the poststructuralist critique of the originary genius' in 1970s and 1980s, did not help the cause of women and other marginalized groups within the industry, who might have benefitted more from the status and visibility accorded by Romantic auteurism.[10] On the other hand, Angela Martin, among others, has pointed to the 'male-centredness of the *politique des auteurs*' as it arose and argued that '"auteurism" has nothing to do with women's filmmaking'.[11] All these critical responses to authorship in film studies find common ground with directions taken by English studies in relation to Romantic authorship, not least in the continuing return to the author as Romantic genius, enacted in repeated attempts to deny or disperse that figure's individual potency.[12]

Jane Campion as Romantic Auteur

In the context of these debates, the critical industry that has grown up around Jane Campion has increasingly become focused on scrutinizing her position as 'the ultimate auteur'.[13] The story of her career, as told and retold by herself and by numerous interviewers and academic critics, contains a powerful narrative of Romantic genius: her films are described as passionately personal, even autobiographical, and developed in opposition to the system. Yet already this story, which ends in both artistic and commercial success, suggests the contradictions that inhere in Campion's authorial persona. One obvious contradiction is applicable to all commercially successful auteurs – that the narrative of an inspired personal vision is used as an effective marketing ploy; *Bright Star* is 'A Jane Campion Film', partly because it can be sold on her name and her status as a celebrity writer-director. Other contradictions arise from her well-publicized collaborations with cinematographer Sally Bongers, script author Gerard Lee, producer Jan Chapman, and others. Some have found Campion's collaborative practices compatible with Romantic auteurism.[14] Others have seen them as exposing the mythology of an autonomous creative vision. Dana Polan contends, for instance, that this 'dispersion of authorial responsibility' means, ironically perhaps, that 'to call a work a "Jane Campion" film may be to recognize how she helps facilitate work communities where various contributors can all make their mark'.[15] In other words, in her case, the individual directorial name may be taken to imply a collaborative approach to the production process. Campion herself has been equivocal when questioned on this issue. In 1990 she described both conflicted and harmonious relationships with her production team and admitted that collaboration is 'the plus and minus of film-making': 'I'm able and not able to take collaboration'.[16] When, in 1993, she reflected on the making of *The Piano*, however, her position seemed to have shifted: 'Now I totally believe in collaboration because there is no way I could possibly have created this work on my own'.[17] Arguably, an important factor in this vacillation is her identity as a woman filmmaker working at a certain point in history. As Hilary Radner argues, her career

> captures the paradoxical legacy of Second Wave Feminism, which encouraged women of Campion's generation to achieve a singularity of vision while simultaneously promoting a theoretical model that undermined the validity of such achievements, viewing them as potentially anti-feminist.[18]

This feminist inflection of the dilemma we have already encountered in relation to Romantic authorship – 'singularity of vision' versus collaborative creativity – would seem to place extra pressure on Campion, as on other women filmmakers of her generation, to avoid a high Romantic auteurist stance.[19]

Bright Star marked a significant moment in Campion's career in the context of her public image as auteur. She declared that, in the six-year gap between *In the Cut* (2003) and *Bright Star* (2009), she had taken stock and found a new and gentler approach to filmmaking:

> the Keats story is so powerful, you just want to give it its space and feel like you're in the story without the authorship being too present. So I tried to disappear…[20]

> I got pretty sick of director's signatures, fancy shots and the director leading the thinking or the ideas … Bresson's films are very simple. He pretty much disappears.[21]

Here Campion describes herself in terms that embody a new paradox: that of the self-effacing auteur. By insisting on this as a personal project, as opposed to a commercial costume biopic, and by paying homage to Bresson, Campion presented *Bright Star* as the work of a Romantic auteur. Yet she redefined what this might mean by insisting on gentleness and a loss of authorial presence. This authorial persona derives not only from Bresson, of course. It also borrows from Keats's aesthetic of sensitive expressivity combined with his critique of a High Romantic conception of authorship – what he called 'the Wordsworthian or egotistical sublime'.[22] 'Men of genius', Keats writes, 'have not any individuality, any determined Character'.[23] The 'poetical Character ... has no self – it is every thing and nothing – It has no character. ... A Poet is the most unpoetical of any thing in existence; because he has no Identity – he is continually ... filling some other Body'.[24] Campion does not refer to this passage explicitly in the interviews (although, as we shall see, part of it is quoted in the film), but she does cite, as the guiding philosophy for herself and the cast in the making of *Bright Star*, Keats's related theory of '*Negative Capability*, that is when man is capable of being in uncertainties, Mysteries, doubts, without any irritable reaching after fact & reason'.[25] Again, this suggests a surrender of selfhood and of authorial ego (whether by the actors or the director), an ability to accept the existence of other centres of consciousness. It is interesting that Campion should associate her own authorial presence with a Keatsian view of the creative genius as supersensitive, self-effacing and receptive in this way, since, from Keats's time to the present, it has often been viewed as a 'feminine' model of Romantic authorship, by contrast to the virile independence and assertiveness of Wordsworth's or Byron's authorial personae. Campion's identification with Keats encourages an auteurist reading of the film as personal expression, but, within that model, it favours a softer vision of authorial agency than that of the traditional auteur – one more akin to Polan's model of the 'dispersion of authorial responsibility'. Thus, Campion and her marketing team construct for the audience a Romantic, auteurist reading of the film, but only in a modified sense. The emphasis on the 'disappearance' of the auteur shows them keeping one eye on the perceived commercial pitfalls of a director – or a film – projecting wholesale reverence for a high Romantic model of genius.

Bright Star (2009)

As Campion acknowledges, *Bright Star* was inspired by Andrew Motion's biography of Keats.[26] Motion acted as an advisor on the film and there is much in it taken straight from the pages of his book. But, given this relationship, what is more remarkable is the extent to which the version of Keats's life that Campion scripted and directed flies in the face of the Motion biography. Motion started his book by rejecting the Victorian conception of Keats as 'the archetype of the stricken Romantic: a supersensitive soul, brought to an early grave by the hostile reviewers'.[27] More attention had to be given to Keats's engagement with the public and political world, he argued. It was misguided to think that 'he lived in a vacuum, and never described or responded to wider issues'.[28] Motion sold his biography as one that would put this right, describing how Keats's poetry:

> At all times, and in various ways ... tangles with what he called his 'barbarous age' ... he engages with the issue of military power, with the French Revolution and the Napoleonic Wars, with the repressive effects of the Corn Laws, enclosures and the Six Acts, with radicals such as Cobbett ... and his early mentor Leigh Hunt, and with the plight of people working in factories.[29]

This was a public and politicized Keats that clearly drew on the academic historicization of Romantic writers touched on in my introduction, but it was a Keats who held no interest for Campion.

In *Bright Star*, we look at the poet exclusively through the eyes of Fanny Brawne (Abbie Cornish, see Figure 4.1), with the consequence that the wider social and political contexts for his life and art are almost completely bracketed out: we only know of them what Fanny knows. Thus we hear of the reviews of *Endymion*, we venture to Keats's lodgings in Kentish town, we see glimpses of him at the beach on the Isle of Wight, and of his coffin departing from the Spanish steps in Rome, but the world beyond Hampstead is as shadowy for us as it is for Fanny. The Keats we see is the man who remains within Fanny's orbit, and Campion's version of Fanny, like her version of Keats, contrasts significantly with Andrew Motion's. Motion argues that Fanny

> 'was wont to discuss' politics 'with fire and animation', not only with her English neighbours, but with the French exiles who had clustered round Orel House in Hampstead during and after the French Revolution. In so far as her gender and class allowed her to feel part of the wide world, she engaged with it energetically.[30]

But this isn't the Fanny or the Hampstead that Campion projects or that Cornish delivers. Campion chooses instead to show Fanny and her community as intensely inward-looking, domestic and feminine. Motion, too, acknowledged that Fanny's world represented feminine domesticity for Keats – but with this important difference: that as such, he argued, it was in direct *conflict* with Keats's ambitions as a poet. 'How could he love Fanny without compromising his genius?' Motion asks.[31] He claims that Keats withdrew from her at one stage, afraid of her 'smothering domesticity'.[32] Motion's Keats thus oscillates between a desire to submit to his love for Fanny and a wish to assert his separate identity as author. This is a far cry

Figure 4.1 Ben Whishaw as John Keats, the abstracted poet who finds his context in Fanny Brawne (Abbie Cornish) in *Bright Star* (2009).

from Campion's film, which represents Keats's genius as nurtured by Fanny and flourishing harmoniously within her affectionate, domestic world.

So, on the one hand, *Bright Star* returns to a now distinctly old-fashioned vision of Keats as a poet working apart from the great social and political upheavals of his time – and in that sense a solitary genius. But, on the other hand, the film presents the writer as a social creation – dependent on his intimate community – and refuses to take part in promoting the myth of the author as a man whose genius is defined by his separateness from others. On the contrary, the film emphasizes Keats's desire to be sociable within his close circle – and, more particularly, to mingle and mix his identity with that of his lover. The screenplay and imagery of the film represent the poet as happy to surrender his ego. Quoting from his letter on 'The Poetical Character', Keats tells Fanny that the poet 'has no Identity – he is continually in for – and filling some other Body'.[33] Later the film quotes from another of his letters in which, this time, he expresses his desire to merge identities with Fanny: 'My sweet Girl', he writes, 'You dazzled me – There is nothing in the world so bright and delicate'. 'You have absorb'd me. I have a sensation … as though I was dissolving'.[34] The film embodies Keats's imagery in its use of light to dazzle and obscure distinct identity. In one scene, the poet climbs a tree full of blossom, to lie luxuriously on its surface contemplating the spring sky. The camera shoots straight into the sun dissolving his body. The identities of Keats and Fanny intermingle as their relationship develops and the boundaries between self and other fade. The couple sit intertwined, their fingers locked together and they later recite 'La Belle Dame Sans Merci', taking alternating stanzas. In Motion's biography, this poem is interpreted as Keats's attempt to escape from his 'grim anxieties about the identity-*sapping* powers of love'.[35] In the film, the poem is interpreted, by contrast, as an affirmation of the strength of interwoven minds – shared identities. The final verses, describing the knight left on the cold hillside by his lady are significantly omitted from this scene, and replaced by a cut to the maid, Abigail (Antonia Campbell-Hughes), crying after having been seduced and made pregnant by Keats's poet-friend Charles Brown (Paul Schneider). No such conflict is to be brooked between Keats and Fanny in their mutual rapture.

Campion's film is a love story, but it also, of course, describes a *creative* relationship, between Keats's poetry and Fanny's needlework. Here too, the boundaries of self dissolve and the hierarchy of poetry over fashion asserted by Brown – or, for that matter of fashion over poetry declared by Fanny – is replaced by a creative equality. The poet is no longer the autonomous, originating self, but a mind and body produced through domestic relationships. It is an interaction conveyed in imagery of interwoven lines, lines of thread and of poetry, of male and female voices intertwining in song and recitation, of woven fabrics and embroidery, gauzy curtains or skirts against the light, washing flapping in the breeze, tangled reeds and branches. As Keats says to Fanny before their final parting: 'We have woven a web you and I, attached to this world, but a separate world of our own invention'.

To some extent in this film, Keats is still the Romantic genius as god-like creator. He is the author of his and Fanny's world at Hampstead: the imagery of dazzle and delicacy, beauty and transience is a visual translation of Keats's own words in his letters and poetry. But, if this is true, then, particularly in the first half of the film, Fanny is subtly present in the role of *co-author*, even in her own way as a kind of originating genius too: 'All I wear I've sewed and designed myself,' she says. 'I have *originated* the pleats on my dress.' The film's imagery of butterflies illustrates the way in which Campion suggests Keats and Fanny as co-creators of their world. In a letter from the Isle of Wight, the historical Keats writes, 'I almost wish we were butterflies and liv'd but three summer days – three such days with you I could fill with more delight than fifty common years could ever contain'.[36] The butterfly, a symbol of the soul, alludes to Keats's meditation on soul-making and his 'Ode to Psyche'. In *Bright Star*, however, the metaphor is literalized and so, after Fanny reads the letter, the butterflies of Keats's epistolary imagination become *manifest* as real insects in Hampstead: we see them being netted by her brother and sister in the meadow outside her house and then imprisoned in Fanny's bedroom. Keats's words have, it seems, been allowed to author Fanny's reality. Then, however, we remember that Fanny herself has already been glimpsed at a dance earlier in the film, with butterflies in her hair. These were fabric butterflies, stitched by herself as accompaniment to her 'triple-pleated mushroom collar', her own extravagant expression of the themes of natural beauty and transience. Fanny has already anticipated Keats's image: when, therefore, the butterfly hunting scene occurs, it is to be understood as a manifestation not of one creative mind, but of *two* – minds, and souls, interlinked, Fanny's material butterflies intermingling with Keats's metaphorical ones. And in the bedroom scene, this mixture is suggested by the fact that whilst some of the species are real enough and might well have been found in Hampstead in 1818, others – the great blue ones for instance – are conspicuously exotic, fantastical, imported less from the English meadow than from the heightened world of the imagination.

Bright Star thus detaches the Romantic poet from his wider political and social contexts but then enmeshes him again within a feminine, domestic community. It represents Keats as a collaborative and, to this extent, a self-effacing, author, his poetry the result of emotional and intellectual interactions with those closest to him, above all, Fanny; his reader, fellow creator and lover. In so doing, the film reflects on Campion's own much debated status as auteur and on the wider question of authorship in literature and film. The film is still deeply implicated in an ideology of Romantic genius – that is, of autonomous creativity agency – but one that is countered by a vision of the creative process as far from solitary, dependent on intimate human relationship, and above all, perhaps, on the interactions between author and audience. The inexorable progress of the narrative is towards the death of the author and to his afterlife, which is, of course, dependent on his readers. In the context of the film these readers are represented by Fanny, who survives to recite his poem 'Bright Star' in the final long tracking shot, and by Campion, whose film is presented as a way of bringing the poetry to a new audience. Yet, despite this power of mediation granted to Keats's female readers, the film is ambiguous as a meditation on female creativity. Creativity is shown as bound up in love, but love also has the capacity to override it. *Bright Star* ends up representing Fanny as the tragic handmaiden to Keats's genius, her own energies entirely focused on her emotional involvement with her lover. In interviews, Campion presents the touching love story as what first interested her in the project, and the romance eventually supersedes the film's discussion of creativity. This comes as no surprise in one respect: it follows a long line of literary biopics in which the same is true. Authorship on screen is rarely perceived to be commercially viable except as a pretext for a grand, and usually tragic, love. Yet the balance does not have to swing this way, as my next example, Julien Temple's *Pandaemonium*, demonstrates.

Julien Temple as Romantic Auteur

Director Julien Temple has been the focus of far less media and academic attention than Campion. This is perhaps partly because, having made his name in music video and documentary, Temple has made relatively few feature films, and none which has met with the sort of commercial or critical success to rival Campion. He is, then, no celebrity auteur. Across his diverse output, though, there are recognizable directorial signatures. One of these is Temple's focus on the lives of anti-authoritarian, creative figures, who, he makes known, have been personal heroes and inspirations to him as a filmmaker. His portrait of Coleridge and his circle in *Pandaemonium* (2000) came soon after the more conventional biopic homage to Jean Vigo, *Passion for Life* (1998), and hard on the heels of his documentary on The Sex Pistols, *The Filth and the Fury* (2000). All three films explored individual and collective creativity – whether in literature, film or music – within a context of social and cultural revolution. Although *Pandaemonium* was the only one to take a Romantic-period poet as its hero, Temple's representations of Coleridge, Vigo and Johnny Rotten were all underpinned by a Romantic ideal of the artist as visionary original, fuelled by opposition to the establishment and the need to find free expression. In each case, the films were also presented as personal, and in some ways autobiographical, statements by the director. Although Temple was a mostly unobtrusive presence behind the anarchic montages of film footage, TV archive, animations, stills, and interviews that composed *The Filth and the Fury*, his director's commentary made it clear that this was not just a record of The Sex Pistols' moment of glory in 1976–7, but was also a look back at his own creative initiation as a young film student trailing the band: 'that was my time ... I saw the world through music'. He describes opening the rusty film canisters containing his student footage of the band as a strange journey back into his own past as well as into theirs. The interchange between his own creative energy and that of The Sex Pistols is also suggested in the film's formal structure – Temple's 'cut-up' or 'ripped-up' technique as a documentary maker expresses 'the essence of the group'.[37]

Pandaemonium was another self-reflexive portrait of the artist, this time with a concerted effort to frame the film as the project of a Romantic auteur.

Interviews with the cast on the DVD and a lengthy director's commentary all worked towards selling the film as a deeply personal project by a man who not only loved Coleridge's poetry but also had much in common with the poet. Actors Emily Woof (Dorothy Wordsworth), Samantha Morton (Sara Coleridge) and Linus Roache (Coleridge) endorsed *Pandaemonium* by saying that they took part in the film because it was a personal vision of the period, by Frank Cotterell-Boyce (screenplay) and Julien Temple, rather than a conventional costume drama. Temple called it 'a very personal project for me' and identified himself specifically with Coleridge, as 'a man who has been important to me throughout most of my life really. It's something I've been obsessed with for a long time'. The scene in which Coleridge, Dorothy and William Wordsworth experiment with Oak Apple is revealed to be based on Temple's own experiences in his student days. He also tells us that, like Coleridge, he grew up in Somerset, where *Pandaemonium* was set and filmed. At school he found Coleridge 'to be incredibly relevant to me – incredibly alive and vivid … he really spoke to me … for many years I wanted to make a film about him'. Throughout the commentary, Temple and his cast stressed the importance of getting away from the idea of period drama set in aspic, and making history provocatively alive and present. Again, this worked to integrate the film with Temple's personal vision as a director interested in music and politics in post-war and contemporary Britain. Thus, Coleridge is compared to Lennon, and Wordsworth (the betrayer) to McCartney, Thatcher and Blair ('It was meant to wind up and annoy a lot of crusty old Wordsworth Professors'). Coleridge is akin to the leaders of The Sex Pistols not only in appearance: he, like them, is also a radical rabble-rowser. The scene in which he delivers a firebrand speech to the crowd at Bristol was rehearsed, Temple tells us on the voice-over commentary, to the accompaniment of 'Anarchy in the UK'.[38]

Unlike the Campion of *Bright Star*, Temple does not attempt to efface himself as Romantic auteur. Just as he celebrates a masculine independence of vision embodied in his cultural heroes, so he publicizes his films, unabashedly, as personal and even autobiographical statements pitted against the establishment. *Pandaemonium* itself does not neglect the collective context for creativity. It situates Coleridge within his close circle of political and literary allies, family and friends and, as part of this, shares with *Bright Star* an interest in the relationship between the male genius and his female, domestic community. Yet, in Temple's film, the poet is the meeting point of more sharply conflicting desires – for the social world on the one hand, and solitary transcendence on the other.

Pandaemonium (2000)

In contrast to *Bright Star*, *Pandaemonium* is a film that insists upon the wider political and social contexts for authorship. Coleridge is not only seen making political speeches at Bristol, as the soldiers march in to break up the crowds; he is shown, with Sara and the Wordsworths, visiting Thelwall (Andy Serkis) at his printing press (Thelwall here merged with Joseph Cottle), and later distributing pamphlets from a hot air balloon supplied by Humphrey Davy (Dexter Fletcher). Wordsworth's and Coleridge's *Lyrical Ballads* is not plucked from thin air: it is a radical volume, a part of the print culture of the period, an experiment arising from its revolutionary times. It is also the product of personal interactions between the poets, their family and friends. Both Sara and Dorothy are important sustaining influences for the poets through their affectionate nurturing. There is much attention in the film to domestic interiors, to Sara's role as mother and wife and to Dorothy's as sister and friend, both offering affectionate support to the men as they wrestle with their poetry. A prolonged reading of 'Frost at Midnight' with Coleridge holding his baby son, Hartley, up in the moonlight in their garden at Nether Stowey, celebrates the domestic context of the 'Conversation Poems'. Dorothy is also presented as offering active creative sustenance as the poets' co-author. If Campion's Fanny Brawne recites Keats's lines, then Temple's Dorothy actually supplies and improves Wordsworth's: 'I wandered lonely as a cow,' muses Wordsworth; 'Perhaps cloud would be better William,' Dorothy interjects. She also suggests lines for 'Tintern Abbey' and key events in 'The Rime of the Ancient Mariner'. She is represented as an originator of the experiment of *Lyrical Ballads*, from which she then, however, feels the need to eliminate her own contribution in the public account. As she says: 'We are working on a book together – well, William and Sam are working on a book together.'

Creativity is therefore shown to be communal, even when not fully acknowledged as such in the world beyond. Yet, creative communities are fragile in this film. Most centrally, the personal and working relationship between Coleridge and Wordsworth breaks down, due to Wordsworth's jealousy of his fellow poet, and, we learn at the end of the film, his betrayal of their radical politics. The support offered by Coleridge's female domestic community fragments too, for unlike Campion, Temple refuses to assimilate Romantic genius to the feminine, domestic world and represents the two as frequently in conflict. Not only does Dorothy compete with Sara for Coleridge's affections, she scorns Sara's world: 'the soul does not live by nursing babies … must a woman be like a farmyard animal … with no ambition, nor intelligence?' She finds Coleridge's 'Conversation poems' 'narrowly domestic and lacking in ambition' and prefers his visionary work, 'The Rime of the Ancient Mariner' and, above all, 'Kubla Khan'. Coleridge himself is shown as caught between Sara and Dorothy, the domestic and the visionary. The communal harmony and naturalistic imagery of the 'Frost at Midnight' sequence is countered in the film by recitations of 'The Rime', against images of Coleridge, alone, strapped heroically to a mast on a stormy sea, in imitation of the Gustave Moreau engravings, or wallowing in mud against the backdrop of Hinckley Point nuclear power station; and of

'Kubla Khan', against an opium-fuelled vision of the poet struggling though a gushing river in his journey through an underground cavern towards a distant panorama of the stately pleasure dome. These are powerful visualizations of the solitary poet's transcendent, Romantic imagination, but also of the director's: Temple's use of fantasy and anachronism breaks the realist illusion to signal the presence of the auteur.

The film's frame narrative, showing the Highgate years, captures the human tragedy of the collapse of a creative community. Coleridge has retreated into a solipsistic world of opium addiction, as has Dorothy. Yet they still emerge heroically – especially by contrast with the turn-coat Wordsworth and the literary establishment of which he is now part. Southey (Samuel West) has received the laureateship that Wordsworth was expecting, the betrayer is betrayed and his efforts to suppress 'Kubla Khan' fail too. The film ends with Dorothy reciting the poem to the stunned London crowd. In some ways it is a similar closing scene to the final shot of *Bright Star* – the former lover paying homage to the poet by reciting one of his poems. But, unlike 'Bright Star', 'Kubla Khan' is not a love poem. Here, and in keeping with the focus of *Pandaemonium* as a whole, it is the inspiration of 'Kubla Khan' as a mysterious prophecy that is commemorated, rather than the lost relationship with Coleridge. Again, at this point, the realist illusion is broken and Temple's presence as auteur is felt as we move into the present day to see Coleridge reading the poem, to two children, from a pop-up picture book.

Pandaemonium, released in 2000, is millennial in theme. Coleridge's pleasure dome merges (bathetically in retrospect) with the Millennium Dome, seen at the end when the credits roll over images of Coleridge taking a bewildered ride on the London Eye to the strains of 'Xanadu' by Olivia Newton John. Where Campion adopts an ambiguously self-effacing presence as director, avoiding 'fancy signature shots', and sheltering Keats in nineteenth-century domestic Hampstead, Temple embraces the role of Romantic auteur, cutting between realism and fantasy, juxtaposing meticulous historical accuracy with exuberant anachronism, releasing Coleridge onto the streets of twenty-first-century London. *Bright Star* turns inwards to investigate how in Keats's life, tenderness and creativity intertwined. *Pandaemonium* insists on the contemporary relevance of Coleridge's poetry, with its warning against breaking the bond with nature. The fact that Campion, a woman, favours an introverted domestic approach to her subject, while Temple embraces a buccaneering Romanticism, should not encourage us to make crude distinctions along gender lines between these filmmakers and their work. As I have suggested, Campion's stance as the self-effacing auteur may in part be a response to her position as a female director, whose films (especially after *The Piano*) have been marketed to a female audience. Yet neither the directors of *Bright Star* and *Pandaemonium*, nor the films themselves encourage obvious conclusions about the relationship between gender and creativity. The films have different biases, but both contest the Romantic model of genius upon which they depend. In so doing they stand in contrast to recent biopics of female authors, such as *Sylvia* (dir. Christine Jeffs, 2003), *Miss Potter* (dir. Chris Noonan, 2006) or *Becoming Jane* (dir. Julian Jarrold, 2007), which all tell the story of the woman writer as an heroic struggle for creative autonomy, counterpointed by tragic romance. Critics objected to the fact that, in *Becoming Jane*, Austen's novels seemed to have been written as a compensation for her doomed love affair with Tom Lefroy, but nowhere in that film is Lefroy shown to have been Austen's co-creator in the way that Fanny is Keats's in *Bright Star* or Dorothy is Coleridge's and Wordsworth's in *Pandaemonium*. The myth of the solitary, Romantic genius is enshrined in the self-projections of Campion and Temple as directors, and in their films, but it is also continually measured against the dependency of genius on creative community.

Notes

1. See J. North, *The Domestication of Genius: Biography and the Romantic Poet* (Oxford: Oxford University Press, 2009).
2. See, for example, J. Stillinger, *Multiple Authorship and the Myth of Solitary Genius* (New York: Oxford University Press, 1991); G. Russell, *Romantic Sociability: Social Networks and Literary Culture in Britain, 1770–1840* (Cambridge: Cambridge University Press, 2002); and S.J. Wolfson, *Romantic Interactions: Social Being and the Turns of Literary Action* (Baltimore, MD: Johns Hopkins University Press, 2010).
3. Quoted in B.K. Grant (ed.) *Auteurs and Authorship. A Film Reader* (Oxford: Blackwell Publishing, 2008), p. 3.
4. M.H. Abrams, *The Mirror and the Lamp: Romantic Theory and the Critical Tradition* (Oxford University Press, 1971); J. Caughie (ed.) *Theories of Authorship* (London: Routledge, 1981, 2001), pp. 17–21, 24–5.
5. Caughie (1981, 2001), p. 11.
6. Caughie (1981, 2001), pp. 200, 32.
7. T. Schatz, *The Genius of the System: Hollywood Filmmaking in the Studio Era* (London: Faber and Faber, 1988, 1998), p. 5.
8. T. Corrigan, *A Cinema Without Walls: Movies and Culture after Vietnam* (New Brunswick, New Jersey: Rutgers University Press, 1991), p. 103.
9. R.L. Carringer, 'Collaboration and Concepts of Authorship', *PMLA*, CXVI (2) (March, 2001): 370–79 (374). Carringer favours 'collaboration analysis' because it retains a recognition of the importance of the agency of the director while taking account of the collaborative context for that agency.
10. V.W. Wexman, *Film and Authorship* (Chapel Hill: Rutgers University Press, 2003), p. 2; and see D.A. Gerstner and J. Staiger (eds.) *Authorship and Film* (New York: Routledge, 2003), p. 49.
11. Quoted in Grant (2008), pp. 129, 128; and see p. 126, for Claire Johnston on collectivity in women's film.
12. See D. Polan, 'Auteur Desire', *Screening the Past*, XII (March, 2001): 8.
13. L. Borden quoted in H. Radner, A. Fox and I. Bessiere (eds.) *Jane Campion: Cinema, Nation, Identity* (Detroit, MI: Wayne State University Press, 2009), p. 20. For Campion as auteur, see e.g., D. Polan, *Jane Campion* (London: British Film Institute, 2001); K. McHugh, *Jane Campion* (Urbana: University of Illinois Press,

2007); Radner, Fox and Bessiere; and D. Verhoeven, *Jane Campion*, Routledge Film Guides (London: Routledge, 2009).

14. See H. Margolis (ed.) *Jane Campion's 'The Piano'* (Cambridge: Cambridge University Press, 2000), pp. 7, 12: 'Campion's originality cuts across these collaborations … her career has been characterized by the near absence of subordinate positions on others' projects as well as an unusual degree of artistic control over her own projects.'

15. Polan, *Jane Campion* (2001), p. 12.

16. Speaking in 1990, quoted in V.W. Wexman (ed.) *Jane Campion: Interviews* (Jackson MI: University Press of Mississippi, 1999), p. 79; and, quoted (undated) in Margolis, p. 7. See also a 1986 interview on the strains of collaboration, quoted in McHugh (2007), p. 150.

17. Speaking in 1993, quoted in Wexman (1999), p. 121.

18. In Radner, Fox and Bessiere (2009), p. 20.

19. See, for example, Sally Potter interviewed by Kristy Widdicombe, 'The Contemporary Auteur: An Interview with Sally Potter' (2003). At: http://www.bfi.org.uk/filmtvinfo/publications/16+/potter.html (accessed 1 February 2012): 'the better director you are, the more you draw out *other* people's ability, their genius.'

20. Interviewed by Nick James, *Sight and Sound*, XIX (12) (December, 2009). At: www.bfi.org.uk/sightand sound/feature/49582 (accessed 1 February 2012).

21. Campion quoted in Maria Garcia, 'A Sweet Unrest: Jane Campion Recreates the Love Affair between Poet John Keats and Fanny Brawne', *Film Journal International*, CXII (9) (September, 2009).

22. Keats, letter to Richard Woodhouse (27 October, 1818). See Hyder Edward Rollins (ed.) *The Letters of John Keats, 1814–21*, 2 vols (Cambridge MA: Harvard University Press, 1958), vol. 1, p. 387.

23. Keats, letter to Benjamin Bailey (22 November 1817). *Letters*, vol. 1, p. 184.

24. Keats, letter to Richard Woodhouse (27 October 1818). *Letters*, vol. 1, p. 387.

25. Keats, letter to George and Tom Keats (21 December 1817). *Letters*, vol. 1, p. 193. For Campion this theory 'became like a kind of charm for us or a kind of guide', a 'belief in the *being* of a character, just the *presence* of them', seeking a style of acting that was 'unmotivated, just true … no apparent effort' (*Bright Star* DVD extra 'Working with Jane').

26. Andrew Motion, *Keats* (London: Faber and Faber, 1997).

27. Motion (1997), p. xix.

28. Motion (1997), p. xxii.

29. Motion (1997), p. xxiii.

30. Motion (1997), pp. 324–5.

31. Motion (1997), p. 326.

32. Motion (1997), p. 411.

33. Keats, Letter to Richard Woodhouse (27 October 1818), *Letters*, vol. 1, p. 387.

34. See Keats, letters to Fanny Brawne, (11 and 13 October 1819). *Letters*, vol. 2, pp. 222–3.

35. Motion (1997), p. 376.

36. See Keats, letter to Fanny Brawne (1 July, 1819), *Letters*, vol. 2, p. 123.

37. Julien Temple (dir.) *The Filth and the Fury* (2000), DVD, director's commentary.

38. Julien Temple (dir.) *Pandaemonium* (2000), DVD, director's commentary.

5

The 'tables of memory': Shakespeare, cinema and the writing desk

Megan Murray-Pepper

> So Orlando stood gazing while the man turned his pen in his fingers, this way and that way; and gazed and mused; and then, very quickly, wrote half-a-dozen lines and looked up.[1]

Virginia Woolf's sketch of an (anonymous) Shakespeare at work captures a cultural preoccupation as familiar now as it was in 1928: the desire to 'gaze', like her hero/ine Orlando, on the scene of authorship – which is itself characterized by an enthralling combination of intense glance and rapid motion. Addressing the transference of this scene to the film screen, this chapter explores the ways in which the site of Shakespearean composition has been cinematically conceptualized throughout the twentieth century. Repeatedly configured as an act of mysterious inspiration, the depiction of writing on the film screen has usually obscured the actual conditions of Early Modern authorship increasingly detailed by recent scholars.

Diverse titles including *Shakespeare Writing Julius Caesar* (dir. George Méliès, 1907), *Old Bill Through the Ages* (dir. Thomas Bentley, 1924), *The Immortal Gentleman* (dir. Widgey R. Newman, 1935), *Time Flies* (dir. Walter Forde, 1944), *Prospero's Books* (dir. Peter Greenaway, 1991) and *Shakespeare in Love* (dir. John Madden, 1998) each rewrite the scene of 'Shakespeare at work'. To differing degrees, they preserve the glamour that inheres in an unfathomable process, inflected by the Romantic purview that 'locates the essence of genius in *the scene of writing*'.[2] Jane Kingsley-Smith, in her study of three of these films, has identified what she calls an 'inherently conservative' tendency: though they 'question the poet's originality by identifying his work as collaborative', they do so in the service of returning him to a comfortably exalted pre-eminence.[3] In considering this wider number, I am concerned to identify the *framing* of the compositional scene and the ways in which it manipulates the gaze of the (Orlando-esque) spectator.[4]

In particular, I focus upon the extent to which visual realizations of Shakespeare are invested in the trope and the geometry of the study scene itself, and the writing desk or table that (often) forms its metonymic centre. Both speculative and spectacle, the configurations of authorship presented in these pictures variously position the viewer so as to cultivate a (knowing) complicity in the construction of familiar Shakespearean verse. They invite the collaboration of the spectator while rejecting that which appertained to the Early Modern playhouse.

In doing so, they pose a strategic memorialization of Shakespearean composition which employs the visual shorthand of the table as an index of labour (the stronger the focus upon the formation of the desk, the more *work* is seen to take place). Here a curious recalibration of Early Modern theatre practice does takes place, in echoing its use of the table-*book* as a compositional device, in what has recently been labelled a 'mnemonic dramaturgy'.[5] It is to this figure that I shortly turn, in order to illustrate the multiple resonances attached to this signifier, some of which are transferred into the cinema; there, as in Woolf's scene above, concentration in the act of writing is (supposed to be) translated into the rapt attention of the spectator.

In *A Room of One's Own* (1929), Woolf suggested Shakespeare as a model for the ideal androgynous mind that is 'naturally creative, incandescent, and undivided'.[6] Her essay ushered in an oft-cited paradigmatic association between study space and successful output that has undoubtedly inflected the cinema's recent love affair with authorship, manifest in the tortuous creative dramatization of luminaries such as Shakespeare, Woolf, Jane Austen and John Keats.[7] In this subgenre of literary biopic, cinema renders visible on a large scale the praxis of authorial composition. Its effective obfuscation of the boundaries of ivory tower and public (movie) theatre enacts – with a frisson – the apparent exposure of creativity to the gaze of the multitude.

This current popularity is all the more remarkable in light of theoretical convolutions of the past half-century that have threatened, if not the author's death, then a replacement of *creation* with *production*; as Pierre Macherey has remarked: 'One can create undiminished, so, paradoxically, creation is the release of what is already there: or, one is witness of a sudden apparition, and then creation is an irruption, an epiphany, a mystery'.[8] Impatient with the illogical reverence for creativity contained within humanist models, Macherey describes here an effacement of ideological and institutional practices that serves to mystify literary outputs and their enabling conditions. Even if the author is accepted as an isolated and productive entity, the actuality of composition is arguably by no means a glamorous process, but what Paul Arthur calls a 'solitary, static labour performed in dull locations over excruciating stretches of time' featuring 'internal matters of confusion, frustration, and the pressures of the unconscious'.[9] Cinematic exhibition thus requires both condensation and the injection of pace into the confused, frustrating and excruciatingly attenuated process Arthur describes; making exterior that which is interior and intangible.

Both of these models pose practical difficulties for visual rendition, outlining a tension between the Romantic compulsion to imagine the (apparently spontaneous) scene, and the material frame in which the cinema must body it forth. Skilfully handled, the material properties encoded with frustration (witness the screwed-up papers and inked-slashed false starts at *Shakespeare in Love*'s opening) might, in fact, make for excellent montage.

At least one of these cinematic examples, however, perpetrates an outright evasion of the specific conditions in which Shakespeare might have written. To a great extent, Widgey R. Newman's film *An Immortal Gentleman* (1935)[10] condenses the essentially Romantic vision of impulsive imagination, while occluding a vision of the writing process itself. In contrast to the study scenes explored in other releases, this film depicts Shakespeare (Basil Gill) enjoying a Southwark drinking session with fellow poets Ben Jonson (Edgar Owen) and Michael Drayton (Hubert Leslie), and reflecting on the genesis of his most triumphant scenes from *Hamlet, Romeo and Juliet, The Merchant of Venice, The Taming of the Shrew* and *Twelfth Night* – which are then acted out through a series of dissolves into theatrical staging.[11] It deliberately intersects with other performances and with iconic Shakespeare images: Hamlet (Terence de Marney) posing with Yorick's skull, and the backlit pose in which he resembles Caspar David Friedrich's classic Romantic painting 'Wanderer above the Sea of Fog' (1818).

In this version, Shakespeare draws inspiration from the characters of all types that inhabit the tavern. This is the city poet as a jocular, stationary species of *flâneur*, his keen eye reading traits and humours in each countenance. But he is also a point of origin against which that world may be judged. Where there is disaffection, where there is emotion, he has anticipated it: 'It was so I saw my Juliet.' In a transparent intercutting of his flourishing 'seven ages of man' recital with close-up shots of representative embodiments through the tavern, all of human life seems to populate this chamber, just as it inhabits – so runs the insinuation – the wonder cabinet of the playwright's own dramatic *oeuvre*. The film exemplifies a creative paradigm in which naturalized Shakespearean instantiations border and effortlessly anticipate real-life situations and character; while, with a final (slightly sinister?) shot to camera – 'I shall live forever' – the author insists on his own changeless immortality.

An organic link is proposed here between life and Shakespeare's art, which bypasses the writing scene itself, and its assorted paraphernalia, including the desk. Incarnated in this picture as a self-satisfied wit, Shakespeare dissevers himself from the mechanistic objects of praxis: 'My pen wrote it;

I only thought of it.' This fluidly instinctive process is further exposed in his assessment of writing *Twelfth Night*:

> When the wine's in, the wit flows out. Why, were we not tippled in this very room the day I wrote my merry kitchen scene in my play *Twelfth Night*? Ah, no truly sober man could have written that. No ... such scenes should be written in grape juice, not ink!

Naturalizing a link between drink and dramatic output, Shakespeare slyly erases any trace of his own efforts: in Macherey's formulation, he 'creates' what is already there. The film is situated alongside the tradition of anti-quarian John Aubrey who suggested in the late seventeenth century that 'Jonson and he did gather Humours of men dayly wher ever they came', echoed by G.B Harrison just two years prior to Newman's film in the contention that Shakespeare 'borrowed from life, peopling his tragedy with those whom he knew'.[12] Both of these accounts contain an implicit debt ('borrowed'), which the film strategically repositions in suggesting Shakespearean emotion as precursive to that seen within the tavern walls. At the same time, *An Immortal Gentleman* marginalizes professional collabo-ration by establishing Shakespeare's fellow dramatists Jonson and Drayton as virtually silent foils.[13]

Yet, in picturing Shakespeare (almost) discussing his work with fellow playwrights, we are offered a tentative glimpse of a social theatrical culture on London's South Bank, which has subsequently been the site of much scholarly interest. John Aubrey famously described the living conditions of Shakespearean contemporaries and co-authors Francis Beaumont and John Fletcher: 'They lived together on the Bank-side, not far from the Play-house, both batchelors, lay together, had one Wench in the house between, which they did so admire; the same cloathes and cloake etc between them.'[14] In Jeffrey Masten's reading, writing space is included within this intense cohabitation, though little consensus has been reached regarding the practice of such cooperative endeavour.[15] Nevertheless, the emphasis on an institutionally collaborative and textually unstable period of literary production constitutes what Jeffrey Knapp has called a 'new orthodoxy' in the academy.[16] Rather than fixed monuments, plays themselves are 'only written testaments to moments in the life of an unstable text' – one produced by the multiple agencies of playwright(s), playing company, and printing house.[17]

The drama of Shakespeare's period does sometimes imagine the author, in John Day's words from 1606, as 'close in his studie writing hard'.[18] If Shakespeare's own uses of the study location primarily reflect its patrician and monastic origins, Lena Cowen Orlin has recently shown that its func-tions as part of the 'cultural landscape of private life' were proliferating, and might be as social as they were secluded.[19] And it is in fact in the enactment of the materials of composition upon the public stage to which a model for twentieth-century figurations can be partially traced.

The Tables of Memory

Within Shakespeare's metaphorical schemas, the writing 'table' operates as a nexus for the sophisticated correspondence of portraiture, composition and remembrance. In *Two Gentlemen of Verona* Julia addresses her maid with the endearment, 'thee / Who art the table wherein all my thoughts / Are visibly charactered and engraved' (II.vii.1–5).[20] Julia conjures up a figurative system within which Lucetta's image is a book bearing the inscription both of friendship and of memory, and she emphasizes the specifically visual dimension of what is nevertheless conceived as a textual event. Such a bibliographic system is exploited in greater depth in *Hamlet* when the prince responds to the Ghost's injunction to remember:

> Remember thee?
> Ay, thou poor ghost, while memory holds a seat
> In this distracted globe. Remember thee?
> Yes, from the table of my memory
> I'll wipe away all trivial fond records,
> All saws of books, all forms, and pressures past (1.5.95–100).[21]

Hamlet's image signals the 'memory theatre' derived from classical arts in which information is assigned a place or locus, often in a design thought to bear resemblance to the Globe itself.[22] He offers to erase his current system of recall in order to concentrate solely on the act of revenge. The redirection of his thoughts, however, rapidly leads him to call for a physical site of inscription: 'My tables! Meet it is I set it down / That one may smile, and smile, and be a villain' (1.5.107–108). The 'table-book' is a portable property used on stage to record or compose information, as in John Marston's *Antonio's Revenge* (1602) when Balurdo, hearing phrases he wants to retain, '*drawes out his writing table, and writes*' (1.3).[23] A similar action is implied by Hamlet in calling for his 'tables' in which he will 'set down' the maxim that he has just composed: they operate as '*aide-memoire*'.[24] The 'table' thus becomes a figurative surface upon which the act of writing is a potent metaphor for the composition of memory itself.[25] It is with this play of meanings in mind that I consider how, in cinematic terms, the writing table is represented as an index of labour, rather as the Early Modern 'table' might metonymically figure forth the site of dramatic composition.

Frame(s) of His Own

In the series of films examined here, I focus on how the site/sight of the creative act is configured to discursively evoke both the presence and process, if not of that most slippery category, 'genius', then of an authorial effort that constitutes collective cultural event. The film frame becomes the waxen tablet on which the memory of composition is itself manufactured, and repeatedly re-inscribed, though still bearing traces of the 'forms, and pressures past'.

Attention to the scene of authorship dates from the flowering of narrative film in the first few years of the twentieth century. As also discussed in the Introduction and in Laura Marcus' chapter in the current volume, in 1907 the Shakespearean presence on screen was inaugurated by George Méliès' short silent picture *Le Rêve de Shakespeare* or *La Mort de Jules César*, translated as *Shakespeare Writing Julius Caesar*. Though the film is now lost, the *Star* film catalogue scenario describes Shakespeare (played by Méliès) 'seated in his study' making unsuccessful attempts to write the play's crucial assassination scene. (See Figure I.2 for the configuration of the writing desk.) Frustrated, he paces the room and finally, sitting in his armchair, is struck by inspiration: 'his thoughts take life, and right before him appears an old Roman forum' (Figure I.3). As the bodies of the other actors in Shakespearean character push the writer to the margins of the frame, the scene then plays out before him as 'interested spectator' before dissolving back into the parameters of the study where he begins to 'stalk about excitedly'.[26]

Contemporary audiences (including the *Star*'s writer) saw here the metatheatrics of authorship take life upon the screen. Méliès' scheme makes literal and visible the pressures of the artistic unconscious, inscribed in Shakespeare's physical movement within the space of the chamber and the film frame – his excited 'stalking' – and his embodiment as Macherey's 'witness to a sudden apparition'. A surviving still photograph (Figure I.3) shows the writer ensconced in a wooden chair at the extreme right of the frame while the conspirators gather amid the pillars of a Roman *mise-en-scène*.[27] Making theatrical spectacle of intellectual endeavour, this performative configuration also incidentally recalls the design of the indoor Blackfriars theatre, with Shakespeare occupying the position of audience gallant on the edge of the stage. In effect, the entire frame has become the surface of composition writ large. By positioning Shakespeare as gazing from the margins at his own imaginative venture, Méliès elides the distinction between author and spectator and showcases his own creative uses of film technology.

As an ex-magician, the actor-director brings a dazzling sleight of hand to bear upon this embodiment; his final 'trick photography' dissolve into Shakespeare's bust surrounded by international garlands encodes, in Judith Buchanan's words, 'a sentimental vision of universal, and universalizing Shakespeare'.[28] Despite this gratuitous flourish, the writer's witnessing of creative epiphany lends credence to the previous labour, as theatrical enactment is contained *within* the study space.

In 1924 Shakespeare appeared as a supplementary character in the time-travel burlesque *Old Bill Through the Ages* (dir. Thomas Bentley).[29] The film documents the adventures of the title's Bill (Syd Walker), an absurdly moustachioed soldier from World War I and exemplar of the plain and heroic working man, whose perambulations are provoked by enthusiastic consumption of the mighty volume *A History of England* alongside a dubious tin of lobster.[30] Displaying the Renaissance as signified by the twin poles of Shakespeare and Elizabeth I, a reactionary thrust against an outmoded elitist culture is enacted through the bombing of Shakespeare (Austin Leigh) *offstage* during a declamatory performance at the Court.[31] He is originally framed in pretentious stance at the lectern that constitutes the writing table of the authorial poser (and surrounded by a bizarre ''arem' of tutu-clad assistants) – a gesture that rather emphasizes his *lack* of serious work. Shakespeare's subsequent and violently symbolic disappearance is induced by the delivery of what are presented as senselessly fragmented quotations; Bill's disdain for the staging of empty theatrical rhetoric strikes a blow for the aggressively democratic medium of cinema as a mainstay of popular culture.

It was to be a short suppression, however. Shakespeare's return to prestige in *The Immortal Gentleman* is ironically sited in the populist locale of the tavern. In the intercutting of Shakespeare with the enactment of set-piece scenes evoked by the Southwark clientele, the same actors transmute into their theatrical counterparts (in a nod towards the doubling conventions of Early Modern theatre). Verbal bridges between the two 'stages' attempt to marry Shakespearean dialogue with that of the everyday, in a manner pre-emptive of *Shakespeare in Love*; Shylock's 'better my instruction' dissolves gracelessly into Shakespeare's witty cue, 'My instruction? My usual!' Here, the memory of previous performance(s) is used to prove Shakespeare's originality; as he outlines the conjunction of wine and wit, and the frame dissolves into his famous 'kitchen scene', the spectator glimpses the Shakespearean mind as coexistent with staged performance. Public theatre is aligned with private imagination, and leaves precious little space for the collaborative agencies within the playhouse.

The space of the Globe Theatre however intrudes much more forcefully in Walter Forde's *Time Flies* of 1944. A group of time-travelling American students happen to 'land' in the Theatre, where they encounter Shakespeare (John Salew) seated at a desk on the stage struggling with *Romeo and Juliet*. Here the act of composition is literally produced or showcased on the site of performance, and doubly framed by the stage and then the film screen. This location is both impractical and unlikely; but it operates as a code for authorship that gestures towards the conflation of written page and physical stage. Time-travelling Susie supplies Shakespeare's missing line, in a circular process that links past and future; if, as Kingsley-Smith contends, 'the words she gives him are his own', they are also Susie's (and ours) by a process of cultural assimilation.[32]

Time travel, explored by *Time Flies* and by *Old Bill Through the Ages*, becomes a clearly established trope within which Shakespeare is able to signify particular historical period while (at least in Forde's picture) transcending history in order to render the act of composition as simultaneous in past and present. There follows an apparent hiatus of almost half a century in the cinematic production of Shakespearean authorship; when the subject re-emerges on the cinema screen, it is with some evidence of the technological and theoretical revolutions of the intervening years, and with a renewed desire to foreground Shakespeare's composition as central.

Step forward Peter Greenaway's *Prospero's Books* (1991). Emerging from this silence as both ostensible adaptation of *The Tempest*, and as Shakespearean authorial narrative of radical alterity, it combines a strikingly humanist reverence for scholarly composition with metafictional strategies embedded in the post-modern. Shakespeare himself is subsumed within the character of Prospero (John Gielgud) as learned author-magician or 'prime originator' of the drama that unfolds (Figure 5.1).[33] The film thus partakes of the well-established tradition – the logic of the epilogic – of the play as Shakespeare's last; and its interest in surveying artistic practice is acute.[34]

More than any other in the series, this film subjects the angles and aesthetics of the study and compositional processes to persistent investigation. This is Prospero/Shakespeare as Renaissance scholar-cardinal whose magic island is visually built around the study as focal point (see also Figure 9.1), and rendered in a vibrant bricolage of image, text and digital paintbox technology. Insistently locating frames within frames, the film not only blurs and distorts distinctions between media but acts, in Douglas Lanier's

Figure 5.1 John Gielgud as Prospero/Shakespeare in Peter Greenaway's *Prospero's Books* (1991).

phrase, as an 'extended interrogation of those representational codes by which we make order of reality'.[35] In doing so, it not only negotiates a complex fetishization of the textual artefact, but engages with the extremes of fantasy that underpin our notions of authorial process.

The film's opening is marked by the regular visual and aural interpolation of a vivid ink droplet falling. Linking a naked Prospero in the bathhouse with the scratching of quill on paper, the frame expands shot by shot to gradually reveal the complete image of Prospero as author scripting the operation of the scene. The 'poor cell' of his study (actually rich and ornate) is framed with curtains drawn back as though to expose its inner workings to the gaze. Stylistic and intellectual centrepiece, and site of return throughout the film, the partially enclosed desk is closely modelled on paintings of the medieval scholar St. Jerome in his study.[36] In Greenaway's words:

> It is the study or writing room where Prospero thinks and reads, speculates and ruminates and dreams – and, on occasion – sleeps. Prospero has always felt most at ease in a study surrounded by books. It is a place where he can think most readily of his past and contemplate most pertinently what is left of his future. It is the place where Prospero would plan a revenge on his enemies.[37]

It is also, in this opening image (a view repeated at the beginning of the film and near its climax) theatrically staged here as spectacle. And it is principally the site of power, making a collage of the past and future mentioned by Greenaway through Prospero's fantastical manipulations of language and reality. It demonstrates, like Prospero's *Book of Motion*, 'how ideas chase one another through the memory'. The words of Shakespeare's text are whispered, written, altered, revised, Prospero himself voicing all of the other characters until the final reconciliation; Judith Buchanan has noted discrepancies and developments that activate readership in inviting comparison to the First Folio text.[38] The relation between speech and textual inscription remains fluid, with text-in-composition often palimpsestically loaded onto the compositional scene. Shots of flowing ink drops usually anticipate the visual return to the desk as the site of artistic origin; suggestively, the frequency of these re-establishing shots replaces the (silent) cinematic practice of intertitles for orientation.

The desk itself is shot from a wide variety of different angles, continually repositioning the spectator and reconfiguring the angle of vision from which the writer in action can be discovered and observed. Moreover, it appears in different guises, from the bare table top to a high ledger to flat surface cluttered with pillars and objects, reflecting the qualities of fantasy. Sometimes bristling with quill tips as a symbol of compositional fertility, sometimes shown in profile to emphasize the quantity of books from which Prospero's inspiration is derived, this playfully unstable geometry evokes a compositional process in flux. It proposes the space itself to be produced as reflection of the writer's (fluctuating) mind. (Mirrors constitute another perpetual motif). The narrative – and its author – is continually reiterated, remade, positing Prospero-*qua*-Shakespeare as an author who evades temporal fixity, always writing at a/his desk, and the desk itself as continually re-written. In fact the *portable* quality of the desk implies it is designed to be moved and reconstructed anywhere, and conceivably on any screen – a fact underlined by its transmediation from the painting of St. Jerome in an act of specific visual quotation.

Where Greenaway's film is firmly arthouse, John Madden's *Shakespeare in Love* (1998) is fully mainstream.[39] While the film's post-modern and meta-cinematic qualities have been documented, less regard has been paid to some of its historical precursors whose characteristics it partly condenses and re-calibrates.[40] A triumph both at the box office and at the Oscars, Tom Stoppard and Marc Norman's script portrays a hapless and creatively frustrated Shakespeare whose latent powers of production are released by his tragic affair with the cross-dressing aristocrat Viola de Lesseps. Like *Old Bill*'s penny farthing, the film enjoys playful historical anachronisms (the mug as 'a present from Stratford-on-Avon);[41] like *An Immortal Gentleman* (though with greater sophistication), it weaves together knowingly famous lines alongside contemporary idiomatic phrasing: 'I had that Christopher Marlowe in my boat once.' However, Madden's film is more much inclined to disperse the play's lines among a colourful Elizabethan world: witness the zealous street preacher pronouncing 'a plague on both your [play]houses'.

Composition here is typified by energy: the dashingly white-shirted figure of Shakespeare (Joseph Fiennes) scribbling in his wooden garret, whose *mise-en-scène* is a pastiche of objects – manuscript, quills, candles – supposed to signify authorial practice. The romantic portrait initially delineated, scratching quill pen and ink-stained fingers seen in loving close up, is upset as the frustrated poet abandons his desk and delivers a savage kick to the stool. He soon returns from the world, though, seemingly fired with inspiration from an encounter with the devious Rosalind. In the centre of the frame is the wooden table, before which Shakespeare performs a ritual twirl-and-spit as superstitious prequel to the fraught act of writing. Once seated, his sequence of gaze, pause, scribble reads like the scene scripted by Woolf for the entrancement of Orlando. Though the proper site of inspiration here will be the welcoming bed of ardent Viola rather than the severe study of scholarly Jerome, the film returns with energetic regularity to the table-bound image (or rather series of images in close-up) that characterize the authorial pose at the desk. The characteristic montage of composition that follows Shakespeare's first meeting with Viola remarkably rejoices in the quill-stripping, knuckle-cracking physical hardships of long labour, and exactly prefigures the rapturous scenes of love-making for which it is a potent analogue.

In partially restoring Shakespeare's creativity to a domain inflected by both chaos and contingency, *Shakespeare in Love* attempts to perform a considerable popularization of the institutional conditions of the playhouse – signalling the competitive cut-and-thrust of theatre manager Henslowe and the amicable rivalry between Shakespeare and Marlowe. Yet as Kingsley-Smith has noted, it signally fails – in a repetition of previous titles' obscurations – to acknowledge the prior existence of *Romeo and Juliet* in Arthur Brooke's poem of 1562, and the period's investment in literary source material (acknowledged elsewhere by the bibliophilia central to *Prospero's Books*).[42]

On these various screens, sites of Shakespearean composition are fabricated and inscribed with the traces of works (or words; the 'real' material) supposedly constructed there. This process is literalized in *Prospero's Books* by the overlay of script upon the authorial furniture. These 'memories' are then played out and simultaneously created by the film's articulation in the present, with the co-option of the audience's textual recollections and cultural knowledge into the creation of coherent narrative. For the spectator, viewing pleasure hinges partly on the recognition of familiar quotations whose origins are made (sometimes spectacularly) visible even while they anticipate the rest of the text – a text perhaps already encoded in their memory.

Though we owe notions of Shakespeare's innate genius to the Romantics, the Wordsworthian ethic of tranquil recollection is nevertheless anathema to the highly strategic drama of authorship that these pictures epitomize. Purporting to represent the release of the instinctual, in most cases they ultimately stage a prolonged mystification of creativity itself – and thereby demonstrate the cinema's own talents for epiphany. Frequently, the 'magic' actually lies in seductive montage and in technological verve, as in *Prospero's Books* when the reversal of a short sequence restores the chaos of swirling papers to their rest in the library. In frames that repeatedly draw the gaze back to the site of the desk as the surface to which composition can be materially ascribed, *Shakespeare in Love* and (to an even greater extent) *Prospero's Books* configure the cinematic table as the figurative book in which authorial labour scripts collective textual recollection. The Early Modern table-book, once a way for writers to remember, becomes in the framing of the desk a way for us – as viewers and readers – to re-member the writer. In committing Shakespeare's writing practices to the screen, these films invite us to own and enjoy Orlando's rapt gaze.

Notes

1. V. Woolf, *Orlando: A Biography* (1928), Brenda Lyons (ed.) (London: Penguin, 1993), p. 16.
2. J. Bate, *The Genius of Shakespeare* (New York; Oxford: Oxford University Press, 1998), p. 82 (emphasis original).

3. J.E. Kingsley-Smith, 'Shakespearean Authorship in Popular British Cinema', *Literature/Film Quarterly*, 30(3) (2002): 158–65 (162, 158).
4. In using the term 'gaze' I do not attempt to negotiate the significant body of film theory that has developed on this topic. See, for example, Laura Mulvey, 'Visual Pleasure and Narrative Cinema', *Screen* 16(3) (Autumn 1975): 6–18. I am following Woolf's use of the term in *Orlando*, which describes a rapt visual attention (often shared by the spectator and the writer being pictured).
5. L. Perkins Wilder, *Shakespeare's Memory Theatre: Recollection, Properties, and Character* (Cambridge: Cambridge University Press, 2010), p. 1.
6. V. Woolf, *A Room of One's Own* (1929; London: Penguin, 2004), p. 114.
7. *Shakespeare in Love* (dir. John Madden, 1998), *The Hours* (dir. Stephen Daldry, 2002), *Becoming Jane* (dir. Julian Jarrold, 2007), *Bright Star* (dir. Jane Campion, 2009).
8. P. Macherey, *A Theory of Literary Production*, trans. Geoffrey Wall (London: Routledge, 2006), p. 77.
9. P. Arthur, 'The Written Scene: Writers as Figures of Cinematic Redemption', in Robert Stam and Alessandra Raengo (eds.) *Literature and Film: A Guide to the Theory and Practice of Film Adaptation* (Malden, MA; Oxford: Blackwell, 2005), pp. 331–42, (331).
10. A print is available to view at the British Film Institute's National Film Archive.
11. MGM also released an 11-minute film in 1936 entitled *Master Will Shakespeare*, a short biographical sketch.
12. J. Aubrey, *Brief Lives; Together With, An Apparatus for the Lives of our English Mathematical Writers; and, The Life of Thomas Hobbes of Malmesbury*, John Buchanan-Brown (ed.) (London: Penguin, 2000), p. 290. G.B. Harrison, *Shakespeare at Work 1592–1603* (London: George Routledge & Sons Ltd, 1933), p. 75.
13. See Kingsley-Smith (2002), 161.
14. J. Aubrey (2000), p. viii (original spelling retained).
15. J. Masten, *Textual Intercourse: Collaboration, Authorship, and Sexualities in Renaissance Drama* (Cambridge: Cambridge University Press, 1997), p. 62. See also G.E. Bentley, *The Profession of the Dramatist in Shakespeare's Time, 1590–1642* (Princeton University Press, 1971), p. 227; G. Ioppolo, *Dramatists and their Manuscripts in the Age of Shakespeare, Jonson, Middleton and Heywood: Authorship, Authority and the Playhouse* (Abingdon: Routledge, 2006), p. 32.
16. J. Knapp, 'What is a Co-Author?', *Representations* 89 (Winter 2005), 1–29 (1).
17. T. Stern, *Making Shakespeare: From Stage to Page* (London: Routledge, 2004), p. 2.
18. J. Day, *The Isle of Guls As it Hath been Often Played in the Blacke Fryars, by the Children of the Reuels* (1606) G.B. Harrison (ed.) (London: Oxford University Press, 1936), A2.
19. L.C. Orlin, *Locating Privacy in Tudor London* (Oxford: Oxford University Press, 2007), pp. 3, 5, 316. 'The early modern phenomena of private areas and private literatures are related in popular understanding, because the small enclosed chamber – a room of one's own – has long been assumed to be the condition of possibility for thinking and writing' (p. 3).
20. W. Shakespeare, *The Two Gentlemen of Verona*, William Carroll (ed.) (London: Arden Shakespeare, 2004).
21. W. Shakespeare, *Hamlet*, Ann Thompson and Neil Taylor (eds.) (London: Arden Shakespeare, 2006).
22. F. Yates, *The Art of Memory* (London: Routledge and Kegan Paul, 1966), p. 334. See also Perkins Wilder (2010), p. 15.

23. J. Marston, *Antonio's Revenge* (1602), W. Reavley Gair (ed.) (Manchester: Manchester University Press, 1999), p. 67.

24. P. Beal, 'Notions in Garrison: The Seventeenth-Century Commonplace Book', *New Ways of Looking at Old Texts: Papers of the Renaissance English Text Society, 1985–1991*, W. Speed Hill (ed.) (Binghampton, NY: Medieval and Renaissance Texts & Studies, in conjunction with Renaissance English Text Society, 1993), pp. 131–47, p. 134. See also Adam Smyth, *Autobiography in Early Modern England* (Cambridge: Cambridge University Press, 2010).

25. On the role of memory in the Shakespearean theatre more generally, see Perkins Wilder (2010), *passim*, and p. 13 for further references.

26. Quoted in R. Hamilton Ball, *Shakespeare on Silent Film: A Strange Eventful History* (London: Allen and Unwin, 1968), pp. 35–6.

27. This image is reprinted in Hamilton Ball (1968) in an insert after p. 96 (illustration number 5).

28. J. Buchanan, *Shakespeare on Silent Film: An Excellent Dumb Discourse* (Cambridge: Cambridge University Press, 2009), p. 119.

29. Available to view at the British Film Institute's National Film Archive. Two (quasi-) biographical dramas were produced before this, including British and Colonial's *The Life of William Shakespeare* (dir. Frank R. Growcott/ J.B. Macdowell, 1914), and Thanhouser's *Master Shakespeare, Strolling Player* (dir. Frederick Sullivan, 1916). From the descriptions provided by Hamilton Ball, they sound more interested in speculation on romantic intrigue than in the act of composition.

30. Comparable to *Master Shakespeare, Strolling Player* (1916), in which the heroine falls into a delirium during the Mexican war and is transported to the sixteenth century to become entangled in the Shakespeare-Bacon authorship dispute. See Hamilton Ball (1968), p. 228.

31. On the frequent conjunctions of Shakespeare and Elizabeth see H. Hackett, *Shakespeare and Elizabeth: The Meeting of Two Myths* (Princeton, NJ; Oxford: Princeton University Press, 2009). On *Old Bill* in particular, see pp. 188–91.

32. Kingsley-Smith (2002), p. 161. I am deeply indebted to Kingsley-Smith for the description of this film, a viewing copy of which has so far eluded me.

33. P. Greenaway, *Prospero's Books: A Film of Shakespeare's* The Tempest (London: Chatto & Windus, 1991), p. 9. Greenaway is explicit about this conflation: 'at times they [Prospero, Shakespeare, Gielgud] are indivisibly one person' (9).

34. See G. McMullan, *Shakespeare and the Idea of Late Writing: Authorship in the Proximity of Death* (Cambridge: Cambridge University Press, 2007), pp. 331–50, for a fuller exploration of this tradition and of the conscious practice by which Prospero functions also as epilogue for actors including Gielgud and Mark Rylance (who plays Ferdinand in Greenaway's film).

35. D. Lanier, 'Drowning the Book: *Prospero's Books* and the Textual Shakespeare', in *Shakespeare, Theory and Performance*, James C. Bulman (ed.) (London: Routledge, 1996), pp. 187–209 (193).

36. For the considerable correspondences between Prospero and Jerome, see Judith Buchanan, *Shakespeare on Film* (Harlow: Longman-Pearson, 2005), pp. 224–9.

37. Greenaway (1991), p. 50. Compare to Tamora's direction in *Titus Andronicus*: 'Knock at his study, where, they say, he keeps, / To ruminate strange plots of dire revenge' (5.2.5–6). W. Shakespeare, *Titus Andronicus* Jonathan Bate (ed.) (London: Arden Shakespeare, 2006).

38. Buchanan (2005), p. 223.

39. At the time of writing, the authorship controversy film *Anonymous* (dir. Roland Emmerich) is scheduled for release in September 2011.
40. See for example T.F. Davis and K. Womack, 'Reading (and Writing) the Ethics of Authorship: *Shakespeare in Love* as Postmodern Metanarrative', *Literature/Film Quarterly*, 32(2) (Salisbury, 2004): 153–62 (155).
41. Hackett (2009), p. 189.
42. Kingsley-Smith (2002), p. 161.

6

Brit-lit biopics, 1990–2010

Andrew Higson

The 1990s and 2000s saw the release of a surprising number of British and American films depicting the lives of prominent British writers and focusing in some way on the process of writing.[1] We might label these films Brit-lit biopics. In fact, there have been at least sixteen such films in twenty years – that is, almost one a year, from *Shadowlands* (dir. Richard Attenborough, 1993) and *Tom and Viv* (dir. Brian Gilbert, 1994) in the early 1990s, via *Shakespeare in Love* (dir. John Madden, 1998) and *Iris* (dir. Richard Eyre, 2001) around the turn of the century, to *Miss Potter* (dir. Chris Noonan, 2006) and *Bright Star* (dir. Jane Campion, 2009) in the late 2000s (see Table 6.1). These films covered writers as diverse as William Shakespeare and Oscar Wilde, Jane Austen and Iris Murdoch, J.M. Barrie and C.S. Lewis, Beatrix Potter and Dylan Thomas. There was also *The Hours* (dir. Stephen Daldry, 2002), which, though hardly a biopic, nevertheless offers scenes from the life of Virginia Woolf.

How do these films work for their audiences? At one level, of course, these films are simply literary biopics, depicting the lives of prominent writers. To riff on Roland Barthes, the literary biopic enables us to move beyond the death of the author to his or her reincarnation. But, if actors impersonate particular, historically specific writers, the characters they create on screen also make flesh the *function* of the author in a more generalized sense; in effect, they incarnate the concept of literary authorship. Alongside their status as biopics, however, these films are also designed, promoted and received in two other key ways.

First, most of the Brit-lit biopics are female-friendly films designed to appeal to feminine sensibilities and to attract female audiences. Thus, most of them work as both romantic dramas and costume dramas, genres traditionally associated with female audiences; and many of them have female protagonists. Admittedly, while eleven of the Brit-lit biopics listed in Table 6.1 are about male writers, only five are about female writers – *The Hours*, plus the four films that have recognizably female names as titles, *Iris*, *Sylvia* (dir. Christine Jeffs, 2003), *Miss Potter* and *Becoming Jane* (dir. Julian Jarrold, 2007).

Table 6.1 Brit-lit biopics, 1990–2011

Film	Date	Main writer(s) depicted
Hedd Wynn	1992	Welsh poet Ellis Evans
Shadowlands	1993	C.S. Lewis
Tom and Viv	1994	T.S. Eliot
Carrington	1995	Lytton Strachey (and Dora Carrington)
Wilde	1997	Oscar Wilde
Shakespeare in Love	1998	William Shakespeare
Pandaemonium	2000	Coleridge and Wordsworth
Iris	2001	Iris Murdoch
The Hours	2002	Virginia Woolf
Sylvia	2003	Sylvia Plath
Finding Neverland	2004	J.M. Barrie
The Libertine	2004	John Wilmot, Earl of Rochester
Miss Potter	2006	Beatrix Potter
Becoming Jane	2007	Jane Austen
The Edge of Love	2008	Dylan Thomas
Bright Star	2009	John Keats

However, women also figure centrally in almost all of the films as narratively significant romantic partners.

Second, these Brit-lit biopics are also tasteful, refined, middlebrow dramas, 'quality' films in the parlance of the business, either solid art-house fare or commodities that are able to move between the art-houses and the multiplexes. This is a question of tone, taste and sensibility, and it applies not just to the films themselves, but to their afterlives, the way they are promoted and circulate on video, DVD, television and download, or provide images for book covers. These are films that appeal primarily to university-educated middle-class audiences, to whom they offer an engagement with respectable literary culture that plays on, but also goes beyond, the adaptation of canonical novels and plays. As such, these films are in many ways typical of the Anglo-American heritage cinema trends of the period, reworking familiar stories, characters and iconographies of British national history.[2] They thus bring together ideas of middlebrow culture, literary heritage and the British past, inviting audiences to read them in relation to adaptations of canonical novels, enriching the idea of what we might call the literary film.

The Literary Film and 'Literate' Cinema

What I mean by the literary film is broader than the literary biopic or the literary adaptation. In particular, I want to draw a connection with films that certain critics and audiences regard as 'literate' by comparison with the mainstream model of the action-led and effects-laden blockbuster. The literary film in these terms is a form of cinema that depends on overt links with literary culture, and which therefore draws on some of the same values as so-called serious literature.

We can see this link being made in critical discourse about such cinema, with professional critics invoking the literary as a means of both praising what they perceive as 'good' cinema, and recommending that cinema to well educated, 'literate' audiences. Several reviewers described the adaptation of *Howards End* (dir. James Ivory, 1992), for instance, as a 'literate' film – where literate meant intelligent, subtle, civilized entertainment, as opposed to the 'mindless' attractions of mainstream Hollywood cinema; as one critic put it, the adaptation 'achieved just the right balance between the literate and the cinematic'.[3] *Ladies in Lavender* (dir. Charles Dance, 2004), an adaptation of a short story, was described in similar terms as 'a warm and literate film', a film with a 'kind of charm and sweetness and class' that distinguished it from 'the usual fare', films 'dedicated to numbing the brain and deadening the senses.'[4] *Stage Beauty* (dir. Richard Eyre, 2004), an adaptation of a play, was also 'refreshingly literate',[5] 'the sort of thoughtful, well-crafted movie intelligent film-goers yearn for'.[6]

Films without any obvious literary connections could also be described as literate, however. Thus, *Gosford Park* (dir. Robert Altman, 2001) and *To Kill a King* (dir. Mike Barker, 2003), both costume dramas but both also made from original scripts rather than adapted from literary sources, still depended on what critics called a 'literate' script,[7] while *Elizabeth* (dir. Shekhar Kapur, 1998) was promoted in the UK as a 'prestige' production ideal for an 'upscale, literate dinner-party crowd'.[8]

If the, strictly speaking, non-literary *Gosford Park*, *To Kill a King* and *Elizabeth* could be described as 'literate' films, it is no surprise that self-consciously literary biopics are also described in these terms. After all, they deal with literary authors and the process of writing, and they are designed to impress critics and audiences looking for a literate cultural experience. Thus the Oscar Wilde biopic *Wilde* (dir. Brian Gilbert, 1997), for instance, could be applauded for its 'intelligent, literate script',[9] while *Shakespeare in Love*, was commended as 'one of the most satisfying – and literate – romantic comedies in years'.[10]

The prevalence of this 'literate' branding in both promotional materials and critical discourse invests products with specific commercial as well as cultural significance. It is, therefore, used not only to establish an aura of quality and intelligence around a cultural practice more often addressed to and understood in terms of the mass market, but as, in itself, a marketable commodity, albeit one addressed to a highly specific niche audience.

The literate film is a key element of middlebrow cinema, and the subjects of the Brit-lit biopic are carefully chosen and developed in this context. At one level, we might say that a very diverse range of British writers appears on the screen in the 1990s and 2000s: writers for children as well as adults, from a range of genres and from every century from the sixteenth to the twentieth, from the early modern playwright to the modern British novelist. But if these biopics seem diverse in their literary subjects, in market terms, they are all of an ilk. Irrespective of historical status or social provenance, the lives of these diverse authors are all transformed into tasteful, literate, middle-brow products, romantic costume dramas and generically conventional heritage films, catering for a well-defined, middle-class audience. Even the children's writers Beatrix Potter and J.M. Barrie – creators of Peter Rabbit and Peter Pan respectively – appeal to nostalgic middle-class fantasies.

Shakespeare in Love may have been immensely successful at the box-office, it may have crossed over from being a small-scale, middlebrow niche product to a genuinely popular rom-com, but that was precisely because it could work at two levels simultaneously. It was, thus, 'a literate crowd pleaser',[11] tapping very successfully into popular romantic culture, but also, like all Brit-lit biopics, engaging with literary culture in various ways. Part of its success was therefore that it could find and engage audiences attached to a more traditional literary culture than to mainstream popular cinema, audiences for whom Shakespeare was an important part of their cultural capital.

There are thus three separate but closely related markets or audiences for these literary biopics: the 'literary' audience; the audience for middlebrow costume drama; and the female audience for romantic drama. For some of these audiences, it is vital that these are 'quality' films about the lives of writers. For others, the protagonists of these films just happen to be authors: what is of real interest is their romantic lives.

The Conventions of the Brit-lit Biopic

Brit-lit biopics tend to adopt a romantic vision of key moments in the life of a writer, a romantic vision that often purports to throw light on the creative process or the source of the fiction produced by the writer in question. Romance, it seems, is the fountainhead of the creative process. To write may be an individual act, but it depends upon a social experience, albeit a very private and intimate form of social activity: as the promotional taglines for *Becoming Jane* have it, 'Jane Austen's most extraordinary romance was her own', and this, her own 'love story[,] was her greatest inspiration'.[12]

The writer protagonists of the Brit-lit biopics are for the most part understood in relation to an idea of young love – and they are often highly photogenic to boot.[13] As one of the promotional taglines for *Bright Star* puts it, 'First love burns brightest.'[14] The course of true love rarely runs smooth in these films, however, and is often thwarted, frustrated or tragically denied; romantic love is thus complicated by illness or social conventions, as in *Tom and Viv*, *Carrington* (dir. Christopher Hampton, 1995), *Wilde*, *Shakespeare in Love*, *Miss Potter* and *Bright Star* – as well as *Shadowlands*, albeit there with middle-aged characters.

The mythology of the writer as a romantic individual, and of the relationship between creativity and desire, is almost invariably tied to another discourse, the discourse of historical authenticity. Circulating around these literary biopics are the usual claims made by filmmakers and distributors about historical authenticity, fidelity, accuracy and truth. At the same time, such films by definition personalize and individualize the historical project, organizing the representation of the past around desire and romance. The titles of *Shakespeare in Love* and *Becoming Jane* are thus indicative in the way that they foreground romance and individual biography, as opposed to depicting the wider literary or political contexts within which the individual operates. Biopics are always about dramatizing a life, but as such there is always a tension in these films between biographical depth and historical substance on the one hand and, on the other, the need to create a compelling cinematic drama with an engaging narrative drive and a beguilingly attractive *mise-en-scène*.

At one level, recent biopics about British characters, and especially biopics about British writers, have developed their own standard narrative and aesthetic formulae; at another level they draw on the well-worn conventions of other more popular genres and modes of filmmaking. As Steve Neale has pointed out, Hollywood has long 'modelled the lives it depicted [in biopics] according to dramatic, generic and fictional formulae which it also used and applied to its fictions'.[15] Darryl Zanuck, for instance, producer of several biopics, 'was constantly aware of the need to tailor the events they depicted and the stories they told so as to conform with what he saw as Hollywood's aesthetic values'.[16]

In the same way, the Brit-lit biopics of the 1990s and 2000s adopted the conventions of romantic drama, costume drama and heritage drama, seeking to create an aesthetic experience that would work both for more mainstream audiences and for more self-consciously refined, middlebrow audiences. While the films necessarily dwell on the lives of their writer protagonists, or at least on brief episodes from those lives, they must also work generically as tasteful costume dramas and conventional romantic stories. The writer protagonists are thus almost always in some way situated within a familiar heritage space and a heart-tugging romantic plot.

The Austen Franchise and Literary Authorship

One of the most widely discussed Brit-lit biopics of the 1990s and 2000s was the Jane Austen biopic, *Becoming Jane*. In developing a case study of this film, I want first to situate it in the wider context of the Austen film and television franchise, and the way that franchise engages with ideas of literary authorship. Austen, of course, was one of the most adapted of English authors in the 1990s and 2000s. The mid-1990s was the moment of what various cultural commentators at the time called Austenmania, with four film adaptations and two television series appearing in the space of a couple of years. Central to this moment was the BBC serialization of *Pride and Prejudice* (dir. Simon Langton, 1995). The first half of the 2000s saw another flowering of *Pride and Prejudice*, from the *Bridget Jones* films (2001, 2004),[17] via the Mormon rom-com *Pride and Prejudice – A Latter-Day Comedy* (dir. Andrew Black, 2003) and Gurinder Chadha's *Bride and Prejudice* (2004), to Joe Wright's version of *Pride and Prejudice* (2005). The late 2000s saw cultural commentators coin a new Jane-ite pun, dubbing this the moment of Austen Power; this was mainly a televisual phenomenon, but for my purposes the key text is the celluloid biopic *Becoming Jane*.

The Austen franchise typifies the ways in which classical literature and its authors are taken up by the film and television businesses and pitched to particular markets and audiences. First, there are the apparently more authentic period adaptations, from the Emma Thompson/Ang Lee version of *Sense and Sensibility* (1995) to Joe Wright's *Pride and Prejudice*. Second, there are contemporary dramas that rework the Austen source material in more radical ways, from *Clueless* (dir. Amy Heckerling, 1995) to *Bridget Jones's Diary* (2001), to *Bride and Prejudice* – makeover films, as Deborah Cartmell describes them,[18] that emphasise those elements of Austen that might work as chick flicks, date movies and romantic comedies. Third, there are biopics like *Becoming Jane*, and the TV drama *Miss Austen Regrets* (dir. Jeremy Lovering, 2008), and various other spin-off texts like *The Jane Austen Book Club* (dir. Robin Swicord, 2007), about a group of modern-day Californians, mainly women, who meet to read and discuss Austen's novels, and inadvertently live out some of her plots.

The fact that two Austen biopics appeared as part of the moment of Austen Power, one on film (*Becoming Jane*) and the other on television (*Miss Austen Regrets*), indicates the extent to which film and programme makers were keen to exploit the possibilities of both the Austen industry and the market for literary cinema and television – and more generally, the market for 'traditional' English drama. To look at the Austen franchise is also to reveal a much broader sense of the cinematization of literary authorship, of how the writer is put on screen, one that extends from writing to reading, from production to reception, from branding to rewriting, and from a reverential treatment of the canonical Austen to a more playful form of fan fiction.

When Kenneth Branagh wrote Mary Shelley's name into the title of his film *Mary Shelley's Frankenstein* (1994), and Baz Luhrman followed suit in *William Shakespeare's Romeo + Juliet* (1996), they acknowledged the market boost that the literary property of an authorial name can carry, and therefore showcased that name as prominently as possible. Equally, of course, Austen's name and cultural reputation have been crucial to the cultural status and marketability of the 'well-made' period adaptations of her novels. The author's name is used, in effect, as a means both of securing an audience and branding a product. Some adaptations, however, go further than this and specifically evoke the author as a metaphorical screen presence within the drama. Thus Fanny Price (Frances O'Connor), as the author of Austen's juvenilia in Patricia Rozema's *Mansfield Park* (1999) (Figure 6.1), takes on a persona that is equivalent to that of Jane Austen (Anne Hathaway) in the literary biopic *Becoming Jane*; the heroine of *Pride and Prejudice – A Latter-Day Comedy* is also a writer, while Bridget's (Renée Zellweger) diary-writing does not just record the plot, but becomes its engine, in *Bridget Jones's Diary* (dir. Sharon Maguire, 2001).

While a central character in an adaptation can be configured as a writer in this way, and so echo the authorial process, in the literary biopic, the inverse is also often true, writers becoming, in effect, characters in their own fictional worlds. Thus, in *Becoming Jane*, Jane becomes another Austenian character in another Regency drama, another way of working out Austen's stories on screen for a twenty-first century audience. In this sense, as Cartmell has suggested, *Becoming Jane* might be read as yet another adaptation of *Pride and Prejudice*.[19] In effect, *Becoming Jane* fictionalizes Austen's life, dramatizing various historical personages and episodes according to the conventions of romantic drama, heritage costume films and especially Austen adaptations. Austen the writer, Austen the creator of a particular literary universe, is inserted into her own fictional world. We also see her producing versions of the fiction she would later publish, her creativity inspired at one level by her romantic encounter with Tom Lefroy. In such instances, the author as character, the author as historical personage and the author's stories become blurred and interchangeable in the costume drama of the literary biopic.

One consequence of this intermixing is that contemporary literary biopics, while still adhering to the more general conventions of the quality English costume drama, nevertheless give each author his or her distinctive treatment. If a biopic about Austen has to be Austenian in tone, therefore, so a biopic about a Romantic poet has to be romantic in tone, a Shakespearean biopic Shakespearean, and so on. In this way such films rework and reproduce a particular idea of the author, an idea that is shaped as much by her or his literary creations as by how those creations have themselves been adapted, reworked and represented as films and television programmes. And of course the commercial benefits of the adaptation process cross media in the other direction, as when film adaptations are used to remarket the books on which they are based.

The concept of literary authorship thus works in part as a marketing tool, a promotional hook, a brand name, addressed both to fans and other specialist readers, and to a wider literate public. Branding is a marketing strategy, in this case selling a film by invoking and circulating the singular and distinctive name of a canonical author; but the imaginative representations of writing, reading and rewriting in fact create *multiple* manifestations of the same author; audiences engage with the author in different ways through these different processes; in effect, as I've suggested, authorship is a function of these representations of writing, reading and rewriting.

Becoming Jane

How is Austen represented in *Becoming Jane*? How is she made flesh? How is this particular commodity pitched in the market-place? How does the name of the author compete with other attractions, other selling points?

In casting a Hollywood star to play an English icon, *Becoming Jane* is typical of the small-scale English literary film in its endeavour to appeal to mainstream audiences attuned to the Hollywood star system. In *Becoming Jane*, Anne Hathaway plays Austen; in *Shakespeare in Love*, Gwyneth Paltrow plays Shakespeare's muse; in *Finding Neverland* (dir. Marc Forster, 2004), Johnny Depp plays J.M. Barrie, while in *The Libertine* (dir. Laurence Dunmore, 2004), Depp is Rochester; and in *Miss Potter*, Renée Zellweger plays Beatrix Potter. Add to this Paltrow's performance in *Emma*, Nicole Kidman's Woolf in *The Hours*, Frances O'Connor's Fanny Price in *Mansfield Park*, and Cate Blanchett's Queen Elizabeth I in the two *Elizabeth* films, as well as Zellweger's turn as another sort of English icon in the *Bridget Jones* films, and the strategy looks both concerted and extensive. It is a strategy that also clearly appeals to a certain type of Hollywood star, keen to demonstrate his/her acting ability to create convincing characters in refined, literate, middlebrow products.

One of the taglines used to promote *Becoming Jane* proposed the film's storyline as 'the inspiration behind Jane Austen's greatest love stories'. In so doing, it captured the dual appeal of the film: on the one hand, this was a serious literary film, part of the Austen franchise; on the other hand, it was a love story, another romantic drama. This double address, both to those that want a literate film and those that prefer a romantic drama, was central to the way the film was conceived and put together. At the start of the film, for instance, it is early morning and Jane is writing; she is delighted when she conjures up some choice words, but her elation awakens the whole house and causes some consternation. Her mother's response is precise: 'that girl needs a husband'. Thus from the outset, both the literary and the romantic are carefully signalled, with the mother's response triggering a typically Austenian storyline about romance, subtle class differences and the problems of inheritance.

The production was designed from the outset to work in these complementary contexts. With funding, distribution deals and pre-sales from a variety of European and American sources, the package was typical of modestly budgeted cinema addressed to crossover audiences, with the goal of attracting both a youthful mainstream audience and a more mature audience interested in 'literate films'. The British trade paper *Screen International*, for instance, predicted that 'the chemistry between [the] co-stars ... and their combined marquee value should position *Becoming Jane* as a potent middlebrow, mainstream attraction, especially in the UK.'[20] As it transpired, the film in the end did not fare as well as expected at the box office.

The initial plan was to release *Becoming Jane* in the USA in June or July of 2007, through a strategy known as counter-programming, whereby so-called small, quality films would be released in the same week as one of the big summer blockbusters. It was also seen as 'a seven-day movie' – that is, not one that relies solely on the opening weekend of its release for the bulk of its income, but the sort of film that would play well throughout the week, and gradually build up audiences as its run developed.[21] But if *Becoming Jane* was perceived as a small-scale, intelligent, literary film that might appeal to middlebrow, adult audiences, it was also a romantic comedy-drama with up-and-coming young stars, and was therefore also expected to play well to younger, more mainstream audiences.

At one level, then, this was another Austen film, a quality English period drama, not quite a literary adaptation, but certainly designed to make the most of its proximity to such films. It thus tapped into a prominent cultural vein and thereby sought to engage with a sizeable pre-established audience. Productions such as this carefully signal the literary Austen, the iconic Austen, using that as a lure for certain audiences – but then find ways to address other audiences as well. They thus both engage with and disengage from the literary Austen.

The film itself clearly engages with the literary Austen from the outset, and images of Jane writing become a key motif of the film, along with scenes of her reading the stories she has written, defending her work and her interests, and discussing the relationship between writing and experience. As Jane moves through the drama, we witness her blending her experiences and observations into an early draft of *Pride and Prejudice*, with the Tom Lefroy character (James McAvoy) played out in the film as a model for Darcy. As the film shows the gradual fictionalizing of a life, it also engages sympathetically with some of the difficulties of female authorship.

The producers of the film stressed the film's historical credentials – 'it is taken from research, culled from a lot of biographies'[22] – and drew attention to the fact that the script was based on an historical biography, *Becoming Jane Austen: A Life*, whose author, Jon Spence, was employed as a historical consultant on the film.[23] The star of the film, Hathaway, also claimed in several interviews to have researched her part carefully, including having read 'every one of Austen's letters in the British Library'.[24] Meantime her co-star, McAvoy, observed: 'we wanted the production to have some integrity and not just be a British rom-com in tights'.[25] Julian Jarrold's stated aim as director was 'to bring Austen up to date by roughening her up a bit', arguing that Austen adaptations were too often 'a little bit picture-postcard and safe and nice and sweet. I want more life and energy and fun'.[26]

If an effort was made to establish a sense of historical authenticity and deal with the familiar, there was also therefore a concern to ensure a modern spin. 'We wanted to bring [an] element of modernity to *Becoming Jane*', explained co-producer Robert Bernstein.[27] 'It is young love. It is Jane Austen in love, something you've never seen before, a complete departure from the usual oblique portrait of her as a spinster.'[28] Like his producer, Jarrold felt that audiences other than Austen purists would be put off by the traditional image of the author as 'a middle-aged spinster obsessed with manners and propriety. That's one of the things that attracted me – that one is able to breathe a little life into it.'[29] This of course was hardly a new way of thinking about Austen; indeed, it was very much a re-run of the debates provoked by *Persuasion* (dir. Roger Michell, 1995), *Emma* (dir. Douglas McGrath, 1996) and *Mansfield Park* (dir. Patricia Rozema, 1999).[30]

However, if the production was to develop a new, more modern image of Austen, it was to be a more restrained modernity than the one embodied by Alicia Silverstone in *Clueless* (1995) or Billie Piper in the ITV adaptation of *Mansfield Park* (2007), and it is less shockingly erotic than Patricia Rozema's 1999 version of *Mansfield Park*. 'The film is not titillating or gratuitous', assured Douglas Rae, of Ecosse Films; on the contrary, 'It's very chaste! There is only one kiss!'[31] That didn't stop more conservative commentators trying to create a moral panic around the kiss, of course (see Figure 6.2). If the film was to be as intimate as possible, that intimacy would be hemmed in by the constraints of late eighteenth-century customs: 'There is a lot of passion in the film, but it is passion across the ballrooms and the soirees and walks with other people.'[32]

There was then a careful balancing act going on around the figure of Austen. On the one hand, as Rae explained, 'what we've tried to do is convey the intelligence and energy and humour of the woman – to keep the integrity and spirit of Jane Austen'; on the other hand, '[we've tried to] make her story and her passion more accessible'.[33] The casting of Hathaway and the focus on Austen's early adulthood were central to this strategy of renewal. 'I wanted to get away from the old-fashioned, nostalgic, chocolate-box English period drama thing', explained Jarrold. 'Having an American, or someone from a different background, a different way of acting, seemed kind of interesting.'[34] What Jarrold wanted to establish was an image of the young Austen as 'feisty … full of energy', instead of the usual 'prim and proper' image, someone 'that anyone could relate to'. 'There was something very interesting', he suggested, 'about looking at her before she became an iconic image'.[35]

The discourse is again very familiar: these were exactly the terms in which *Elizabeth* had been conceived a decade earlier. And of course, the idea of presenting a 'modern' Austen accessible to contemporary mainstream audiences had been central to the Austen project since at least the mid-1990s. Hathaway's presence was vital in this respect. Where *Clueless* had revisioned Austen's *Emma* as a high school romantic comedy for teens, *Becoming Jane* sought to tap into this same vein through the casting of someone who had

Figure 6.1   Frances O'Connor as Fanny Price in *Mansfield Park* (1999): author and character implicitly elided.

Figure 6.2   Anne Hathaway and James McAvoy in *Becoming Jane* (2007): romance the wellspring of creativity.

made her name in the two *Princess Diaries* films (2001, 2004),[36] Disney's pre-teen and young teen comedy-dramas, in which Hathaway plays an American girl who discovers she's actually European royalty:

> We went with Anne because we know she will bring a young teen audience with her to the film. Many of the 11-year-olds who fell in love with

her in *The Princess Diaries* are now just turning 15. They are the right age for Austen.[37]

Of course, by the time *Becoming Jane* was released, Hathaway had also made the much edgier teen flick *Havoc* (dir. Barbara Kopple, 2005), as well as having taken on more adult roles in *Brokeback Mountain* (dir. Ang Lee, 2005) and *The Devil Wears Prada* (dir. David Frankel, 2006). Such roles would only extend her potential appeal in *Becoming Jane*. Austen purists, however, were unimpressed, and there was a predictable outcry among Jane-ites on the Internet, prompting the mainstream press to report that Austen fans were 'livid' about Anne Hathaway, a beautiful American woman, 'playing their beloved authoress'.[38]

The film had a mixed reception. Some critics perceived a disappointingly middle-of-the-road film, 'a pleasant, picturesque if pedestrian biopic ... solidly directed' but overall 'bland and ... too much like Sunday night telly'.[39] Certainly many of the characters, plot developments, relationships, desires, conversations and settings seem overly familiar. Of course, in part, this was intentional: the filmmakers had to try to recreate the sorts of attractions that had worked in previous period films and literary adaptations; they also deliberately drew parallels between the imagined biography of Austen and the plots and characters of her novels.

The tensions between the literate film and the rom-com were also explicitly brought out in reviews. 'As literary biography it's about as tenable as *Shakespeare in Love*,' suggested one critic, 'but as a romantic comedy-drama for those who like big frocks and stately homes, it's wittier than most Austen film adaptations'.[40] It was all about what was expected of the film and how it could be used by its audiences:

> Feminist critics might take exception to the idea that the inspiration for Austen's success stemmed from a stymied heart, while literary scholars may bleat about liberties taken and history imagined. But for thousands of love-hungry couples seeking a mutually agreeable reason to cuddle up at the flicks, it's terrific – eye candy for blokes and girls alike, with a smartly sneaking sense of the reality of relationships.[41]

One woman's magazine confidently declared 'you absolutely must not miss this bright, funny, romantic, heart-breaking triumph',[42] while a film magazine described it as 'a warm, charming, bittersweet romance – destined to make a thousand dates.'[43] 'Guys, take her to see this one', proposed an American television reviewer: 'She'll love you for it!'.[44] But the film was always going to work in two different ways, for different audiences. As a result, for some reviewers, the film was 'more than just a handsomely mounted chick-flick'.[45] On the contrary, it was 'a beautifully crafted biography'[46] about the 'quintessential English author Jane Austen'.[47]

Conclusions

Becoming Jane was in many ways typical of the Brit-lit biopic, period versions of Austen and the modestly scaled, literate film; but while it was carefully addressed to the niche market for so-called 'quality' films, it was also addressed to mainstream audiences seeking a romantic comedy-drama. Its dual address was carefully strategized, and designed in part to enable audiences to decide whether they wanted to engage with, or disengage from, the literary Austen. The film made it possible to renew and extend the Austen franchise, which had proved to be such a potent aspect of culturally English filmmaking (and television programme-making) in the 1990s and 2000s. It also functioned as a way of putting the writer on screen, embodying the author as a character who precisely creates fictions on the page, and suggesting that romance is the wellspring of such creativity. But the film also situates the figure of Austen as a character in her own fictional world, blurring the boundary between the author as historical personage and Jane as a character in yet another Austenian fiction. If authorship is one of the themes of literary biopics like *Becoming Jane*, the vision of the writer is as a romantic soul who creates stories and characters out of the world she inhabits. On screen, that world – irrespective of the historical specificities of its source story – becomes the generically conventional world of the 'tasteful' middlebrow costume drama. The market appeal of that world is enlarged, however, by blending it with the generic conventions of the more mainstream romantic drama.

Notes

1. This chapter, and especially the case study of *Becoming Jane*, draws on material in A. Higson, *Film England: Culturally English Filmmaking Since the 1990s* (London: I.B. Tauris, 2011). I'm very grateful to Judith Buchanan for her expert editorial interventions.
2. See A. Higson, *English Heritage, English Cinema: Costume Drama since 1980* (Oxford: Oxford University Press, 2003).
3. P. French, 'Be-All and End-All for Triumph', *The Observer* (3 May, 1992): 52; J. Salamon, 'Film: Merchant Ivory's "Howards End"', *Wall St Journal* (12 March, 1992), Section A: 10; T. Crow, 'Regarding *Howards End*', *Los Angeles Village View* (17–23 April, 1992): 15.
4. R. Reed, 'Grim Flicks Creep out Toronto', *The New York Observer* (27 September 2004): 24.
5. D. Rooney, 'Stage Beauty', *Variety* (10–16 May 2004): 50.
6. *Night & Day Magazine, Mail on Sunday*, quoted on Official Website, at http://www.radiotimes.com/stagebeauty/pressquotes.html (no longer available).
7. P. Howlett, 'Film Choice: Gosford Park', *The Guardian Guide* (21 March 2009): 53; Derek Elley, 'Quite a Royal Send-Off', *Variety* (19–25 May 2003): 27.
8. Telephone interview with PolyGram Filmed Entertainment staff, 23 November 1998.

9. P. French, *The Observer*, quoted on Samuelson Entertainment's website for *Wilde*, at http://www.oscarwilde.com/newrev5.html

10. M. Goodridge, 'Shakespeare in Love', *Screen International* (18 December 1998): 19.

11. O. Gleiberman, *Entertainment Weekly*, quoted in Miramax advertisement in *Screen International* (11 December 1998): 7.

12. Used in promotional materials including posters and DVD covers.

13. See Geoffrey Wall's 'Literary biopics: a literary biographer's perspective', Chapter 7 in this volume.

14. Used in promotional materials including posters and DVD covers.

15. S. Neale, *Genre and Hollywood* (London: Routledge, 2000), p. 61.

16. Neale (2000), p. 61.

17. *Bridget Jones's Diary* (dir. Sharon Maguire, 2001); *Bridget Jones: The Edge of Reason* (dir. Beeban Kidron, 2004).

18. See Deborah Cartmell's 'Becoming Jane in Adaptations of Austen's Fiction', Chapter 9 in this volume.

19. Cartmell, Chapter 9 in this volume.

20. A. Hunter, 'Becoming Jane', *Screendaily.com* (8 March, 2007).

21. A. Thomas, 'Italian audiences love "I Want You"', *Variety* (13 March 2007), at http://www.variety.com/article/VR1117961060?refCatId=13

22. R. Bernstein, co-producer, quoted in Hugh Davies, 'Jane Austen at 19: The Real Life Love Story' (6 April 2006), at http://www.telegraph.co.uk/news/uknews/1514932/Jane-Austen-at-19-the-real-life-love-story.html

23. J. Spence, *Becoming Jane Austen: A Life* (London: Continuum, 2003).

24. See e.g. N. Reynolds, 'I Could Only Become Jane by Reading all her Letters, Admits Star', *Daily Telegraph* (7 March 2007), at http://www.telegraph.co.uk/news/uknews/1544587/I-could-only-become-Jane-by-reading-all-her-letters-admits-star.html

25. Quoted in C. McLean, '"Sexing up" Jane Austen', *The Daily Telegraph* (2 March, 2007), at http://www.telegraph.co.uk/culture/film/starsandstories/3663499/Sexing-up-Jane-Austen.html

26. Quoted in S. Williams, 'Not so Plain Jane', *Telegraph Magazine* (17 February, 2007), at http://www.telegraph.co.uk/culture/3663235/Not-so-plain-Jane.html

27. Quoted in Williams (2007).

28. Bernstein, quoted in Davies (2006).

29. Jarrold, quoted in W. Ide, 'Breathing Passionate Life into the Nation's Favourite Spinster', *The Times* (8 March 2007), http://cma.staging-thetimes.co.uk/tto/arts/film/article2426130.ece

30. See A. Higson, *Film England* (2011), chs. 5 and 6.

31. Quoted in Williams (2007).

32. D. Rae, quoted in Jack Malvern, 'Austen's Movie "A Fanciful Affair"', *Timesonline* (18 March 2006), at www.timesonline.co.uk (no longer available).

33. Quoted in Williams (2007).

34. Jarrold, quoted in Ide (2007).

35. Julian Jarrold, in 'Behind the Scenes', special feature on *Becoming Jane* DVD, (2Entertain Video Ltd., 2007).

36. *The Princess Diaries* (dir. Garry Marshall, 2001); *The Princess Diaries 2*: *Royal Engagement* (dir. Garry Marshall, 2004).

37. C. Hastings, B. Jones and S. Plentl, 'Jane Austen to be the Latest Teenage Sensation', *The Sunday Telegraph* (4 February 2007), at http://www.telegraph.

co.uk/news/uknews/1541509/Jane-Austen-to-be-the-latest-teenage-sensation.
html
38. L. Benedictus, 'Calamity Jane?', *Guardian Unlimited*, at http://www.guardian.co.uk/
film/2007/mar/02/3 (accessed 12 December 2012). On Jane-ite concern on the
Internet, see especially the copious material on www.austenblog.com
39. C. Tookey, 'Perfectly Pleasant, but this Jane still Falls Short', *Daily Mail* (9 March,
2007), at http://www.dailymail.co.uk/tvshowbiz/reviews/article-441197/Perfectly-
pleasant-Jane-falls-short.html
40. N. Barber, 'Becoming Jane', *The Independent* (11 March 2007).
41. N. Pierce, 'Becoming Jane', *Total Film*, 126 (April 2007): 36.
42. R. Witcher, *Grazia*, quoted on Ecosse Films website, http://www.ecossefilms.com/
film_becoming.aspx
43. Pierce, 'Becoming Jane' (April 2007): 36.
44. Jeffrey Lyons, on NBC's *Reel Talk*, quoted on the official DVD website, at http://
video.movies.go.com/becomingjane/
45. McLean (2007).
46. Hunter (2007).
47. Hunter (2007).

7
Literary biopics: a literary biographer's perspective

Geoffrey Wall

There is a surprisingly plain psychological truth enfolded somewhere in our conversations about literary authorship. We want to meet the author, see the author, hear from the author. When I tell my 16-year-old son that I once met W.H. Auden, I rise in his estimation. Auden thereby makes more sense to him. Something mysterious, something extra-textual has been transmitted, across the years, from Auden to me, from me to my son. How does this happen? Why that lingering desire for the author?

Authorship is of course pervasively, historically contingent. The exuberant mutability of authorship is evident in current efforts to codify intellectual property for the digital age, to enforce copyright across cyberspace and tighten the grip of corporate interests on all forms of cultural value. Once disconnected from the archaic vocal apparatus, the one originally used to speak this text to an audience physically present, my discourse can be packaged and labelled and made to circulate in chastely disembodied and perfectly commodified form. Once received, it can be consumed as silently internalized speech. If we can download the audio-book, do we still need the bard reciting the song of the tribe by torchlight in the great hall? Interestingly, we do. Our everyday notions of authoriality have been radically historicized in the past fifty years, since the textual turn of the 1960s, and the digital turn of the 1990s. The legal codification of all the diverse forms of intellectual property proceeds apace. In this context of continuously contested cultural, legal and technical mutation, literary authorship looks like one of those *good old things* that Brecht so incisively contrasted to all the *bad new things*.[1] Perhaps for that reason alone, we need to study authorship from a comprehensively political perspective, asking what it used to do, what it does and what it might yet do.

Centuries of techno-mediation have liberated the magisterial word from the primitive requirement of mutual presence, speaker and listener. Masters of abstraction we may be, and yet at some other level all of this arduously acquired sophistication counts for nothing. We never feel at home in a text.

Stubbornly, surreptitiously, endearingly, we ritualize the scene of reading, in the hope of raising spirits, communing with the mighty dead, face to face, off the record, in some strange unlicensed cultural space. Literary biographers have consecrated this ambiguous pursuit. By their means, we retrieve something precious and satisfying from the triumphant abstraction of print.

We contrive, publicly and privately, to connect with our authors. We draw them down to earth, or we keep them safely aloft. We celebrate their genius, and then take revenge on its intolerable supremacy. We connect with our authors. We scrutinize their humanity, investigate their peculiarities. We do all of the above, all at the same time. We invest immensely in the name and the image and the history of the author. We attach our stories and our images to the textual thing. It keeps that thing circulating, animates it, infuses it with our desire.

What are we hoping to see? Where, or what, or who is the object of this intemperate curiosity? Those images and those stories of authoriality, whether meticulously true-to-life or passionately distorted: what is it that they add? Why picture the author? Why not take her at her word? Some things, such as authorship and parental intercourse, we were never meant to see. When we catch a glimpse, it's fascinating but we don't quite understand what we've seen. Those images become the material of fantasy. We work them over, we work them up. Literary authorship and the scene of parental intercourse have at least this much in common. They are the primal scenes of human creativity, cultural and biological.

Compulsively imagined or carefully disavowed, these scenes remain quite properly *veiled*, perpetually, teasingly, imperfectly visible. Jokingly we invoke the muse. We acknowledge that this thing, whatever it is, partakes of the sacred. That's a hazardous substance, the sacred: approach it at your peril. Something must intercede. Better call it the unconscious and populate it with fabulous dark agents.

For two years, from 2007 to 2009, the *Guardian* newspaper ran a compelling weekly series entitled *Writers' Rooms*. The series was subtitled 'Portraits of the spaces where authors create'. One hundred and sixteen rooms were photographed and then described by the inhabitant. We see the room, the private space, the things in the room, the intimate clutter, the immediate material context for the activity of writing. We don't see the writer. And why should we? There is nothing much to see.

The writer writing is ever imperfectly alone, in her fantasy, alone with the language, for the moment at least. More prosaically, perhaps, alone with the institutions of literature, the literary agent, the commissioning editor, the accountant. The writing hand is moving steadily. The writing fingers skip across the keyboard. The eyes are wandering, in search of the *mot juste*. The lips move, as they voice the shape of the sentence in progress. A smile, a frown, a sigh, a gesture of despair, a whispered invocation to some benign guardian presence. That's all there is. The action is inward. A mental process, a history that can scarcely be narrated, let alone represented in a flow of images.

In the mind of the writer, in the timeless subjective moment of writing, nobody is looking. You don't want real people watching you, reading you, over your shoulder, when you're writing. You want some imaginary admirer. Or perhaps, more strenuously, your intellectual hero watching you, from beyond the grave, nodding approval of the particularly felicitous sentence just composed. Once you've stopped, surrendering exhausted to the familiar fact of imperfection, that's the moment to show your face, to make an appearance, to be short-listed, photographed, interviewed, sounding decorously successful. Plucked from habitual obscurity, from the crowded solitude of composition, you do your best to look the part, according to the cultural templates of creativity, past and present. But you know all along that this performance has almost nothing to do with the writing.

The elaborate mediating cultural fiction of literary authorship is several centuries older than the cinema. At a surprisingly early moment in its evolution, the printed book began to include, on the title page, a portrait of the author. In these images we are invited to observe the public face of the writer, composed, smoothed out, plausibly idealized, socially consecrated, according to the edifying conventions of elite portraiture and the technical limitations of line engraving.

Erasmus, emblem of the emergent secular intelligence, was among the first to impose the image that would complement his print persona. Lisa Jardine's book-essay, *Erasmus Man of Letters*,[2] describes how skilfully Erasmus had himself represented, visually. For his portrait, he borrowed the pose and the costume and the material setting of St. Jerome as represented in the paintings of Ghirlandio. In 1510 Jerome was the very type of spiritualized intellectual labour. This adoptive strategy needs a name – Jerome-ification, let us say: drape the new in the dignity of the old.

Might some of our modern Anglophone cinematic versions of authorship engage in Jerome-ification? From the perspective of a literary biographer – this one at least – literary biopics can seem tightly corseted by a profoundly conservative aesthetic code. Let's gently unhook that corset, one tight little hook at a time, and consider what might be done differently. Let us imagine along the way a biographical-cinematic genre that has miraculously caught up with the best of literary biography.

What are the peculiar virtues, the distinctive powers of literary biography in the modern English tradition? Briefly, the tradition has its origins in that curious Edwardian cultural formation, the man of letters. It has remained, in the words of biographer Michael Holdroyd, the affair of 'a maverick crew of self-employed amateurs'.[3] Holdroyd's phrase celebrates the marginality, the residuality, the mildly disreputable status of the literary biographer in the age of the academic professional. Writing for the market, under contract to a trade publisher, brings a certain freedom from the theoretical imperatives and protocols of intellectual work within the university. On the other hand, it imposes adherence to the generic expectations, however sophisticated, of the paying readership.

There is general agreement that the modern school of British biography begins in 1918, with the publication of Lytton Strachey's *Eminent Victorians*. In Strachey's five gleefully impertinent portraits of the cultural heroes of the previous century, biography took a decisive comic-satiric turn. Strachey was influenced by the Bloomsbury ethos of cool critical intimacy, by the radical emergent influence of Freud, and by the ideological turmoil of the war that had not yet ended. Strachey renounced the obligatory idealization of the biographical subject. Impudent joking at the expense of the powerful was, of course, an ancient liberty. Inexplicably, by 1918, it had been mislaid for some years. Under this new and mildly subversive dispensation, the biographer was henceforth licensed to practise a flamboyantly ironic brevity, cutting the over-mighty and self-important subject down to size. The biographer was also licensed to explore the more obscure dimensions of the subject's mental life, especially, of course, his or her sexuality. I quote from Strachey's 'Preface':

> Not by the direct method of a scrupulous narration ... if he is wise the explorer of the past will adopt a subtler strategy. He will attack his subject in unexpected places; he will fall upon the flank or the rear; he will shoot a sudden, revealing searchlight into obscure recesses hitherto undivined. ... the duty of the biographer ... is to maintain his own freedom of spirit. It is not his business to be complimentary; it is his business to lay bare the facts of the case as he understands them.[4]

Seen in retrospect, Strachey's book, though influential, was also perhaps a dead end. Such a thing could only be done once, and perhaps only at that unique 1918 moment. Strachey's mockery cleared the air, but it would be many years before these new freedoms could be consolidated into an agreed ethics of biography in the age of psychoanalysis. That new understanding of sexuality implied deep attendant discontinuities of identity. This new sense of self soon complicated irrevocably the relation between biographer and subject. Biographical truth, whatever it had once been, would never be the same. In 1936, 'aroused by the threat that you wish to become my biographer', Freud wrote to Arnold Zweig:

> Whoever undertakes to write a biography binds himself to lying, to concealment, to hypocrisy, to flummery, and even to hiding his own lack of understanding, since biographical truth is not to be had and if it were it could not be used.[5]

Alongside Strachey, in my Hall of Fame, I have assembled a select but imposing array of monumental literary biographies. They are all slightly larger than life, in the great tradition of decorous marmoreal portraiture. Each commemorates a distinctive contribution to the genre. We shall consider them briefly in turn: Graham Greene, *Lord Rochester's Monkey* (1974)[6] for its cool intimacy with the transgressive; Ian Hamilton, *Keepers of the Flame* (1992)[7] for its account of the comedy of manners generated by various valuable literary estates; Richard Holmes' *Footsteps: Adventures of a Romantic Biographer* (1984)[8] for its affectionately mock-heroic portrait of the biographer in pursuit of departed spirits; Timothy Garton Ash, *The File: A Personal History* (1997),[9] though a personal memoir rather than a literary biography, for its exploration of the specialized forms of biography practised by the secret police of East Germany; Peter Ackroyd, *Dickens* (1990)[10] for reviving the imaginary conversation. Though far from being the whole story, these recent books are my personal choices as a practitioner of the genre.[11] These are the books I come back to. Taken together they have defined, for me at least, the possibilities of the literary biography. How do current cinematic versions of authorship compare with the achievements of this group? And what, we might ask, could cinema learn from literary biography?

First, the question of length. The current norm for literary biography is 400 pages, 140,000 words in total. The length of the book is specified in the contract that the biographer signs with the publisher. The published work is intended to describe, in a more or less orderly, more or less continuous fashion, as far as the evidence will allow, the evolution of the biographical subject. Thus constrained, both by contract and convention, the biographer observes a loosely implicit pre-modernist chronological decorum. Richard Ellmann's *Oscar Wilde* (1987),[12] Hermione Lee's *Virginia Woolf* (1996),[13] Roy Foster's *W.B. Yeats* (1997),[14] and Richard Holmes's *Coleridge* (1989)[15] all conform to this pattern. Here's no clever stuff: simply a comprehensive narrative intelligence. For all that, the form can, of course, accommodate minor novelties. Two recent examples come to mind. Teasingly, Peter Ackroyd begins his *Dicken*s (1990)[16] on the authorial deathbed, and Claire Tomalin's *Thomas Hardy* (2006)[17] opens on a funeral. However, in both cases, the larger narrative model remains linear.

In the cinema, an operational consensus seems to determine that the depiction of a life lasts for around two hours, and this simple fact makes a world of difference. The cinematic form dictates a briskly elliptical narrative line; there is no time to explore historical context, early experience, family history, intellectual formation. All that luxurious and evocative abundance of significant biographical detail is stripped away, leaving behind only that which is essential to narrative coherence. Obliged to be compellingly concise, the biopic resorts biopictorially to a simplified, improvised visual notation. We are invited, as spectators, to dwell upon what I shall call the curious signs of creativity. I can think of various examples from recent work.

In *Shakespeare in Love* (dir. John Madden, 1998), the poet's wonderfully improbable green leather jacket testifies to his genius. In *The Hours* (dir. Stephen Daldry, 2002), Virginia Woolf chain-smokes her roll-ups with passionate intensity as she settles to writing *Mrs Dalloway*. In *Barton Fink* (dir. Joel Coen and Ethan Coen, 1991), the apprentice screenwriter's gleaming Underwood portable typewriter affirms his uneasy modernity. These notations all tell us, with persuasive immediacy, '*This* is how writers do what they do. This is the intimate truth of all the asocial labour of literary composition.'

The literary biographer's primary aim is to render the subject, however exalted, comprehensively and disconcertingly human. As Graham Greene puts it, with disarming simplicity, remembering his own work on a biography of the poet Rochester, 'The longer I worked on his life the more living he became to me.'[18] To work on another person in this way is to compose the whole pattern of a life, not just one corner of it. For all its chronological decorum, perhaps indeed by means of that decorum, a certain virtuosity in the evocation of deep time is one of the principal intellectual pleasures of the biographical genre. Formatted so differently, the film biography would be hard pressed to convey in the conventional space of two hours that sense of biographical deep time.

What do I mean by 'deep time'? It sounds, perhaps, Jungian, as if it has to do with archetypes and the collective unconscious. But that's not it. Biographical deep time is closer to the anthropologist's concept of thick description. Beneath the surface flow of narrative, the biographical subject inhabits simultaneously, joyfully and invisibly, many dimensions, both temporal and psychic. In this, the multiple self of biographical deep time, the remembered and the misremembered past, the imagined future and the ever-volatile present, are fused together. The visible life is not the only one. There is another, an unseen life, equally significant.

The literary biographer is committed to the forward movement of narrative. But that narrative must embrace all the years, the many selves unfolding, often alongside each other: the real, the imagined and the never realized. 'A secret, at least tacit life,' Richard Ellmann wrote, 'underlies the one we are thought to live'.[19] Disconcertingly, according to Michael Holroyd, 'the lies we tell are part of the truth we live.'[20] We need a good ear, for the secret and the lie and the half-truth; we also need to be attuned to something more elusive – the subjunctive mood: that mode of the imagination for which there is no visual cinematic equivalent. The subjunctive is woven deftly into the fabric of every life, but it is probably a more conspicuous feature of the life of the writer.

I turn now to questions of biographical evidence. To make the story flow, the biographer makes connections, gently stretching the available evidence, linking the singular biographical subject to the larger, circumambient history. This is not to fictionalize. It requires a measure of disciplined imaginative identification, a certain venturing-out beyond the facts. Informed and legitimate conjecture flows from the biographer's sustained, playful, obsessive, inward, conversation with the chosen subject. Conjecture certainly needs to come clean, to identify itself as such, allowing the reader to be the judge of what is on offer. Quality and consistency of conjecture are a good measure of the ambition and the inwardness of any literary biography.

The biographer is master of the archive, guided by a commitment to the known facts of the case. She is equally the master of uncertainty, of non-factuality. Without that lucidly affectionate union of the archival and conjectural, how can the biographer produce that compassionate effect of the real, that sudden and delicately compelling enlargement of human sympathy that constitutes both the intellectual pleasure and the ethical imperative of the genre? I wonder: can the film life ever reach into this dimension? Perhaps the pace is simply too brisk, the visual image too explicit, the whole too fixed in the indicative mood?

The biographer is master of uncertainty. We work all the time with incomplete information. We expect it, are resigned to it: we do our best with what has been preserved. We learn to decipher the gaps and the erasures, to work with the fact of the destruction of primary evidence such as personal letters. The information is always partial in the other sense too; it's predictably tendentious. We read the distortions, we sense the cumulative peculiarities of a particular source, or the peculiarities that cluster around testimony on a topic which is especially difficult. If you're in luck there will be other sources. They will allow you to correct for the known bias of the first source. You will never have the complete picture, but you will avoid mere credulity. You're immersed in the material intellectually, analytically and speculatively. You keep with it, you keep it going in your head when you're not actually writing, as if the known outcomes were not yet known. Your wilder hypotheses live in your notebooks. They testify to one's impatience at the paucity of the real evidence for the inner life of the subject. Deployed cautiously, they can impart a sharp sense of the subject's complex temporality, woven from their thwarted hopes, their cherished imaginings.

There's no avoiding that condition of persistent disciplined uncertainty. There is, of course, no definitive biographical truth, nothing finally to satisfy biographical desire. But no cause for despair either. You learn to indicate implicitly the degree of certainty in relation to any particular biographeme. This is the work of style. You don't need footnotes to spell it out. Once you've mastered the full discursive etiquette, established a narrative presence, then you can add one or two discrete biographical jokes. They're a kind of secret signature, moments at which you suddenly appear and the work of biography becomes instructively visible.

Among the many things I need to know, my subject's favourite things, her special objects, will figure consistently. These objects, chosen for their private evocative powers, are often present, literally and symbolically, at the scene of writing. They supplement the rational labour of composition with a welcome touch of magical omnipotence. Freud's writing desk was crowded with his cherished collection of miniature statues of Greek and Egyptian deities.[21] Flaubert's writing-room was equally haunted. His deceased younger sister, the beloved Caroline, presided in that room, in absentia, all through the years of the composition of *Madame Bovary*. A life-sized marble bust – it was based on her death mask – stood in the room. More prosaically, the scene of writing included a green morocco leather couch on which the writer spent much of the writing day, sprawled in a state of reverie. When I see Flaubert writing, I see these two objects close at hand. To be more precise, I see Flaubert on his green morocco leather couch seeing that image of his sister. In the film version of this scene, I want to see these two objects through his eyes. Special objects of this sort could be woven into any film narrative. Often they are not. In *Becoming Jane* (dir. Julian Jarrold, 2007), for example, we do not see the writing desk that Jane Austen's father gave her for her twentieth birthday, the gift that was a decisive gesture of encouragement.

For reasons we might question, we want the writer to look the part. Consider two recent cinematic examples. There's Ben Whishaw's young Keats, reposing in glory on the leafy, blossoming crown of a tree in *Bright Star* (dir. Jane Campion, 2009). There's Anne Hathaway's Jane in *Becoming Jane*, posed in an interior lit like a Vermeer, her bonnet cast aside, writing a letter to her sister Cassandra. The joyful unalienated labour of creativity is supposed to look good, meant to remind us how it felt, on a good day, to be immersed in child's play, that perfect gratuitous unity of being.

On the other hand, one might question the persistent visual pleasure of the Lovely Frock. The act of visualising the everyday life of the pre-industrial past often involves some surreptitious ideological magic. Ever since *Gone With the Wind* (dir. Victor Fleming, 1939), cinema has excelled at this meticulous and seductive celebration of the material culture of extinct social elites. But at what price this sumptuous aesthetic? We are served not with a soberly instructive effect of the real, but with a melancholic effect of the past, a rich lament for lost splendours, for all that pre-industrial elegance of the everyday, the hand-embroidered silk waistcoats, the beautiful riding boots, the provincial ballroom etiquette, the conservative gender roles. This is not inevitable, this surface gloss takes our mind off other things. Borrowed from period costume drama, it's no essential part of how we might screen literary authorship. These imperatives of primary visual pleasure also dictate a fixation on the more photogenic years of the subject's life. This will inevitably skew the biographical narrative towards beginnings. John Keats is, in this sense, the ideal subject.

Authorship in the age of the printed book remains visually elusive. Painters, musicians, actors, dancers and sculptors all put on a show. Writers are such dull creatures, by comparison. They just sit about. Among the many possible visible signs of the authorial, the hand observed in the act of writing is the most intimate and the most obvious. The close-up shot of the hand in motion, as if seen by the writer herself, or as if from over her shoulder, takes us into the inner chamber, the very stuff of creativity, the work in progress. But how unilluminating this is compared to the biographer's account of the manuscript page as it records that discontinuous, intermittent process of composition that is too complex, in its many layers of temporality, to be dramatized.

The logic of cinematic representation normally requires that quotation be dramatically embedded. We don't want to see the author reading direct to camera: this restricts what can be quoted, and it doesn't allow for the slow pleasures of reading. *Bright Star* is exceptionally ingenious in allowing for the performance of brief extracts. I am thinking of the moment when Fanny Brawne's younger sister reads aloud, in a beguilingly childish voice, famous lines from the newly published copy of Keats's poem *Endymion*. The pleasure of this moment lies in the fact that these lines are, within the film narrative, not yet well known. We watch their on-screen audience hearing them for the very first time. Fanny interrupts the reading. She takes the book from her sister and lies back to read silently for herself. This is something that cinema can bring to life. Not the scene of writing, but those earliest scenes of reading, the drama of reception, the social circulation of the text, often a livelier occasion than its faltering creation. Once again, in *Bright Star* towards the end, the two lovers recite alternate couplets from 'La Belle Dame sans Merci', the recitation dramatically embedded with real imaginative tact. We get to hear the familiar lines with a poignant difference.

The only other way to stage quotation is to break from dramatic context. I suspect this only works cinematically at beginnings and endings, on the boundaries of the dramatic representation. So *Bright Star*, for example, ends with the voice of Keats. His death has just been discovered and yet we can hear him reading the full text of 'Ode to a Nightingale'. The voice accompanies the credits to their end. The effect is odd: the minimal image, with just the credits rolling, pulls strongly and prosaically against the posthumous voice of the poet. Helpfully, however, this disjunction suggests the afterlife of the poem.

That creative play at the boundaries of the narrative is a distinctive feature of *Bright Star*. Elsewhere, narrative logic is often insidiously restrictive. For example, *Becoming Jane* makes no sustained use of Austen's letters to her sister Cassandra. It also omits all of Austen's intimacy with her exotic cousin Eliza. In place of those relationships we are offered the drama of the failed elopement with Tom Lefroy. These plot decisions impose a strongly narcissistic singularity on the central character. We are simply not shown that distinctive moral quality that we know from Austen's biography:[22] the receptive, ventriloquizing, imaginative, self-mocking, role-playing aftermath of her affair with Tom Lefroy.

That pleasantly simplified singularity of the film is imposed at the cost of misrepresenting literary production by eliminating its more elusive collective dimension. There is no time to explore literary apprenticeship, the imitation of the masters, the assimilation of precursors. Austen is prompted by Tom Lefroy to read *Tom Jones*. But there is no time to explore her response to it, other than to imply that Lefroy is another Tom Jones. *Becoming Jane* doesn't follow the formation of Austen's style, her reading of Samuel Johnson for example. How could that be incorporated without stalling the love-story? There's just never enough time, cinematically, for the author to do any reading.

Tom and Viv (dir. Brian Gilbert, 1994), *Shakespeare in Love* (1998), *Nora* (dir. Pat Murphy, 2000), *The Hours* (2002), *Sylvia* (dir. Christine Jeffs 2003), *Becoming Jane* (2007), *Miss Austen Regrets* (dir. Jeremy Lovering, 2008) and *Bright Star* (2009) all focus on the intimate emotional life of the author. All are more or less eloquently unhappy love stories, the conventional plot in each case infused with compelling dramatic energy by the rhetorical authority and transgressive imagination of the writer.

This narrow generic choice in favour of the love story is surely not inevitable. What are the other stories we might want to tell about our writers? Where are the examples of the writer as dissenter, as dissident, as satirist, as the critic of state power, as the scourge of privilege and injustice? Looking only at the English possibilities, where's the Milton, the Bunyan, the Blake, the Wollstonecraft, the Shelley, the D.H. Lawrence, the George Orwell? Does their remarkable absence have anything to do with the historical accident of our sharing a language and a cinematic culture with a more powerful neighbour, and with its dominant determination of market demands?

We can all imagine a hybrid form of literary biographical cinema, a form committed to story-telling, engaging with the inner and the outer histories of authorship, but telling it differently, exploring the possibilities opened up by practitioners working in cultural forms less constrained by The Money. I have no desire to renounce the unreconstructed primary visual pleasures of commercial cinema. I want to preserve that exuberantly detailed and startlingly expensive surface, that narrative drive which engages desire at the simplest level. Nevertheless, I want more, all around the edges. I want stories of authorship that are more comprehensive, that reach out beyond the writing desk, the family circle and late adolescence, stories that are licensed to explore the more complex and less instantly photogenic realities of authorship.

In conclusion, I want to consider the mutations in the depiction of a notorious seventeenth-century life, that of the Earl of Rochester. I follow this life across five texts, from comedy of manners to literary biography to stage play to feature film: George Etheredge, *The Man of Mode* (1676);[23] Samuel Johnson, *The Life of John Wilmot, Earl of Rochester* (1780);[24] Graham Greene, *Lord Rochester's Monkey* (1974); Stephen Jeffreys, *The Libertine*

(1994),[25] a theatre text based on the last years of the life of Rochester; and Laurence Dunmore, *The Libertine* (2005), a feature film loosely based on Jeffreys' play.

John Wilmot, 2nd Earl of Rochester (1647–1680), was the younger London contemporary of John Milton and Samuel Pepys. These three men walked the same city streets, and knew of each other by report. Milton would have included Rochester among the company of the damned. Pepys on the other hand kept a copy of Rochester's darkly erotic poems hidden in a secret drawer in his office. Rochester's friend, the dramatist George Etheredge, portrayed him on the London stage of the day as the effortlessly ingratiating Dorimant in *The Man of Mode*. It was a flattering portrait. A century later, in a more censorious age, Johnson's *Life of Rochester* lowered a monumental slab of disparagement upon both the life and the work. Neither the man nor his poetry would rise again for 150 years. Observe how Johnson lays out the meaning of Rochester's life in a single magnificently compendious sentence:

> Thus in a course of drunken gaiety, and gross sensuality, with intervals of study perhaps, yet more criminal, with an avowed contempt of all decency and order, a total disregard to every moral, and a resolute denial of every religious obligation, he lived worthless and useless, and blazed out his youth and his health in lavish voluptuousness; till, at the age of one and thirty, he had exhausted the fund of life, and reduced himself to a state of weakness and decay.[26]

It is delightful to see how in that sentence a defiantly imaginative impulse of compassion quarrels with the dominant impulse of denunciation. Johnson is also generously perceptive when he takes the measure of Rochester's 'blaze of reputation':

> Lord Rochester was eminent for the vigour of his colloquial wit, and remarkable for his many wild pranks and sallies of extravagance. The glare of his general character diffused itself upon his writings; the compositions of a man whose name was heard so often, were certain of attention, and from many readers certain of applause. This blaze of reputation is not yet quite extinguished; and his poetry still retains some splendour beyond that which genius has bestowed.[27]

Graham Greene, when still a young aspiring novelist, discovered Rochester in the early 1930s, at a time when – for fear of prosecution – Rochester's poetry could not yet be published in anything other than a private limited edition. Excited by that prohibition, charmed both by the poems and by Rochester's complex reputation for conscience-stricken sexual extravagance, Greene researched and wrote his only biography, *Lord Rochester's Monkey*.

'It was a blow to me,' Greene wrote, 'when my biography was turned down by my publisher, Heinemann, and I hadn't the heart to offer it elsewhere.'[28]

Not then published until 1974, this is a novelist's biography, spare and elegant, though thankfully not novelized. It is fully researched, and notably generous in quotation of the primary texts. 'I have tried hard,' said Greene looking back, 'to avoid any unacknowledged use of the imagination'.[29] Nonetheless, Greene's Rochester is a characteristic study in the poetics of damnation. In the words of one reviewer, 'it has the originality, thoroughness, and alertness to affairs of conscience that one finds in his fictional manhunts.'[30] In Greene's agreeably contrarian opinion, it was Rochester rather than T.S. Eliot's Marvell who was the true poetic and spiritual heir of John Donne: '[Rochester's] unbelief was quite as religious as the Dean of St Paul's faith'.[31]

Stephen Jeffreys' intricately researched Rochester drama, *The Libertine* (1994), had its first production at the Royal Court Theatre in London. It was directed by Max Stafford-Clark and performed in repertoire with George Etheredge's *The Man of Mode*. This was a clever combination. As well as foregrounding the recurrent theatrical theme, it allowed the two reincarnations of Rochester to be considered alongside each other. Etheredge's Rochester, disguised as Dorimant, explores an elegantly poised moral ambiguity which 'superimposes the Reformed Rake pattern onto that of the libertine trickster.'[32] Jeffreys' Rochester is altogether darker and more self-destructive. The play depicts only the last years, a time of quickening physical and moral decay, streaked with a cruel and self-loathing eloquence that grows ever wilder as syphilis and alcoholism take hold. It's not a pretty picture, but it is perfectly compelling.

Laurence Dunmore's film *The Libertine* (2004) uses a screenplay by Stephen Jeffreys. Much of the set-piece eloquence of the stage version has been trimmed to fit with the protocols of cinematic story-telling. Coming to feature films via graphic design and music videos, Dunmore imposed a distinctive indie visual signature – handheld camerawork and candlelight for all interior scenes – that provoked mockery from American reviewers more attuned to the production values of, for example, *Pirates of the Caribbean* (dir. Gore Verbinski, 2003).

How do they compare, these three modern versions of Rochester, Greene's book, Jeffreys' play and Dunmore's film? Greene's biography incorporated generous quotation from poems and letters, as a circuitous way of publishing texts that could not yet, in the 1930s, be published in their own right. There's no time in either play or film for much of Rochester's writings. We are given only snippets of the poetry and then a few phrases incorporated from Rochester's letters to his wife.

Less obviously, the mode of authorship of book, play and film differs substantially. Greene was the singular author of *Lord Rochester's Monkey*, whereas Jeffreys and Dunmore were always partners in collaborative projects that mingled legal, financial, technical and artistic imperatives. Jeffreys' text was originally commissioned by Max Stafford Clark for his theatre company, Out of Joint. Dunmore's film was financed by Miramax and produced by John Malkovich who had previously played Rochester in the American stage version of Jeffreys' play.

Such differences suggest that cinema, with its intricate industrial division of labour, loves to dwell upon literary authorship precisely because writers represent an archaic mode of apparently unconstrained individual cultural production. Writers can be conscripted to embody simple genius, the fantasy magical version of aesthetic value. Literary authorship, as conventionally imagined on-screen, has perhaps become our modern version of pastoral.

Notes

1. W. Benjamin, *Understanding Brecht*, translated by A. Bostock (London: Verso, 1998), p. 121.
2. L. Jardine, *Erasmus Man of Letters: The Construction of Charisma in Print* (Princeton NJ: Princeton University Press, 1993).
3. M. Holroyd, *Works on Paper: The Craft of Biography and Autobiography* (Washington DC: Counterpoint, 2002), p. 29.
4. L. Strachey, *Eminent Victorians* (London: Modern Library, 1918), p. 5.
5. E. Jones, *Sigmund Freud: Life and Work*, vol. 3: *The Last Phase 1919–1939* (London: Hogarth Press, 1957), p. 208.
6. G. Greene, *Lord Rochester's Monkey: Being the Life of John Wilmot, Second Earl of Rochester* (London: Bodley Head, 1974).
7. I. Hamilton, *Keepers of the Flame: Literary Estates and the Rise of Biography* (London: Hutchinson, 1992).
8. R. Holmes, *Footsteps: Adventures of a Romantic Biographer* (First pub. 1985, New York: Viking, 1996).
9. T. Garton Ash, *The File: A Personal History* (New York: Random House, 1997).
10. P. Ackroyd, *Dickens* (London: Sinclair-Stevenson, 1990).
11. G. Wall, *Flaubert: A Life* (London: Faber, 2001).
12. R. Ellmann, *Oscar Wilde* (London: Hamish Hamilton, 1987).
13. H. Lee, *Virginia Woolf* (London: Chatto and Windus, 1996).
14. R.F. Foster, *W.B. Yeats : A Life* (Oxford: Oxford University Press, 1997).
15. R. Holmes, *Coleridge: Early Visions* (London: Hodder & Stoughton, 1989).
16. Ackroyd (1990).
17. C. Tomalin, *Thomas Hardy : The Time-torn Man* (London: Viking, 2006).
18. Greene (1974), p. 4.
19. Holroyd (2002), p. 30.
20. Holroyd (2002), p. 19.
21. L. Gamwell and R. Wells, *Sigmund Freud and Art: His Personal Collection of Antiquities* (London: Thames Hudson, 1989 [1943]).
22. D. Nokes, *Jane Austen* (London: Fourth Estate, 1998).
23. G. Etheredge, *George Etherege: The Man of Mode*. (London: A & C Black, 2007).
24. S. Johnson, 'Rochester', in R. Lonsdale (ed.) *The Lives of the Most Eminent English Poets: With Critical Observations on Their Works* (Oxford, Clarendon Press, 2006).

25. S. Jeffreys, *The Libertine*, new edn (London: Nick Hern Books, 1994).
26. Johnson (2006), vol. 2, pp. 11–16 (12).
27. Johnson (2006), vol. 2, p. 12.
28. Greene (1974), p. 9.
29. Greene (1974), p. 10.
30. V.S. Pritchett, 'Rogue Poet', *The New York Review of Books* 21 (1974), p. 15.
31. Greene (1974), p. 10.
32. J. Barnard, 'Introduction', in *George Etherege: The Man of Mode* (London: A&C Black, 2007), p. xvi.

Part II
Cinema's Authorial Proxies and Fictional Authors

8
Hemingway adapted: screening the star author

R. Barton Palmer

Autobiographical Fabulizing

Novelist Milan Kundera, speaking for many a modern writer, concedes how deeply the author's life is embedded in his work. He believes that life, in fact, constitutes verbal art's only inevitable source. And yet, in a gesture that crystallizes the incompatibility of self-justifying form with its material source in extra-textual experience, Kundera advises strongly against autobiographical readings:

> According to a well-known metaphor, the novelist demolishes the house of his life and uses its bricks to construct another house: that of his novel. From which it follows that a novelist's biographers unmake what the novelist made, and remake what he unmade. Their labor, from the standpoint of art utterly negative, can illuminate neither the value nor the meaning of a novel.[1]

This provocative metaphor interestingly postulates the interchangeability of the constructive elements of fiction, imagined as building blocks that can be reoriented as biographical lexemes. From these, a 'house' of a different kind might be (re)constructed, suggesting the material fungibility that Kundera reprehends, even if the secondary agent upon whom this process depends deals only in the supposed paratextual, in the confection of a text he believes – and wrongly according to Kundera – might constitute a welcome supplement for the reader. Kundera, in fact, constructs a false binary: one can have either the work in itself (a creative rebuilding of the life) or the writerly life, which is furnished by a reading that is nothing more than a misguided rebuilding of a rebuilding, now pointlessly demolished.

   In Kundera's imagining, the literary biographical is a parasitical form dependent on textual demolition, not the provision of an authorial context in which fabulation, acknowledged as a form of life writing, might be appreciated. But that the fictional can assist in the (re)making of the biographical establishes the potential reversibility of the fabulizing process; the novelist is a figure whose talent, thoughts, and experiences mark his work as original in the sense that an origin in the self proclaims a lack of origin. And yet the life – or, more accurately, the material for formal reorientation that living inevitably, and in this view solely, provides – is indispensably dispensable to an informed encounter with the resulting fiction. The blind spot of this insight, of course, is that the writer's life can be constructed for the reader in ways other than by textual demolition.

Interestingly, Kundera does not think the activity of the house-building writer as a form of imitation, for to do so would allow the life to be signified, however slantwise, by the work that somehow also embodies it; the house of fiction is built by him from experience, not to represent but contain it. Conceived as representation, however, the novelist's life would then constitute a parallel form of narrative in symbiosis with any fictional reimagining. For Kundera, what the writer experienced cannot be a useful point of reference that enables readers to approach the author written into the fiction. Author and form brought into more intimate contact would perhaps dismantle the freestanding, 'built' nature of the fictional house, reconfiguring it as a message cast in disposable form.

But what of the artist's life not as textualized but as lived? Writers in the public eye (one thinks of Mark Twain and Charles Dickens as useful early examples of a trend that has only accelerated) often determine to build two houses, so to speak, constructing a public persona meant to be of interest not only in itself, but also to be read against and with the fabulizing for which that life serves as a rich source. As performing selves, Twain and Dickens created rich, appealing, and ostentatiously physical versions of their writerly selves, which became particularly effective promptings for the kind of intrasubjective construct imagined by the Russian formalist thinker Boris Tomashevsky as necessary for any act of reading. The author's life in this sense is not an existential fact, but a complex image drawn from different sources that, as Tomashevsky argues, 'operates in the reader's consciousness … a traditional concomitant to artistic work.'[2] There are always intriguing (dis)connections between the artist 'made known' to readers through his living and revealed, tantalizingly if indirectly, in the body of works. 'The truth is,' literary biographer Leon Edel reminds us, 'that, however much we may isolate a picture on a wall and try to keep our eyes within its frame, we do not wholly lose our awareness of the wall or the adjacent pictures'. As Edel admonishes, 'the literary voice is not one of the "voices of silence"; it cannot be separated … from the speaker or from the listening world.'[3]

Even if they do not advertise themselves on the lecture circuit, as did Twain and Dickens, many writers foreground the relationship between speaker and literary voice, staging a continuing drama that unfolds in range of that 'listening world' of readers. Ernest Hemingway is a notable case in point. In his instructive history of celebrity, *The Frenzy of Renown: Fame and its History*, Leo Braudy argues that, like that notable 'aristocrat of the air', Charles Lindbergh, Hemingway worked diligently – and at great cost to his health – to construct his public image as that of the 'new, young American – strong, bold, without pretension', an ethos, anticipated by the writerly selves of Owen Wister and Jack London, that he represented formally in a 'spare, direct style that spoke of action, feeling, and the hard edges of things rather than their fretful nuances'.[4] The antithesis of drawing-room chroniclers like Henry James or William Dean Howells, Hemingway created characters who were 'often in quest of a cleansing adventure that would involve action, combat, and a stretching of the self beyond the comfortable limits of its civilization'.[5]

The truth of Hemingway's vision of the world was authenticated by his carefully self-promoting participation in the same quest for meaning that occupies his characters. This extraordinary life was lived, as Hemingway often reminded his readers, in aid of providing material for a series of fictional 'rebuildings' that referenced the same experiences. Through the lens of the creative act, the lived is brought into sharper, more vital focus, but this did not mean that readers should neglect the relevance of the truth-establishing contours of one of modern literature's best documented public lives. The appeal of fictional avatars like Frederic Henry (*A Farewell to Arms*), Nick Adams (in the series of stories in which he figures as protagonist), Robert Jordan (*For Whom the Bell Tolls*), and Thomas Hudson (*Islands in the Stream*), among others, is, in part, that the author offered himself as the model for their hard-won, rigorous standards of behaviour, their expert knowledge of how things work and how work should be accomplished, their susceptibility to life-changing romantic attachment, and, perhaps above all, their inclination toward a quixotic and often self-sacrificing idealism. In this rivalry between creator and created, the fictional side of the Hemingway phenomenon did not prove triumphant, never emerging as the dominant object of popular interest. In contrast, as Braudy observes of the American novelist, 'short of death, his heroes could rarely compete with the array of wounds, breaks, and bruises that year by year accumulated on Hemingway's own body'. The public self became the master "text" against which its various fictionalized configurations came to be closely read.

As Braudy argues, the result was that 'the man and his work' became 'as much of a "we" as Lindbergh and his plane', a twinned phenomenon that anticipated the way in which, in our currently highly mediatized culture, authors have become commodities that collapse any difference between self and works.[6] 'To become a celebrity is to become a brand name', complained novelist Philip Roth after the success of *Portnoy's Complaint* convinced the reading public that the author was one with the book's sex-obsessed protagonist.[7] And yet Roth in some sense embraced that depersonalizing reification, offering in his later fiction not only a thinly disguised version of himself struggling with the fact of notorious celebrity à la *Portnoy* (in his Nathan Zuckerman novels), but also a seemingly straightforward autobiographical reminiscence that paradoxically grounds the contrafactual speculations of *The Plot against America* in an accurately remembered childhood. The collapse in the public mind between the authorizing self and what is offered as a fabulized version of the same was, decades earlier, Hemingway's fate as well, which, perversely, he railed against while continuing to encourage the confusion, anticipating Roth's more playful and sardonic manufacturing of 'lived' selves.

By the 1930s, after the sensational success of both *The Sun Also Rises* and *A Farewell to Arms*, Hemingway had become one of American publishing's most marketable brand names, famed for his artistry.[8] Like all cultural stars, he was soon freighted with the paradoxical representation of key elements of the evolving national character, not the least of which was the connection that his well-publicized living (as a big game hunter and fisherman, as a risk-taking war correspondent, as a man enamoured of women and always in search of fulfilling romantic experience) ostentatiously established between manly derring-do and the quite different qualities required for its subsequent textual embodiment: moralizing intelligence, a keen eye cast on social experience and self, as well as the discipline to refrain, in order to write, from restless adventure. Made known to the public (if only in retrospect earlier in his career), his living was a gathering of the material that would authorize the essential truth of its subsequent representation, expressing the productive permeability between world and text that readers quickly found compelling. And yet his text-making found not only its source but a reinforcing parallel in this notorious living; they were both paths to the celebrity Hemingway craved and, having obtained, assiduously cultivated.

Thus the Hemingway text is metafictional in an interesting sense, depending upon a productive tension between the distancing, idealizing effects of fictionalization, with its confection of alternative selves, and its particularizing gesturing toward the life of the author. A writer who became, in some ways, as famous as the nation's most celebrated aviator (yet another thrill seeker), Hemingway in time saw his novels and stories sold to Hollywood. It was inevitable that movie producers would find these pre-sold properties irresistible, even as these works posed an interesting, if far from unique, challenge to the process of screen versioning. The film adaptation of literary texts customarily faces difficulties that are both institutional (for example, long novels must be abridged to suit commercial exhibition) and formal (for example, cinematic equivalents must be found for the distinctive tone of a narrative voice). But a more difficult problem is posed by the desire to represent (or make reference to) the author whose life stands behind these fictionalizations. In the early, and some later, screen versions of Hemingway's fiction, this possibility of metafictional resonance is ignored. *A Farewell to Arms* (dir. Frank Borzage, 1932), *For Whom the Bell Tolls* (dir. Sam Wood, 1943), *To Have and Have Not* (dir. Howard Hawks, 1944), *The Killers* (dir. Robert Siodmak, 1946), *The Macomber Affair* (dir. Zoltan Korda, 1947), *Under My Skin* (dir. Jean Negulesco, 1950) and *The Breaking Point* (dir. Michael Curtiz, 1950) offer nothing beyond different forms of the Hemingway type of hero. In the event, only *Farewell* and *Bell* are deeply autobiographical, but Hemingway is present in the film versions only through an implicit invocation of his public self; Gary Cooper, the star in both, emerges as a Hemingway hero (quietly passionate and interior, committed to violent action, concerned to live up to his image of himself, an American willingly marooned in an exotic landscape) rather than as a more personalized version of the author. Though often in the public eye because of his role as a war correspondent, Hemingway would only toward the end of the 1940s be transformed into the unpredictably irascible but often avuncular *eminence*, enjoying a middle age marked by increasing portliness and a substantial grey beard. Christened 'Papa Hemingway' by his admirer and collaborator, A.E. Hotchner, in the biography that crystallized his place in twentieth-century cultural history some five years after his suicide,[9] this version of the author has been etched so indelibly into the national imaginary that it is difficult to conjure him up in his earlier avatar as the darkly handsome and impressively athletic budding writer of short fiction, the supposedly starving artist of 1920s Paris provenance.

The post-war era witnessed a startling transformation in Hemingway's fortunes as his literary reputation suddenly and spectacularly peaked after a period of decline. The only modest success of *The Short Happy Life of Francis Macomber*, *Under My Skin* and *The Breaking Point* as well as the poor sales of, and even poorer critical reception accorded to, his long-awaited 1950 fictional treatment of World War II, *Across the River and Into the Trees*, seemed to promise a lessening of public interest. But this was not to be, as, beginning in the 1950s, the novelist's standing with both his readers and the literary establishment was to reach unexpected heights. This trend continued after his suicide in 1961, fuelled by the wildly successful publication in 1964 of a nearly completed project, the so-called 'Paris book' that his literary executor, fourth wife Mary Hemingway, entitled *A Moveable Feast*, following a suggestion by Hotchner.[10] Readers responded deeply to the evocation of an era increasingly idealized in literary history (the American émigré Paris of the 1920s) and to the author's deeply felt, almost maudlin nostalgia for a *temps perdu* (a theme embraced by the national literary culture and played for gently satiric laughs in Woody Allen's 2010 film *Midnight in Paris*). This now-golden past is dominated not only by a remembered sense of deep dedication to the development of a distinctive writerly style, but by Hemingway's failure, as the result of a disastrous extramarital dalliance, to keep his marriage to Hadley Richardson intact. This is a loss that the older and wiser self of the book sees as an occasion for great regret.

Responding in the next twenty-five years to this renewed celebrity, Hollywood managed to find ways in three key adaptations to screen the author along with his text(s). The screen versions of *The Snows of Kilimanjaro* (dir. Henry King, 1952), *Hemingway's Adventures of a Young Man* (dir. Martin Ritt, 1962), and *Islands in the Stream* (dir. Franklin J. Schaffner, 1977) do not simply reconfigure literary fiction in cinematic form. In these cases, the filmmakers found ways to signify, or even contain, the author's authenticating presence, rewriting the fictional narrative to push it further toward the hagiography that the viewing public was now presumed eager to consume and which the novelist in his own way had long been seeking. This approach to adapting Hemingway is best illustrated by what Hollywood did with his most celebrated short story, 'Snows'. Eager to repeat the effective formula of this biographical adaptation, a few years later filmmakers followed this same approach with less success in *Adventures*. This later project was based on Hotchner's turning selected Nick Adams stories into something of a biographical narrative, reinforced at points by references to commonly discussed aspects of Hemingway's life, including not only his service in the Italian ambulance corps during World War I, but also his problematic relationship with an overbearing and controlling mother. It is the melodramatized 'escape' from that parental trap that gives *Adventures* a bildungsroman conclusion. As its title suggests, the film offers viewers not only a bricolage of fictional elements drawn from Hemingway's short fiction (and in some respects from *Farewell* as well), but also a somewhat sensationalized biography. Henry King's *Kilimanjaro* did more honour to both Hemingway's writing and his extraordinary life.

'Not my complete works': *The Snows of Kilimanjaro*

Hemingway did not take the trouble to review Casey Robinson's script before production began, and so he was shocked and more than a little peeved when he attended a viewing of *The Snows of Kilimanjaro*, which had ostensibly adapted from his famous short story of the same name, first published in *The Fifth Column and the First Forty-Nine Stories* (1938). 'I sold Fox a single story,' the author fumed, 'not my complete works. This movie has something from nearly every story I ever wrote in it'.[11] As was his wont, Hemingway exaggerated for rhetorical effect, but he was not far wrong. Certainly, material from some of his other stories was incorporated into the film. An early episode, for example, derives from 'The End of Something', one of the author's better-known Nick Adams stories. But Hemingway would have been justified in complaining that the script Robinson constructed recycles characters and incidents from three of his best-known novels: *The Sun Also Rises* (1926), *A Farewell to Arms* (1929) and *For Whom the Bell Tolls* (1943). In his version of *Snows*, screenwriter Robinson creates a love interest named Cynthia for the story's main character, the writer Harry, and in doing so offers an intriguing and complex mixture of otherwise heterogeneous Hemingway elements.

Cynthia is quite obviously modelled on Lady Brett Ashley from *Sun*. Both are sympathetic versions of the new woman whose vivacity and allure allow her to enjoy the sexual and intellectual freedom of the age; both are associated with Paris (where Cynthia meets Harry, who is a journalist and writer, like Hemingway himself). Echoing *Sun*'s portrait of a self-indulgent 'lost' generation, the film presents Paris as one of the era's more permissive environments, a world of seemingly endless alcohol-fuelled café nights, where no harm attends a chequered romantic history. In fact, a failed relationship or two, even a distinct whiff of promiscuity confers instead a compelling form of appeal on Cynthia. The couple's love affair, obviously soon consummated after a chance meeting in a café, leads to a cohabitation that is never sanctioned by marriage. This was a plot development that involved the bending of the Production Code, still very much in effect at the time in Hollywood, and it reflected Hemingway's racy, if always carefully vague (he was no D.H. Lawrence), handling of pre-marital sex in all of his novels, one of the most attractively controversial aspects of his fiction-making. It is worth noting that Cynthia is played, and convincingly, by Ava Gardner, who is cast, and once again appropriately, as Brett in the 1957 film version of *The Sun Also Rises*, also directed by Henry King, who can hardly have missed the resemblance between the two characters when taking on the job of adapting the famous novel.

These resemblances are worth documenting. Although a playgirl committed at first only to her own pleasure, Cynthia's eventual desire to have a family and domesticate Harry in *Kilimanjaro* destroys their relationship. Subsequently, she displays a yen for political commitment when civil war breaks out in Spain. She volunteers to assist the cause of democracy as an ambulance driver and nurse on the Republican side, thereby in effect conflating the main characters of *A Farewell to Arms*: not only Frederic Henry, the American ambulance driver volunteer, but also Catherine, the nurse he falls in love with. Cynthia and Harry had parted when the pair was travelling in Spain, particularly to attend the bullfights, and she had gone off with a young matador, once again recalling central elements in the narrative of *Sun*. Sometime later, Harry returns to Spain to find her, joins the Republican cause himself, and the two enjoy a battlefield reunion. She dies in his arms, and this destroys the possibility of their future happiness in a finale that recalls the tragic ending of *Farewell*. That this poignant, if somewhat improbably melodramatic, series of events unfolds during the Spanish Civil War of course cannot help but recall *Bell*. Itself a kind of reprise of *Farewell*, *Bell* also features a doomed romantic relationship between the politically committed American who travels to Spain to defend the cause of another people and the Spanish Republican partisan, Maria.

It is easy enough to understand Robinson's dilemma as he tackled writing the screenplay for *Kilimanjaro*. He was faced with adapting what had already become the best known and most admired story from one of the country's most famous practitioners of that genre. His screenplay had to discover a way of expanding the undramatic materials of a tale that offers more an account of feelings than action: a writer, dying of gangrene on African safari, reviews the important events of his life in a series of poetically composed interior monologues, passing judgment on both his romantic and also his professional failures, even as he reconciles himself to the inalterability of the gruesome fate that awaits him. In the story, Harry is not a version of Hemingway, but of the failed writer, full of self-loathing, that Hemingway might have become in his second marriage to the well-off Pauline Pfeiffer, had he surrendered his artistic gift in order to enjoy the life of ease and expensive diversion she could have provided. As is generally recognized, the story is deeply autobiographical, drawing on an actual incident that occurred during the African safari largely funded by his wife that Hemingway made in 1933. It ended with the author, gravely ill, being airlifted from the campsite for medical treatment at a nearby hospital.

At the beginning of the 1950s, Hemingway was more celebrated for authoring the three best-selling novels just discussed, and their popularity must have had something to do with Robinson's decision to confect the character of Cynthia and the events in which she is involved by drawing on notable elements from them. And yet Hemingway's reputation as a writer of short fiction was well established early in his career and had an enduring life of its own. It is worth remarking that the *Fifth Column* collection in which 'Snows' had first been published was preceded by four other anthologies of stories reprinted from magazines, with the first, *Three Stories and Ten Poems*, appearing in 1923 even before Hemingway had begun to make a name for himself as a novelist with the sensational release of *Sun*. The republication of selected early stories in *Fifth Column* was followed thirteen years later in 1961 by yet another collection of short republished fiction: *The Snows of Kilimanjaro and Other Stories*. As its exploitation as a headlining item by the publisher suggests, 'Snows' was a property that was still pre-sold even more than a decade after its original publication, and it might have proved commercially disastrous to alter its structure too radically, harming or perhaps even destroying its appeal. So, in writing his screenplay, Robinson had to expand without adding anything that would have seemed inauthentic in terms of the author's well-known ideas and values. Because he borrows liberally from other works by the same author, the screenwriter can hardly be accused of plagiarism in the normal sense, but such appropriation was unusual enough, perhaps even spectacular. Undeniably, as the novelist himself recognized, *Snows* became a multi-level bricolage of Hemingway images and motifs that alludes to the most popular of his novels, while providing what was, in many ways, a faithful version of his most famous piece of short fiction.

However, there is another way to describe this screen versioning. In the story, Harry's experiences parallel only roughly those of the author, while in the film Harry is transformed into an unmistakable, if idealized, version of the Hemingway so well known to the American public of the era (Figure 8.1). The particular form that Robinson's fictional stew assumed suggests that the screenwriter had in mind not only solving the problem of expanding undramatic material from a short story into a feature film. Drawing on fictional

Figure 8.1 Hemingway's authorial presence is conspicuously refracted through central character Harry (Gregory Peck) in *The Snows of Kilimanjaro* (dir. Henry King, 1952).

sources that had already been established in the public mind as deeply autobiographical, *Snows* became a film that clearly referenced the famous Ernest Hemingway whose hunting expeditions in Africa, whose sympathies for the Spanish Republican cause and heroic career as an ambulance driver on the Italian front in World War I, whose boyhood spent in the deep woods of Michigan, and whose early career in Paris as a journalist and struggling author were the essential markers of a writerly life like no other. None of these touch points is omitted in *Snows*.

A concern with personal voice and self, moreover, dominates in a series of effective voice-overs that reproduce the story's interior monologues. Their constant subject is sardonic self-criticism, centring on the question of how to live properly; this is a theme picked up from the story, but made much more prominent in the screenplay, which in an early flashback provides Harry with an avuncular relative (Leo G. Carroll) who advises him against romantic entanglements that might compromise his writerly career. By 1950, Hemingway's dedication to the pursuit of adventure and to his writings was transforming him into an authority on the purpose-driven life, a reputation soon to be cemented by his poignant rendering, also largely in interior monologue, of a heroic struggle endured by a simple fisherman in the novella *The Old Man and the Sea* (1952). The release that year of the film version of *Snows*, which is meditative in the same sense, strongly expressed Hemingway's constant insistence on the strict code that should guide the behaviour of the honourable man who intends to fulfil what he understands is his reason for living (the struggle for authenticity that has become a cliché of the Hemingway style). Interestingly, his reputation as a writer concerned with the question of how to live well endures, as demonstrated by such recent publications as *The Good Life According to Hemingway* (2008), a coffee-table volume, assembled by Hotchner, that weaves together vignettes and memorable quotations in order to construct the author as a kind of folksy philosopher, who embraces recklessness and monumental drinking even as he lives a life conforming to traditional male values, especially as tested in big-game hunting and fishing.[12] It is impossible to imagine similar volumes devoted to other American novelists, even those whose fiction takes up pressing moral questions. *The Good Life According to F. Scott Fitzgerald? The Good Life According to William Faulkner?* A tragic version of this form of Hemingway's self (the writer as self-defeating, self-betraying, too attached to the comforts a woman can offer, too devoted to indulgence) dominates in 'Snows', as Harry simply runs out of time before he can complete the writing to which he should have more properly devoted his life. In contrast, the film provides Harry with a physical, spiritual and romantic cure, thus offering the kind of happy ending that Hollywood generally required but – and this is the crucial point – also constructing its Harry (now a thinly-disguised Hemingway portrayed, unsurprisingly, by one of the era's most darkly handsome and sensitive male leads, Gregory Peck), as a man whose drive for writerly perfection is renewed after a period of artistic blockage and who finally succeeds in his quest for satisfying romance with a woman able to be his equal companion in dangerous adventure.

The film's version of Hemingway in effect answers two of the questions that his public life had been posing for some years. Would Hemingway repeat the success he had achieved in the 1930s as a bestselling novelist? Would the man whose first three marriages, the last two of which had ended in well-publicized bitter, recrimination-filled divorces, find happiness at last with wife number four (Mary Welsh, whom he married in 1946)? A spunky reporter whom Hemingway found delightful as a hunting and fishing companion, Mary Welsh Hemingway seems clearly evoked by *Kilimanjaro*'s Helen (Susan Hayward), the latest wife accompanying Harry on the doomed safari. It is Helen who literally saves Harry from dying by heroically lancing the gangrenous boil on his leg, shooting game for the party to eat and patiently supporting Harry in his desire to regain his spiritual and writerly balance. These are elements that Robinson added to the story's very thin portrayal of Harry's rich wife. In the film, when the long-expected plane arrives to take Harry to hospital, the moment is anti-climactic. Through the aid of a caring and capable woman and his own considerable capacity for self-criticism, Harry has already been saved from the rot, both physical and spiritual, that was killing him.

Robinson's screenplay establishes the doomed Cynthia as the love of Harry's life, but the plot also posits Helen as someone capable of taking her place, giving Harry in effect a second chance at romantic happiness and a proper balance between self-indulgence and the pursuit of literary excellence. Two scenes set in Paris after Cynthia's death effectively anticipate the ending. In the first, a dismayed Harry sees Helen getting into a car and accosts her, thinking against hope that it is Cynthia. A later night-time meeting sees this mistaken wish come true. A drunken Harry contemplates leaping from the Pont Neuf, but he surrenders his thoughts of suicide when Helen fortuitously turns up and manages to blunt the pain of his grief. Harry's problem is that he does not fully accept Helen's love until he lies dying and she saves him once again. None of this is in the original story, where the female figures are drawn only sketchily. *Snows* hints at a renewal of creative energies for Hemingway after a decade marked by a distinct lack of productivity featuring only one novel (and an inferior one at that). The career revival predicted in *Snows* was already in full swing because of the sensation aroused by the publication of *Old Man* when that film hit the nation's theatres in 1958. Hemingway received the Pulitzer Prize the same year, establishing beyond further argument a literary greatness that had seemed in jeopardy only a few years before. It was a recovery every bit as remarkable as that of the author's avatar in *Snows*. In the Hemingway manner that screenwriter Casey Robinson so effectively assumed, Harry is rescued by the kind of grace under pressure that the author admired, especially in the woman whom he expected to share a life of adventure as his equal in braving danger. *The Snows of Kilimanjaro* suited perfectly the era's developing image of the older and wiser novelist.

Coda: *Islands in the Stream*

If the 1950s began with an extraordinary renewal of Hemingway's reputation, and the promise of a more satisfying romantic relationship, the decade ended badly. The marriage deteriorated, while his many injuries and self-destructive drinking led to a series of health problems and, finally, to an inability to continue writing. His career seemingly finished, Hemingway saw no reason to go on living and committed suicide in 1961. Inglorious and almost pathetic, this finale hardly suited the image of the writer that emerged, helped by his own considerable participation, in the 'frenzy of renown' that had caught him up during his early career and had transformed him into one of the country's most notable and admired public figures. A heroic death eluded him. Interestingly, however, along with hundreds of other partly completed works, he left behind an unfinished novel whose two sections his widow Mary assembled and edited for publication (the third part of this 'sea novel' had been published independently as *The Old Man and the Sea*). While the work, as it was presented to the public in 1970, hardly reflected the author's structural intentions (Mary had incorporated an independent short story, 'Islands in the Stream', to compensate for the earlier excision), *Islands in the Stream* pointed toward the possibility of a different ending for the writer, one more suited to the image of himself he had carefully constructed. Mary may not have realized it, but *Islands* was in many ways a suitable epitaph, a culminating image in its fictionalized autobiography of the artist who had entranced two generations of readers with his fiction and two generations of Americans with the high adventures of his living.

Islands' protagonist, Thomas Hudson, is a painter who, after a tumultuous personal life, has sought solitary refuge on the island of Bimini, where he devotes himself to his work and, in moderated fashion, to the pleasures of drinking and male companionship. A transforming event is the arrival of his sons, from two failed marriages, for a summer visit. Having reconnected with the boys, Hudson learns not long after their return to the mainland of their deaths in a car accident. Deeply saddened, he gives himself over to a long period of mournful inaction in a Havana where he haunts local bars and seeks solace in conversation and drink; in Cuba he learns of the death of his eldest son in the war. Eventually, he takes up a semi-official assignment from the US Navy to track German submarines in the area; in a fire fight with submariners who have just massacred a village of Cubans, Hudson is wounded, perhaps fatally, and the novel ends with an interior monologue in which he talks to himself, in the manner of Robert Jordan at the end of *Bell*, chronicling his accomplishments and failures and clinging to a desperate hope for the future even as life drains from him:

> You can paint the sea better than anyone now if you will do it and not get mixed up in other things. Hang on good now to how you truly want to do it. You must hold hard to life to do it. But life is a cheap thing beside a man's work.[13]

The novel's last section contains some of Hemingway's finest 'philosophical' writing. Reflecting that meditative mood, Franklin J. Schaffner's 1977 film adaptation of the novel deepens the biographical references and improves on its idealizing wish fulfilment, providing viewers with a fictionalized finale that is truer to the writerly self that had emerged in both *Farewell* and *Bell* decades before. The film's Hudson is incarnated by a George C. Scott who resembles with remarkable closeness the Papa Hemingway of the 1950s. Hudson is roused from his isolating self-concern not just by the arrival of his three sons, whom he successfully introduces to his manly world. In a notable sequence, the middle son, Davy (Michael James-Wixted) harbouring resentment against the father who deserted him, shows his mettle in a game fishing sequence reminiscent of the encounter with the giant marlin in *Old Man* that assuages at least some of his disappointment. In the film's middle sequence, which owes nothing to the novel, Hudson is visited by his first wife Audrey (Claire Bloom). Still deeply in love with each other, the couple is divided by the memory of Hudson's faithlessness, which, despite his sorrow and deep apologies, prevents any but the most unhappy of reconciliations. They embrace when Hudson suddenly realizes she has not come to resume a love affair whose passion has never died, but instead to tell him of the horrific death of their son Tom (Hart Bochner), who had been flying with the RAF.

The film's finale does not detail the improbable and foolish sub-chasing presented in the novel (based on Hemingway's own experiences with self-appointed international vigilantism), and it rightly ignores the interminable bar-room scenes that slow the novel's middle sections to a tortuous crawl. Instead, Schaffner constructs a more poignant and fitting finale for the artist who has finally come to grips with the pain caused by his weakness and neglect, by his selfish devotion to his talent and his inconstant pleasures. Interestingly, the model for this section seems to be another Hemingway property, at least of a sort: John Huston's adaptation of the novella *To Have and Have Not* (1944), which features the conversion of the hitherto self-concerned main character, fishing boat owner, Harry Morgan (Humphrey Bogart), into a patriot devoted to the Allied war effort. Hemingway had seen this novel transformed into yet another version of the eminently popular *Casablanca* (dir. Michael Curtiz, 1942), and he would perhaps have been amused to see Thomas Hudson become, like Morgan, a would-be rescuer of those dispossessed by the war. Morgan survives his transport of French Resistance leaders to a Vichy-dominated Martinique, but Hudson dies while attempting to land Jewish refugees in Cuba. Death comes only after he escapes his self-imposed isolation, re-establishing himself as his sons' father and admitting his guilt for the collapse of his marriage to Audrey. If in the novel, Hudson's last thoughts, like those of Harry in 'Snows', are mostly on an artistic vocation still unfulfilled, in the film the dying artist thinks of those he loves: an imagined reunion in which Audrey and all the boys are present. In the midst of a terrible tragedy that deepens his sense of an ungrasped opportunity for a fuller life, Hudson is at least able to confess his love for her and receive hers in return. The sense of loss that haunts the confessional *A Moveable Feast* finds moving, dramatic expression in the film, if not in the source novel, as a reunion of sorts is staged with fabulized, if recognizable, versions of first wife Hadley and son John. An older, wiser Papa finds the 'good' death that had always eluded him, as a house of fiction, constructed by Hemingway, wife Mary, and screenwriter Schaffner, emerges to embody and reference the remarkable life that was his, and provide it with a fitting finale.

Notes

1. M. Kundera, *The Art of the Novel* (New York: HarperCollins, 2000), p. 146.
2. B. Tomashevsky, 'Literature and Biography', in L. Matejka and K. Pomorska (eds.) *Readings in Russian Poetics* (Cambridge, MA: MIT Press, 1971), p. 47.
3. L. Edel, *Literary Biography* (New York: Anchor Books, 195, [1957]), p. xiii.
4. L. Braudy, *The Frenzy of Renown: Fame and its History* (New York: Oxford University Press, 1986), pp. 25–6.
5. Braudy (1986), p. 26.
6. Braudy (1986), pp. 25–6.
7. Quoted in J. Moran, *Star Authors in America* (London: Pluto Press, 2000), p. 101.
8. For full details see the very readable account in L.J. Leff, *Hemingway and his Conspirators: Hollywood, Scribners, and the Making of American Celebrity Culture* (New York: Rowman & Littlefield, 1997).
9. A.E. Hotchner, *Papa Hemingway: A Personal Memoir* (New York: Random House, 1966).
10. The enduring power of this book is suggested by Woody Allen's *Midnight in Paris* (2011), which offers a cinematic homage to both the memoir and the literary/artistic circle of émigré Americans, including F. Scott Fitzgerald and Gertrude Stein, who are Hemingway's subjects.
11. Quoted in G.D. Phillips, *Hemingway and Film* (University of Michigan: Ungar, 1980), p. 6.
12. A.E. Hotchner, *The Good Life According to Hemingway* (New York: Ecco, 2008).
13. E. Hemingway, *Islands in the Stream* (New York: Scribner, 1970), p. 444.

9

Becoming Jane in screen adaptations of Austen's fiction

Deborah Cartmell

Austen's popularity as a novelist has always been, for better or worse, intertwined with her mystique as a single woman. The fact that she left so little evidence of her personal self behind has led readers to seek in her fiction clues reflecting the author's own life. This stubborn refusal to free the author from her fiction is especially present in adaptations of the two novels that provide bookends to her career: *Pride and Prejudice* and *Persuasion*,[1] variously interpreted on film and television as portraits of the author as a young and middle-aged woman. In the BBC television biopic, *Miss Austen Regrets* (dir. Jeremy Lovring, 2008), the attempt by Austen's niece, Fanny, to prevent Cassandra Austen from destroying her sister's letters (as she did in real life) is met with the response: 'You still believe there is a secret love story to uncover?' Cassandra implies that such a quest would damage the reputation of her sister. Fanny, however, is not alone in her belief in an undisclosed love story and this television biopic both denies and affirms the existence of such a story. Rather than telling the story of a single woman's triumph in an overwhelmingly patriarchal society, as it seems to gesture towards in its opening stages, *Miss Austen Regrets* falls into the biopic trap of presenting writing as inextricably connected with love. The film therefore implicitly presents Austen's writings as the by-products of an unfulfilled life, with female authorship the consolation for a failure to produce her own personal love story.

The belief in a secret Austen love story and the need to fill in the numerous gaps in Austen's biography is covertly present in the so-called 'straight' adaptations of Austen's fiction. In its focus on the failed opportunities of its central character's youth, the narrative of *Miss Austen Regrets* is closest to *Persuasion*. However this Austen (Olivia Williams) is no angel in the house. There has been a longstanding tendency to view the long-suffering heroine of Austen's last novel, the repressed romantic Anne Elliot, as a self-portrait of Austen herself. Anne Thackeray's comments of 1871, the year after the publication of the biography (or hagiography), the *Memoir of Jane Austen* by the author's nephew, James Edward Austen-Leigh, illustrate this tendency with particular clarity:

> Anne Elliot must have been Jane Austen herself, speaking for the last time. There is something so true, so womanly, about her, that it is impossible not to love her. She is the bright-eyed heroine of the earlier novels, matured, chastened, cultivated, to whom fidelity has brought only greater depth and sweetness instead of bitterness and pain.[2]

Thackeray's biographical reading of the novels chimes uncannily well with the portrayal of the writer on screen from 1940 to the new millennium.

As I have demonstrated elsewhere, 'straight' screen adaptations of *Pride and Prejudice* have shown a noticeable tendency to interpret the novel as autobiography.[3] At the beginning of Robert Z. Leonard's 1940 adaptation – the first major screen adaptation of Austen – Elizabeth, played by Greer Garson (in her mid 30s and by today's standards, a disturbingly old Elizabeth Bennet), is positioned looking out of the window, the film objectifying her as a piece of art or a fictional creation, framing her for us to look at. Elizabeth continues to be shown by windows in the latter half of the film too, but now with a modestly signalled but significant adjustment in point of view: the audience increasingly looks *with* rather than *at* her, the perspective shift discretely moving her from 'character', to be looked at, to 'author', to be looked with. Joe Wright's 2005 film begins, in contrast, with Elizabeth (Keira Knightley) looking in through the window, set apart from her family as an outside observer, while by the end of the film, she is on the inside looking out. And, as in the earlier film, she is implicitly likened to Rapunzel in her prison, waiting for her knight in shining armour to release her, but also like the Greer Garson Elizabeth, in control of the (authorial) gaze. This Elizabeth shares the omniscient author's ability both to objectify her family and to articulate the novel's prevailing sense of domestic entrapment, both of which are major challenges to screen adaptation.

The 2005 film begins with a steadicam shot following Elizabeth up the garden path to Longbourn. This enables Elizabeth to introduce the film through a reading of a novel, closing the book as she draws near her home, with a sigh of pleasure. The book's presence at the beginning of the film calls attention to the movie as an adaptation, with a referential nod to the Disney technique (discussed, for example, by Richard Burt in Chapter 10, this volume) of commencing a film with the opening of a book that metamorphoses into moving pictures, intimating that the moving images to come will be even more magical than the book upon which it is based. Close inspection (discoverable only on DVD pause) reveals the book to be *Pride and Prejudice* itself, a witty declaration of the film's source and status as an adaptation. Additionally the presence of the book may serve as intertextual reference to the Bollywood-style *Bride and Prejudice* (dir. Gurinder Chadha,

2004), a film which uses the same trick, with the Elizabeth figure, Lalita (Aishwarya Rai Bachchan), reading *Pride and Prejudice* on the beach in the company of Darcy (Martin Henderson) and the Caroline Bingley figure, Kiran (Indira Varma). David Roche reads this meta-adaptive moment in Joe Wright's film as an announcement of the film's infidelity to Austen: the adaptation will leave the book behind to create something new.[4] However, Elizabeth's possession and absorption of the book (and of her own story) also establish a discrete connection between author and heroine. Hence the two film versions of *Pride and Prejudice* (1940 and 2005) invite a subtle identification between Jane Austen and her central character, implicitly 'reading' the novel as concealed autobiography. In Leonard's *Pride and Prejudice* the book's famous first line ('It is a truth universally acknowledged, that a single man in possession of a good fortune, must be in want of a wife')[5] is visualized through images of the women shopping and ogling the new male arrivals in the town, giving expression to the binary oppositions of love and materialism, or shopping and courtship present in Austen's celebrated opening.[6] By contrast, the line is absent from Joe Wright's 2005 film. Wright adopts other strategies for associating Elizabeth with her author, especially through the emphasis on Elizabeth's eyes (or the speaking 'I' with the seeing 'eye'). The film is dominated by half face shots of Elizabeth's (Keira Knightley's) eyes, referencing Darcy's attraction to Elizabeth's 'fine eyes' ('I have been meditating on the very great pleasure which a pair of fine eyes in the face of a pretty woman can bestow')[7] while often allowing the viewer to see the fictional world through these same eyes, that is to share Elizabeth's point of view.

In a similar, if not quite so obvious manner, the BBC TV adaptations of *Pride and Prejudice* of 1980 and 1995 both encourage comparisons between Austen and Elizabeth by giving versions of Jane Austen's famous opening line to Elizabeth. In the 1980 mini-series adaptation (dir. Cyril Coke), the line is divided between Charlotte Lucas and Elizabeth (linking the materialistic with the romantic characters' views on marriage), while in the 1995 version (dir. Simon Langton), Elizabeth speaks the line, thus being invited to share the ironic perception of Austen's narrator in partial mockery of Mrs Bennet's ambitions. Meanwhile, Mrs Bennet's enthusiastic nodding in decidedly unironic response to Elizabeth's declaration acts as the convenient foil to emphasize the aligned superiority of Elizabeth and the narrator and their shared remove from too sullying an involvement in the commerciality of marriage.

The implicit associations previously drawn between Elizabeth and Austen are nowhere more explicit than in the biopic *Becoming Jane* (dir. Julian Jarrold, 2007) that can be interpreted as a logical extension of previous adaptations' strategies to unite central character and author. The Romantic notion that art is inspired by love is strikingly central to many films depicting the life of an author. While normally despised by both film and literary critics for being both notoriously inaccurate and crudely formulaic, 'author biopics' continue to be a popular source of entertainment in the early twenty-first century, given the list of titles, including *Iris* (dir. Richard Eyre, 2001), *The Hours* (dir. Stephen Daldry, 2002), *Sylvia* (dir. Christine Jeffs, 2003), *Finding Neverland* (dir. Marc Forster, 2004), *Miss Potter* (dir. Chris Noonan, 2006) and *Bright Star* (dir. Jane Campion, 2009). *Becoming Jane* fits effortlessly into the author biopic template which focuses on the 'becoming' of the author, concentrating on life-defining moments involving a conflict between 'true love' and art and the sacrifice that this entails. The film opens with Jane reading an excerpt of her work to a family party (after which she overhears the hero contemptuously dismissing it – 'Well, accomplished enough, perhaps, but a metropolitan mind may be less susceptible to extended juvenile self-regard' – echoing Darcy's famous overheard rebuke of Elizabeth in *Pride and Prejudice*); it ends with a mature and now successful Jane reading to an enthralled audience, including an enraptured hero. Jane has completed her canon; she begins the film as Elizabeth Bennet and ends it as Anne Elliot, sacrificing love for what she perceives to be the greater good and taking consolation in her fame as a leading novelist. However, while the film celebrates her as both novelistic character and novelist, it also hints that for this novelist, the life of an unmarried writer was second choice.

It is undeniably the case that screen adaptations of Austen and scholarly work on Austen adaptations are second in quantity only to those of Shakespeare. Similarities between Shakespeare's most famous film biography, *Shakespeare in Love* (dir. John Madden, 1998), and *Becoming Jane* (2007) have to be more than just coincidental.[8] In *Shakespeare in Love*, *Romeo and Juliet* and *Twelfth Night* are adapted by screenwriters Marc Norman and Tom Stoppard who rewrite, and reconceive, the little we know about Shakespeare's life to reflect an author who writes from the heart, his most powerful expressions inspired by the personal experience of love. As Richard Burt argues, while critiquing mass culture, *Shakespeare in Love* depends 'on a very conventional way of representing literary authorship: Shakespeare's composition is privatized, and the sonnets and plays about love are granted a privileged generic status precisely because they are to be read as autobiographical documents'.[9] *Becoming Jane* similarly romanticizes authorship by depicting 'real life' inspiration, privatizing Austen's fiction by 'reducing' it to personal reflections on the self, something akin to diary entries. The similarities between *Shakespeare in Love* and *Becoming Jane*, especially the fetishization of the authors' telltale inky fingers, are impossible to miss. Even the publicity images are noticeably alike, dominated by embracing lovers with a tiny picture of the author below them – a composition visually suggestive of a love triangle: an author caught between the love of her/his life and the demands of art.[10]

While *Becoming Jane* emulates *Shakespeare in Love*'s design as an obvious marketing ploy to capture a similar audience, it takes the symbolism a stage further. In the main image of Anne Hathaway's Jane and James McAvoy's

Tom, the lovers are literally separated by the pen in Jane's hand. The pen (or quill in the case of *Shakespeare in Love*) is a defining image of both biopics, symbolic of frustrated desire as well as a rival or replacement desire (see Figure 9.1). Shakespeare's account to the apothecary, alchemist, astro-loger, seer, interpreter of dreams, and priest of psyche, Dr. Moth (Anthony Sher) of his inability to write is an obvious confession of sexual impotence and confirmation of the biopic's compression of romantic/erotic love and authorship:

> I have lost my gift.
>   not finding this easy)
> It's as if my quill is broken. As if
> the organ of the imagination has dried
> up. As if the proud tower of my genius
> has collapsed.[11]

Becoming Jane similarly insists upon a vital connection between artistic inspiration and 'true love'. It also focuses very much on the pen in the hand, an image which, as Graham Holderness has demonstrated in the opening chapter of *Nine Lives of William Shakespeare* (2011), has become symbolic of the writer himself:

> The image dovetails with our romantic idea of the writer, physically engaged in putting words on paper, transferring thoughts and emotions from the mind, via the muscles and nerves of arm and finger, through the writing implement that makes immediate contact with the paper.[12]

Figure 9.1   Still from *Becoming Jane* (dir. Julian Jarrold: Hanway/Miramax, 2007).

Holderness demonstrates how the quill has become virtually synonymous with the writer, a must-have souvenir for visitors to Stratford-upon-Avon, somehow ambient of Shakespeare himself. Consequently, it is the key image in biopics from *Shakespeare in Love* (1998) (Figure 9.2) to *Anonymous* (dir. Roland Emmerich, 2011) whose poster features the Earl of Oxford (Rhys Ifans) – in this film, the true author of Shakespeare's plays – from behind, ink splatters encircling him, with a quill tellingly featured in his right hand. The quill functions to reveal that this is the figure of the writer, the 'real Shakespeare'.

Becoming Jane is an adaptation of *Pride and Prejudice* insofar as it magnifies parallels between Jane Austen's life and the novel. The film is set just prior to 1796 when the novel, originally entitled *First Impressions*, was begun. As well as an adaptation of Austen's novel and of numerous other film adaptations of her work, the film is also an adaptation of Jon Spence's biography of the author, *Becoming Jane Austen* (2003), in which Spence contends that *Pride and Prejudice* was inspired by the novelist's relationship with Tom Lefroy, the Irish nephew of Jane Austen's friend and neighbour. Tom Lefroy, Spence writes, 'did not dwindle into insignificance: he found his natural place in her imagination, and remained there for the rest of her life'.[13] Like *Shakespeare in Love*, this film leaves no doubt about the author's sexuality (and her reasons for not marrying); and ultimately the prospect that Jane can exist without a man is quickly dashed in the closing sequence, coming hard on the heels of the scene of the lovers' parting. At the close of the film, the circling shot of the painted ceiling, adorned with putti, accompanied by the music of Mozart, momentarily plants the impression in the audience's mind that we are in Heaven. But no, Tom Lefroy's reappearance, several years later, completes the circle with Jane finally satisfied in the knowledge that she is, more than ever, appreciated by the man she once loved. Rather than the author being celebrated for her work alone, the revelation of Tom's

Figure 9.2   Still from *Shakespeare in Love* (dir. John Madden: Universal/Miramax, 1998).

daughter's name, 'Jane', provides the film with its romantic climax and, possibly, that which this Jane regards as her finest work.

Associating the heroine of the story with Austen herself is not an approach confined to *Pride and Prejudice*. Most prominently, Frances O'Connor's Fanny Price in *Mansfield Park* (dir. Patricia Rozema, 1999) invites comparisons between author and heroine via the addition of an authorial role for Fanny; however it is Elizabeth alone who allows for a far more glamorous portrait of the artist as a young woman. Such screen readings, which defiantly write the historical Austen into her fictions, making Austen 'more becoming', are in diametrical opposition to André Bazin's observation that adaptations can only be valued once we cast off what is, after all, a very modern and possibly flawed idea of the author.

Anticipating Roland Barthes's 'The death of the author' (1968), Bazin writing twenty years earlier, asserts:

> The ferocious defense of literary works is, to a certain extent, aesthetically justified; but we must also be aware that it rests on a rather recent, individualistic conception of the 'author' and of the 'work', a conception that was far from being ethically rigorous in the seventeenth century and that started to become legally defined only at the end of the eighteenth.[14]

For Robert Stam, the poststructuralist devalorization of the author enables us – as adaptation critics – to look at adaptations not as a quest to uncover 'the "spirit" or "self-presence" of "authorial intention"', but 'as orchestrations of discourses, talents, and tracks, a "hybrid" construction mingling different media and discourses and collaborations'.[15] But while we, as critics, might approach adaptations by determinedly downplaying the role of the author and, consequently, the 'original', these screen readings of Jane Austen ostensibly do the reverse; inflating the figure of the author and fleshing her out in her central characters.

Paradoxically, the biopic – in particular the film biography of an author – uses genre both to kill and resurrect the author. Unperturbed by concerns over the intentional and affective fallacies that so revolutionized the manner in which literature was interpreted in the mid-twentieth century, screen adaptations of Austen's work seem to doggedly cling to old-fashioned biographical approaches to fiction that equate interpretation with finding out 'truths' about the author. The attraction of this approach to fiction and to literary biography is summarized by John Worthen in terms that could equally apply to the biopic:

> The fact that we *want* an emergent sense of the inevitable development suggests the enormously soothing quality which biographies have come to have in our age. Not only do biographies suggest that things as difficult as human lives can – for all their obvious complexity – be summed up, known, comprehended: they reassure us that, while we are reading,

a world will be created in which there are few or no unclear motives, muddled decisions, or (indeed) loose ends.[16]

This need for an author is almost always present in adaptations of Austen's fiction, even in the 'adaptation-savvy' 2008 TV mini-series, *Lost in Austen* (dir. Dan Zeff), in which Elizabeth's absence from her world is explained by the fact that she is away writing a book, a book that is, almost certainly, *Pride and Prejudice* itself. Elizabeth, the most modern, knowing and allusive character in *Lost in Austen*, can be seen as yet another portrait of the artist as a young woman.

While *Pride and Prejudice* has been adapted into two major films, several television adaptations and numerous spin-offs,[17] and has an influence that extends to popular romantic fiction and the romantic comedy film genre,[18] *Persuasion* has enjoyed more moderate screen success. If Jane Austen has been reincarnated as Elizabeth Bennet, she is perhaps yet more convincingly re-imagined as Anne Elliot in the 1995 and 2007 television adaptations (dirs. Roger Mitchell and Adrian Shergold respectively) and in the biopic *Miss Austen Regrets*. The title of this biopic makes manifest the mood of regret that permeates Austen's novel, even at its conclusion in the heroine's regret for her earlier failure to seize the day and rebel against those who regulated her behaviour, sentencing her to a life of solitude and yearning. But as Sandra M. Gilbert and Susan Gubar observe, unlike Austen's previous novels, *Persuasion* is concerned with the liberation rather than the submission of the heroine: rather than subduing an overactive female, the novel narrates the coming to life of 'an angelically quiet heroine who has given up her search for a story'.[19] Effectively, Anne, unlike Austen's previous heroines, takes charge of the pen, creating her own story. This image of the pen – as we have seen in *Becoming Jane* – becomes increasingly visually prominent in screen adaptations of *Persuasion*, resonating with the famous introductory question in Gilbert and Gubar's monumental *Madwoman in the Attic* of 1979: 'Is a pen a metaphorical penis?'[20] This question, unambiguously answered in *Shakespeare in Love* (as indicated above), has become a part of the fabric of later adaptations of Austen's fiction that increasingly draw associations between author and heroine. Links between the author and the heroine in the last two television adaptations are immediately present in the appearance of the heroines – played by Amanda Root (dir. Roger Michell, 1995) and Sally Hawkins (dir. Adrian Shergold, 2007). Their appearances are specifically designed to be similar to Jane Austen herself (as she appears in the surviving portrait by her sister Cassandra). This is in marked contrast to the earlier screen Anne Elliot played by Ann Firbank (dir. Howard Baker, 1971) who is blonde with full hair and a large face. The first screen Anne Elliot, Daphne Slater (dir. Campbell Logan, 1960), had portrayed Elizabeth Bennet in a previous series (dir. Campbell Logan, 1952), suggesting, albeit unconsciously, a continuity between the youthful and older Austen as represented by the characters of Elizabeth and Anne.

While there is no disputing that Nick Dear and Roger Michell's 1995 adaptation of *Persuasion* was eclipsed by Andrew Davies and Simon Langton's *Pride and Prejudice* of the same year, this adaptation deserves to be remembered for its departure from the norm: in what has now become known as a 'muddy hem' adaptation, in which the heroine isn't typically beautiful, some of the clothes are worn and dirty and some of the houses are grubby.[21] In this more sombre adaptation, Anne is seen as observer rather than writer, biting her tongue while visually digesting the subtle gestures made towards her by Captain Wentworth, the suitor whom she had regretfully rejected eight years earlier. While there is a visual connection between this Anne Elliot and Jane Austen, Anne does not start to act 'authorially' until her confidence begins to be restored, recommending (as she does in the novel) in lines that seem to be spoken by Austen herself, that the melancholic and poetry-addicted Captain Benwick should 'include a larger allowance of prose in his daily study'. As in the novel, it is Wentworth who holds the pen at the close of the film, reflecting Anne's uncharacteristically outspoken rebuke to Captain Harville that 'Men have had every advantage of us in telling their own story. Education has been theirs in so much higher a degree; the pen has been in their hands.'[22] In this adaptation, however, the pen is passed from Wentworth to Anne; and we see her writing on something that looks like a writing desk aboard Captain Wentworth's man-of-war in the film's final minutes. The film leaves us with the image of Anne as author, finally holding the pen – which, as discussed above, has become a potent shorthand image of the author.

A prominent 'biographical' feature in Austen adaptations is the presence of the portable writing desk, unmistakably alluding to the desk thought to have been a gift of encouragement for the budding young writer from her father, the Reverend George Austen.[23] It makes its appearance in 2007 in *Becoming Jane*, *Northanger Abbey* (dir. Jon Jones) and *Persuasion* (1995). This latter adaptation, like its predecessor, begins with the 'shrouding' of Anne's ancestral home, Kellynch Hall (recalled in Joe Wright's 2005 *Pride & Prejudice* in the covering of dustsheets over the furniture of Netherfield). The 'shrouding' symbolizes the death of the heroine's hopes, so dependent on the place for any future happiness, and perhaps implicitly, the 'blank sheets', the stifling of the source of inspiration.[24] The despair is communicated in Anne's diary, with tears staining the page, helplessly erasing the words, accompanied by Anne's voiceover. The adaptation returns to Anne at her writing desk at the close of the film, this time filling the page with happy words; the fusion of Austen and Anne is now complete. With Captain Wentworth returning her to her home at the close of this adaptation, Anne's dearest wish that 'one day I might hope to return' is realized. The return home, or the seeming recovery of the past, however, as in the novel, is clouded by the differences between then and now, tinged with the regret for time lost and the fragility of the author/heroine. Austen's own back story, a career cut short because of her early death, cannot help but inform this and other adaptations of *Persuasion.*

The plot of *Persuasion*, though perhaps less amenable to romantic comedy than *Pride and Prejudice*, still exerts an influence on 'Hollywood-style' romances such as *The French Lieutenant's Woman* (1969; film, dir. Karel Reisz, 1981), *When Harry Met Sally* (dir. Rob Reiner, 1989), *Bridget Jones: The Edge of Reason* (1999; film, dir. Beeban Kidron, 2004) and *The Lake House* (dir. Alejandro Agresti, 2006). This most recent film is perhaps best described as a time-travelling rom-com. In it, *Persuasion's* gender roles are reversed as it is Keanu Reeves's character, architect Alex Wyler, who must wait to catch up in time with the subject of his affections, Dr. Kate Forster (Sandra Bullock), who writes to him from two years into the future. Together again for the first time since *Speed* (dir. Jan de Bont, 1994), Bullock and Reeves are reunited like the characters they play, with a knowing nod to their predecessors, Anne and Wentworth. In fact, Austen's novel, *Persuasion*, literally, brings the lovers together, providing a diegetic source for the film's love story (as the presence of the novel, *Pride and Prejudice*, does in the films, *Bride and Prejudice*, *Pride & Prejudice* and *Lost in Austen*). The novel, a cherished gift to the heroine from her father, is recovered on a train platform by Alex just as the doors close, propelling Kate beyond the reach of her would-be lover (with echoes too of David Lean's *Brief Encounter* (1945)). The novel provides a talking point for the couple's first meeting and reappears under the floorboards of Kate's apartment where it had been placed purposely by Alex two years earlier. Austen's novel underlines the film's representation of a love that literally transcends time, characterized by loss and waiting.[25]

A remnant of the story of lost opportunities is also present in David Nicholls' bestselling novel, *One Day* (2007), made into a film in 2011 (dir. Lone Scherfig) starring Anne Hathaway in what for many fans can be regarded as a reprisal of her role as Jane Austen in *Becoming Jane*. *One Day* is, in many ways, a *tour de force* adaptation, recreating not just one period, but twenty, painstakingly reconstructing minute changes to sets and costumes over a period of twenty years. In her portrayal of Emma Morley, Hathaway's more robust Jane Austen/Elizabeth Bennet has turned into a version of Jane Austen/Anne Elliot and like the heroine of *Persuasion* lives to regret her early cautiousness, finding love only after much self-sacrifice and waiting. The inability to seize the day has its consolations, however, and the years of waiting for emotional fulfilment give her the time to become what she really wants to be: an author. But her ultimate life-time achievement, like Jane Austen's and (perhaps) Anne Elliot's, is short-lived – the consequence of her own (gendered) fragility.

Equating Charlotte Brontë with her fictional character Jane Eyre has become commonplace in screen adaptations. As is evident in the reception given to the 2011 film directed by Cary Fukunaga, this is now considered something to be taken for granted, unworthy of note. The conventionality of this position perhaps emerges from the associations that Charlotte Brontë's biographer, Elizabeth Gaskell, first drew between novel and life.[26] Given audiences' appetite for attractive leading characters in popular films, it is easy to understand the tendency to turn author into Hollywood star, but the seeming need to translate Hollywood star or character into author is not so easily explained. In Austen adaptations, it is often the case that, rather than the author becoming her heroine (as in *Jane Eyre*), the heroine becomes the author, a version of Jane Austen, the writer. The ways in which Austen has been repeatedly and increasingly linked to her heroines, Elizabeth Bennet and Anne Elliot, over the course of her screen history is a transformation part-popularised by the taste for the make-over story. Like the effortful make-over of Harriet Smith in *Emma*, however, this is frequently not 'true to the spirit' of the original. The 'lack' of an author – which Bazin identifies as the illogical root cause of film's barrier from acceptance into the pantheon of the arts, a prejudice that still dogs the academic acceptance of adaptations[27] – is seemingly defiantly repudiated in these adaptations of Jane Austen's fiction which 'authorize' the films with an increasingly and paradoxically fictional representation of Austen herself. These productions are not simply intent on giving Austen 'a life', that which so many critics and fans have lamented she lacks: there is also a discernible inclination in adaptations of *Pride and Prejudice* and *Persuasion* to give her heroines 'authority', by putting the pen firmly into their hands.

Notes

1. Austen's 'Elinor and Marianne' (a first draft of *Sense and Sensibility*) was probably written in 1795; 'First Impressions' (to become *Pride and Prejudice*) in 1796. *Sense and Sensibility* was published in 1811, *Pride and Prejudice* in 1813, and *Persuasion* posthumously in 1817 together with *Northanger Abbey*. See 'Chronology', P. Rogers (ed.) Jane Austen, *Pride and Prejudice* (Cambridge: Cambridge University Press, 2006), pp. xv–xxi.
2. 'Anne Thackeray on Jane Austen', 1871 (from *Cornhill Magazine*, 1871, xxxiv), in *Jane Austen: The Critical Heritage*, Volume II: 1870–1940, B.C. Southam (ed.) (Abingdon: Routledge, 2001, 1987 rpt.), pp. 164–7 (167).
3. See D. Cartmell, 'A more gentle sensation towards the original': *Pride and Prejudice* as concealed autobiography', *Screen Adaptations: Jane Austen's 'Pride and Prejudice'* (London: Methuen, 2010), pp. 109–22.
4. D. Roche, 'Books and Letters in Joe Wright's *Pride & Prejudice*: Anticipating the Spectator's Response through the Thematization of Film Adaptation', *Persuasions On-line*, 27(2), (2007), at: http://www.jasna.org/persuasions/on-line/vol27no2/roche.htm
5. J. Austen, *Pride and Prejudice*, ed. Douglas Gray (New York and London: Norton, 2001, 1966 rpt.), p. 3.
6. For a discussion of screen adaptations of the materialism of *Pride and Prejudice*, see L. Brosh, 'Consuming Women: *Pride and Prejudice* and *Wuthering Heights*', in *Screening Novel Women: From British Domestic Fiction to Film* (Basingstoke: Palgrave, 2008), pp. 19–44.

7. Austen (2001), p. 19.
8. Connections between *Shakespeare in Love* and *Becoming Jane* are noted by L. Hopkins, *Relocating Shakespeare and Austen on Screen* (Basingstoke: Palgrave, 2009), p.142, and M.C. López and Rosa M. García-Periago, 'Becoming Shakespeare and Jane Austen in Love: An Intertextual Dialogue between Two Biopics', *Persuasions On-Line* 29(1), (2008), a: http://www.jasna.org/persuasions/on-line/vol29no1/cano-garcia.html
9. R. Burt, 'Shakespeare in Love and the End of History', in M.T. Burnett and R. Wray (eds.) *Shakespeare, Film, Fin de Siècle* (Basingstoke: Palgrave, 2000), pp. 203–231 (216).
10. Other instances in which one DVD cover visually recalls another in order to bid for a similar audience is Joe Wright's *Pride & Prejudice* (2005) and Ang Lee's *Sense and Sensibility* (1995). The covers are remarkably alike in similar shades of yellow, green and brown with the film's title dividing two pictures and the central figures (Emma Thompson and Keira Knighley), both dressed in brown, with similar hairstyles, gazing to their right.
11. *Shakespeare in Love* by Marc Norman and Tom Stoppard, *The Internet Movie Script Database*, at: http://www.imsdb.com/scripts/Shakespeare-in-Love.html
12. G. Holderness, *Nine Lives of William Shakespeare* (London: Continuum, 2011), p. 24.
13. J. Spence, *Becoming Jane Austen* (New York: Hambledon Continuum, 2003), p. 116.
14. A. Bazin, 'Adaptation, or the Cinema as Digest', in James Naremore (ed.) *Film Adaptation* (New Brunswick, NJ: Rutgers University Press, 2000), pp. 19–27 (23).
15. R. Stam, 'The Theory and Practice of Adaptation', in R. Stam and A. Raengo (eds.) *Literature and Film: A Guide to the Theory and Practice of Film Adaptation* (Oxford: Blackwell, 2005), pp. 1–52 (9).
16. J. Worthen, 'The Necessary Ignorance of a Biographer', in J. Batchelor (ed.) *The Art of Literary Biography* (Oxford: Clarendon Press, 1995), pp. 227–44 (231).
17. For example, see *Lost in Austen* (2008) and revisions, such as Helen Fielding's 1996 novel and Sharon Maguire's 2001 film, *Bridget Jones's Diary* (in which the central figure is also a diarist and with the central message, if you can't find a boyfriend, then write).
18. George Bluestone, as early as 1957, observes how the characteristics of shooting-scripts have a 'remarkable resemblance to the components of Jane Austen's style – a lack of particularity, an absence of metaphorical language, an omniscient point of view, a dependency on dialogue to reveal character, an insistence on absolute clarity'. 'The world of *Pride and Prejudice*,' he continues, 'meets the requirements of Hollywood's stock conventions and, at the same time, allows a troubling grain of reality to enter by the side door. It depicts a love story that essentially follows the shopworn formula of boy meets girl; boy loses girl; boy gets girl'. G. Bluestone, *Novels into Film: The Metamorphoses of Fiction into Cinema* (Berkeley and Los Angeles: University of California Press, 1957), pp. 117–18 (144).
19. S.M. Gilbert and S. Gubar, *The Madwoman in the Attic*, 2nd edn (New Haven and London: Yale University Press, 2000 [1979]), p. 175.
20. Gilbert and Gubar (1979), p. 3.
21. See S. Parrill, *Jane Austen on Film and Television: A Critical Study of the Adaptations* (London: McFarland, 2002) in which this adaptation is contrasted to 'heritage promotion pieces' (p. 151).
22. J. Austen, *Persuasion* (London: Vintage, 2008), p. 23.
23. See C. Harman, for instance, *Jane's Fame: How Jane Austen Conquered the World* (Edinburgh: Canongate, 2009), p. 15.

24. For a commentary on this scene in the 1995 adaptation, see J. Wiltshire, *Recreating Jane Austen* (Cambridge: Cambridge University Press, 2001), p. 94, and K. Sutherland, *Jane Austen's Textual Lives: From Aeschylus to Bollywood* (Oxford: Oxford University Press, 2005), p. 346.

25. For a discussion of the film as an adaptation of *Persuasion*, see M.C. López, '*Persuasion* Moves to Chicago: Rewriting Austen's Classic in *The Lake House*', *Persuasions On-Line* 29:1 (2008), at: http://www.jasna.org/persuasions/on-line/vol29no1/cano-lopez.html

26. See E. Gaskell, *The Life of Charlotte Brontë*, Elisabeth Jay (ed.) (Harmondsworth: Penguin, 1997) for associations drawn between Charlotte Brontë and Jane Eyre, especially in the similarities Gaskell notes between Lowood in *Jane Eyre* and Cowan's Bridge, the school attended by the Brontë sisters. The presence of George Richmond's chalk drawing of Charlotte Brontë on book covers of *Jane Eyre*, together with the novel's subtitle, 'An Autobiography', invites further comparison between heroine and author. See, for instance, *Jane Eyre* (Harmondsworth: Penguin Audiobooks, 1994), *Jane Eyre* (Harmondsworth: Penguin, 1985) and E. Gaskill, *The Life of Charlotte Brontë* (Cambridge: Cambridge University Press, 2010 [1908]).

27. For a discussion of the absence of twentieth-century critical attention to adaptations, see T. Corrigan, 'Literature on Screen, A History: In the Gap', in D. Cartmell and I. Whelehan (eds.) *The Cambridge Companion to Literature on Screen* (Cambridge: Cambridge University Press, 2007), pp. 29–44.

10

Duplicated and duplicitous self-configurings in Kaufman's *Adaptation* (2002)

Gennelle Smith

Our first glimpse of the screenwriter Charlie Kaufman (Nicolas Cage) in *Adaptation* (dir. Spike Jonze, 2002) captures our subject unawares. Through the lens of an unseen video camera, Charlie peers nervously from the sidelines on the set of *Being John Malkovich* (dir. Spike Jonze, 1999), the real Kaufman's first filmed Hollywood script. His obvious unease at the peripheries of this set sits oddly with his designation as the primary character of the film we are watching, a role established by his anxious voiceover monologue just seconds before. He has been formally identified as 'Charlie Kaufman, Screenwriter' across the bottom of the screen and the camera's interest in him as a subject is evident. But despite these privileging gestures in the narrative set-up, the first assistant director's sharply dismissive; 'You. You're in the eye-line. Can you please get off the stage?'[1] is sufficient to confirm Charlie's sense of his own interloper status. In the face of such confident demonstrations of on-set authority, Charlie, the production's writer, is scared from the set. As the scene demonstrates, Cage's Charlie already has sweat-inducing issues with his function as screenwriter, author and, more acutely yet, as a human being. As a fictional version of the 'real' Charlie Kaufman in a semi-fictional cinematic space created by Kaufman,[2] the character Charlie is constantly overwritten by the real Kaufman's anxieties about authorship, screenwriting and artistic sincerity. Yet, importantly, Charlie's search for a meaningful adaptation of another person's work suggests that in a twenty-first-century world simultaneously fascinated by true feeling and cracked apart by its deteriorating belief in 'reality',[3] *Adaptation's* bold, postmodern wrapping can scarcely conceal an emphatically modernist search for an honest, and singular, truth.

The filmmaker's quest for truth does not, however, wed him to local acts of truth telling. On the contrary: it is difficult to imagine a film more committed to deceiving its audience than *Adaptation*. Indeed, as Kaufman populates his storyline with a parade of different authors – novelists, journalists, scientists, screenwriters – it becomes more difficult to discern which of Kaufman's authorial proxies (Charlie and his twin brother Donald only the most obvious of the available candidates) comes nearest to its creator. My analysis will investigate two related threads running through *Adaptation*: first, Kaufman's anxious negotiation between the profession of screenwriting and the status of author; and second, his use of duplication and duplicity in exploring himself and his authorial identity on-screen. Further, I shall argue that throughout this film Kaufman uses acts of duplicity to distil the true from the inauthentic – in other words, harnessing the power of lies to find the truth in human nature.

Hollywood has long been interested in the conflicted figure of the screenwriter. Traditional iterations of the hardworking yet underpaid movie scribe appear memorably in films such as *Sunset Boulevard* (dir. Billy Wilder, 1950), narrated by a dead screenwriter; *Barton Fink* (dir. Coen Brothers, 1991), featuring a screenwriter struggling with writer's block; and *State and Main* (dir. David Mamet, 2000), which follows a first-time screenwriter just entering Hollywood. Significantly, all three characters share an inherent anxiety about the opportunity to be personally recognized for their work in an essentially collaborative industry. Similarly, in *Adaptation*, Charlie is struck by the dangers inherent in being a writer in Hollywood. When commissioned to adapt the non-fiction work *The Orchid Thief*, he decries formulaic screenwriting, telling studio executive Valerie (Tilda Swinton) that he doesn't want to have to compromise 'by making it a Hollywood thing, you know, like making it an orchid heist movie or turning the orchids into poppies and making it about drug-running, you know?'[4] Kaufman's (and Charlie's) fear of the formulaic seems validated when, later in the movie, Valerie attempts to allay Susan Orlean's (Meryl Streep) anxieties about adapting her own work for the screen with the over-quick reply, 'Oh, don't worry ... We have screenwriters to write the screenplay'.[5] In referring to them in the plural, Valerie alludes to a stable of apparently interchangeable jobbing writers. This marks 'them' as other – hired hands working to someone else's vision and therefore clearly institutionally distinguished in the hierarchies from an author of Susan's standing. In the event, the type of 'hack' alluded to in both Charlie's fears and Valerie's chirpy reassurances finds direct expression in the film in the character of Charlie's twin brother Donald. Donald worships screenwriting guru Robert McKee's 'principles' of screenwriting and, by directly implementing those, writes an unapologetically formulaic thriller called *The 3*. The fact that he later sells this cynical work of writing-by-numbers for a six-figure sum vindicates both Valerie's cheeriness and Charlie's sense of dread, illustrating as it does the commercial efficacy of 'the system' and the industry's habitual privileging of the generically tested and market-affirmed.

The screenwriter's status as a contracted worker rather than as an author remains, at least in part, a symptom of uneven copyright law across different forms of published fiction in the United States. Unlike novels, books and plays, a screenplay legally belongs to the commissioning employer, not to the hired screenwriter.⁶ This institutional ownership of a script, working in concert with *auteur* theory's influential deference to the director as the creative 'voice' of a film,⁷ contributes to the uncertain status of the screenwriter. In *The Screenplay: Authorship, Theory and Criticism*, Steven Price accounts for the screenwriter's marginalization by placing him/her outside the bounds of single authorship, a form of creative authority that has held artistic supremacy since the Romantics. Rather than a screenplay being read as 'an act of personal expression', Price contends that 'notions of authorship in relation to screenwriting tend to be displaced by legal and contractual relationships and, often, by notions of collective, evolving, and even anonymous authorship'.⁸ As a result, the screenplay becomes 'an inherently unstable text',⁹ subject to countless interventions by uncredited, contracted writers, through spontaneous changes during production, and in the edit during post-production. What is excised, elided, included and altered is outside the screenwriter's control, thus de-centring his or her status as originator.

While these displacing elements have the potential to dismantle the screenwriter's authorial voice, they actually contribute to a purer understanding of the scriptwriter's creative process. In contrast to the Romantic author's poetic metaphors, screenwriters trade in technicalities; in their line of work, the clues to a normally hidden writing process – the cues, the character notes, the fades-to-black – lay exposed. Price argues that these elements of the process inform all forms of writing, not only screenplays. However, because screenplays conspicuously foreground the processes behind many acts of literary creation by revealing their ongoing collaboration with editors, agents and others, they lose their claim to creative autonomy. In implicitly acting as the sole originator of their creative labour, literary 'Authors' themselves perhaps perform by default their own kind of duplicity.¹⁰ This (culturally required) duplicity creates a sense of authorial stability within traditionally published literature, rendering our imaginative engagement with books and novels slightly more seamless and, consequently, more comfortable.¹¹

This assumed seamlessness is perhaps why, in the context of Hollywood's system of shared, unstable *cinematic* authorship, Kaufman has repeatedly and emphatically marked his place as primary author of his work. As James Mottram notes, Kaufman is 'one of the very few screenwriters in Hollywood – perhaps the only screenwriter – whose authorial identity supersedes the director's'.¹² This strategically constructed perception of Kaufman as author (as opposed to merely institutional writer) partly results from his wholly original screenplays, replete as these are with idiosyncratic introspection and a set of personal preoccupations. These include an interest in memory, time passing, death and the absurd elements of daily life. Kaufman's bundle of thematic hallmarks is stretched across his screenplays by repeated references to Franz Kafka, Marcel Proust, Alexander Pope, Samuel Beckett and other authors linked by related philosophical enquiries. For instance, in Kaufman's latest film, *Synecdoche, New York* (dir. Charlie Kaufman, 2009), characters refer to at least ten canonical writers who can be considered part of an existentialist or even Modernist tradition similar to Kaufman's.[13] Kaufman's philosophical consistency has even sparked the recent usage of the term 'Kaufmanesque' to describe any film engaged with similar issues.[14] Evoking the word 'Kafkaesque' in both its acoustics and its philosophy, the term 'Kaufmanesque' refers to a certain type of cinematic world-building that is identifiably Kaufman's own, but which echoes Kafka's similar ability to 'name [a] world' or to bid a world into being, a style of poetics outlined by Heidegger in his landmark 1950 essay 'Language'. While specifically discussing poetry in his writings, Heidegger also contends that other forms of art can be considered 'language spoken purely', or 'that in which the completion of the speaking that is proper to what is spoken is, in its turn, an original'.[15] Kaufman's remarkably original screenplays, the uniqueness of which is brought about by his honest approach to his own preoccupations, fit within this broader view of a Heideggerian 'true poetics'.

The 'Kaufmanesque', however, transcends a mere collection of thematic interests. Rather, Kaufman actively asserts his authorial voice in a variety of ways across his body of work. 'I like the idea of being more in charge of creating the whole thing, from beginning to end',[16] he has remarked, and his frequent collaborator, French director Michel Gondry, agrees: '[Kaufman] is the author of the thing to the end ... If you work with Charlie, you have to accept that'.[17] Furthermore, Philip Seymour Hoffman (who plays Caden in *Synecdoche*) identifies Kaufman as 'one of those auteur-type people. And they're a specific type of person, you know'.[18] Kaufman's unusually systematic, and successful, projection of his own authority reaches back to his early screenwriting days. After parting ways with a regular writing partner in the mid-1990s Kaufman says he 'decided to collaborate with myself', combining disparate story ideas with his 'familiar thoughts' and seeing what arose.[19] In doing so, he notionally pays homage to the idea of screenwriting, and filmmaking, as a collaborative process, while actually cementing the emphatically individual character of his own authorship by himself occupying both halves of the putative collaboration.

Perhaps unsurprisingly, then, Kaufman places the role of the writer on a similar footing to that of the director. In an interview with writer-director David Cronenberg, Kaufman remarks:

> One of the things that I found really helpful ... is that being a neophyte in directing, I feel like I have a kind of authority simply because I'm the writer as well ... Certainly on *Synecdoche, New York* we had discussions and arguments, but I felt like I had authority.[20]

In response, Cronenberg quips that this was 'undoubtedly an illusion' and laughs, providing another glimpse into how writers are typically perceived in Hollywood. Kaufman's self-positioning here – affirming the creative value in a writer's assumption of control of his or her project – is decisively outside the mainstream. Kaufman's exceptional status in this respect is underscored by the little-known fact that in addition to being the sole credited writer on all of his films (excepting the rather extraordinary case of *Adaptation*, which officially carries Donald's name as well), he is also credited as executive producer or producer on all of them. Being present in all stages of the production in this way, and at all levels, inevitably further concretizes his personal ownership of, and authority over, his projects.

Beyond his involvement in the production process, however, Kaufman pointedly inserts himself into his screenplays by inscribing onto his main characters an authorial presence frequently evocative, and sometimes even directly imitative, of his own. His protagonists are almost exclusively artists and writers frustrated by creative blockages, such as puppeteer Craig (John Cusack) in *Being John Malkovich*, artist Joel (Jim Carrey) in *Eternal Sunshine of the Spotless Mind* (dir. Michel Gondry, 2004), and theatre director Caden in *Synecdoche, New York*. In addition, supporting characters in Kaufman scripts include actors (John Malkovich, *Being John Malkovich*, hundreds of extras in *Synecdoche*), novelists (Lila Jute, *Human Nature*), and self-help writers (Madeleine Gravis, *Synecdoche*). Kaufman's obsessive self-configuring in his screenplays emphasizes his fundamental concern as both a subject of investigation and as the investigating artist: himself. As actor Mike White comments: 'I think Charlie Kaufman, while he doesn't act in his films ... puts himself in them. There's certainly an effort to put himself out there and make sure he is associated with his material.'[21] Kaufman's appearance in his own work therefore emerges less as a by-product of the artistic process and more as an emphatic assertion of personal authorship, accompanied, as a matter of course, by a questioning of its validity.

With *Adaptation*, however, Kaufman's decision to insert 'Charlie Kaufman' into the screenplay prompted some commentators to sniff at his perceived vanity and presumption. Critic Rick Kisonak wrote: 'In the real world, if your employer gives you an assignment and you don't complete it, that's called failure. In the motion picture industry, it's called bold innovation.'[22] As ever, Kaufman anticipates, even legitimates (and so partially defuses) the jibe, having Charlie explicitly worry that 'I've written myself into my screenplay ... It's self-indulgent, it's narcissistic, it's solipsistic, it's pathetic.'[23] From documenting the excess of these processes of self-configuration, Kaufman tends to emerge looking more neurotically insecure than egomaniacally vain; as, in effect, a man without sufficient quietude to consider other options for subjects beyond himself (Figures 10.1, 10.2). As Kaufman's proxy Charlie muses in one key scene: 'It's like the only thing I'm qualified to write about is myself.'[24] *Adaptation* good-humouredly suggests that not only is Kaufman apparently unqualified to write about anything other than himself, but, more than that, doing so is all but an imperative: he *must*,

Figure 10.1 The on-screen character Charlie Kaufman (Nicholas Cage) worries over his script in *Adaptation* (2002).

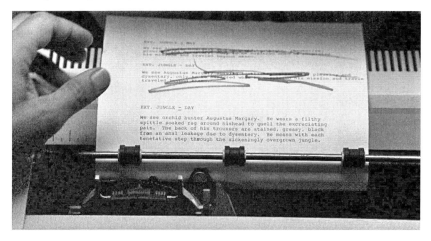

Figure 10.2 Charlie's script is marked by vigorously self-critical deletions.

it seems, write about himself in order to try and know, define and be reconciled to that troubled self.

Importantly, though, the portrayal of self in *Adaptation* involves duping the audience. Since the term is key to my enquiry, it may be helpful here to pinpoint what I mean by 'duplicity'. The word most often serves to describe 'deliberate deceptiveness'[25] by someone or something, indicating a concerted effort to withhold or distort the truth. Crucially, however, it also means to do so by doubling, a meaning contained within its Latin root 'duplo' ('to double'), whose charge is felt explicitly in the alternative

English stem 'duplication'. Donald understands the potential storytelling and thematic advantages of duplicatory devices and even tells Charlie after his screenwriting seminar with McKee: 'Because of my multiple personality theme, I've chosen the motif of broken mirrors to show my protagonist's fragmented self. Bob says an Image System greatly increases the complexity of an aesthetic emotion.'[26] Whereas acts of duplication can indeed help emphasize themes and add weight and interest to a narrative (though are shown to do so under strain in Donald's conspicuously unsubtle application of the lesson), duplicity, on the other hand, adds something darker to the idea of doubling. *Adaptation* is played out at the point where duplicity and duplication meet – in the fine space shared by the duplicitous and the duplicatory. Kaufman deceives his audience in two main ways: he uses cinema's structured dishonesty to lull us into belief, and he duplicates his authorial presence multiple times through his invention and reinvention of Charlie, Donald, Susan and the orchid poacher John Laroche (Chris Cooper).

Adaptation is, in fact, another example of what McKee terms Kaufman's 'suspicious realities'. Blurring the line between reality and fiction habitually forms the basis for Kaufman's work, whether in the absurd realism of Spike Jonze's *Being John Malkovich* or *Adaptation*, or the whimsy of Gondry's hand-made aesthetic in *Human Nature* (2001) and *Eternal Sunshine of the Spotless Mind*. Even in *Confessions of a Dangerous Mind* (dir. George Clooney, 2002), the one film Kaufman had no part in beyond adapting, the plot plays with the discrepancies between what is claimed as real by its memoir-writing protagonist, Chuck Barris (Sam Rockwell), and what is recorded as true. Indeed, Kaufman, Jonze and Gondry's lack of interest in conscientiously recreating the reality of the extra-cinematic world and their layered questions about the meaning, value and location of the real have led many movie goers to identify Kaufman's screenplays as postmodern.

Despite this claim, however, Kaufman's films differ significantly from the depthless references of Wes Anderson's *The Royal Tenanbaums* (2000) or the repurposed pop songs of Baz Luhrmann's *Moulin Rouge!* (2001). This is not to say that Kaufman does not relish cinema's capacity for layered invention: this is, of course, his stock-in-trade. Just as, according to Shakespeare, 'The truest poetry is the most feigning', Kaufman's cinematic truth-telling is firmly couched in the false realities he creates.[27] To examine this idea and Kaufman's duplicatory/duplicitous strategy more closely, I will look at one key scene from *Adaptation*: the point at which Charlie and Donald switch places in order for Donald to interview Susan, and then discuss what they have just experienced.

Charlie begins by insisting that his brother should not only resemble him in looks and personality, but must actually *be* him, telling Donald: 'You've gotta be exactly me. I have a reputation to maintain ... Don't laugh how you laugh'. Donald's sincere response – 'I'm not gonna laugh. I get to have people think I'm you. It's an honor' – emphasizes the understood hierarchies between them, underscoring Charlie's constant struggle to distinguish himself from his guileless brother and his brother's admiration for his intellectual twin. For Charlie, the only value in their identical looks would be if their personalities match, too. Yet, despite Charlie's fears, Donald's lack of intellectualism actually improves the interview he conducts with Susan. He relaxes Susan enough to ask her whether she still keeps in touch with Laroche, venturing that he 'detected an attraction to him in the subtext'. Susan is taken aback; with 'a practiced casualness', as Kaufman expresses it in the screenplay, she responds that their relationship 'was strictly reporter-subject. I mean, certainly an intimacy does evolve ... But the relationship ends when the book ends'. Susan's careful denial prompts Donald to murmur 'Mendacious deceit' as he notes it down, sparking a 'What?' from Orlean. Donald's tautological juxtaposition of 'mendacious' with 'deceit' both provides further evidence of his lack of linguistic subtlety (are both words needed here?) and simultaneously, through its duplicatory emphasis, inadvertently throws light on the functioning of both duplication and deceit within the film. So it is, therefore, that while Susan is, indeed, a 'mendacious deceiver' (one, that is, who both deceives and who seeks to deceive), Kaufman, by contrast, wants to be a non-mendacious deceiver, or perhaps a mendacious truth-teller – one, that is, who consistently deceives at a local level while seeking to communicate a bigger truth not dependent upon local accuracy.

In this endeavour, he inserts into his film not one but two starkly differentiated versions of himself and his self-interrogating mind world bearing the 'Kaufman' name. Jonze highlights the twins' alter-ego identities by frequently framing them in two-shots, despite the technical difficulties presented by the double casting of Cage in this respect. As the brothers spy on Susan from a distance, for example, Jonze's framing and Cage's finely differentiated acting helps us not only distinguish the two brothers, but to discern through them two distinct aspects of Kaufman's own authorial identity: the neurotic, self-doubting introvert and the fun-seeking extrovert.

The invention of Donald Kaufman is, of course, the most obvious of Charlie's duplicitous duplications, but it is not the only one. Beyond the ego/alter-ego argument favoured by critics, his existence may also be, as others have suggested, 'a cinematic means to dramatize Charlie's inner conflicts to an audience'.[28] The dialogue between the on-screen Kaufmans that the creation of Donald makes possible may be a sign that off-screen Kaufman initially heeded McKee's advice to avoid resorting to voiceover to explain inner emotion. Even the Charlie and Donald double presence, however, proves insufficient to represent the totality of Kaufman's multifaceted psyche. As the film goes on, Kaufman's interest in devolving his authorial identity across multiple characters develops beyond a simple storytelling tool. Like a cripplingly more self-aware version of Donald's fictional cop with multiple personality disorder, in *Adaptation*, as McKee himself articulates it, Kaufman '[gives] each faction [of himself] a characterization taken from so-called reality, then declare[s] war on himself'.[29] As a result, the third member of that scene, Susan Orlean, becomes another of the screenwriter's many on-screen proxies: she is everything Charlie is not, and yet is also his intellectual soul mate. As Kaufman teases out the parallels between the two, we begin to see that Susan is a more loyal double for Charlie than his gregarious brother. While Donald causes Charlie to mutter 'You and I share the same D.N.A. Isn't that sad?', it is the enviable stability of Susan's authorial self that Charlie most aspires to share.

By configuring Susan as a partial version of both Charlie and himself, however, Kaufman also draws clear lines between the screenwriter's authorial value and that of the novelist. In one early scene, Charlie is static, paralyzed by the blank page; Susan, by contrast, is imaginative and compelling, industriously typing at a computer in her New York apartment. As Charlie uses a typewriter and consults maps of Florida, Susan is on location researching her subject and recording her thoughts in a notebook. She is offered as the ideal modern-day author, in charge of her own material, making a good living and most importantly, drawing meaningful conclusions from her work, something Charlie values as a fellow writer. As he tells Valerie, he thinks that 'Orlean makes orchids so fascinating. Plus, her, her musings on Florida and orchid poaching ... It's great, sprawling *New Yorker* stuff, and I'd want to remain true to that.'[30] The 'great, sprawling' nature of Orlean's writing, however, remains difficult to achieve for a screenwriter constrained by deadlines, temporal restrictions, structure (or lack thereof) and an innate feeling of authorial inadequacy.

The burden of telling the story does not, though, rest entirely on Charlie. As Frank P. Tomasulo points out, Susan narrates parts of the film as well.[31] When Charlie reads her book, he often hears Susan's pensive voice speaking the words, articulating the polished thoughts of a writer who, unlike himself, has moved beyond the research phase and is now communicating in published form. Her tone indicates a certain distance from both the past events that inspired the book and from the reader consuming it in the present. This subtle yet unshakeable sense of distance exemplifies Steven Price's theory of the deceptive author: if we are to believe the ubiquity of her calm narration, Susan is the *only* author of her work. The details of her creative relationship with Laroche, with her editors and agents, are nowhere to be seen, a benefit for an author seeking to assert her sole authority over a piece of work. This sort of literary patina bothers Kaufman, who explains that:

> stories are things that are polished and seen from a distance, [but] I want to try and do stuff where it feels like it's immersed, where I'm immersed in it when I'm working on it, and that the audience will experience that immersion or the chaos and confusion of actual existence, as opposed to

a story ... that doesn't really seem part of the actual moment-to-moment life that I have.[32]

Despite the lure of authorial stability articulated by Charlie in *Adaptation*, Kaufman himself also values the creativity to be found in the provisional, the unpolished, the process-exposing truths of what he terms this 'messy, junky world'.[33] Indeed, as Chris Dzialo argues, 'for [Kaufman] as "author" there seems to be a frustrating and ultimately unrealized desire to live in the reversible, mutable, contingent, and complex time of consciousness'.[34] In order for emotion to ring true onscreen, though, there have been times when he has had to court the impression of decisive and stable knowledge; as he remarks on his directorial experience with *Synecdoche*: 'If the actors had some sort of emotional situation, I had to be stable, which was really good practice for me because it is not the way I normally am.'[35]

The *instability* that is Kaufman's more usual place of rest(lessness) finds vicarious expression in *Adaptation* in the person of John Laroche. As well as being a published author ('both in magazine and book form' as he himself insists),[36] Laroche also personifies another facet of Charlie's growing multiplicity of selves – the passionate adventurer/lover. If Susan can be considered an adventurer, she is a cautious one; Laroche, meanwhile, flits from passion to passion. Indeed, like Susan, Charlie spends most of the film wishing he could feel an intense desire for something as Laroche does. While the two writers both intellectualize their pursuit, however, Laroche prefers to experiment, to expand his knowledge through gritty experience. As an orchid poacher, his professional life is predicated upon a deceit (if in pursuit of higher ends) and he ascribes a comparable propensity for deceit to his beloved orchids, which themselves engage in duplicity in order to lure in their 'double'. Laroche eloquently explains the process:

> [W]hat's so wonderful is that every one of these flowers has a specific relationship with the insect that pollinates it. There's a certain ... orchid looks exactly like a certain insect, so the ... insect is drawn to this flower. Its *double*. Its soul mate.[37]

Though Susan hears this as a compelling metaphorizing of her own nascent relationship with Laroche, it also incidentally evokes the 'little dance' of duplicated identities embarked upon by all four of the film's main characters, Charlie, Donald, Susan and Laroche. If we read the narrative as a conflict between the 'warring factions' of Kaufman's psyche, as McKee puts it, then Laroche's and Donald's deaths near the end of the film, and Charlie's final contemptuous dismissal of Susan in the swamp, represent the painful but necessary expulsion of some of those competing elements within Kaufman, enabling him to move towards the less conflicted singularity of settled self-hood and productive authorship in evidence by the film's conclusion.

Perhaps the most expressive, but least conventional, of all Kaufman's self-revealing proxies, however, is the screenplay itself. *Adaptation*'s reputation as unique stems from its remarkably mutable screenplay. This seems to interpret 'adaptation' not just as the theme that drives the drama but as an imperative governing its own structural development: the screenplay itself therefore undergoes a remarkable, and transformative, adaptation during its third act. As has been argued elsewhere,[38] the screenplay begins as a meditation on the impossibility of truly representing someone else's work and concludes on a triumphantly formulaic note satirizing the dominance of the market in shaping the evolution of most films. Kaufman himself is in no doubt about the centrality of the emerging screenplay in the film:

> To my mind, the main character in *Adaptation* is the screenplay itself, and the evolution of the screenplay from its initial intents to its ultimate ... corruption. And to me, that's kind of the tragedy of this creature, this screenplay that never was able [to] reach the fruition that Charlie had hoped. He never was able to make a movie about flowers.[39]

Indeed, the screenplay is the purest articulation of Charlie's, and Kaufman's, dilemma. It reflects their frustration, yet also indicates their growth – a process that Charlie initially rejects, preferring instead to portray 'a story where nothing much happens ... Where people don't change, they don't have any epiphanies. They struggled and are frustrated, and nothing is resolved. More a reflection of the real world'.[40] By the end of the film, however, Charlie does reach an epiphany. Driving away from Amelia, he decides on the ending to his script: 'It feels right. Conclusive. So ... Kaufman drives off from his encounter with Amelia, filled for the first time with hope. I like this. This is good.'[41] Though the hyperbolic conventionality of this happy ending is clearly driven by a heavy dose of Kaufmanesque irony, nevertheless Charlie's discovery of this proclaimed truth cannot be fully contained by the irony in which it is so conspicuously couched. The film's ending, therefore, covers its own embarrassment in embracing the epiphanic and the unproblematically resolved by dressing itself up as pure self-satire, while simultaneously sincerely enjoying the *discovery of something* and the *emergence into something* in the wake of all the self-interrogating dead-ends that have preceded it. Does Kaufman here, despite himself, reward his own search for meaning, while duplicitously pretending he is purely ironizing the reward of such searches? I think so. After all, we do experience happiness sometimes, and is that not a truth in itself – and one to which this ending surreptitiously pays tribute?

At one point in *Adaptation*, in the course of a discussion of Donald's writing, Donald explains to Charlie the symbolism behind his inclusion in his screenplay of a snake eating its tail. 'It's called Ourobouros', replies Charlie morosely: 'I'm Ourobouros ... I've written myself into my screenplay.' The sinister and visceral image of the self-consuming snake clearly holds a perverse appeal for the self-loathing Charlie. However, in Donald's earlier image of multiple fragmented mirrors, the film provides an alternative, and more pertinent, symbolic analogy for Charlie than the one he draws down accusingly upon himself. Charlie's anxiety about achieving the status of author in an industry that does not value the screenwriter is made manifest by the competing authors whom he configures marching through his psyche. As so often in the film, it is Donald who encapsulates an important truth for which Charlie has been reaching, and he does so in stunningly simple language: 'Art always tells the truth. Even when it's lying.' Charlie's multiple selves in this film constitute a big lie, or at least, a decisive departure from the truth as locally and accurately conceived. But they also collectively generate a truth about identity and selfhood that transcends its local (and manifold) layers of deceit. Since this film is so much about *process*, and so suspicious of *products*, however, perhaps – despite his audacious invention of a cinematic Charlie Kaufman – Kaufman did not actually *put* himself in his screenplay at all. Perhaps Charlie's – and Donald's, Susan's, Laroche's and the screenplay's – on-screen existence attests to the fact that, as playwright Alan Bennett remarks, 'You don't put yourself in your screenplays. You find yourself there.'[42] That, surely, is a paradox of Kaufmanesque dimensions.

Notes

1. C. Kaufman and D. Kaufman, *Adaptation: The Shooting Script* (New York: Newmarket Press, 2002), p. 3.
2. For clarity, I refer to the fictional Charlie Kaufman as Charlie and the real-world screenwriter as Kaufman.
3. T. Vermeulen and R. Van Den Akker, 'Notes on Metamodernism', *Journal of Aesthetics & Culture* 2 (2010): 1–14.
4. Kaufman and Kaufman (2002), p. 5.
5. Kaufman and Kaufman (2002), pp. 47–8.
6. S. Price, *The Screenplay: Authorship, Theory and Criticism* (New York: Palgrave Macmillan, 2010), p. 13.
7. C.P. Sellors, *Film Authorship: Auteurs and Other Myths* (London: Wallflower Press, 2010), p. 2.
8. Price (2010), p. 9.
9. Price (2010), p. x.
10. The paratextual apparatus (such as acknowledgements or dedications) can of course compromise this impression.
11. Similarly, I note that although my name appears as sole author of this chapter, there have, of course, been other inputs.
12. J. Mottram, *The Sundance Kids: How the Mavericks Took Back Hollywood* (New York: Faber and Faber Inc., 2006), p. 319.
13. A few examples include writers such as, or works by Harold Pinter, Beckett, Arthur Miller, Marcel Proust, Fyodor Dostoevsky, Antonin Artaud, Henrik Ibsen and Kafka.

14. For example, *Cold Souls* (dir. Sophie Barthes, 2009), starring Paul Giamatti as a version of himself who puts his soul 'in storage', was labelled 'Kaufmanesque' by some upon its Sundance Film Festival debut. *IndieWire's* Eric Kohn found the term both apposite and derivative, a symptom of film audiences' search for familiar tropes within cinema, while conceding that 'the basic outline for "Cold Souls" does suggest a Kaufman-esque dreaminess, and the atmospheric parallels are definitely there if you look for them'. E. Kohn, 'The Peculiarities of Soullessness: Sophie Barthes' "Cold Souls" (Sundance '09)', at: http://www.indiewire.com/article/the_peculiarities_of_soullessness_sophie_barthes_cold_souls_sundance_09

15. M. Heidegger, *Poetry, Language, Thought* (New York: HarperCollins Publishers, 2001 [1971]). Translated by Albert Hofstadter, p. 192.

16. C. Kaufman, interview with Marit Kapla. Göteburg International Film Festival, 29 January 2011, at: http://www.youtube.com/watch?v=xpjgjJqayxI

17. J. Tanz, 'Charlie Kaufman: Hollywood's Brainiest Screenwriter Pleases Crowds by Refusing to Please', *Wired* (October 2008): 233.

18. Tanz (2008), p. 233.

19. Kaufman, interview with Marit Kapla (2011).

20. D. Cronenberg, 'Charlie Kaufman'. *Interview Magazine* (November 2008), at: http://www.interviewmagazine.com/film/charlie-kaufman/

21. Mottram (2006), p. 320.

22. R. Kisonak, 'Adaptation', *Film Threat*, 17 Jan. 2003, at: http://www.filmthreat.com/reviews/4182/

23. Kaufman and Kaufman (2002), p. 60.

24. Kaufman and Kaufman (2002), p. 58.

25. 'Duplicity', *The Oxford English Dictionary*, online.

26. Kaufman and Kaufman (2002), p. 51.

27. W. Shakespeare in B. Mowat and Paul Werstine (eds.) *As You Like It* (New York: Washington Square Press, 1992), Act 3, scene 3, ll.15–17.

28. F.P. Tomasulo, 'Adaptation as Adaptation: From Susan Orlean's The Orchid Thief to Charlie (and "Donald") Kaufman's Screenplay to Spike Jonze's Film', in J. Boozer (ed.) *Authorship in Film Adaptation* (Austin: University of Texas Press, 2008), p. 168.

29. R. McKee, 'Critical Commentary' in *Adaptation: The Shooting Script* (New York: Newmarket Press, 2002), p. 132.

30. Kaufman and Kaufman (2002), p. 5.

31. Tomasulo (2008), p. 165.

32. Kaufman, interview with Marit Kapla (2011).

33. C. Kaufman, *Being John Malkovich* (London: Faber and Faber Ltd., 2000), p. ix.

34. C. Dzialo, 'The Screenplays of Charlie Kaufman' in W. Buckland (ed.) *Puzzle Films: Complex Storytelling in Contemporary Cinema* (Chichester, UK: Wiley-Blackwell, 2009), p. 109.

35. Kaufman, interview with Marit Kapla (2011).

36. Kaufman and Kaufman (2002), p. 16.

37. Kaufman and Kaufman (2002), p. 24.

38. Geoff King gives a characteristic overview of the plot in his observation that 'What *Adaptation* offers, then, is an extremely reflexive, metafictional narrative, in large part focused on what appears to be its own process of gestation'. G. King, *Indiewood, USA* (London and New York: I.B. Tauris, 2009), p. 51.

39. Kaufman, interview with Marit Kapla (2011).

40. Kaufman and Kaufman (2002), p. 68.
41. Kaufman and Kaufman (2002), pp. 99–100.
42. T. Adams, 'Enter, finally, the real Alan Bennett', *The Guardian*, (8 November 2009), at: http://www.guardian.co.uk/stage/2009/nov/08/alan-bennett-habit-of-art

11

Writing the endings of cinema: saving film authorship in the cinematic paratexts of *Prospero's Books*, Taymor's *The Tempest* and *The Secret of Kells*

Richard Burt

In this chapter I examine the appearance of books and illuminated manuscripts being written/produced in the closing sequences of two adaptations of Shakespeare's *The Tempest* – Julie Taymor's *Tempest* (2010) and Peter Greenaway's *Prospero's Books* (1991) – and of *The Secret of Kells* (dir. Tomm Moore, 2009), the animated feature film about The Book of Kells. I analyse these films, all three of which are concerned with the process of writing medieval and early modern books, in relation to two developments in the history of the cinematic paratext: first, opening and end sequences that show the credits printed on turning pages of a book; and, second, the increasing expansion and development of end credit sequences since 1980.[1] I take note of some specific developments that increasingly both co-ordinate and differentiate the opening and end title sequences to shed light on two principal questions: (i) why cinema turns to textual media for the paratext and (ii) why books remain, in the age of digital cinema as much as of celluloid cinema, ideal filmic multimedia referents – and particularly in animated feature films.

Before discussing these three films, let me make some preliminary remarks on the ways in which the cinematic paratext and the medium of the book bear on writing in film. Why has the book become such a commonly used medium for opening title sequences? In large part, I suggest, because it provides a solution to an authorship problem specific to film. Because 'filmmaking involves a comparatively large division of labor', observes Georg Stanitzek:

> a film cannot be attributed to one author ... the opening credits (or *génerique*) constitute a paratext that uses a number of the paratextual forms found in books – as a kind of imprint for film – but so in a specifically filmic way ... Just as the book has two covers, a title, an imprint, and so on, a film .... has opening and closing credits, and so on. A book can function as a filmic organizer of communication, as a kind of natural delineation of the entire work.[2]

The homology Stanitzek finds between book and film paratexts allows, I maintain, for a typographical regularization of film authorship by singling out the director in the credits as author, or *auteur*, in a number of ways. Whereas, for example, the name of the screenwriter(s) often appears in a frame alongside others who have worked on the film, the director's name is typically given a frame to itself, a large font size and the significance of being positioned as the final credit of the opening title sequence. As a result of these multiple privileging strategies, one might conclude that film author and film are more strongly connected paratextually than are book author and book.[3] As 'a kind of imprint', the film paratext defaults clearly to an *auteur*, director-as-writer notion of film authorship.

Equally, though, opening title sequences of films begin (and sometimes end) with the studio logo in a more prominent display of institutional authorship than is typically afforded to a publisher in a book's paratextual apparatus. Whereas a publisher's 'introduction' of a book is usually overlooked by readers, the cinematic equivalent cannot be skipped over or fast-forwarded by film viewers as projected in movie theatres or watched on DVD/Blu-ray players. A viewer of a DVD or Blu-ray edition of a film will therefore be forced to 'read' the entire paratext. The peritext of a book (that part of the paratext included in the work's contents) may be said to have been written in a kind of invisible ink; the peritext of a film, the alphabetic text of titles and credits, however, is engraved, as it were, on the image. No wonder, then, that, since the 1950s (when credits first started to be systematically integrated into the film as prologue material to the story itself), the succession of credits has often appeared through the analogy of the turning pages of a book.

Yet if the medium of the opened bound book proposes answers, by way of analogy, to major questions of film authorship (Do films have authors? Yes they do. Who is the 'writer' of the film? The director), it also opens up new questions about film authorship. Title sequences are almost always outsourced, and their 'authors' are frequently not credited. In some exceptional cases, the designer of the opening title sequence is credited, two famous examples of this being Saul Bass in Alfred Hitchcock's *Vertigo* (1958) and Kyle Cooper in David Fincher's *Se7en* (1995). More often, the outsourced agency gets a corporate credit (for example, 'Titles: Pacific Title Company'). The design of the very sequence that asserts the film's authorship is, therefore, frequently undertaken by an anonymous, corporate agent, thereby reinscribing in the film, albeit in a barely noticeable way, the problem of authorial determination (a film being the product of a collaborative team) that the imprint of the book (with the author on the furthest margin of the peritext, the book's spine) would otherwise appear to have resolved.

Stanizeks's important insight that the film paratext tends to default to the medium of the book misses the way a bibliocentric notion of film authorship depends on a spectralization of the writer of the cinematic para-text, a spectralization already happening in books: as Gérard Genette points out, 'the author's name is not necessarily always the author himself'.[4] The author's name is put on the title page and cover outside the main body of the text in a way that creates a mutually legitimating relation between writer and publisher:

> [W]ith respect to the cover and title page, it is the publisher who presents the author, somewhat as certain film producers present both the film and its director. If the author is the guarantor of the text (*auctor*), this guarantor himself has a guarantor – the publisher – who 'introduces' him and names him.[5]

This 'introduction' provides for an opening, but not necessarily for a smooth entry into the book. The most exterior parts of a book's paratext – the cover and title page – paradoxically unify writer and pub-lisher by splitting the author from himself. The publisher's 'introduction' is often followed by another paratext, namely, the author's preface. As Genette notes, 'one of the normal functions of the preface is to give the author the opportunity to officially claim (or deny) authorship of his text' (49). I consider this supplement to the publisher's 'introduction' to be a way of saving not only the writer of the book but the book itself: the supplement serves as a paratextual back-up loosely analogous to an auto-recovered 'saved' digital document.

William H. Sherman has offered a useful corrective to Genette's con-ceptualization of the paratext that focuses almost entirely on a book's introduction.[6] Sherman explores how the paratext significantly shapes the ways in which we finish reading books. Work on the cinematic paratext, however, has followed Genette in focusing on opening title sequences and ignoring the endings and end credit sequences of films.[7] The analogy of front and back book covers with opening and closing film sequences (an analogy specifically evoked by film endings in which the book that opened the film closes just before 'The End' appears), has further broken down or been reworked in ways that turn the closing credit sequence into multiple, individuated stories about the main characters. As I will show at the end of this chapter, Disney's hybrid animated and cinematic feature film *Enchanted* (dir. Kevin Lima, 2007) begins with a book much as Disney's *Snow White and the Seven Dwarfs* (dir. David Hand, 1937) and *Sleeping Beauty* (dir. Clyde Geronimi, 1959) do, but ends with a sequence that serves as a mini-sequel. For the moment, let me note the impossible way in which the ending of *Sleeping Beauty* recalls the beginning.

After the opening title sequence, the film begins conventionally enough with a copy of a book entitled *Sleeping Beauty*, its illustrated pages turning automatically with writing that is also heard in voice-over. The camera

Figure 11.1a–d   The architecture of a book frames the narrative of *Sleeping Beauty* (dir. Clyde Geronimi, 1959). At its opening, the book opens onto the action (a and b); at its close the action is then re-enclosed within the book's covers (c and d).

zooms in on a particular image of the book and passes into the narrative of the animated film. With predictable symmetry, the film reverses this transition at its close, showing the inverse passage from an animated image to that image on the last page of the book, with 'And they lived happily ever after' at the bottom of the page (see the sequence in Figure 11.1). Yet, paradoxically, the book does not close from right to left to arrive at the back cover of the book, as one would expect. No, instead, the book closes from left to right so that we return to the front cover upon which 'The End' and 'A Walt Disney Production' are then superimposed, or 'written'. Even the most conventional manner of using the medium of the book to frame and shape the film's narrative could, therefore, produce bizarre results.

Since the 1990s, end sequences have expanded beyond rolling credits in a markedly wide variety of ways that include epilogues, interviews with characters in the film while still in character, experimental 'aftershots' that some viewers will undoubtedly miss since most audiences leave the theatre or turn off the DVD or Blu-ray when the end credits begin.[8] The end of the film does not bookend the opening so much as it opens new pages of a new book. The differences between the writing of the opening and end sequences are also formal. Stanitzek writes:

> when watching the film at a the cinema or on video or a DVD, viewers see several minutes of carefully prepared closing credits presented in the same typography as that found in the opening credits, and music is provided to help viewers exit the film narrative.[9]

Yet Stanitzek is hardly describing the norm. More often than not, the typography of the closing credits differs completely from the font of the opening titles. So does the music. The studio logo did appear in the same way at the beginning and end of the film for a long period of time, but more recently, logos have become film sequences in themselves (Dreamworks being a good example). The animated logos typically play at the start of the film but not at the end, whereas matte-painted logos of 1930s films often appeared both at the very beginning and very end.[10] I now turn to the endings of Taymor, Greenaway and Moore's films. Here I examine specific ways in which the closing sequences adapt the book written and the book being written. I will consider how these sequences both unify the film and complicate a sense of its ending, of how complete a narrative film is, of when the narrative stops and the closing paratext begins, and so of when one can legitimately exit the cinema or turn off the disc player. Can one still afford to write off the end of film when the end credits begin? Or is one compelled, for fear of missing something, to stay seated and keep watching even after 'The End'? Such announcements of seeming completion can sometimes, of course, be duplicitous, acting as teasing herald to further moments in the textual/paratextual endings beyond 'The End' that loop back the closing paratext to the earlier text of the film. I address these questions and others in a necessarily tentative manner by discussing the extent to which the end sequences of Taymor, Greenaway and Moore's films paradoxically save the film author as a writer in the fullest sense by destroying or disintegrating the book (*auteur*, you will recall, means 'author' in French and has a much higher cultural status than the more everyday *écrivain*, or writer).

Prospero's books do not need to exist materially in *The Tempest*. There are references in Shakespeare's text to his staff and cloak as required stage props, but not to his 'book' or 'books' as necessary stage presences: these exist exclusively through references to a significant but unseen book (or books) elsewhere. Shakespeare's text therefore makes no provision, for example, for us to see Prospero drown his book.[11] The seven-minute-long end-title sequence of Taymor's *Tempest*, designed by Kyle Cooper, however, gives expressive form to the moment when Prospero 'drowns' his book: as the credits roll and the camera is submerged under water, we watch Prospera's books (in plural form) float slowly towards the ocean bottom, musically accompanied by a haunting version of Shakespeare's epilogue, scored by Elliot Goldenthal. Taymor originally cut Prospero's epilogue from the film script but ended up restoring it. In *The Tempest*, the book published as companion piece to the film, Taymor writes:

> The film's last image of Prospera on the ocean cliff, her back to the camera, tossing her magic staff to the dark rocks below, and the staff's subsequent shattering, is the ending. But when all was cut and timed and scored and mixed, the rhythm of the end of the film felt truncated, incomplete. I asked Elliott [Goldenthal] to take these last great words [the epilogue]

and set them to music for the seven-minute-long end-title sequence. And to that haunting female vocal, sung by Beth Gibbons, the credits rolled and we drowned the books of Prospera in the deep dark sea.[12]

Taymor enlarges authorial agency beyond the individual in the 'Rough Magic' preface to the book, reporting that 'we (sic) drowned the books of Prospera' (21). Yet this enlargement of cinematic authorship implicitly extends beyond the production team who helped to implement the Taymor vision for this film to more spectral collaborators also. The end-title sequence during which we witness the visualized consequences of Prospera's declared intent to 'drown' her 'books' allows Taymor to 'double graft' her already gender-bent Prospera to an implicitly invoked 'Shakespeara' as author and to Taymor herself as *auteur*. I read Taymor's film as an allegory of the immersion of the book into a residual paratexual storage space. Taymor accommodates a readerly and spectatorial desire for an authorial force by encrypting and spectralizing the absent writer of the book. She accompanies this allegorical depiction of displaced authorship with a speech-turned-requiem sung by an extra-diegetic female voice (Beth Gibbons of Portishead). The voice is identified only in the end credit sequence rather than spoken by Helen Mirren (Prospera). The authorial specters of the film are (re)called at the end of the tie-in screenplay. The last two pages of this lavish publication show a still taken from the film's closing credit sequence, a still of a book opening up after it has been plunged into the water (Figure 11.2) with the production and cast credits superimposed over the left-hand page.

Filming an adaptation of *The Tempest* allows Taymor to perform a salvage operation on the book, an operation that paradoxically does not save it: precisely because the drowning books apparently lack a paratextual apparatus

Figure 11.2   A drowning book from the visually poetic end sequence of *The Tempest* (dir. Julie Taymor, 2010). This image covers the final double spread of the tie-in screenplay, with credits listed down the left-hand side.

(no titles or authors are visible on the covers), the book as a medium, in its paratextually near-blank form as configured here, serves as a metaphorical storage unit for film, a book cover like the metal canisters used to house rolls of celluloid film that contain, as it were, the author. This paradox may be vividly grasped in the tie-in book of the film *The Tempest*. In a paratextual space usually left blank, namely, the inside back cover and facing page, the film credits for the director and actors are printed just to the left of an 'uncredited' book falling through water (Figure 11.2). The book of the film thus showcases a book displaying neither title nor author while simultaneously recording Taymor as the film's 'author' (asserted via her multiple credits here as writer, director and producer, in combination with the prominence of her name on both front and back covers): since Shakespeare is also, of course, credited as her source at the requisite paratextual moments, it's a kind of hybrid authorship Taymor claims here and one that perhaps extends to the untitled, unauthored book that drifts towards the sea bed on the final page of the volume. By focusing on Prospera's books opening as they fall underwater, Taymor invites us to ask a new question, namely, what does it means to 'drown a book' rather than burn one? Phrased another way, we might ask: Why does Prospero not follow Caliban's instructions to Stephano and Trinculo – 'burn but his books' – in order to destroy them? By shooting them in medium-long shot in murky sea water, Taymor quietly insists on making Prospera's drowned books unidentifiable; even though the pages are open, they are unreadable, and therefore symbolically a repository for other authorial reflections.

Greenaway performs a very different kind of salvage operation in *Prospero's Books*. Cataloguing and displaying the twenty-four books (twenty-five if we include *The Tempest*) of Prospero's library in separate sequences, the film has an epilogue but no closing sequence beyond that. In the final shot, the words 'The End' appear at the bottom of the screen and remain there with additional logo information as the shot fades to black. The opening title sequence consists of one of Greenaway's characteristic tracking shots, the camera moving at a steady pace as it tracks right in one long take. The sequence unfolds much like a scroll; a huge book in the opening title sequence whose pages are turned by a naked man is just one of many bizarre and heterogeneous scenes. By contrast, the interpolated serial book sequences that interrupt the dialogue from *The Tempest* are all set up and set off with the use of a digital paint box. Greenaway visualizes the (extra-textual) book drowning in the film's final *tour de force* montage that ends with the two final book sequences. Prospero's last books – Shakespeare's yet to be completed First Folio and *The Tempest* – prove to be exceptions to the drowning requirement. All of the plays have been printed in the Folio, the narrator tell us, except for *The Tempest*, which is written in a bound book the same size as the Folio. The first page on which Prospero was writing in the film's prologue returns first as a blank space in a facsimile of the Folio and then as a film prop, a bound, completed manuscript of *The Tempest* we saw Prospero begin to write in the prologue.

The permanently blank pages of the First Folio become an empty yet potentially redemptive allegorical space. 'There are thirty-five plays in the book and room for one more,' the narrator says; 'nineteen pages have been left for its inclusion right at the front of the book, just after the preface' as the camera shows the First Folio page with the poem entitled 'To the Reader'. As Caliban surfaces from the water and recovers the floating books, the narrator offers the ostensible reassurance that, 'We still have these two books, safely fished from the sea.'

Of course copies of the First Folio are extant, but in the film these books exist only as props, as referent effects. Shakespeare's safely fished books both expand and diminish Shakespeare's authorial presence: on the one hand, the collected works are completed; on the other, their completion means splitting the manuscript of *The Tempest* from the other, thirty-four printed plays (and implicitly superimposing Prospero on Shakespeare as author of *The Tempest*). In any case, the drowning of Prospero's books but not Shakespeare's is only part of Greenaway's rewriting of the play. Prospero ends by liberating Ariel and delivering the epilogue, a close-up talking-head shot shrinking into a progressively smaller frame until it occupies only its centre and is surrounded by black. In an extra-textual epilogue, Prospero (John Gielgud) is shot in close-up on a stage set, and as the camera dollies back smoothly in what Greenaway calls 'a single, bravura take' (163), we see Ariel (played by three different actors) running towards the camera as a text is superimposed over the applauding audience of courtiers. This last composite shot of the film ends as Ariel is shot in slow motion jumping out of the frame and over the camera.

In a moment of what Latour and Wiebel term 'iconoclash', or uncertainty about whether this liberation from the page is creative or destructive, the manuscripts of *The Tempest* and the First Folio are saved.[13] However, they are saved only, as Judith Buchanan has pointed out, 'within the confines of the film' that becomes not only 'their guardian and vehicle of transmission' but also finally 'the gleeful agent of [their] displacement.'[14] The published screenplay records that Greenaway had intended the film's ending to loop back to the beginning to recover its own non-literary opening: 'A series of ever decreasing splashes drip and plop into the black water … thus the beginning of the film is reprised. A final splash plops … all water-movement ceases and the screen is a black velvet void.'[15] The envisaged symmetrical neatness of this imagery is not, however, where the film itself ends. In the film's unscripted epilogue, the book returns as an unreadable work of art: a single, unbound page resembling an abstract multimedia painting (Figure 11.3c).

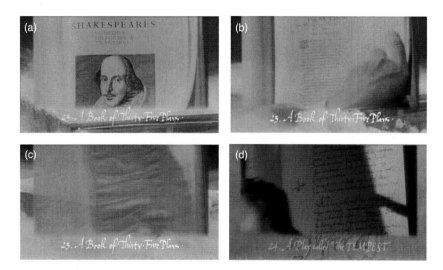

Figure 11.3a–d   The First Folio in *Prospero's Books* (dir. Peter Greenaway, 1991).

The film sequences with 'Prospero/Shakespeare's' (164) books had already begun to make them partially unreadable. The First Folio is submerged even before it is drowned so that the date at the bottom of the page cannot be read (Figure 11.3a). Similarly, the shot of the page with Ben Jonson's dedicatory poem in the First Folio omits the words 'To the memory of my beloved' at the top of the page, showing just 'The AUTHOR MR. WILLIAM SHAKESPEARE: AND what he hath left us' (Figure 11.3b). *The Tempest* is similarly defaced: the manuscript is shot in such extreme close-up that the film frame cuts off the top and bottom parts of the page (Figure 11.3d). Writing becomes automatic. A close-up of the word 'boatswain' we saw Prospero write in the prologue returns in the First Folio sequence, along with Gielgud's voice pronouncing it (and, additionally, 'master') off screen (Figure 11.4a). But this time a question mark is added after 'boatswain' not by the hand of a visible writer bearing a visible quill, a hand which by now we know well, but rather through the apparently agent-less processes of animation (Figure 11.4b).

Similarly, in the final shot, unreadable letters are written backwards in the upper right of the screen through animation and run right to left, some letters disappear as others appear in a recursive cycle (Figure 11.4c). 'The End', the date of *Prospero's Books*, and the film's production companies appear first at the bottom of the final page but then only on the otherwise black screen (Figure 11.4d). Genette's account of the publisher's introduction (consisting chiefly of the author's name on the book cover and title page) is transformed by Greenaway into an 'exit' that involves reading one's way out of his film.

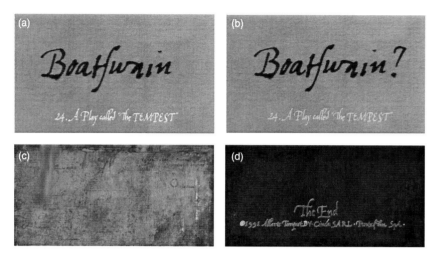

Figure 11.4a–d From the closing sequence in *Prospero's Books* (dir. Peter Greenaway, 1991).

In order to explore briefly the ways in which the book as written and the book being written plays new roles in ending the cinematic paratext as cinema has shifted from analogue to digital, I close with a discussion of the completion of an illuminated manuscript at the end of *The Secret of Kells*. Lev Manovich observes that animation, marginalized when cinema became primarily narrative-based, has returned to the centre in the wake of digital film.[16] Yet animation has also occupied a new paratextual margin: the animated feature film end sequence is noticeably expanded in animated films like *A Bug's Life* (dirs. John Lasseter, Andrew Stanton, 1998). Every Pixar animated feature film ends with an integrated epilogue and end credit sequence. Writing in 2002, Manovich could not have foreseen new developments in immersive cinema that introduce new kinds of books in the cinematic paratext along with new uses of the book as a cinematic medium: the return and continued run of 3D cinema, the 3D effect of LCD flat-screen computers and television sets, 3D television sets, and moving holographs.[17] The end titles of *Kung Fu Panda* (dirs. Mark Osborne, John Stevenson, 2008), for example, unfold horizontally and continuously as a remarkably long Chinese scroll, recalling the scroll that is central to the plot of the film.

The Secret of Kells combines 2D and 3D animation and is explicitly about saving the book. The book in the picture in need of finishing is also made analogous to film – the illuminated manuscript projects light, and, in an act of synecdoche, *The Book of Kells* is reduced to one final page, the Chi-ro page. The book appears neither in opening or closing sequences, but it does appear at the end of the film. Brendan (voiced by Michael McGrath), one of the story's two monkish illuminators, returns as an adult to the Abbey of Kells where he was thought to have been killed long ago by Viking invaders and his book destroyed along with the Scriptorium. Abbot Cellach (voiced by Brendan Gleeson) tells Brendan that all he has left is a fragment of the manuscript, a single page which he unfolds. Brendan consoles him by giving him the now completed book and giving it a new title: *The Book of Iona* has become *The Book of Kells*. This sequence follows a previous one in which we see the master illuminator, Brother Aidan (voiced by Mick Lally), hand the completed book to his assistant Brendan, telling him to take it 'to the people' (Figure 11.5).

Brendan's return to the Abbey is followed by Cellach's vision of the blindingly illuminated and momentarily animated book. Seven close-up shots of details from the book punctuated by a blinding white light (Figure 11.6) are followed by the complete Chi-ro page (Figure 11.6c). The Chi-ro page apparently then seemingly assumes three-dimensions as the camera begins to pass through it (Figure 11.6d). The credit sequence follows as the aftermath of this unreadable vision of depth, mystery and beauty.

The Secret of Kells saves *The Book of Kells* insofar as the book is retitled, fragmented into animated close-ups that freeze on the page, then condensed to a single page, which is then itself dismantled as the camera moves through it. The canniness of *The Secrets of Kells'* quasi-mystical salvage operation (derived from Celtic rather than Christian mythology) may be grasped more fully if we compare the film to two animated films made the same year, films also related to medieval books. In the opening title sequence of *The Tale of Desperaux* (dirs. Sam Fell and Robert Stevenhagen, 2008), we see pages of

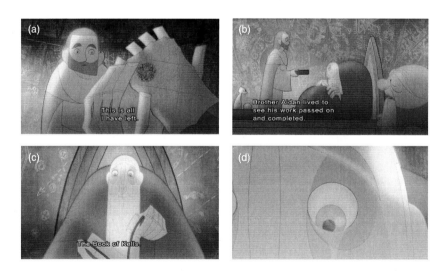

Figure 11.5a–d   Master illuminator Brother Aidan tells his assistant Brendan to take the completed book 'to the people' in the closing sequence to *The Secret of Kells* (dirs. Tomm Moore and Nora Twomey, 2009).

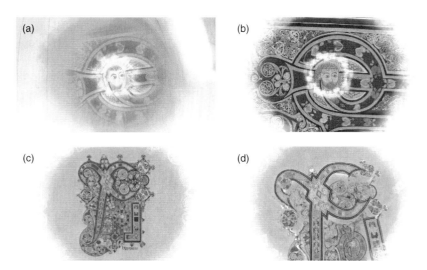

Figure 11.6a–d   The camera passes into the depth of the manuscript's Chi-ro page in the final moments of *The Secret of Kells* (2009).

two different books but the dominant metaphor is an animated thread that makes its way through various surfaces. The film title appears for a final time at the end of a long paper for the 'scrolling' credits, only this time next to a needle and thread. Disney's hybrid film *Enchanted* (dir. Kevin Lima, 2007), which combines animated and live action, begins by recalling the use of books at the beginning of the earlier Disney films that it parodies such as *Sleeping Beauty* (dir. Clyde Geronimi, 1959) and *Snow White and the Seven Dwarves* (dir. William Cottrell et al., 1937). *Enchanted* opens with a book on a stand, but immediately departs from the earlier films as the book opens up as a series of three pop-up book pages before entering the animated prologue of the film. The film ends with a series of happy endings rendered alternately in live cinema and in animation, all held together through pop-up pages that serve as wipes from one scene to the next, the pop-up pages providing in 2D cinema an effect evocative of 3D. 'The End' becomes the final pop-up page, folds it up, and when it closes we see the *Enchanted* book just where we saw it at the beginning of the film.[18] Happy endings can be evenly distributed through a 3D effect that (un)folds live action into animation and, blurring the line between the end of the film and the beginning of the paratextual scrolling title sequence, follows the shot of the book of *Enchanted* closing itself up. Rather than have pages of an ordinary printed book being turned over to open and close the film, as in *Sleeping Beauty*, the pop-up book in *Enchanted* affords a closing and reopening of the ending into multiple endings.[19] Through its idiosyncratic animation style, the ending of *The Secret of Kells* provides a very different complete 3D-effect 'vision' of the illuminated book as animated filmic medium. The completion of the book in the film and its completion of the film's narrative in the book's visualization depends both on rendering the book as unreadable vision and on the complete elimination of the book from the opening and end sequences.[20]

In different ways, then, the endings of Taymor's, Greenaway's and Moore's films save film authorship while showing the book disappearing at the very boundary limits of film. Through its absence or its placement, the ordinarily unwatched end credit sequence becomes specifically readable as a kind of double writing, an epilogue in the form of a reprieve for film authorship that at the same time constitutes a kind of unrecognized mourning that follows the ending of a film. Film authorship is saved, but the crypt within which it may be preserved is provided by images of another medium, the book, and another kind of writing that, in obscuring its own origins, becomes largely unreadable.

Notes

1. The date 1980 is significant in the legal history of film production, marking the introduction of union-negotiated contracts over title sequences. However, the date is somewhat artificial given that graphic design developments in the cinematic paratext are never fully standardized and innovations can be dropped or become the norm decades later. For examples of innovations in opening title sequences never adopted elsewhere, see the opening titles of BBS films from the 1970s such as *The King of Marvin Gardens* (dir. Bob Rafelson, 1972) and *A Safe Place* (dir. Jack Nicholson, 1971). For similarly exceptional innovations, see the last shot of Nicholas Roeg's *Walkabout* (1971) and the parodic rolling end titles during the epilogue of *Strange Brew* (dirs. Bob and Doug McKenzie, 1983).

2. G. Stanitzek, 'Texts and Paratexts in Media', translated by E. Klein, *Critical Inquiry* 32 (1) (Autumn 2005): 27–42 (37, 38). On the book and film, see G. Blanchard, 'Le Scriptovisuel ou Cinémato-Graphe', in *L'Espace et la lettre: Écritures, typographies* (Paris, 1977), pp. 411, 422. For more on the cinematic paratext and the book, see R. Burt, *Medieval and Early Modern Film and Media* (New York: Palgrave, 2008, rev. 2010). On opening title sequences as text to be read in relation to the film, see Tom Conley, *Film Hieroglyphs*, 2nd edn. (Minneapolis: University of Minnesota Press, 2006), pp. xxv–xxvii.

3. The introduction of *The Girl Can't Help It* (dir. Frank Taschlin, 1956) is an exception to the rule. Lead actor Tom Ewell talks to the audience out of character before the film begins and seems to enlarge the aspect ratio of the film from Academy ratio (33.1) to Cinemascope (widescreen aspect ratio) by pushing on the left and right sides of the film image. Similarly, Cecil B. DeMille comes out from behind a theatre curtain and faces the camera directly as he speaks into a standing microphone to introduce *The Ten Commandments* (1956).

4. G. Genette, *Paratexts: Thresholds of Interpretation*, translated by Jane E. Lewin (Cambridge: Cambridge University Press, 1997), p. 46.

5. Genette (1977), p. 46.

6. W.H. Sherman, 'The Beginning of "The End": Terminal Paratext and the Birth of Print Culture', in H. Smith (ed.) *Renaissance Paratexts* (Cambridge: Cambridge University Press, 2011), pp. 65–90. See also Sherman, 'On the Threshold: Architecture,

Paratext, and Early Print Culture', in S.A. Baron, Eric Lindquist, and Eleanor Shevlin (eds.) *Agent of Change: Print Culture Studies and the Legacy of Eisenstein* (Amherst: University of Massachusetts Press, 2007), pp. 67–81.

7. In his brilliant essay, 'Upon Leaving the Movie Theater', in *The Rustle of Language* (New York: Hill and Wang, 1990), pp. 345–6, Barthes ignores end credit sequences and endings.

8. As a central, perhaps inaugural, example, see the closing sequence of *Se7en* (dir. David Fincher, 1995). It is now often possible to see DVDs/ Blu-rays of films from the 1930s to the 1980s on DVD/Blu-ray, released with overture, entr-acte and/or intermission and exit music.

9. Stanitzek (2005).

10. Even logos have sometimes become brief narratives. For example, the Dreamworks logo sequence shows a boy fishing while sitting on a crescent moon. The animated logo sequences of Pixar animated feature films are also memorable, notably in the inventive, extended animated logo sequence at the end of *Wall-E* (dir. Andrew Stanton, 2008). Animated studio logos were used back as far as 1930s. Universal films featured a scale model of the earth being circled by an airplane (not built to the same scale). Clint Eastwood uses this now old logo at the beginning of *Changeling* (2008) in order to make it consistent with the historical period of the film's narrative. Similarly, *The Wolfman* remake (dir. Joe Johnston, 2010) begins with the Universal Studios logo that opened the original 1942 film directed by Curt Siodmak.

11. See B. Mowat, 'Prospero's Book', *Shakespeare Quarterly* 52(1), (2001): 1–33. Shakespeare's *The Tempest* refers, Mowat notes, both to a singular book ('I'll to my book'; 'I'll drown my book') and to plural books ('books I priz'd above my dukedom'; 'burn but his books'). Mowat insists that Prospero's book is present even though there is no stage direction for it in the text: 'Prospero's always-offstage book' is the 'one book essential to his magic, the one that he goes offstage to consult before the series of spirit spectacles begins in Act 3, the same one that near the end of the play he promises to drown as he abjures his magic' (p. 1). Prospero's strangely singular and clearly spectral singular-plural book/s 'appear' only as phantom referents in the printed script of the play. It makes no sense at all to make a prop for the actor playing Prospero to consult off-stage. What are we to make of a phantom prop that is referenced both in the singular and the plural without ever being shown on stage? What is the relation between the book/s and the spirits Prospero commands? Greenaway and Taymor address these questions in very different ways by materializing what is missing.

12. J. Taymor, *The Tempest, Adapted From the Play by William Shakespeare* (New York: Abrams, 2010), p. 21. Peter Greenaway's tie-in book, *Prospero's Books: A Film of the Shakespeare's The Tempest* (Four Walls Eight Windows, 1991) serves as a paratextual commentary on the film, providing information about the sources of each of the twenty seven books shown in the film and giving their titles once again as they are drowned (see pp. 161–2). *The Secret of Kells* Blu-ray edition includes a comic booklet version of the film.

13. B. Latour and P. Weibel (eds.) *Iconoclash: Beyond the Image Wars in Science, Religion and Art* (Cambridge, MA: MIT Press, 2002). Latour and Wiebel write: 'Icono*clasm* is when we know what is happening in the act of breaking and what the motivations are for what appears as a clear project of destruction of art; icono*clash*, on the other hand, is when one does not know, one hesitates, one is troubled by an action for which there is no way to know, without further inquiry, whether it is destructive or constructive' (14).

14. J. Buchanan, *Shakespeare on Film* (Harlow: Longman-Pearson, 2005), pp. 229–30.
15. P. Greenaway, *Prospero's Books: A Film of the Shakespeare's The Tempest*, p. 164.
16. L. Manovich, *The Language of New Media* (Cambridge, MA: MIT Press, 2002).
17. On immersive cinema, see A. Griffiths, *Shivers Down Your Spine: Cinema, Museums, and the Immersive View* (New York: Columbia University Press, 2008). Griffiths focuses on IMAX cinema, not 3D. See also the motionless 3D hologram of the Fabargé egg sequences in *Ocean's Twelve* (dir. Steven Soderberg, 2004) and Anne Eisenberg, 'Holograms Deliver 3-D, Without the Goofy Glasses', *New York Times* (4 December 2010).
18. Pages from the book that opens Walt Disney's *Sleeping Beauty* return in the final shot to reorient the viewer, like a voice-over narrator. In Taymor's films, books are never seen with paratexts but they are all bound. No covers, no titles, no author's names. Prospero's books are bound, with paratexts, but without covers. They have peritexts inside, but are identified by title and author when they are destroyed with the exception of Shakespeare's First Folio. The cover shows the initials 'W.S.' goes between unbound books, sometimes damaged, sometimes disintegrating, sometimes burning both in the diegesis and in the interpolated sequences as opposed to bound books of Shakespeare.
19. The ending of *Enchanted* develops the practice of earlier, much briefer epilogues in films such as *American Graffiti* (dir. George Lucas, 1973) and already parodied in *Animal House* (dir. John Landis, 1978) in which a shot of a character is matched to written text that outlines what became of him or her later in life. For an ending similar to *Enchanted*'s that uses pop-up book pages as a book medium for film, see *Baby Moma* (dir. Michael McCullers, 2008).
20. Both the opening and end sequences have voice-overs. Aisling (Christen Mooney), a fairy who resides near Kells and helps Brendan find berries to make ink for what will become *The Book of Kells*, gives a voice-over prologue in the scrolling credits, and an unidentified and uncredited voice-over speaks briefly in Latin (the Latin text presumably to be found in *The Book of Kells*) in the final credits as well.

12
Deliveries of absence: epistolary structures in classical cinema

Clara Rowland

Part I

In a late sequence from François Truffaut's *Stolen Kisses* (1968), Antoine Doinel (Jean-Pierre Léaud) sends a letter by 'pneumatic post'. It is a farewell letter: 'our feelings will die of the same impossibility of Félix de Vandenesse's love for Madame de Mortsauf'. We see him writing the letter, discarding an early draft, writing it again and posting the letter at night in a Montmartre street while, in voice-over, we hear its contents read aloud by its author. The camera then follows the letter, in its delivery capsule, through an intricate network of underground tubes, until it is delivered on the other side of town where, at dawn, it is opened by a female hand. We then return to the street where the letter originated. Fabienne Tabard (Delphine Seyrig) has crossed Paris to deliver her reply personally to Doinel, proposing a contract with him, whereby she offers herself to him for a few hours: 'Look at me. You wrote me yesterday and the answer is ... me.'

Everything in this sequence, which I take as my departure point, seems to suggest a mirror pattern: a set of oppositions is established and enacted in the relation between the letter and its reply. The whole episode could be described as the doing and undoing of an epistolary situation. Antoine's love letter seems to encompass, under a sole figure, ideas of writing, literature, distancing and projection: sent at night, conveyed through voice-over, its underground trajectory mapping the city through signposts with the names of the corresponding streets, while the transmission process is handled by anonymous human machinery. Fabienne Tabard's reply is, in every way, the opposite of this: she walks through Paris to join Doinel in his room, talks about her own physicality in doing so and about the city she saw on her way, asserts their uniqueness and denies their identification with Balzac's *The Lily of the Valley*.

'I am not an apparition, I am a woman, which is just the opposite', she says to Antoine, thereby crystallising the conflict at the heart of this episode. In the rejection of the epistolary frame of reference summoned by the earlier

sequence, Fabienne also thereby rejects other forms of substitute, representative presence: indeed, in her personal appearance as simultaneously author
of the reply and the unmediated delivery mechanism for it, the immediacy
of vision seems to be restored. In fact, through a game of denial and affirmation, the letter and its reply reveal a tension in the idea of presence that
inevitably encompasses the medium of representation. In this answer to the
letter, the film seems to be affirming something about, in Laura Mulvey's
phrasing, 'its uncertain relation to life and death':[1] in other words, through
the medium of the letter, film is engaging with its own ontology. Can the
cinematic letter bear this sort of representative weight? I believe it can for
the letter opens up a divide where ideas of disembodiment and absence
necessarily surface. One might think of Kafka's description of the love letter
in *Letters to Milena*:

> How on earth did anyone get the idea that people could communicate
> by letter! Of a distant person one can think, and of a person who is near
> one can catch hold – all else goes beyond human strength. Writing let-
> ters, however, means to denude oneself before the ghosts, something for
> which they greedily wait. Written kisses don't reach their destination,
> rather they are drunk on the way by the ghosts. It is on this ample nour-
> ishment that they multiply so enormously. Humanity senses this and
> fights against it and in order to eliminate as far as possible the ghostly
> element between people and create a natural communication, the peace
> of souls, it has invented the railway, the motorcar, the aeroplane. But it's
> no longer any good, these are evidently inventions being made at the
> moment of crashing. The opposing side is so much calmer and stronger;
> after the postal service it has invented the telegraph, the telephone, the
> radiograph. The ghosts won't starve, but we will perish.[2]

Kafka's letter, one of literature's most uncanny depictions of epistolarity, is
also a depiction of writing: Kafka describes 'one's own ghost' secretly evolving 'inside the letter one is writing or even in a whole series of letters' and
addressing the ghost of the recipient. In the spatial and temporal interval
opened up by letters, a phantasmatic dimension is inevitably conjured.
From this stems the famous opposition of two 'orders' of inventions: trans-
portation technologies, where touch is possible and bodies are brought
together; and then, an army of ghosts equipped with letters, telegraphs or
telephones enacting a form of disembodied communication. As Deleuze
once noted, photography and cinema would be part of this second order.[3]
The sequence from *Stolen Kisses* is built upon the same opposition. Truffaut,
I suggest, encapsulates in these few minutes some of the uncanny and
agonistic tensions at stake.

My hypothesis is that the conflict between the opposing concepts in
this example illustrates the functioning of the letter in film. I will look

at how this problem is approached differently in two near-contemporary features: Max Ophüls' *Letter from an Unknown Woman* (1948) and Joseph L. Mankiewicz's *A Letter to Three Wives* (1949). Both are structured around epistolary motifs and both signal a clear interest, within classical cinema,[4] in the circulation of writing. My analysis of both films will examine the conventions of epistolary representation, with its elaborate articulation of voice-over strategies and flashback structures. As has been often recognized, in these two films these conventions are boldly taken to their limits, and I want to suggest that the way in which they engage with their own form can be assessed through the tensions inscribed in the letter as a rhetorical figure. The idea of a separation between voice and body is to them especially relevant – either in the form of a disembodied voice-over, as in *A Letter to Three Wives*, or in the form of a posthumous voice in *Letter from an Unknown Woman*. In this, both films seem to enact what I would like to call a cinematic response *to* the letter, where ideas of writing and cinema are questioned and addressed. In fact, as I shall argue, two opposite responses emerge: denial and subscription.

Part II

> As in the story of the spartan – in Plutarch's Apophthégmata lakoniká – who plucked a nightingale and, finding very little meat, scorned: 'You are just a voice, and nothing more!' (João Guimarães Rosa, 'Aletria e Hermenêutica').

I begin with *A Letter to Three Wives*. In the famous scene where the letter is delivered, the three women are leaving on a boat for a day-trip. Addie Ross's letter is handed to them as they are about to board the boat. They read it together, Addie's voice-over doubling the words on the page, with its disturbing announcement: 'You see, girls, I ran off with one of your husbands.' Hesitating, they obey the captain and climb the stairs. While the boat prepares for departure, the three of them stand on the deck, casting a long, frustrated look at a public telephone on shore.

Although this letter has been visible to the viewer since the title credits, it is only at this point that its importance as a narrative object is established. it is also at this point that this film reveals itself to be based upon the defining polarities of communication. It does so obliquely: for the letter, through its material deployment and integral reading, is presented as an apparently delimited element within the space of the film. Its effects, however, will be difficult to circumscribe. At the level of plot, the letter sets up a question (to whom is it addressed?) that will remain active until the very end. And through an articulated series of displacements in the film's structuring, the two elements conventionally associated with letters (voice-over and flashback) will be sundered from what nonetheless remains their source, beginning either before or after the letter. Such a scene establishes the most significant tension at stake here: the tension between the letter *in* the film and the letter as the structuring device *of* the film.[5] As we shall see, a similar effect will define *Letter from an Unknown Woman* as a 'double letter'.[6]

It is tempting to see the opposition between letter and telephone in the light of a suggestion made by Tom Gunning: 'If the telephone had not existed, film would have to invent it'.[7] As a creation of modernity, the telephone perfectly illustrates cinema's affinity for technology. In itself, the telephone stands for something eminently cinematic, drawing attention, by contrast, to the specifically literary character of the letter. The scene of the women holding the potent letter and gazing from the deck of their departing boat at the inaccessible phone box clearly states the film's entrance in what one might call an 'epistolary mode': the divide between letter and telephone becomes a divide between deferral and immediacy, setting up the particular temporality that will structure the film until the boat's return. The three flashbacks that make up the movie take place in this interval, which is transformed by Addie's letter into a suspended period of waiting and retrospection. Significantly, one of the wives will describe the three women as 'beginning to behave as in some movie about a women's prison'. Until their return to shore, *A Letter to Three Wives* is on the side of the letter.

This distinction between modes of communication reinforces the letter's role in this film as a figure of deferral. However, from a broader perspective, the telephone cannot be entirely isolated from it. If we consider the part radio will play during the second flashback, where the marriage of Rita (Ann Sothern) is threatened both by her work for the radio *and* by Addie Ross, we may begin to see how the family of ghostly forms of communication interacts in the film. What letters, radio and the telephone appear to have in common in *A Letter to Three Wives* is a connection to the idea of a disembodied voice. Proust admirably described the telephone as an instance of separation between voice and body in his character's first phone call in *The Guermantes' Way*:

> Suddenly I heard that voice which I mistakenly thought I knew so well; for always until then, every time that my grandmother had talked to me, I had been accustomed to follow what she said on the open score of her face, in which the eyes figured so largely; but her voice itself I was hearing this afternoon for the first time. And because that voice appeared to me to have altered in its proportions from the moment that it was a whole, and reached me thus alone and without the accompaniment of her face and features, I discovered for the first time how sweet that voice was . . . It was sweet, but also how sad it was ...; 'Granny!' I cried to her, 'Granny!'

and I longed to kiss her, but I had beside me only the voice, a phantom as impalpable as the one that would perhaps come back to visit me when my grandmother was dead.[8]

The telephone functions here as a marker of the same polarity that, according to Janet Altman, is constitutive of every letter: bridge/barrier.[9] The threat of separation is always implicit in its connective function. The possibility of death is discovered and anticipated through the encounter with nothing but a voice. This effect is, as in Kafka, reliant on the mediation of absence, on the fact that bodies are beyond reach. Separated from the face and its readability, this voice becomes the voice of the dead. Michel Chion has read this passage as an example of *acousmatic voice*,[10] connecting its uncanny effect to the cinematic device of *voice-over*. As Mary Ann Doane has stressed, the separation of the voice from its source through *voice-off* or *voice-over* effects entails, in the classical film, the risk of 'exposing the material heterogeneity' of the medium; a risk that is often covered up by the integration of this voice within the dramatic framework, and by its anchoring to a visible body.[11] Provocatively, in *A Letter to Three Wives*, this 'integration' is denied. Addie's voice-over, initially identified as the source of the film, will never be linked to an image. Her voice seems to be hovering over and around the space of a film that, at the same time, seems to revolve around her absence.

In the two examples proposed, the unsettling of the body-voice relation is dependent upon a third element: the inscription of writing. If letters are typically represented through voice-over strategies, we may ask what is at stake when epistolary structures prevent the reintegration of voice and image. These films associate letter writing with a denial of the image in very different ways. Perhaps in these cases the problematic anchoring of the voice depends more on the presence of writing that on the absence (or posthumous impossibility) of a body; or perhaps the uncanny effect of these voices stems from the fact that their source is an absence bodied forth in the form of a letter.

Part III

> Of such a letter, death himself might well have been the post-boy (Melville, *Moby Dick*).

Recognition may be said to be the subject of Stefan Zweig's 1922 novella 'Letter from an unknown woman' from which the Ophüls film was adapted. It becomes a leitmotiv throughout the woman's confession. For her, to be visible is to be recognised as an 'enduring picture' through the intelligibility of memory. It has often been remarked that the fundamental difference between the Ophüls/Koch screenplay and the literary text it adapts is the man's inability to remember. Žižek, for example, briefly summarizes this view:

> What is especially interesting here is the difference between the film and Zweig's story, a difference that confirms the superiority of the film (and thus refutes the commonplace about the Hollywood 'vulgarization' of literary masterpieces). In the story, the pianist receives the letter, reads it, and remembers the woman only in a few hazy flashes – she simply didn't mean anything to him.[12]

Robin Wood, listing the major differences in the adaptation, also notes this distinction: 'Stefan [Louis Jourdan], even at the end, never manages to remember Lisa [Joan Fontaine], and her letter has no discernible effect on his life'.[13] Yet, the idea of a 'discernible effect' is the problematic focus of the novella's last paragraphs: if the writer is unable to form a discrete image of the woman in his mind, the text ends, nonetheless, with an immaterial perception of 'death and (...) of deathless love'. Avrom Fleishman was right in suggesting that 'by having the protagonist go out to die, the film's finale acts out the story's metaphysical rhetoric of a transaction with the dead'.[14] The novella's complex interplay of remembrance and recognition is essential to an understanding of the film's remediation of its source.

Both of my central case study films, in fact, inherit the epistolary motif from their source texts. *A Letter to Three Wives* was adapted from John Klempner's novella 'A Letter to Five Wives' that had been published in *Cosmopolitan Magazine* in 1945. Everything in the film reinforces the epistolary situation created by Klempner, beginning with the film's central idea, Addie Ross's invisibility (claimed by some to have been the suggestion of producer Sol Siegel).[15] But Ophüls' film is adapted from a text that is itself built upon a doubled structure: the Zweig novella places the long, uninterrupted letter-text inside a very brief narrative frame that explicitly questions the effects of reading. This, I believe, cannot be separated from the issue of recognition. The novella is staging writing through writing, while at the same time placing a writer in the position of the reader: this series of doublings is of crucial importance in considering the relations between writing and film. In the novella, the very first thing we are told about R., the novelist, is that he is reminded of his own birthday by glancing at a newspaper's date. We could see this as a premonition of the way the letter will entail a revelation of mortality. But we could also think of this man as being described through Theuth's warning: 'Trust in writing will make them remember things by relying on marks made by others, exterior to them'.[16] In any case, the question this novella asks is one concerning the powers and pitfalls of writing. And, on a broader scale, the same is true of the films themselves.

This is the major issue at the end of the Zweig 'Letter from an unknown woman' novella, when the narrative frame describes the writer's reaction to having read the anonymous letter:

> The letter fell from his nerveless hands. He thought long and deeply. Yes, he had vague memories of a neighbour's child, of a girl, of a woman in a dancing hall – all was dim and confused, like a flickering and shapeless view of a stone in the bed of a swiftly running stream. Shadows chased one another across his mind, but would not fuse into a picture. There were stirrings of memory in the realm of feeling, and still he could not remember. It seemed to him that he must have dreamt all these figures, must have dreamt often and vividly – and yet they had been the phantoms of a dream. His eyes wandered to the blue vase on the writing table. It was empty. For years it had not been empty on his birthday. He shuddered, feeling as if an invisible door had been suddenly opened, a door through which a chill breeze from another world was blowing into his sheltered room. An intimation of death came to him, and an intimation of deathless love. Something welled up within him, and the thought of the dead woman stirred in his mind, bodiless and passionate, like the sound of distant music.[17]

The novelist is unable to remember her. His inability to see is described as an inability to form an intelligible image from scattered flashes (beginning, middle and end: the child, the girl, the woman), shaping them into a consistent visual whole. The tension between the fleeting impression of her body in time and the endurance of memory, as described in the letter, returns here in the opposition between the running stream and the shapeless stone: her image is to him unattainable. However, after restating his blindness, the text depicts an act of perception: the man's eyes wander to his writing desk, where he perceives the absence of the white flowers. Invested by her narrative with a metonymic dimension (these were *her* flowers), the emptiness of the vase depletes the trope and becomes an image of death: the writer thinks of the invisible woman (die *Unsichtbare*, in the German text) as a void, her existence paradoxically acknowledged by its negation (dematerialized: in bodiless thought, like a distant sound). Only in a blank figuration can this recognition of death, brought by a posthumous letter, take place. We are not far here from Zweig's description, in another novella, 'The Invisible Collection', of the blind collector in unknowing contemplation of the blank sheets that have been substituted for his treasured prints:

> I shuddered as the unsuspecting enthusiast extolled the blank sheet of paper; my flesh crept when he placed a fingernail on the exact spot where the alleged imprints had been made by long-dead collectors. It was as

ghostly as if the disembodied spirits of the men he named had risen from the tomb.[18]

It is this same problem that is brought to Ophüls' film by Zweig's 'Letter from an unknown woman', both in terms of the rendering of the letter and of the film's relation to its source. If the perception of a void is the effect of this posthumous reading, can the film put forth what the text itself denies? And how do we relate the voice-over to the articulation between images and writing? These are central questions to Ophüls' work, which, according to Marie Claire-Ropars, 'claims, at the same time, reference to Literature and the self-sufficiency of film'.[19] *Letter from an Unknown Woman* clearly enacts this conflict by foregrounding the letter's materiality through scenes where it is being written and read, counterbalanced, in a complex use of flashback convention, by images in which Lisa's narrative is visually rendered. By doing so, the unknown woman is given not only a name, but also a face. And if the story is *about* recognition, it is also clear that what is impossible in Zweig's text – the reader's remembrance of the nameless writer – becomes possible in the film, where the protagonist can finally act in answer to the letter. Stefan is held back by the letter and prompted by its reading to sacrifice himself in the final duel.

One should not, however, jump to the conclusion that the film responds to the denial of the image in Zweig's story through its flashbacks. In fact, those images are clearly framed by writing. V.F. Perkins has called attention to the fact that the film has a palindromic pattern: the beginning and the end are marked by a series of symmetrical repetitions, such as Stefan's gesture in covering up his eyes, first employed immediately before washing his face, and subsequently echoed, though now in despair, immediately after reading the letter. 'The effect is to lend weight to the containment of Lisa's story within Stefan's, and so to balance our sense of Lisa's letter as the frame within which the events of the past are accessed.'[20]

I would like to take this idea further, by focusing on how the doubling between writing and voice-over is introduced. The letter is delivered to Stefan by his mute butler as he enters his apartment and gives instructions for his departure. He moves around his chambers, throws the letter on his writing desk, takes it to the bathroom where he washes his eyes. At that moment, he is attracted to the letter by its first sentence, which arrests his movements and brings him to the text: 'by the moment you read this letter I may be dead'. We read this sentence through a close-up, *before* it is repeated by the voice-over as Stefan sits down to his reading. From that moment on, the flashback is triggered. The voice comes into play as a deferred doubling of writing. There are only two shots in the film where Lisa's text is *readable* on the screen, in close-ups in which writing figures as both a verbal *and* visual inscription: the beginning of the manuscript was the first. We return to an image of writing, and to the clear repetition of text and voice, only at the end of the flashback. Lisa's final uttered words (*If only...*), interrupted by death as she writes them,[21] are the *raccord* to a voiceless shot of the same words on that last page, now in Stefan's desk, handwritten by Lisa and sealed by the partially typewritten announcement of her death by the sister-in-charge (significantly, these words have no voice-over). The structure is indeed palindromic, in Perkins's terms, or perhaps we should call it chiastic: the uttered words follow or precede the writing, and delimit the complex perspective of the flashback in which Lisa is depicted. The letter functions as the mediator between the two spaces. The impossible co-presence of Lisa and Stefan – writing and reading separated by death, the condition for the letter's delivery – is enacted *through the letter* in its deferred doubling of sound (and as the voice ceases, images get blurred). This, I think, sheds some light upon the issue of invisibility raised by Zweig's text. For if the body of the woman has been constantly shown to us throughout the flashback, and her name has been literally shouted at our ears, what Stefan actually sees is *writing*. The ironic construction of the film seems to enact his blindness through our ability to see, while the status of the voice-over, as the transitional element between writing and the images, is brought into question. In this complex temporality, Lisa's death is revealed at the end of the letter (and of its reading) as having already occurred, being the condition to its delivery. Her voice is reread as the writing that survives her body: anchored to the letter, it has become a posthumous voice.

Part IV

> Dead letters! does it not sound like dead men? (Melville, *Bartleby the Scrivener*)

To understand this better, I propose a return to the celebrated voice-over in *A Letter to Three Wives*. Initially presented as an omniscient narrator, Addie is then revealed to be part of the fictional world she describes and is finally deprived of her apparent control: her letter turns out to be undone by events she couldn't predict. 'A man can change his mind', reads the script: the husband she has run off with returns home. This movement, which is at the heart of the film's comic reversal, should draw our attention to the temporal status of her presumed knowledge.

The film opens with a fixed shot of a train leaving a station by the river. A woman's voice is heard: 'To begin with, all the incidents and characters in this story might be fictitious, and any resemblance to you, or me, might be purely coincidental.' Two things strike me as important here: the first is the way in which the film plays with the conventional written disclaimer. If this begins to establish the paradoxical construction of Addie's movements in and out of the fictional world she supposedly depicts, it also reveals a trope important to the film as a whole: Addie's voice doubles writing, or stands for writing. And not just her writing: towards the end, Addie's voice will be heard over a text that is clearly not hers. Moreover, the initial sequence can be seen, retrospectively, as the moment when the letter is shipped, when we learn that Addie sold her car and left town; and we also learn that Porter (Paul Douglas) was actually seen at the station that morning. The beginning of the movie presents what we will discover to be two opposing movements: the train leaves with Addie while the letter is sent to the wives – Addie's departure is the condition for its delivery. From this stems the particular temporality of Addie's knowledge: her voice knows, one could say, what the letter knows; the letter functions in her absence and her action is confined to its consequences. The intermittent return of her voice can be more or less directly traced to the letter's effects and implications. And the script's provocative insistence upon her body's invisibility is a form of negative affirmation: the voice is anchored to the presence of her absence, in the form of her letter.

It is possible, then, to see the plot's final reversal as the film's undoing of this ghostly presence, much like in Truffaut's example. This letter began its circuit by stating the problem of identifying its addressee (which wife?). The wives then pass from the recognition of themselves as candidates for that position (all three are addressed) to the reassurance of the security of their marriage (none is addressed). The three flashbacks make clear that Addie is a shadow in each of these women's relationships; yet it is also through the doubt instilled by the letter that the film becomes, once the boat returns to shore, a kind of remarriage comedy, in Cavell's terms,[22] in which the threat to marriage and 'the ordinary' is overcome through a reassessment of an open past. The necessary condition to the confirmation of marriage is presence: 'being there' is the answer given by two of the husbands to the women's fears.[23] With this movement, the letter becomes, at one and the same time, unanswerable (Addie has left no address) and undeliverable: it has become a dead letter. Addie can thus be 'the dear departed', or the invisible 'body under the table'[24] only until her absence is relevant. With the plot's final clarification, her disembodied voice takes leave with the famous shot of the glass breaking on the empty table. This radical figuration of an aural void is elided – with the film it signs – in the restoration of presence.

Part V

> Nobody could fight his way through here even with a message from a dead man. But you sit at your window when evening falls and dream it to yourself. (Kafka, 'An Imperial Message')

We can now return to the ending of *Letter from an Unknown Woman* and to the problem of its voice-over. As we have seen, the voices that double these belated letters are affected by the constitutive absence of their authors.

In the end, as the letter is emptied of meaning, Addie's voice takes leave. But in Ophüls' film, Stefan remembers Lisa. Finishing the interrupted letter, he looks away from the page, only to see the seven repeated shots that cause him such horror; the 'spell of his blindness', as Zweig has put it, seems to be broken. But those images are now contaminated by the consciousness of death. Between their first appearance, invisible to Stefan and framed by the written words, and their return, filtered through her death and shared by him, the film enacts a visual quotation that begins to suggest, through repetition, the overlapping between words and images, letter and memory. But just as the letter is still incomplete, this recognition is nothing but partial. For the seven shots Stefan recalls are all related to two of Lisa's three forms: the woman and the girl. What is missing is the image of the child, impossible for him, yet, to recall, since their first encounter is the beginning of Lisa's story (her second birthday, as she says), and can be perceived as such only through the 'retrospective revelation of the law of the whole' of her narrative.[25] For Stefan, to remember it is to recognize the story as *his* story, to recognize himself in it, and to identify that moment as the beginning of a narrative that has now achieved closure. It is here, I think, that the question of this film's response to the letter, and to the ending of Zweig's novella, is most clearly articulated: the condition for this sighting, for the retrieval of the original encounter, is death.

The decision to fight the duel inserts Lisa's letter into what we may call a deadly correspondence, a transactional exchange in which suicide may prove the impossible answer to a posthumous letter. It depends upon the revelation of the name by John, bearer of the letter, figure of the film and inscribed witness to their common past:[26] the letter reaches closure only when the possibility of a reply arises, that is, when it becomes part of a chain of address, giving Lisa her own name.[27] If Lisa uttered Stefan's name just before she died, as we are told by the sister-in-charge, Stefan can at this point double the mute writing of her name in his own voice. It is now that the film's rigorous structure of demarcations between seeing, hearing, writing and reading may be set aside. The letter breaks out of its frame in an open display of contaminations that fully enact a coincidence (a correspondence) between letter and film: now the film *is* the letter. In this, invisibility is reversed: image and sound, now, in a mode of absence, are on the side of the letter. Lisa's voice is heard, outside the flashback, over the image of the vase filled with her roses, and the child's spectral image, by the door, leads him to death. The beginning of their story has become the end.

In an earlier sequence of the film, Lisa and Stefan are walking through the Prater. They talk of wax statues. Lisa wonders whether they'll ever make one of Stefan. 'If they do, will you pay your penny, to come in and see me?' he asks. 'Only if you'll come alive', is Lisa's reply. Between this exchange and its reversal in the end (death as a condition to vision), the film imparts its beautiful uncanny ambivalence, of which the letter is a figure.

Notes

1. L. Mulvey, *Death 24 x a second* (London: Reaktion Books, 2006), p. 18: 'To see the star on the screen in the retrospectives that follow his or her death is also to see the cinema's uncertain relation to life and death. Just as the cinema animates its still frames, so it brings back to life, in perfect fossil form, anyone it has ever recorded.'
2. F. Kafka, *Letters to Milena* (New York: Schocken Books, 1990), p. 223.
3. G. Deleuze, *Cinema 1. L'Image-mouvement* (Paris: Minuit), p. 142.
4. The presence of epistolary structures in Hollywood cinema is strongly indebted to Howard Koch's writing. Besides *Letter from an Unknown Woman*, he wrote the script of two other major 'letter films': *The Letter* (dir. William Wyler, 1940) and *The Thirteenth Letter* (dir. Otto Preminger, 1951).
5. M. Vernet, suggests a doubling in the fact that the letter's circuit (written in the absence of the recipients and received in the absence of the writer) imitates the functioning of the cinematic device. *Figures de l'absence* (Paris: Cahiers du Cinéma, 1988), p. 114.
6. S. Cavell, *Contesting Tears. The Hollywood Melodrama of the Unknown Woman* (Chicago: University of Chicago Press, 1996), p. 108.
7. T. Gunning, 'Fritz Lang Calling: The Telephone and the Circuits of Modernity', in J. Fullerton and J. Olsson (eds.) *Allegories of Communication: Intermedial Concerns from Cinema to the Digital* (Rome: John Libbey, 2004), pp. 19–37, (24).
8. M. Proust, *In Search of Lost Time*, vol. 3 (London: Everyman, 2001), pp. 419–21.
9. J. Altman, *Epistolarity: Approaches to a Form* (Columbus: Ohio State University Press, 1982), p. 186.
10. M. Chion, *The Voice in Cinema* (New York: Columbia University Press, 1999), p. 32; and *Film: A Sound Art* (New York: Columbia University Press, 2009), p. 466. Chion has described the acousmatic voice as a voice whose source is impossible to identify. Its power, he argues, is usually undone through the materialization of the source as a discrete body.
11. M.A. Doane, 'The Voice in Cinema: The Articulation of Body and Space', *Yale French Studies* 60 (1980): 33–50 (35). For a recent detailed analysis of female voice-over in the frame of feminist theory, see B. Sjogren, *Into the Vortex: Female Voice and Paradox in Film* (Chicago: University of Illinois Press, 2004).
12. S. Žižek, *Looking Awry: An Introduction to Jacques Lacan through Popular Culture* (Cambridge, MA: MIT Press, 1991).
13. R. Wood, *Sexual Politics and Narrative Film: Hollywood and Beyond* (New York: Columbia University Press, 1998), p. 203.
14. A. Fleishman, *Narrated Films: Storytelling Situations in Cinema History* (Baltimore, MD: Johns Hopkins University Press, 2004), p. 150.
15. P. Mérigeau, *Mankiewicz* (Paris: Denoël, 1993), p. 99.
16. Plato, *Phaedrus* (Oxford: Oxford University Press, 2002), p. 70.
17. S. Zweig, 'Letter from an Unknown Woman', reprinted in *Selected Stories* (London: Pushkin Press, 2009), pp. 119–120.
18. Zweig (2009), p. 149.
19. M-C. Ropars, 'L'Oubli du Texte', *Cinémas* 4 (1), (Fall 1993), 11–22 (14).
20. V.F. Perkins, 'Same Tune Again! Repetition and Framing in *Letter from an Unknown Woman*', *CineAction* 52 (2000), 40–8 (46).
21. Ropars describes the image of Lisa writing as the sole moment where the suppressed 'graphic gesture' takes over the film, establishing a 'declared *faux raccord*'

between reading and writing as the point of tension between text and film. Ropars (2000), 15.

22. Cavell (1996), p. 108.

23. Porter and Deborah (Jeanne Crain): 'Brad didn't run away with Addie. I did.' 'But how? You're here!' 'A man can change his mind, can't he?'

24. Rita and Deborah: 'There's a fine relaxed atmosphere at this table. It's as if there were a body under it.' 'What was it that you called Addie down at the peer? The dear departed? Maybe that's who's under the table. Only it's Brad.'

25. J. Hillis Miller, *Ariadne's Thread. Story Lines* (New Haven: Yale University Press, 1992), p. 18.

26. For the association between the butler and the director, see Cavell (1996), p. 109; for his description as bearer of the script see Perkins (2000), p. 45.

27. As Branka Arsić suggests: 'The unaddressed do not have a name, however they may be called.' 'Afterword: On Leaving no Address', in P. Kamuf, *Book of Addresses* (Stanford, CA: Stanford University Press, 2005), p. 286.

13

'Far from literature': writing as bare act in Robert Bresson's *Journal d'un curé de campagne* (1951)

Erica Sheen

> I want to be as far from literature as possible, as far from every existing art. ... Until now I have found only two writers with whom I could agree: Georges Bernanos, a little, not too much, and, of course, Dostoevsky. I would like the source of my films to be in me, apart from literature. Even if I make a film from Dostoevsky, I try always to take out all the literary parts. ... I don't want to make a film showing the work of Dostoevsky. When I find a book I like, such as *Country Priest*, I take away what I can feel myself. What remained was what I could have written myself.[1]

Robert Bresson's films present some of the most challenging examinations of authorship and the act of writing in the history of cinema: Agnes' fateful letter in *Les dames du Bois de Boulogne* (1945), adapted from an episode in Diderot's *Jacques le fataliste*; *Journal d'un curé de campagne* (*Diary of a Country Priest*), with its sustained presentation of a young priest's diary, adapted from Georges Bernanos; Michel's diary in *Pickpocket* (1959), with its record of his fascination with Lambert's *Prince of Pickpockets*, adapted from Dostoevsky's *Crime and Punishment*. With such a pedigree, his comments to Paul Schrader in an interview in 1976 may seem surprising. By his own account, his approach to film-making is resolutely un-, even anti-literary. His highly personal use of the term 'cinématographe', recorded in the 'Notes' which were surely the off-screen model for his on-screen preoccupation with private journals,[2] draws on a distinction between the practices of writing that underpinned his own work and the role of adaptation in mainstream production. So elusive in its relation to 'movements' like French New Wave or the American Independents, yet so powerful in its influence on individual directors, Bresson's work has been fundamental to the post-war emergence of an international cinema that rejects an aesthetic of mass production and reimagines film-making as a radically personal synthesis of its full range of creative practices.[3]

Notwithstanding his desire to distance himself from the idea of literature, literary terms of reference appear repeatedly in appraisals of Bresson's work. According to Jacques Rancière, his 'alterations' to the 'normal expectations … of mainstream cinematographic practice … share some properties with literary procedures'.[4] For Marguerite Duras, 'what has been accomplished in poetry, in literature, Bresson has done with the cinema'; for Bernardo Bertolucci, Bresson's work is 'a kind of film *manifesto* for poetic rigour.' More recently, Mireille Raynal-Zougari found Bresson's 'poésie' in his 'reconfiguration' of Bernanos, and suggested that 'on peut alors voir en Bresson un poète, ou un nouveau roman-cier'.[5] While the analogy is a valuable starting point for a discussion of Bresson's stylistic originality, part of the point of this chapter is to question any version of the tendency to allow 'literature' to assert itself as a master-category for the analysis of film and cinema. In the discussion that follows, I argue that *Journal d'un curé de campagne* (hereafter *Journal*) presents what I will refer to as a 'bare act' of writing: an act of writing that, in its onscreen presentation *as* act, strips away the parasitically literary values of the adaptive process to reveal a radically non-literary understanding of the role of writing in the making of film.

My use of the term 'bare act' takes its point of departure from a philosophical tradition of commentary on the nature of perception. Writing in 1728, Zachary Mayne referred to 'the bare act of perceiving an idea', a state of affairs in which 'the mind can have no notion at all; that is, in other words, it can have no understanding or intellectual knowledge and discernment of what it perceives'.[6] Clearly, this is not to say that such an act cannot, at least potentially, give rise to understanding, knowledge or discernment; only that it can be identified as a distinct event in the process of cognition. For my purposes here, the term acts usefully as a restraint on post-modern assumptions that consciousness is 'always already' engaged in interpretation, as well as the related inference that a mind not so engaged is necessarily an *un*conscious one. It also accords with Bresson's own understanding of the nature of perception, and with the way he applied it to the making of film. P. Adams Sitney suggests something of its scope for my analysis in his description of Bresson's 'art' as one in which '"intelligence" is defeated by "automatisme", sound invents silence, emotion takes precedence over representation, and one sees "models" rather than "acteurs"'.[7] According to Roland Monod, who played the pastor in *Un condamné à mort s'est échappé* (1956), Bresson gave him the following description of the act of reading in order to explain an instruction *not* to think about the meaning of his lines:

> When you are reading, your eye just strings together black words on white paper, set out quite neutrally on the page. It's only *after* you have read the words that you begin to dress up the simple sense of the phrases with intonation and meaning – that you interpret them … [A] text should be spoken as Dinu Lipatti plays Bach. His wonderful technique simply releases the notes; understanding and emotion comes later.[8]

Before discussing the film itself, I want to suggest exactly what aspects of Bernanos' novel Bresson 'takes out' in order to find its 'source ... in me'. From his very first phrase, Bernanos' priest is deeply immersed in the European crisis of the 1930s:

> Ma paroisse est une paroisse comme les autres. Toutes les paroisses se ressemblent. Les paroisses d'aujourd'hui, naturellement ... Ma paroisse est dévorée par l'ennui, voilà le mot. Comme tant d'autres paroisses! L'ennui les dévore sous nos yeux et nous n'y pouvons rien. Quelque jour peut-être la contagion nous gagnera, nous découvrirons en nous ce cancer. On peut vivre très longtemps avec ça ... Je me disais donc que le monde est dévoré par l'ennui.[9]

Note those first two words: 'ma paroisse'. We are introduced to the priest as a man who defines himself by his relation to his parish, not the written page as in Bresson's film. The repetition of 'paroisse' rings like a bell across the first paragraph, opening an unfolding horizon which takes our eye from 'ma...' to 'toutes...' and then to 'le monde', the world. This spatial dynamic underpins our understanding of Bernanos' priest, unlike Bresson's, as a man fully and actively 'in the world'. We might also note that we are introduced immediately to the idea of cancer, from which the priest is later revealed to be suffering, as an image of this social condition rather than a general expression of personal alienation, as in the film.[10]

It is only after this highly developed contextualization that we arrive at the point at which the film starts:

> Je ne crois rien faire de mal en notant ici, au jour le jour, avec une franchise absolue, les très humbles, les insignifiants secrets d'une vie d'ailleurs sans mystère.[11]

In the film, as we shall see, this opening statement initiates a sustained and intense focus on what I have called a bare act of writing. Here, the previously established connection between 'paroisse' and 'monde' underpins the representation of a life that is 'sans mystère' because it *is* 'in the world', not because it is apart from it. Bernanos' priest's poverty is a historical poverty: it has been in his family for generations ('je descends d'une lignée de très pauvres gens, tâcherons, manœuvres, filles de ferme, le sens de la propriété nous manque, nous l'avons sûrement perdu au cours des siècles').[12] But we also learn that, despite a childhood of savage deprivation, he enjoyed academic success at the seminary that has resulted, as the Dean of Blangermont observes, in a biting awareness of the injustice of wealth:

> Mon enfant, a-t-il repris d'une voix plus douce, je crains que vos succès scolaires n'aient jadis un peu faussé votre jugement. Le séminaire n'est pas le monde. La vie au séminaire n'est pas la vie.[13]

It is above all this sense of injustice, and the authoritative voice it gives him in his writing, which makes us aware of its writer as an *author*: as the Dean puts it, 'Je vous soupçonne d'être poète (il prononce poâte).'[14] This is nowhere more apparent than in his Dostoevskian dialogues with the Curé de Torcy, in which we become aware that the priest's journal is also 'in the world': a document that is read and discussed by others. The priest believes so strongly in his ideas about the problem of poverty, particularly as they bear on the question of the Church's response to the Russian revolution, that he shows his journal to the Curé, under the pretence that it has been written by a friend:

> J'ai fait lire ces lignes à M. le Curé de Torcy, mais je n'ai pas osé lui dire qu'elles étaient de moi. Il est tellement fin – et je mens si mal – que je me demande s'il m'a cru. Il m'a rendu le papier en riant d'un petit rire que je connais bien, qui n'annonce rien de bon. Enfin, il m'a dit:
> – Ton ami n'écrit pas mal, c'est même trop bien torché.[15]

The two priests discuss the historical difficulties involved in seeking the kingdom of God in the modern world, the role of poverty in God's confrontation with the Devil, and Russia's answer to both. This gives rise to an internal meditation on the part of our priest that is simultaneous with the continuing conversation: 'I too often find myself thinking about the Russians'.[16] The narrative that follows is of Proustian complexity: this iterative statement opens into a general reflection on Russian literature ('If one has known real poverty … Russian writers can bring tears to the eyes'), thence to personal memories of his father's death, mother's illness and the school where a kindly teacher lent the lonely child Gorki's *Childhood Memories*. Although he is aware that Gorki made so much money from his writing that he can 'live in luxury somewhere on the Mediterranean', he confides that this book has given him genuine insight into a 'law' to which he had hitherto submitted 'without understanding':[17] the law of poverty. Once again the idea of a bare act, but here it's taken as evidence of mere ignorance, ignorance that has been replaced, through the experience of literature, by knowledge:

> Il n'y a rien de plus dur que l'orgueil des misérables et voilà que brusquement ce livre, venu de si loin, de ces fabuleuses terres, me donnait tout un peuple pour compagnon.[18]

Bernanos' sense of an international order in which French Roman Catholics and Russian communists could be 'compagnons' in the fight against poverty,[19] and of the privileged role of literature in its construction, is precisely what Bresson's film excludes. On the face of it, this might seem to suggest that Bresson's understanding of the role of film 'in the world' was more reduced than Bernanos' conception of literature; that it aspired less, if at all, to the status of 'engagement'.[20] Some commentators have indeed come to this conclusion – though not, one might add, fellow French filmmakers in the 1950s and 1960s. Writing in the early 1970s, Paul Schrader claimed that 'there are very few cultural elements intermingled with transcendental style in his films ... Bresson is alienated from his contemporary culture' – by which he seems to mean that Bresson's characters do not assassinate politicians or ride bikes across the USA.[21] In fact, there is a glimpse of such possibilities in the priest's brief experience of the open road on Olivier's motorbike, and in the way he is implicated in the Countess' death, but it's in Bresson's presentation of the kinds of experience that close such possibilities down that the *counter*-cultural dimension of his conception of film resides. As we have seen, *Journal* begins at a point that is reached in the novel only after extended contextualization. From the outset, Bresson's interest lies in a far simpler process of writing. As the opening credits begin, we are presented with an image of two notebooks (one to the side, one centrally placed), an inkpot, and a pen. This image remains unchanged until the last credit: 'scenario, adaptation et réalisation de Robert Bresson'. At this point, the credit fades, the last chord of the opening music dies, and a left hand comes across the frame from the bottom left to open the notebook's cover, revealing a much-used sheet of blotting paper. A right hand holding a pen comes up to move this sheet, revealing a page of writing. As the camera moves into a close-up on the page, a voice-over begins, speaking exactly the same words that are written on the page:

> Je ne crois rien faire de mal en notant ici, au jour le jour, avec une franchise absolue, les très humbles, les insignifiants secrets d'une vie d'ailleurs sans mystère.

It's hard to decide the relation of priority between the two (is the written page a transcription of an inner voice, or the voice an enunciation of the written page?); or it would be, if the film gave any hint that it required us to make such a decision. There is a tendency in commentary on this distinctive, multilayered structure of narration – Susan Sontag has called it 'superfluous' narration[22] – to describe it as 'complex'. For Nick Browne, for instance,

> The significant and expressive relations between the voice-over and image in the film are complex. Text is neither a simple commentary on the image, nor is the image a simple illustration of the text. Disjunction, independence, interrogation, and even negation of the image, by the sense of the text, is as much a feature as illustration or duplication.[23]

Offering a brilliant analysis of these complexities, Browne concludes that 'the theoretical model capable of representing the general structure of this sort of narration ... must necessarily challenge and extend existing accounts of narrative theory in film.'[24] Quite so; but would such an account extend our understanding of this film? The overall effect of Bresson's coordination of written text, voice and performance is one of supreme clarity, not theoretical complexity: a sense that a counterpoint of all available strands of expression has simply been released, rather in the way that Bresson describes Lipatti's performance of Bach as 'releasing the notes'.[25] There is an additional element of 'réalisation' in the opening scene that strengthens this reading. Throughout the opening sequence, the image that lies behind the credits looks like a *drawing*, perhaps above all in the unrealistic play of shadows across its surface: the deep shadow of what we can infer to be a wine bottle and glass, lighter grey shading behind the inkpot, and a shallow dark line along the side of the pen, all going in completely different directions. What kind of light source could possibly produce such an effect? Yet, after the last credit, there is an all-but-imperceptible cut as the music dies, and the image begins to move. What seemed to be a drawing has become real; or rather, it has become a film.

Perhaps paradoxically, the range of variations identified by Browne in the relation between text and image (disjunction, independence, interrogation) has the effect above all of sustaining this clarity. In total, there are twenty episodes of writing, with words taken more or less directly from Bernanos' novel.[26] The elements introduced in the opening scene – notebook, inkpot, pen, blotting paper, the hand that writes, the voice-over – all recur, but each in a *mise-en-scène* that is particular to its own episode. For instance, we see the blotting paper again in episode ten, in which the priest reflects on Seraphita's cruelties. The inkpot appears again in episode fourteen, in which the priest records the Countess' death. There are similar variations in location. Sometimes we see the priest at his table writing, but not the page itself; sometimes we see the page in an implied POV, but not the priest. In episode ten, the priest is sitting with his notebooks and pen in his kitchen; in episode seventeen he is sitting on his bed. After he goes to Lille, we see him writing in a café, and then finally in his friend Louis' apartment (episodes eighteen and nineteen). Obviously, basic questions of narrative information are engaged here: we learn where the priest is at given points in the story. But it would not be possible to say that there is *meaning* in these compositional permutations. There's no meaning involved in seeing the blotting paper in episode fourteen; or if the priest is in his bed or at a desk or in his bedroom or in his kitchen; or even, I would argue (against Browne) in the choice of a mid-shot staging showing the priest writing at his desk accompanied by a voice-over, as opposed to a voice-over and POV of the written page.[27] Rather, there is an accumulative principle at work here that I will describe as non-significant variation (not quite the same thing as Sontag's superfluity). An exception to the rule might be the film's treatment of the number of visible notebooks, their accumulation being the most reliable, if not the only, indication of passing time. But even here the principle would seem to apply. The opening scene shows us one notebook in the centre of the frame and one to the side, but we do not know if the one to the side has already been started or if it's a new one waiting to be used, so we do not know, as we do in the novel, if what we are witnessing is the 'beginning'. In episode seventeen, which takes place just before the priest goes to Lille, there is one notebook on the table beside the priest as he sits on his bed writing in a second book. It has a different design on the cover from the one we see at the opening, so it's obviously not that 'first' notebook. When he packs to go to Lille, we see a bundle of six or seven notebooks, which we see again in Lille just before he dies, when he drops, and apparently never picks up again, something like the same number.

There is, in other words, no essential correlation between the *number* of notebooks we see and the way the fact that there *is* a number works as indication of passing time. Like all patterns of repetition and difference, these variations have, above all, the effect of suppressing their own claim to meaningfulness as individual events over the *insignifiance* (the word used in the opening quotation) of the continuing process of daily noting. They are, in other words, themselves bare acts of writing. Contrary to the claims of much recent Bressonian scholarship, they are not primarily 'material' in their effect.[28] This seems to me fundamental. Nick Browne argues that the film 'seem[s] to acknowledge that the handwritten manuscript refers to the fiction of a typographically printed novel as the source'.[29] But we should mark the contrast between the conventional presentation, in such contexts, of a handsome printed volume or page, replete with the parasitically literary values of adaptation, and this unfinished, messy manuscript, which, unlike the journal in Bernanos, lacks any pretension or aspiration to readership, let alone publication. Films that begin with representations of the books they are about to present to their audiences are of course not unusual; they are a conventional feature of the process of adaptation that underpins mainstream cinemas like Hollywood and the French *cinéma de qualité*.[30] Cecil B. DeMille's *Ten Commandments* (1956) provides an instructive example. Like *Journal*, it begins with a cut from graphic to photographic image with voice-over. But here one would hardly describe the transition as 'all-but-imperceptible'. DeMille's manuscript-style catalogue of scriptural 'sources' – 'Philo, Josephus, Eusebius, the Midrash and the Holy Scriptures' – gives way to a massive widescreen image of sunlight breaking through clouds, accompanied by DeMille's own voice authoritatively intoning 'let there be light'. Since the film is preceded by a prologue mimicking a theatrical appearance in front of onscreen cinema curtains, in which DeMille in person spells out the importance of his film in the uncertain international climate of the Cold War, the message is unmistakeable.[31] Nothing could contrast more strongly with the Bressonian *cinématographe* in its refusal to approach film as a debased form of theatre, or make a better case for the usefulness of the idea of the bare act as a way of approaching it.

The physical and temporal indeterminacy of the priest's daily noting process is emphasized by the journal's interaction with other forms of writing, particularly books and letters, but also other handwritten and printed documents interspersed with or inserted within them. When we first see the Countess sitting alone in the château, she appears to be reading a book, but as she glances down at it, a POV shows us that what she is actually looking at is a memorial card for her dead child: an elegantly printed page-sized sheet with a black frame, an oval image of the little boy at the top and beneath it a discreet black Cross. She closes the book, enclosing the card, as she looks towards the priest, who (as far we know) never actually sees that card but later retrieves from the fire the same image of the dead child framed in the Countess' medallion. The priest receives an anonymous letter telling him to leave the village. When he finds Mlle. Louise's missal in the church, inside which she has placed a handwritten copy of *L'Imitation de Jesus-Christ* (from Book 3, '*De la vie intérieure*'),[32] he realizes that the handwriting in the letter is hers. In the extraordinary scene at the confessional, Chantal hands him a letter, a blank white envelope passing in close-up between their hands in a composition that could remind us either of Michelangelo's 'Creation of Adam' or of *Pickpocket*. When he throws it on the fire, anticipating the Countess' later action, we see Chantal's handwriting on the cover, 'à mon père'. The Countess sends him a letter after their fateful interview. After her death, the priest drops it in front of the Count, who bends to pick it up – it is framed in black, like the memorial card – and recognizes his wife's handwriting. It should be emphasized that in several of the episodes cited above, the question of what these letters actually *say* is irrelevant, since their content goes unread: the priest does not read Chantal's letter to her father; the Count does not read his wife's letter to the priest. The point in all of them is how they, and we, respond to basic graphic qualities in the image. Over the course of the film, we become acutely sensitized to often minute differentiations. This increased sensitivity can be calibrated, once again, by contrasting that all-but-imperceptible cut between drawing and film in the opening scene with the climax of the last three shots: the quite shocking transition between the now fragile handwriting of the priest's last entry in the journal, the formally typed letter from Louis reporting his death, and the full screen close-up of the Cross.

André Bazin has described this last image as

> a sublime achievement of pure cinema…; the screen, free of images and handed back to literature, is a triumph of cinematographic realism. The black cross on the white screen, as awkwardly drawn as on the average memorial card, is a witness to something the reality of which is only a sign.[33]

This argument leads to Bazin's famous discussion of the idea of 'fidelity', a critical concept that provides one of the most controversial examples of that tendency to allow literature to provide master-categories for the analysis of film and cinema to which I referred in my introduction.[34] It's one of the great ironies of film criticism that this idea should have been advanced in a discussion not just of Bresson, but of this image in particular. Much as Bazin's description of the Cross 'as awkwardly drawn' is an important acknowledgement of the graphic dimension of Bresson's work, the suggestion that it 'hand[s the screen] back' to literary signification seems to me simply wrong. Its effect is exactly the opposite: it ensures that the *source* of this film emerges, finally, as 'in me', *not* literature. This may seem paradoxical: after all, conventional wisdom (and Cecil B. DeMille) would seem to suggest that sources precede adaptations, not follow them. Bresson's *réalisation* suggests otherwise. Images of the Cross appear throughout the film; indeed, as we have already seen, one of them appears on a memorial card, not awkwardly drawn at all, but beautifully printed. The priest has a Cross on the wall behind his bed, which we see first in medium long shot as we look through the window towards him in bed at night. From this angle, it appears, like the photo on the memorial card and the Countess' later letter to the priest, to be positioned inside a black frame, which closer inspection reveals to be a bare bed-curtain rail, curiously flattened by the angle of the shot. Is it a drawing or an object? Oddly, the fact that the light from the bedside lamp seems to cast against it another of those all-but-imperceptible shadows makes it no easier to decide. In a later scene shot inside the priest's bedroom, the Cross, now free of internal frame but still strangely immaterial, appears behind his left shoulder in the upper right hand corner as he agonises about losing his faith. As the screen fades to black, the Cross disappears into darkness.

By the time we arrive at the final sequence, then, the Cross is deeply implicated in the process that begins in the opening sequence and ends here: the transformation of writing into film. If you look carefully, you will see that here too it looks more like a shadow than a drawing, as it emerges in close-up behind the printed writing of Louis' letter to fill a screen that brightens perceptibly before cutting sharply into darkness. But what kind of light source could possibly produce such an effect...?

I don't think you have to be Roman Catholic, or even religious, to appreciate the power of Bresson's answer to this question. It is appropriate that *Journal d'un curé de campagne* should end, as it begins, with an image that contrasts so intelligently with deMille's extravagantly expensive *fiat lux*. Bresson's *cinématographe* might be described as a filmmaker's version of the priestly law of poverty. Here perhaps is the most important point of faith – not fidelity – between novelist and director. In a conversation with Jean-Luc Godard and Michel Delahaye in *Cahiers du cinéma* in 1967, he found himself in difficulty trying to explain his understanding of his own work, and could only grasp towards the completion of the notebooks that would follow in 1975:

> But I think that we are sinking into far too many subtleties, abstractions. It would be necessary . . . I am going to finish those notes, that book, that I am in the midst of writing, and in which I will explain all that. And I will need many pages to explain what happens, to explain the difference that there is between a professional actor who tries to put himself, tries to forget himself, tries to . . . and who arrives at nothing. ... [I]f I had been willing to accept actors, I would be rich. Well, I am not rich. I am poor.[35]

For Bresson, as for his priest, poverty may be the necessary condition of freedom, but the bare act of writing, insofar as it enables the writer to find himself in what comes after it, is the means of release:

> [I]n all cases it seems to me that I have done the best of what I have done when I found myself resolving with the camera difficulties I had not been able to overcome on paper, and that I had left blank.[36]

Notes

* This essay is dedicated to Plum, who died while I was writing it.

1. P. Schrader, 'Robert Bresson, Possibly', *Film Comment* 13.5 (1977), in J. Quandt (ed.) *Robert Bresson* (Ontario: Cinematheque Ontario, 1998), p. 488.
2. Eventually published as *Notes sur le cinématographe* (Paris: Editions Gallimard, 1975). P. Adams Sitney describes this 'slim but thrilling volume' as 'notes written to himself' (my paraphrase), in which '[Bresson] provided several hints about his theoretical orientation towards his medium, most importantly, his distinction between 'le cinéma', a debased version of theatre, and 'le cinématographe'. (P. Adams Sitney, 'Cinematography vs the Cinema: Bresson's Figures' from P. Adams Sitney (ed.) *Modernist Montage* (New York: Columbia University Press, 1989) in Quandt (1998), p. 145). As we shall see, Bernanos uses the verb *noter* to refer to the priest's diary-writing in the sentence Bresson selects for the first image of the film.
3. I cannot pursue here an argument implicit in a distinction between these 'radically personal' practices – which are also a radical reimagination of the terms for collective experience in post-war Europe – and the ideas of *auteur* and 'art cinema' generally used to address them. This argument will be developed in my forthcoming study, *An Art of Possibility: International Cinema in Cold War Europe*.
4. J. Rancière, 'Aesthetics against Incarnation: An Interview with Anne Marie Oliver', *Critical Inquiry* 35(1), (2008), 172–90. The analysis of the opening shots of *Au hasard Balthasar* (1966), to which this discussion refers, is part of Rancière's critique of the notion of medium specificity in J. Rancière, *The Future of the Image* (London: Verso, 2007).
5. M. Duras in Quandt (1998), p. 530; B. Bertolucci in Quandt (1998), p. 529; M. Raynal-Zougari 'Bernanos-Bresson (*Journal d'un curé de campagne*): le

spectateur du film/lecteur du journal, ou l'image des mots', *French Forum* 33(3) (2008), 105–21.

6. Z. Mayne (1728) *Two Dissertations Concerning Sense and the Imagination with an Essay on Consciousness*, York University Ebooks and Text Archive, at: http:// www.archive.org/details/twodissertations00maynuoft. I'm grateful to Tom Stoneham for this reference, and to Tom and Howard Robinson for discussions of the idea.

7. Sitney in Quandt (1998), p. 145.

8. R. Monod, 'Working with Bresson', *Sight and Sound*, 26 (1957), 30–2.

9. 'Mine is a parish like all the rest. They're all alike. Those of today, I mean. ... My parish is bored stiff; no other word for it. Like so many others! We can see them being eaten up by boredom, and we can't do anything about it. Someday perhaps we shall catch it ourselves – become aware of the cancerous growth within us. You can keep going a long time with that in you ... Well, as I was saying, the world is eaten up by boredom ... .(1–2) All citations from G. Bernanos *Le Journal d'un curé de campagne* (1936) are from *Wikilivres*, at: http://wikilivres.ca/wiki/ Journal_d%E2%80%99un_cur%C3%A9_de_campagne (accessed 14 December 2012). Translation: P. Morris *The Diary of a Country Priest* (New York: Carroll and Graf, 1983).

10. The priest's illness is not identified in the film until his visit to the doctor in Lille just before his death.

11. 'I don't think I am doing wrong in jotting down, day by day, without hiding anything, the very simple trivial secrets of a very ordinary kind of life.' Morris (Bernanos) (1983), p. 7.

12. 'I come of very poor forebears, jobbers, unskilled labourers, farm-girls – we've always lacked a sense of property, or must have lost it in the course of centuries.' Morris (Bernanos) (1983), p. 33.

13. 'My dear lad, I am afraid the academic successes of your boyhood may perhaps have distorted your judgement. The seminary is not the world, you know – real life is not like that.' Morris (Bernanos) (1983), p. 66.

14. 'I suspect you of being a poet', he said. (He pronounced it po-ate.)' Morris (Bernanos) (1983), p. 69.

15. 'I gave the above to M. le Curé de Torcy to read, but I did not dare tell him that I had written it. He is so shrewd, and I'm such a pitiful liar that I still wonder if he believed me. He handed me back the paper with a smirk, a glint in his eye to which I'm accustomed, and that bodes no good. At last he said: "Your friend seems to write rather well, rather too well, if you ask me."' Morris (Bernanos) (1983), p. 47.

16. Morris (Bernanos) (1983), p. 50.

17. Morris (Bernanos) (1983), p. 52.

18. 'There is nothing harder to break down than the pride of the very poor, but suddenly this book of Gorki's, come from so far, from those vast stretches of land, gave me a whole people for my companions.' Morris (Bernanos), p. 53.

19. An element of caution is needed in interpreting this position. It would be easy to assume, particularly from the Curé de Torcy's account of his experiences in a previous parish, from which he was expelled for trying to explain the law of supply and demand to his congregation, that Bernanos' personal sympathies were politically radical. Indeed, such a reading of his position may have been available in the immediate post-war years, when he was known as 'the bard of the Resistance'. However, as John Hellman has argued, in the 1930s his sympathies were Christian anti-capitalist – with more than a tinge of anti-semitism – rather

than socialist or even anti-fascist. See J. Hellman 'Bernanos, Drumont and the Rise of French Fascism', *The Review of Politics*, 52(3) (1990), pp. 41–59.

20. For the influential concept of 'engaged literature' see J.-P. Sartre, *What is Literature? And Other Essays*, trans. B. Frechtman et al. (Cambridge, MA: Harvard University Press, 1988).

21. P. Schrader, *Transcendental Style in Film: Ozu, Bresson, Dreyer* (Berkeley: University of California, 1972), p.60. In the interview quoted at the beginning of this chapter, Schrader suggests the importance of Bresson's influence on his script for *Taxi Driver* (dir. Martin Scorsese, 1976), but refers to the 'fog of misunderstanding' that took place when they finally met: 'there was never the rapport I had hoped for. His answers were not in tune with my questions, or my questions with his answers.' (Quandt [1998], p. 485).

22. S. Sontag 'Spiritual Style in the Films of Robert Bresson', from *Against Interpretation* (New York: Farrar, Strauss and Giroux, 1964) in Quandt (1998), p. 61.

23. N. Browne, 'Film Form/Voice-Over: Bresson's *The Diary of a Country Priest*', *Yale French Studies* 60 (1980) in Quandt (1998), pp. 215–6.

24. Quandt (1998), p. 221.

25. Monod (1957), pp. 31–2.

26. There isn't space in this chapter to provide a breakdown of these episodes. See M. Raynal-Zougari (2008), pp. 117–20, for a 'découpage des séquences mention-nées dans le texte'. The numbers I use here are not the same as hers.

27. Browne's analysis links shot scale and camera movement to 'a complex mode of structure of authority within indirect discourse [which] must certainly be grounded in the distinction in the scope and province of the dramatic "I", the narrative "I" and the camera'. (Quandt (1998), p. 217)

28. Keith Reader, for instance, refers to the 'materialist stress on writing that has pervaded a film in which the suffering body and the body of writing meet as in scarcely other.' K. Reader, *Robert Bresson* (Manchester: Manchester University Press, 2000), p. 39. James Quandt discusses the interplay between the terms 'materialist' and 'transcendental' in recent Bresson scholarship in Quandt (1998), pp. 9–11.

29. N. Browne in Quandt (1998), p. 219.

30. See for instance Claude Autant-Lara's *Le rouge et le noir* (1954), and the trailer, though not the actual film, of René Clément's *Gervaise* (1956), at: http://www.youtube.com/watch?v=TSVKKHBAGeM. I am grateful to Keith Reader for these suggestions.

31. It's worth remembering that the Paramount mountain logo, which appears after the Prologue, was altered for the occasion to look like Mount Sinai.

32. Mireille Raynal-Zougari identifies this text in M. Raynal-Zougari (2008), p. 106.

33. A. Bazin, from *What is Cinema?* (Berkeley: University of California 1967) in Quandt (1998), p. 38.

34. Quandt (1998), p. 39.

35. J.-L. Godard and M. Delahaye, 'The Question' from *Cahiers du Cinéma in English* (London: BFI, 1967) in Quandt (1998), p. 465.

36. Quandt (1998), p. 455.

14

Documentary li(v)es: writing falsehoods, righting wrongs in von Donnersmarck's *The Lives of Others* (2006)

Judith Buchanan

At the heart of the 2006 film *Das Leben der Anderen* (hereafter *The Lives of Others*), written and directed by Florian Henckel von Donnersmarck, are two prominently displayed, and tonally distinct, writing implements: one a pen, the other a typewriter. These sit upon two equally cinematically conspicuous and starkly differentiated desks. The visual scheme of the film depends for much of its aesthetic energy upon the comparison between the writing styles and writing spaces of its two principal characters – spaces which are also, inevitably, invited to act as synecdochic signpost to the writers themselves, the written work they produce and the worlds they occupy.

This comparison animates both the material and symbolic life of the film. Georg Dreyman (Sebastian Koch) is a playwright working in the German Democratic Republic's East Berlin in the mid-1980s before the fall of the Wall. The pen with which he writes the first draft of his plays is one in which there is considerable personal investment. As a birthday present from a writer friend, its value exceeds pure functionality: it is emotionally freighted. And to use it, Dreyman sits at a desk charmingly covered in books, papers, photos, a back scratcher (that his girlfriend tells him is actually a salad server), and plenty of half-read bits and pieces (Figure 14.1). In the proxemical terms of anthropologist Edward Hall, Dreyman's 'intimate space' is clearly inscribed with a vivid and idiosyncratically personal quality.[1] His desk is not only vibrantly worked upon, lived in and lived through, it also carries a generous charge: warmly lit, allowing in light and love and literature, and liberally inclusive into its welcoming ambit not only of non-utilitarian items but also of other people. Moreover, the external visual denotators of an internal literary sensibility (books, papers, photos, quirky objects, idealized lighting) – cinematically con-ventionalized as these things are through a slew of earlier films – are here presented in ways attuned to the established cinematic pattern. Attractive, cinematically clichéd, emphatically encoding both a recognizably shared and a fully personal writing space in emotionally reassuring ways, the image of Dreyman at work is both visually appealing and unashamedly sentimental.

Figure 14.1   Georg Dreyman works on his warmly lit, personalized desk in *The Lives of Others* (2006).

Figure 14.2   Stasi operative Wiesler at his aesthetically bleak, attic work station in *The Lives of Others* (2006).

Directly above Dreyman, in the attic at the top of the apartment block, is a space that has been appropriated by the Stasi to enable them to conduct a full surveillance operation on Dreyman. 'Operation Lazlo', as it is coded, is led by Stasi operative and unconflicted ideologue, Captain Wiesler (Ulrich Mühe), a man committed to excluding from his work and life anything that might problematize the delivery of the state-sanctioned operation. As a cog in the service of the wider machine, Wiesler sits, a grey man with headphones clamped to his ears: he is a brilliantly well-functioning, quasi-mechanized element in the array of surveillance equipment of which he visually and operationally forms part (Figure 14.2). His life, like the observation station he has created, is shown to be bereft of sensuality, drained of anything that might smack of the personal, the improvised, the idiosyncratic or the endearingly out of place. This is a man who has no truck with *affect*. And on the table before him sits the typewriter on which he writes up all the action from the apartment beneath. It is a Stasi-issue typewriter: neutral, grey, institutional, no obvious ticks, no sticking keys, no irritatingly irregular returns, no loud tings. Wiesler's typewriter and desk are, therefore, defined first by their pure functionality and second by the absence of anything else that might compromise the extremity of their contrast with the writing space in the apartment beneath. And unlike the orangeate glow that conspicuously permeates the space of Dreyman's flat, Wiesler's attic is shot through a cool, grey filter to a washed-out palette confirming the non-concessionary character of both its aesthetics and, relatedly, its emotional tenor.[2]

As we view these two work spaces pitted so markedly against each other, the nature of the act of composition upon which each man is engaged inevitably becomes part of our consideration. Dreyman begins the film as a playwright, whose writing serves partly to showcase the acting talents of his own actress-girlfriend Christa-Maria (Martina Gedeck). His plays have a socialist setting and are characterized by moments of high emotion. They dramatize transfiguring experience in the midst of mundanity, but, unlike the work of some of his fellow playwrights, they are not written to be, nor are they received as, a challenge to the political status quo.

Wiesler, by contrast, begins the film as a writer of documentary reports. As one in a busy network of other Stasi operatives similarly employed across the GDR, he is tasked to convert a lived life (Dreyman's, on this occasion) into a vitality-drained textual counterpart of itself, a distilled written account of its salient details relating to daily activity, contacts and political persuasion. The result will be a documentary file whose 'interested' reading and conscientious archiving could in due course be sufficient itself to imperil the life it purports to represent. The quasi-biographical, and acutely politicized, commission to observe a suspect life and produce the state-archived 'file' on it was, of course, a prolifically systematic part of the machinery of power in the real GDR. Given the political-historical setting of the *The Lives of Others*, considering both the construction and impact of such quasi-biographical surveillance reports necessarily invites us to let the film act also as signpost to the lived history of the period, and, reciprocally, to let that history act as part of the interpretive context informing the film.

It has been estimated that, by the fall of the Wall in late 1989, there were between 85,000 and 105,000 paid employees of the Stasi and, beyond these, an unknown proportion of the GDR's citizens (if CIA estimates are to be believed, perhaps as many as one in seven)[3] was at one time or another required to inform for the Stasi.[4] As Neal Ascherson (*The Observer*'s sometime Berlin reporter) expresses it: 'No society in history has been so police-saturated, and the Stasi's job was to know everything about everyone.'[5] The quantities of documentation emerging from this infernal information machine were inevitably vast,[6] including, by 1989, five million personal files.[7] In August 1990, nine months after the Wall came down, the extensive records amassed by the Stasi on individuals and organizations were then declassified and made available to those who could demonstrate they had a legitimate interest in seeing them.[8] It was a move that was both history-revealing and history-making. Among those who duly made appointments to view their own Stasi file was British historian Timothy Garton Ash who had spent time in Berlin on and off throughout the 1970s and 1980s. Garton Ash read with heightened interest the scrupulously documented details about his own movements, *rendez-vous*, friends, acquaintances, lovers, dining habits and leisure activities of years earlier. He wrote up the results of his wondering encounter with these reports in *The File*.[9] He finds himself, for example, comparing the variant reports of his own personal diary with the Stasi file for one particular day in his life:

> The Stasi's observation report, my diary entry: two versions of one day in a life. The 'object' described with the cold outward eye of the secret policeman, and my own subjective, allusive, emotional self-description. But what a gift to memory is a Stasi file. Far better than a madeleine.[10]

However uneasily the file's seemingly fact-driven record of his life maps onto his own impressionistic and differently partial diary entries for the same period, Garton Ash temporarily frees it of its more obvious, and more sinister charge, instead impishly allowing it to outclass Proust's famous madeleine as a helpful *aide-memoire*. Whereas some have claimed, and indeed some of those cited as informants in the files of others have had a vested interest in claiming, that '*die Akten lügen*' (the files lie), Garton Ash's delicately witty first response to his own file seems initially more about an encounter with an unexpectedly recovered *truth*.

The Lives of Others dramatizes a world in which this impressive rate of state-sanctioned textual production is, in line with the historical moment in which it is set, required as a means of countering and containing the myriad 'subversive' texts presumed to be threatening to erupt on every corner.

From the disrespectful joke told by a junior employee in the State Security canteen to Albert Jerska's suspect theatre direction; from the carefully annotated testimony provided in the opening interrogation scene to Dreyman's anonymously written account of the suppressed GDR suicide statistics: texts perceived as seditious abound. And so it is, in response, that the texts of suspect thought are notated, filed and 'analysed' by the state apparatus. *The Lives of Others*, in fact, shows us a regime whose neuroses are fed by, and whose sustained control predicated upon, a well entrenched, if less than intellectually nimble, machinery of textual production and textual analysis. And a regime whose State Security archival vaults, like those of the real GDR, are – as the illuminating shots of the archivist collecting Dreyman's file nonchalantly, but searingly, reveal – crammed floor to ceiling with the resulting texts of potential accusation.

Alerted, post-1989, to the fact that he had himself been subject to these intrusive and reductive processes of 'textualization', the playwright Dreyman, like Garton Ash in the real world, requests access to *his* declassified Stasi file. It is not, though, the scrupulous, if emotionally disengaged, accuracy of the report that strikes Dreyman. Rather he finds, to his consternation, that the account of his life entered onto the official record has been dramatically interfered with: not, as might be supposed, to enhance, but, more astonishingly yet, to *conceal* his guilt in relation to the state. The account's claims to authenticity and accuracy are everywhere imprinted upon it in terms of names, details, Stasi stamps and encoded signatures. These are, however, in this instance, duplicitous signifiers: the self-proclaimed documentary account thus turns out to be itself a work of fiction made up by a Stasi operative known only in the file as HGW XX/7. Dreyman's file is indeed a lie ('*die Akte lügt*'), but, bewilderingly, its untruths have been constructed specifically to protect him. It is the decision of its Stasi author – grey Captain Wiesler in his grey attic – to go literally off-script, living out his commission to *record* a life with such maverick subversiveness, which sits at the heart of the film's dramatic interests.

Wiesler's departures from his political 'script' also require of him a shift in the genre of his writing. At the film's opening, the generic allegiances of Wiesler and Dreyman are both fully secure and tightly differentiated: Wiesler writes documentary reports, Dreyman writes plays. As the film progresses, however, they effectively switch genres. With considerable human courage (if a severely circumscribed dramatic imagination), Wiesler perverts his professional brief to write an unadulterated documentary report by inserting into that report a play written in honour of Lenin's birthday. He brazenly passes off this playscript as the patriotic, and therefore innocence-proclaiming, work of his surveillance subject, Dreyman: in truth, though, Wiesler has scripted it himself. In distorting his commission in this way, Wiesler rewrites his relationship both to himself and to the totalitarian regime he has previously served with such clear political conviction and uncompromising personal zeal. Finding his way into this act of subversion in incremental, and not fully strategic, stages, Wiesler becomes, in von Donnersmarck's own terms, 'an almost-accidental hero'.[11]

In an obliquely analogue move, Dreyman's emerging desire to resist politically takes *his* writing in precisely the other direction, away from dramatic fiction to a fact-driven piece written for *Der Spiegel*. The report he writes is designed to act as an exposé of the GDR's suppressed suicide statistics. While Wiesler's own authorship of the Dreyman file is officially anonymized through the imprimatur of his identity-obscuring operative code HGW XX/7, and his authorship of the playscript contained within it is strategically misattributed, Dreyman's documentary piece for *Der Spiegel* is also necessarily anonymized. Furthermore, it is composed on a clandestine typewriter with an unfamiliar type face in an attempt to thwart subsequent concerted Stasi attempts to trace its authorship.

Wanting to know the authorial origins of a text, however – seeking to de-anonymize it – is the natural impulse of the reader. As discussed in the Introduction to this volume, even in announcing his death and our need to loose our hold upon him, Barthes reminds us how fervently we *desire* the author in some form, if only, in depersonalized expression, as an 'author-function'.[12] Investing not just in an author-function but in the author as a personal force, however, provides a neat, linear model of production and semantic transmission from designing author to receiving reader. Masking the identity of the author only tantalizingly intensifies the need to divine who he or she is and what he or she might be like to have produced such a work: without a disclosed authorial identity, the work feels unanchored and craves the sense of completion that, it is intuitively supposed, might be achieved by being able to attribute to it a personalized point of origin.

If that is fundamentally the case for any text in any place at any moment, the reasons for wanting to know an author in this particular world, the world of *The Lives of Others*' cinematic fiction, transcend the simple psychological satisfaction and intellectual luxury of being able to envisage the uninterrupted trajectory of production through to reception: identifying an author here is a political imperative for the machinery of state and, as a consequence, a pressing professional commission for its functionaries. Thus it is that we see the Stasi apparatus, through the agency of its top graphologist, fervently attempting to decode the self-occluding authoring marks of the subversive text it finds before it in the *Spiegel* article, striving to identify the typeface, in the desire to smoke out, and so indict, its 'dissident' writer.

For their own reasons, both Wiesler and Dreyman become similarly caught up in the desire to establish the authorship of the 'texts' of pressing interest placed before each of them in turn. Thus it is, for example, that having found the preliminary stirrings of something unexpectedly alive within himself in response to Dreyman's play (Figure 14.3), Wiesler turns to the printed theatre programme to discover something about the playwright (Figure 14.4). The programme's brief descriptive blurb on Dreyman, however, merely piques, without satisfying, his interest. Mounting an elaborate surveillance operation gives him a way of feeding his own desire to *know* the author of the play that has unexpectedly tapped something in his own, previously arid, emotional life;[13] and, simultaneously, it supplies the means of perpetuating his newly discovered taste for being an attentive *audience* for the ongoing, passionate, personal life stories of Dreyman and Christa-Maria. 'Operation Lazlo' in effect, therefore, generously augments the theatre programme's biographical notes while prolonging and expanding the personal play-going experience for Wiesler (Figures 14.3 and 14.4).

Wiesler's desire to pursue the identity and character of the author of the play that has engaged his attention finds its precise answering phrase in a paralleled sequence near the end of the film as Dreyman returns the investigative 'compliment'. Once Dreyman has read, in his own Stasi file, Wiesler's invented playlet so idiosyncratically attributed to him (Figure 14.5), he is then himself at pains to convert the codified authorial imprint HGW XX/7 into a real person by tracking down the photo id and personnel card of *its* author (Figure 14.6). Unsatisfied by the bald details of the photo card, in ways directly reminiscent of Wiesler's own desire for more than a minimalist programme entry about Dreyman, Dreyman subsequently traces Wiesler in order to sample the mundane detail of his life – again evoking Wiesler's own surveillance operation on *him*. Having thus teased the anonymous and invisible author of his file into visible human form, he even contemplates crossing directly into his world and making him humanly knowable also. This would shift their relationship from its mediated, textualized expression to something more conventionally socialized. But, like the fan who cannot bear the potentially banalizing disappointment of actually meeting a favoured author in the flesh, and perhaps additionally anxious not to embarrass the man who has previously intervened so expensively on his behalf, he pulls back from a face-to-face encounter. Instead, he replies to Wiesler's textually expressed generosity in correspondingly textual form, both through the title to his next book, *Sonate vom Guten Menschen* (*Sonata for a Good Man*), and through its accompanying, cryptic dedication 'To HGW XX/7, in gratitude'. The publication of the book therefore acts as an attentively crafted thank you letter to Wiesler, expressing a private gratitude for a story whose precise details are known only to the two of them. And in the final moments of the film, we see the mediating novel-as-thank-you-letter being 'received', opened, read and enjoyed by its intended addressee: the letter has reached its destination. Though at root a personal, if indirectly delivered, missive from one man to another, the diplomatic quasi-veiling of the missive in published form necessarily makes its packaging highly conspicuous in the public domain. In fact, within the scheme of the film, publication of this book moves Dreyman's own, once necessarily

Figure 14.3 Wiesler's acute interest in Dreyman's play.

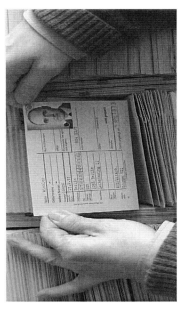

Figure 14.4 Wiesler consults the production's programme to learn more about its author.

Figure 14.5 Dreyman reads the Wiesler-authored file with acute concentration.

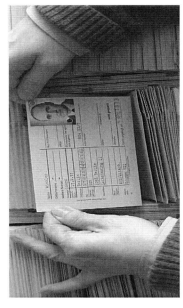

Figure 14.6 Dreyman consults the agent's personnel file card to learn more about its author, inadvertently thereby mimicking Wiesler's pursuit of him.

225

suppressed, authorial identity from the strategically omitted to the now widely publicly promoted. To signal this shift, large marketing photo posters of Dreyman-as-author are seen adorning bookshop window displays. The impact of this is clear: in this post-1989 Berlin, acts of composition and authorship are not only no longer secret, but are now even vigorously and commercially promoted specifically through a well-publicized, personal authorial identity.

From Wiesler's point of view, the indirect literary reply to his own indirect, and quietly expressed, textual heroics is the thing that allows him to own, for the first time perhaps, his individual agency in, and connection to, the human world around him. When, in the final seconds of the film, the shop assistant asks whether he'd like the Dreyman-authored book he is now purchasing gift-wrapped, he replies, in a line with resonance well beyond the immediate circumstances, 'Nein: es ist für mich' ('No: it's for me'). Previously Wiesler has been the man hiding in doorways, lurking in shadows, nameless, a human notebook registering the activities of others. His face has been a concerted study in emotional blankness and personal invisibility. The acknowledgement of the purchased volume as 'for me' symbolically, and significantly, finally allows 'mich' to feature both linguistically and, by implication, socially in public space. Finding an outlet for the owning of self in this way, Wiesler takes a first tentative step out of the voyeuristic shadows and towards being a social entity, with points of connection, even fellowship, not bounded purely by political ideology and professional obligation.[14]

This shift into a sense of connection with the lives of others, however embryonic its articulation, is made possible by having found space in his life for the previously foreign element of *affect* – and having done so, what's more, through the affectively unpromising processes of institutional surveillance report writing. A single moment in the film can serve as telling illustration of his stages of incremental development in this respect: the reading of the report after Wiesler's clod-hopping, unimaginative assistant, Udo, has taken the night shift on 'Operation Lazlo'. The import of the night's events has been entirely lost on the man charged with notating them: as an observer of others, Udo is not, in Geoff Wall's terms, master of the subjunctive.[15] Gloriously unaware of his own interpretive limitations, however, Udo has nevertheless done his unimaginative best not only to report on what he hears but, fearlessly, even to make some interpretive comments upon those things also. The night for Dreyman and Christa-Maria has involved misunderstanding, hurt, political and personal angst about how compromised they both are within the system, passionate, touching love-making as a gesture of recommitment to each other in the face of everything and a decision now to 'do something' (politically). Wiesler returns in the early morning and reads Udo's report on the night passed, allowing the clunkingly unimaginative language in which it is written nevertheless to conjure in his own mind's eye the tonally very different events he imagines the dullard report, for all its conspicuous idiocies, as failing entirely to obscure. The typed report both appears on screen in legibly attentive close-up, as seen from Wiesler's perspective as reader, and is simultaneously heard being 'read' in Wiesler's inner voice. Meantime, the considerable power of the report for Wiesler is demonstrated by the superimposed appearance on screen, overlaid directly upon the typescript report viewed, of the imagined version of enacted events that the report summons for him. Confirming their status as *not quite objectively real*, the images of these imagined events are not accompanied by diegetic sound; rather they are poignantly under-scored by an idealizing melody on strings and piano, and even seen for a few frames in voyeuristically indulgent slo-mo. Wiesler is, in sum, enjoying the heady romance of the silent mini-movie the report prompts in his mind's eye – a transporting drama to which we too are given privileged and revealing access (Figures 14.7–14.10). The alignment of film image track with the conjurations of Wiesler's inner world creates a double inscription on the cinema screen. George Bornstein's account of a palimpsest as 'less a bearer of the fixed final inscription than a site of the process of inscription, in which acts of composition and transmission occur before our eyes' is literally borne out by the layered composition being graphically realized 'before our eyes' here: it is a sequence in which palimpsestic *process* is made visible.[16]

A film scene showing a character's act of writing that then cross fades into the images the text describes was a cinematic convention established early in the film industry's silent era. The 1917 Fox film of *A Tale of Two Cities* (dir. Frank Lloyd) can serve as illustrative example in this respect. In an early scene in the film, an iris opens on the frail, ancient, white-bearded figure of Dr. Manette (Josef Swickard), brightly, almost spiritually, lit from above, as he writes up the traumatic events that have put him in the Bastille (Figure 14.11a). The shot cuts to show us the paper before him on the table. Snippets of his harrowing tale are legible on it: 'On that awful night when I was called from the side of my wife and child to tend a dying...' (Figure 14.11b) Like an accelerated rehearsal of the processes of literary adaptation itself, the words then cross-fade into the visualized version of the story they tell, the images apparently summoned into being by the written memorial account (Figures 14.11c, 14.11d). It is a process that is repeated (Figure 14.11e). At the close of each visualized snippet of the remembered story, the scene cross-fades back to Manette's form feverishly engaged on his writing (Figure 14.11f), or sitting looking ahead in horrified stupefaction as if at an imaginary screen showing him a graphic rerun of his painfully conjured recollections. Thus, the remembered scene plays out episodically, punctuated throughout by the visual reminder of Manette writing as the subjective summoning imagination of the unfolding drama. Once the series of episodic

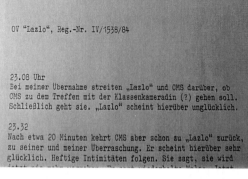

OV "Lazlo", Reg.-Nr. IV/1538/84

23.08 Uhr
Bei meiner Übernahme streiten „Lazlo" und CMS darüber, ob
CMS zu dem Treffen mit der Klassenkameradin (?) gehen soll.
Schließlich geht sie. „Lazlo" scheint hierüber unglücklich.

23.32
Nach etwa 20 Minuten kehrt CMS aber schon zu „Lazlo" zurück,
zu seiner und meiner Überraschung. Er scheint hierüber sehr
glücklich. Heftige Intimitäten folgen. Sie sagt, sie wird

Figure 14.7 Udo's typed report on the night's events as read by Wiesler in *The Lives of Others* (2006).

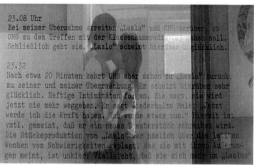

Figure 14.8 The images conjured in Wiesler's imagination by the report create an on-screen word-image palimpsest.

Figure 14.9 The clipped and institutional style of the surveillance report fails to contain the warmth of the images conjured in Wiesler's imagination in response.

Figure 14.10 The images linger on screen beyond the reading of the report, as if now independent of the written account that initially summoned them.

Figure 14.11a–f Dr. Manette writes up his story in *A Tale of Two Cities* (1917), his manuscript cross-fading repeatedly into a graphically realised account of the action. The remembered action is punctuated throughout by a return to Dr. Manette's feverish act of writing from where the story is being conjured.

scenes from Manette's memory ends, the ancient prisoner rests his head on his arms to sob at the vividness of his recollections and at the remembered sweetness of the life that he will never know again.

It is instructive to place alongside the report-reading scene from *The Lives of Others* the cinematic convention as illustrated in this early film of *A Tale of Two Cities*. The comparison highlights a crucial difference between how such a scene conventionally works and how the scene from *The Lives of Others* draws on that convention in order to subvert it. In the 1917 film, there is no competitively fraught relationship between the words shown and the images conjured: indeed we are invited to accept the images we see as the complementary accompaniment to Dr. Manette's written memorial record. In effect words and images complete each other's syntactical constructions, moving fluidly between communicative modes without disruption or disagreement.

In *The Lives of Others*, by contrast, the language of Udo's report cannot account for the significance and weight of the scene upon which he is eavesdropping. 'Heftige Intimitäten folgen', he writes ('Vigorous acts of intimacy follow'): in its institutional insensitivity, the language is humorously adrift from the genuinely moving character of the lived moment – or at least of the moment as Wiesler then reimagines it and we see it. And Udo's attempts at interpreting the import of Dreyman's and Christa-Maria's conversations are yet more ludicrously misplaced. Thus it is, for example, that her articulated commitment to be stronger in the face of institutional blackmailing and enforced seduction is comically misunderstood by Udo as an expression of her desire to keep house better. In his 1986 essay 'Reassembling the dust', Paul Mariani writes about the task of the biographer in the following terms:

> The biographer is both like and unlike the poet. He or she also feels the same strong spur as the poet. But once the biographer has felt that fine delight, that moment of light streaming into the head, the moment of the rainbow, there is still the forbidding pyramid of dust to work with.[17]

Wiesler exceeds his surveillance brief by becoming, like the biographer, interested in finding the poetry in the dust, the rainbow amidst the dancing dust clouds. His assistant, by contrast, is fully absorbed, as indeed he more properly should be, in the diversionary clouds of the dust itself; as a result, he is not equipped to see what might be dancing there. Nevertheless, Udo's clay-footed account proves no bar to finding the poetry in the moment for Wiesler. Wiesler, of course, is a cannily experienced reader of such reports, accustomed to their terse, clinical style, aware of their strategic omissions and in this case, more than happy to supply the gaps, and make the decisive tonal adjustments himself in the act of reading. And so it is that as the competing, graphically visualized version of events is summoned in Wiesler's mind ('*Wiesler stellt sich die Szene genau vor*'; '*Wiesler imagines the scene exactly*'),[18] both the report read and the imagined scene conjured from it are then co-present for us on screen (Figures 14.8 and 14.9). There is, however, no collaborative elision, no harmonizing encounter between the two communicative modes. Rather the report's blundering incomprehension slams up abrasively against the uncompromising idealization of Wiesler's visualized version. The palimpsestic encounter of the two is eloquently, almost comically, tense. And their refusal to reconcile is actively pleasing to Wiesler who declares the report 'good' ('Guter Bericht'). Indeed, the report's banalizing misunderstandings of the politically laden conversations between Dreyman and Christa-Maria are arguably a lifeline for the protagonists. The report is now strategically, and helpfully, wrong in ways that will later become strategically exaggerated.

As used in other contexts, the idea of pure palimpsest tends to imply the semi-obscuration of the earlier inscription, the new text not so much co-habiting on the papyrus in democratic communion, as asserting its dominance by at least part-erasing the prior one. With this in mind, and as played out in this cinematic world, the superimposed encounter of report and life in *The Lives of Others* (Figures 14.7–14.10) potentially provides a dangerously suggestive metaphor. As part of the political landscape of the GDR, the written version of a life (in the form of a surveillance report) could all too easily be used to convict, and so itself then even literally supplant the lived one. By equivocating about how it will be resolved, the formal character of this scene – dramatizing a competitive on-screen tussle between the visuals of the report and those of the life – finds metaphorical expression for this struggle. The sustained co-presence on screen of text and life allows for a question that is not just aesthetically but politically charged: will one medium in the palimpsestic encounter triumph? And in response, one does. In defiance of the alternative, grimmer, possible direction of travel in this respect, the scene comes to rest, surprisingly, in a place that is conspicuously life-affirming,[19] the on-screen text finally ceding to the no-longer-contested image of Dreyman and Christa-Maria peaceably, and post-coitally, wrapped up in each other (Figure 14.10). They now have the screen entirely to themselves, no longer textually 'overwritten' by the thunderingly insensitive report that has apparently conjured their appearance. The scene therefore ends not with the report supplanting the life, but with the potency of the imagined version of the life managing eventually to oust the report from the space of the frame. In this way the imagined visuals of the life as lived claim their own vital and photographic truth, their *more-than-subjectiveness*, thereby symbolically asserting their supremacy in the palimpsestic contest between life and file, image and word, vitality and textuality.

The escape for Dreyman and Christa-Maria from the containing bounds of their subjectively conjured frame here also became one of the most dominantly recycled images of the film in its own marketing. In the film, the image of the passionate embrace up against the wall (Figure 14.8) is clearly subjectively conjured in Wiesler's mind by the report with which it shares the screen. On one of the most frequently employed poster images in the film's international roll-out, by contrast, this same passionate clinch is presented without its textual overlay: the Dreyman/Christa-Maria embrace appears in the left of the image without superimposed text but, instead, now with the large, interpolated figure of Wiesler looking down on them from the upper right of the image. Within the architecture of the poster itself, therefore, a relationship of acute observation is clearly implied. But the particular scene Wiesler apparently 'observes' in this marketing image is, the film itself suggests, actually one he has himself imaginatively *constructed* out of the partial, and uncomprehending, report he reads on events that night. Within the unfolding of the film, therefore, the particular image used in the marketing is a *possible* version of events unseen, or perhaps even Wiesler's preferred *fantasy* version of them. And so, for those who know the film, the poster incidentally concretizes the real subject of the film as 'the lives of others' not as these are lived in the raw, unmediated world of 'out thereness', but, more significantly yet, as creatively constructed within the mind of another. And it is, of course, precisely there, in the world of private empathy and imagination, and in the subsequent textualized expressions of that world, that, as this film allegorizes affectingly, lives can indeed be damned or saved.

In 2007, *The Lives of Others* won seven Deutscher Filmpreis and the Academy Award for Best Foreign Language Film. It has not, however, proved a film to suit all tastes. Its sentimentality about what an exposure to art can do to a moral sensibility, for example, does not, alas, connect perfectly to the lived world of experience (in which Hitler reportedly loved art, Goebbels got a doctorate in Eighteenth-Century Romanticism and Mussolini played the violin). Moreover there are those – notably, for example, the international Australian lawyer and contemporary historian of the GDR, Anna Funder – who object strongly to the implication they see the film as making that a process of empathetic intervention, such as that undertaken by Wiesler, could have formed part of any corner of the Stasi's vast operational organ: 'To believe that a victim could be saved through a perpetrator's change of heart is to misunderstand the totalitarian nature of bureaucratized evil', writes Funder.[20] She sees the film as a 'beautiful fiction' honeying over an 'uglier truth',[21] dismissing as distasteful the implication – even emerging as it does from within a fictional account – that there might have been room for humanity within the Stasi. She even wonders if the film might not be understood as 'an inappropriate – if unconscious – plea for absolution of the perpetrators' of some of the GDR's atrocities. Reading it as a naïve 'fable of forgiveness', she considers it a regrettable part of a disquieting process of 'creeping rehabilitation'.[22] It is, for that reason, 'hard to bear'.[23]

Equally, however, there are those of a very different persuasion and background who object to the film on radically variant grounds. To be personally anecdotal for a moment, let me cite a woman with whom I lunched in the old East Berlin last summer. My lunch companion had been born into a degree of party privilege in the GDR and had grown up as both a beneficiary of, and a believer in, the system. She proved a vigorous proponent of the sort of *Ostalgie* that characterized, for example, *Goodye Lenin!* (dir. Wolfgang Becker, 2003). In stark contradistinction to Funder, she, and others like her, are angered by what they consider the politically motivated demonization of the GDR in West-backed accounts of it since *die Wende* (unification). Unification itself has, to their mind, consistently left the old Ossis (Easterners) economically and professionally disadvantaged. Moreover, the political and economic hardship wished upon them by the West in the present, as they see it, is compounded by the unfairly tough retrospective representational strategy the West is seen as having consistently adopted in relation to the old GDR, damning a whole political system and worthy socialist aspiration through films such as *The Lives of Others*.

The film's concessionary heart about the life of the individual on the one hand but its dystopic vision and cynicism about the corrupt exercise of power by the system in the GDR on the other, have, then, succeeded in arousing acute political sensitivities from diametrically opposed positions. It is, however, possible to acknowledge both the sentimentality of the film's view of what a brush with an artistic sensibility can do to a moral conscience, and the political infeasibility of a Stasi operative shifting allegiance so decisively and surviving, and still appreciate the film as the cinematic equivalent of the wilfully inaccurate report that Wiesler submits within its fiction. Like the impressive, and impressively well-researched, recreation of the material detail of Stasi surveillance operations that characterizes von Donnersmarck's film, Wiesler's report is crammed with the self-authenticating marks of accurate documentary reporting in terms of times, dates, signatures and more. But again like von Donnersmark's film, that anomalous report is also distinctively marked by creatively inventive departures from the fully accurate account of its subject – departures which, to the knowing reader, are as conspicuous as they are well motivated. This is a film that knows its own project: it even incidentally represents it metonymically within the film itself in the form of the fictionalized document that Wiesler files, which is as mismatched to Dreyman's own memory of historical events as it is an imaginative and considerably affecting rewriting of those events. Indeed, the film itself, like Wiesler's effortfully constructed, and personally expensive report, also combines Dreyman's twin writing projects as pursued in his dual identities as a private columnist for *Der Spiegel* and celebrated playwright for the GDR stage: namely to record plainly, and with clear political intent, the hidden horror of the GDR regime on the one hand, and to create a powerful piece of inventive theatre for an invested audience on the other. It is fully understandable, therefore, that this might not be a film for those personally caught up with the real-world history and wanting the film to act politically within that history. However, it finds expression, in beautifully crafted ways, for a deeply human desire to see a rogue act of unexpected empathetic intervention in someone else's life outwit the system. In Wiesler's words, and, not, I confess, unacted upon by the effects of *affect*, I am happy to own it a cinematic fantasy *für mich*.

Notes

1. E. Hall, *The Hidden Dimension* (New York: Doubleday, 1966), pp. 116–19.
2. Director von Donnersmarck was strategic about the colours and overall desired aesthetic through which to represent the GDR: 'I tried to analyze what the visual tendencies were in East Germany. One thing I discovered is that they had different types of colors. I once talked to a chemist why that was and apparently in the Western world there are certain patented color chemicals that allow you to go for those bright, saturated colors that they didn't have in the East ... So the production designer and I spent six months devising the visual world of this film. We saw there were more greens than blues, more orangey-brown colors than actual red. We decided to completely eliminate red and blue and just go with all the greens, grays, and browns and not do it in postproduction. We did not want to do anything digitally. Many people in the East felt the film was a complete resurrection of the GDR.' J. Esther, 'Between Principle and Feeling: An Interview with Florian Henckel von Donnersmarck' *Cineaste* 32(2) (22 March 2007): 40.
3. A. Funder, 'Tyranny of Terror', film review of *The Lives of Others* in *The Guardian* (Saturday 5 May, 2007), at: http://www.guardian.co.uk/books/2007/may/05/featuresreviews.guardianreview12
4. M. Fulbrook, *Anatomy of a Dictatorship* (Oxford: Oxford University Press, 1995), pp. 46, 50.
5. N. Ascherson, 'Beware, The Walls Have ears', *The Observer* (Sunday 11 March 2007), 'Observer Review' Section: 4.
6. Funder asserts that in the forty years of its existence (1949–1989), the Stasi and its informants accumulated more written records than had previously been amassed 'in all of German history since the Middle Ages'. A. Funder, 'Eyes without a Face' *Sight and Sound* 7(5) (1 May 2007): 16–20 (18).
7. Ascherson (2007): 4.
8. P. Cooke, *Representing East Germany Since Unification* (Oxford: Berg, 2005), p. 65.
9. T. Garton Ash, *The File* (New York: Vintage Books, 1998).
10. Garton Ash (1998), p. 12.
11. Esther, 'Between principle and feeling...' (2007): 40 C3.
12. See Introduction, pp. 17–19.
13. In suggesting the surveillance operation for his own reasons, loyal party apparatchik Wiesler inadvertently subjects himself to the indignity of working in support of Minister Hempf's (Thomas Thieme) grubby sexual designs on Dreyman's girlfriend Christa-Maria and of Oberstleutnant Anton Grubitz's (Ulrich Tukur) self-interested careerism.
14. For a psychoanalytic reading of the precise psychological processes (curiosity, passion, mortification, jealousy, projection, introjection, eroticism, vengefulness, emulation, embodied simulation, identification, mentalisation, articulation, empathy) Wiesler undergoes as he learns to empathize and identify with the subjects of his investigation, see Diana Diamond, 'Empathy and Identification in von Donnersmarck's *The Lives of Others*', *Journal of the American Psychoanalytic Association* 56 (2008): 811–32.
15. See Geoffrey Wall, 'Literary biopics: a literary biographer's perspective', p. 126, this volume.
16. G. Bornstein, 'Introduction', in G. Bornstein and R.G. Williams (eds.), *Palimpsest: Editorial Theory in the Humanities* (Ann Arbor: The University of Michigan Press, 1993), pp. 1–6 (4).

17. P. Mariani, 'Reassembling the Dust: Notes on the Art of the Biographer', in S.B. Oates (ed.), *Biography as High Adventure* (Amherst, MA: University of Massachusetts Press, 1986), pp. 104–23 (109).

18. *Das Leben der Anderen* (Frankfurt: Suhrkamp Verlag, 2006), p. 88.

19. That the sequence comes to rest in a definitive place of any sort necessitates a revisiting of the neatness of its illustration of Bornstein's formulation of palimpsest as 'less a bearer of the fixed final inscription than a site of the process of inscription' Bornstein (1993), p. 4. Although the sequence does indeed eloquently dramatize *process*, it also finally, and significantly, allows for a 'fixed final inscription' the import of which, in general terms, Bornstein looks to downplay.

20. Funder, 'Eyes Without a Face' (2007), p. 19.

21. Funder, 'Tyranny of Terror' (2007).

22. Funder quoting Dr Hubertus Knabe, the director of the memorial at Hohenschönhausen prison, 'Tyranny of Terror' (2007).

23. Funder quoting Günter Bormann of the Stasi File Authority, in 'Eyes Without a Face' (2007), p. 18.

Select Filmography

For reasons of space, this filmography lists only those films discussed in this book in which a writer, or an act of writing, is configured. Writer films not discussed in this volume are not listed here. Other films referenced in the book in which a writer does not appear are included in the index but not in this select filmography. (However, this discrimination is not always a self-evident one since configurations of implied authorial presence and of authorial absence feature among the book's interests.) Films listed here are arranged chronologically by year, and, where relevant, alphabetically by title within a single year. The year given in each case is the film's release date for the country in which the film was first released: release dates for international distribution may, of course, vary. Films are listed by their English release title first. Names of writers who appear in the films are given in the final column: writers who had a real historical identity are given in regular font, fictional writers in italic font. The name of the actor is given in parentheses in each case.

Year of Release	Title	Director	Studio/Production Company	Country	Principal Writer(s) Dramatised
1907	*Shakespeare Writing Julius Caesar (La mort de Jules César)*	Georges Méliès	Méliès Star-Film production.	France	William Shakespeare (Georges Méliès)
1912	*Leaves from the Books of Charles Dickens*	(unknown)	Brittannia Films (Pathé)	UK	Charles Dickens (Thomas Bentley)
1914	*The Life of Shakespeare*	Frank R. Growcott and J.B. Macdowell	British and Colonial Kinematograph Company	UK	William Shakespeare (Albert Ward)
1916	*Master Shakespeare, Strolling Player*	Frederick Sullivan	Thanhouser Film Corporation	USA	William Shakespeare (Lawrence Swinburne), Francis Bacon (Robert Whittier)
1917	*A Tale of Two Cities*	Frank Lloyd	Fox Film Corporation	USA	*Dr. Alexandre Manette* (Josef Swickard)
1924	*Dickens' London*	Frank Miller and Harry B. Parkinson	Graham-Wilcox Productions	UK	Charles Dickens (actor unknown)
1924	*Old Bill Through the Ages*	Thomas Bentley	Ideal	UK	William Shakespeare (Austin Leigh)
1934	*The Barretts of Wimpole Street*	Sidney Franklin	Metro-Goldwyn-Mayer (MGM)	USA	Robert Browning (Frederic March), Elizabeth Barrett (Norma Shearer)
1935	*The Immortal Gentleman*	Widgey R. Newman	Bernard Smith Productions	UK	William Shakespeare (Basil Gill), Ben Jonson (Edgar Owen)

(*continued*)

Continued

Year of Release	Title	Director	Studio/Production Company	Country	Principal Writer(s) Dramatised
1936	*Master Will Shakespeare*	Jacques Tourneur	Metro-Goldwyn-Mayer (MGM)	USA	William Shakespeare (Anthony Kemble-Cooper)
1940	*The Letter*	William Wyler	Warner Bros. Pictures	USA	*Leslie Crosbie* (Bette Davis)
1944	*Time Flies*	Walter Forde	Gainsborough Pictures	UK	William Shakespeare (John Salew)
1945	*Les dames du Bois de Boulogne*	Robert Bresson	Les Films Raoul Ploquin	France	*Agnès* (Elina Labourdette)
1946	*Devotion*	Curtis Bernhardt	Warner Bros. Pictures	USA	Emily Brontë (Ida Lupino), Charlotte Brontë (Olivia de Havilland), Anne Brontë (Nancy Coleman), William Makepeace Thackeray (Sydney Greenstreet)
1946	*Great Expectations*	David Lean	Cineguild	UK	*Pip* (Tony Wager, John Mills)
1948	*Letter from an Unknown Woman*	Max Ophüls	Rampart Productions	USA	*Lisa Berndle* (Joan Fontaine)
1949	*A Letter to Three Wives*	Joseph L. Mankiewicz	Twentieth Century Fox Film Corporation	USA	*Addie Ross* (Celeste Holm, voice)
1950	*Sunset Boulevard*	Billy Wilder	Paramount Pictures	USA	*Joe Gillis* (William Holden)
1951	*Diary of a Country Priest (Journal d'un curé de campagne)*	Robert Bresson	Union Générale Cinématographique (UGC)	France	*Priest of Ambricourt* (Claude Laydu)
1952	*The Snows of Kilimanjaro*	Henry King	Twentieth Century Fox Film Corporation	USA	*Harry Street* (Gregory Peck)
1956	*The Ten Commandments*	Cecil B. DeMille	Paramount Pictures	USA	*Voice of God* (Charlton Heston)

1957	*The Sun Also Rises*	Henry King	Twentieth Century Fox Film Corporation	USA	*Jake Barnes* (Tyrone Power)
1959	*Pull My Daisy*	Alfred Leslie and Robert Frank	G-String Productions	USA	Allen Ginsberg (himself), Jack Kerouac (himself, narrator), Pablo Frank (himself)
1968	*Stolen Kisses*	François Truffaut	Les Films du Carrosse, Les Productions Artistes Associés	France	*Antoine Doinel* (Jean-Pierre Léaud)
1977	*Julia*	Fred Zinnemann	Twentieth Century Fox Film Corporation	USA	Lillian Hellman (Jane Fonda)
1978	*Stevie*	Robert Enders	Bowden Productions Limited, First Artists, Grand Metropolitan	UK	Stevie Smith (Glenda Jackson)
1979	*My Brilliant Career*	Gillian Armstrong	Greater Union Organisation (GUO), Margaret Fink Productions	Australia	*Sybylla Melvyn* (Judy Davis)
1983	*Cross Creek*	Martin Ritt	Thorn EMI Screen Entertainment/ Universal Pictures	USA	*Marjorie Kinnan Rawlings* (Mary Steenburgen)
1985	*Out of Africa*	Sydney Pollack	Mirage Enterprises/ Universal Pictures	USA	*Isak Dinesen* (Meryl Streep)
1986	*Gothic*	Ken Russell	Virgin Vision	UK	Mary Shelley (Natasha Richardson), Byron (Gabriel Byrne), Percy Bysshe Shelley (Julian Sands)

(continued)

Continued

Year of Release	Title	Director	Studio/Production Company	Country	Principal Writer(s) Dramatised
1990	*An Angel at My Table*	Jane Campion	Australian Broadcasting Corporation (ABC), Channel Four Films, Hibiscus Films	New Zealand/ Australia/ UK	Janet Frame (Kerry Fox)
1991	*Barton Fink*	Joel and Ethan Coen	Circle Films/Working Title Films	USA/UK	Barton Fink (John Turturro)
1991	*Naked Lunch*	David Cronenberg	Film Trustees Ltd., Naked Lunch Productions, Nippon Film Development and Finance	Canada/ UK/Japan	*Bill Lee* (Peter Weller)
1991	*Prospero's Books*	Peter Greenaway	Allarts/Cinéa/Caméra One	UK/France	*Prospero*/Shakespeare (John Gielgud)
1992	*Hedd Wyn*	Paul Turner	Pendefig Ty Cefn, Sianel 4 Cymru (S4C)	UK	*Ellis Evans/Hedd Wyn* (Huw Garmon)
1993	*Shadowlands*	Richard Attenborough	Price Entertainment	UK	C.S. Lewis (Anthony Hopkins)
1994	*Tom and Viv*	Brian Gilbert	British Screen Productions	UK/USA	T.S Eliot (Willem Dafoe)
1995	*Carrington*	Christopher Hampton	PolyGram Filmed Entertainment, Freeway Films, Cinéa	UK/France	Lytton Strachey (Jonathan Pryce)
1995	*SeZen*	David Fincher	Cecchi Gori Pictures, New Line Cinema	USA	*John Doe* (Kevin Spacey)

Year	Title	Director	Production company	Country	Character (actor)
1995	*Smoke*	Paul Auster and Wayne Wang	Miramax Films, Neue Deutsche Filmgesellschaft (NDF), Euro Space	Germany/USA/Japan	*Paul Benjamin* (William Hurt)
1997	*Wilde*	Brian Gilbert	BBC/Capitol Films	UK/Germany/Japan	Oscar Wilde (Stephen Fry)
1998	*Shakespeare in Love*	John Madden	Universal Pictures/Miramax	USA/UK	William Shakespeare (Joseph Fiennes)
1998	*Vigo: Passion for Life*	Julien Temple	Impact Pictures, Little Magic Films, MACT Productions	France/UK/Japan	Jean Vigo (James Frain)
1999	*Dash and Lilly*	Kathy Bates	A&E Television Networks/Granada Media	UK/USA	Dashiell Hammett (Sam Shepard), Lillian Hellman (Judy Davis)
1999	*Mansfield Park*	Patricia Rozema	Arts Council of England/BBC	UK	*Fanny Price* (Frances O'Connor)
1999	*The End of the Affair*	Neil Jordan	Columbia Pictures	UK/USA	*Maurice Bendrix* (Ralph Fiennes)
1999	*The Passion of Ayn Rand*	Christopher Menaul	Producers Entertainment Group/Showtime Networks	USA	Ayn Rand (Helen Mirren)
1999	*The Talented Mr. Ripley*	Anthony Minghella	Miramax International/Paramount Pictures	USA	*Tom Ripley* (Matt Damon)
1999	*Time Regained*	Raoul Ruiz	Gemini Films/France 2 Cinéma/Les Films du Lendemain	France/Italy/Portugal	Marcel Proust (Marcello Mazzarella)
2000	*Nora*	Pat Murphy	GAM/Natural Nylan Entertainment	Ireland/UK/Italy/Germany	James Joyce (Ewan McGregor)

(continued)

Continued

Year of Release	Title	Director	Studio/Production Company	Country	Principal Writer(s) Dramatised
2000	*Pandaemonium*	Julien Temple	Arts Council of England/BBC	UK	Samuel Coleridge (Linus Roache), William Wordsworth (John Hannah)
2000	*Quills*	Philip Kaufman	Fox Searchlight Pictures	USA/UK/ Germany	The Marquis de Sade (Geoffrey Rush)
2000	*State and Main*	David Mamet	Filmtown Entertainment	France/ USA	*Joseph Turner White* (Philip Seymour Hoffman)
2001	*Bridget Jones's Diary*	Sharon Maguire	Miramax Films/ Universal Pictures/ Studio Canal	UK/ Ireland/ France	*Bridget Jones* (Renée Zellweger)
2001	*Human Nature*	Michel Gondry	Fine Line Features/ Studio Canal	USA	*Lila Jute* (Patricia Arquette)
2001	*Iris*	Richard Eyre	BBC Fox Irish Productions	UK/USA	Iris Murdoch (Kate Winslet/Judi Dench)
2001	*Moulin Rouge!*	Baz Luhrmann	Twentieth Century Fox Film Corporation	USA/ Australia	*Christian* (Ewan McGregor)
2002	*Adaptation*	Spike Jonze	Beverly Detroit/Clinica Estetico	USA	*Charlie Kaufman/Donald Kaufman* (Nicholas Cage), Susan Orlean (Meryl Streep)
2002	*Confessions of a Dangerous Mind*	George Clooney	Miramax Films	USA/ Germany/ Canada	*Chuck Barris* (Sam Rockwell)
2002	*The Hours*	Stephen Daldry	Paramount Pictures/ Miramax Films	USA/UK	Virginia Woolf (Nicole Kidman)
2003	*Byron* (TV)	Julian Farino	BBC Drama Group	UK	Lord Byron (Jonny Lee Miller)

2003	*In The Cut*	Jane Campion	Pathe Productions	Australia/ USA/UK	*Frannie Avery* (Meg Ryan)
2003	*Sylvia*	Christine Jeffs	BBC Films/British Film Council	UK	Sylvia Plath (Gwyneth Paltrow), Ted Hughes (Daniel Craig)
2004	*Bridget Jones: The Edge of Reason*	Beeban Kidron	Miramax Films/ Universal Pictures/ Studio Canal	UK/ France/ Germany/ Ireland/ USA	*Bridget Jones* (Renée Zellweger)
2004	*Finding Neverland*	Marc Forster	Miramax Films	USA/UK	J.M. Barrie (Johnny Depp)
2004	*Stage Beauty*	Richard Eyre	Lions Gate Films/ Qwerty Films/Tribeca Productions	UK/USA/ Germany	Samuel Pepys (Hugh Bonneville)
2004	*The Libertine*	Laurence Dunmore	The Weinstein Company/Isle of Man Film	UK/ Australia	John Wilmot, Earl of Rochester (Johnny Depp)
2005	*Capote*	Bennett Miller	Sony Pictures Classics/A-Line Pictures	USA/ Canada	Truman Capote (Philip Seymour Hoffman)
2005	*Pride and Prejudice*	Joe Wright	Focus Features, Universal Pictures, Studio Canal	France/UK	(implictily) *Elizabeth Bennet* (Keira Knightley)
2006	*Miss Potter*	Chris Noonan	Phoenix Pictures/UK Film Council	UK/USA/ Isle of Man	Beatrix Potter (Renee Zellweger)
2006	*Stranger than Fiction*	Marc Forster	Columbia Pictures/ Mandate Pictures	USA	*Karen Eiffel* (Emma Thompson)

(continued)

Continued

Year of Release	Title	Director	Studio/Production Company	Country	Principal Writer(s) Dramatised
2006	*The Lives of Others (Das Leben der Anderen)*	Florian Henckel von Donnersmarck	Arte	Germany	*Georg Dreyman* (Sebastian Koch), *Hauptmann Gerd Wiesler* (Ulrich Mühe)
2007	*Atonement*	Joe Wright	Universal Pictures	UK/France	*Briony Tallis* (Saoirse Ronan) *Robbie Turner* (James McAvoy)
2007	*Becoming Jane*	Julian Jarrold	HanWay Films/Miramax	UK/Ireland	Jane Austen (Anne Hathaway)
2007	*Mansfield Park* (TV)	Iain B. MacDonald	Company Pictures	UK	*Fanny Price* (Billie Piper)
2007	*Doctor Who 'The Shakespeare Code'* (TV episode)	Charlie Palmer	BBC	UK	William Shakespeare (Dean Lennox Kelly)
2008	*Lost in Austen* (TV mini-series)	Dan Zeff	Mammoth Screen	UK	(allegedly) *Elizabeth Bennet* (Gemma Arterton)
2008	*Miss Austen Regrets* (TV)	Jeremy Lovering	BBC/NOVA/WGBH Boston	USA/UK	Jane Austen (Olivia Williams)
2008	*Synecdoche, New York*	Charlie Kaufman	Sidney Kimmel Entertainment	USA	*Caden Cotard* (Philip Seymour Hoffman), *Madeleine Gravis* (Hope Davis)
2008	*The Edge of Love*	John Maybury	BBC Films	UK	Dylan Thomas (Matthew Rhys)
2009	*Bright Star*	Jane Campion	Pathe Renn Productions/Screen Australia/BBC Films	UK/Australia/France	John Keats (Ben Whishaw)
2009	*Enid* (TV)	James Hawes	BBC/Carnival Films	UK	Enid Blyton (Helena Bonham Carter)

Year	Title	Director	Production company	Country	Character
2009	*The Secret of Kells*	Tomm Moore and Nora Twomey	Les Amateurs/Vivi Film/Cartoon Saloon	France/Belgium/Ireland	*Aiden of Iona, Master Illuminator* (Mick Lally – voice)
2010	*Howl*	Rob Epstein and Jeffrey Friedman	Werc Werk Works	USA	Allen Ginsberg (James Franco) Jack Kerouac (Todd Rotondi)
2010	*The Tempest*	Julie Taymor	Miramax	USA	[Taymor, implicitly]
2011	*Anonymous*	Roland Emmerich	Columbia Pictures	UK/Germany	William Shakespeare (Rafe Spall), Edward De Vere, Earl of Oxford (Rhys Ifans), Ben Jonson (Sebastian Armesto)
2011	*Gnomeo and Juliet*	Kelly Asbury	Touchstone Pictures	UK/USA	William Shakespeare (Patrick Stewart – voice)
2011	*Midnight in Paris*	Woody Allen	Gravier Productions	Spain/USA	*Gil* (Owen Wilson)

Bibliography

Abrams, M.H., *The Mirror and the Lamp: Romantic Theory and the Critical Tradition* (Oxford: Oxford University Press, 1971).

Ackroyd, P., *Dickens* (London: Sinclair-Stevenson, 1990).

Adams Sitney, P. (ed.) *Modernist Montage: The Obscurity of Vision in Cinema and Literature* (New York: Columbia University Press, 1990).

Adams, T., 'Enter, Finally, the Real Alan Bennett', *The Guardian* (8 November 2009), at: http://www.guardian.co.uk/stage/2009/nov/08/alan-bennett-habit-of-art (accessed 14 December 2012).

Altman, J., *Epistolarity: Approaches to a Form* (Columbus: Ohio State University Press, 1982).

Aragay, M. (ed.) *Books in Motion: Adaptation, Intertextuality, Authorship* (Amsterdam: Rodopi, 2005).

Aragay, M. and López, G., 'Inf(l)ecting Pride and Prejudice: Dialogism, Intertextuality, and Adaptation', in M. Aragay (ed.) *Books in Motion: Adaptation, Intertextuality, Authorship* (Amsterdam: Rodopi, 2005), pp. 201–19.

Arthur, P., 'The Written Scene: Writers as Figures of Cinematic Redemption', in R. Stam and A. Raengo (eds) *Literature and Film: A Guide to the Theory and Practice of Film Adaptation* (Oxford: Wiley-Blackwell, 2004), pp. 331–42.

Atwood, M., *Negotiating with the Dead: A Writer on Writing* (Cambridge: Cambridge University Press, 2002).

Aubrey, J., *Brief Lives; Together With, An Apparatus for the Lives of our English Mathematical Writers; and, The Life of Thomas Hobbes of Malmesbury*, J. Buchanan-Brown (ed.) (London: Penguin, 2000).

Austen, J., *Northanger Abbey* (Ware, UK: Wordsworth Editions Ltd; Reprint edition, 1992).

Austen, J., *Persuasion* (London: Vintage, 2008).

Austen, J., *Pride and Prejudice* (New York: Charles Scribner, 1918).

Austen, J., *Pride and Prejudice*, Douglas Gray (ed.) (1966; New York and London: Norton, 2001).

Austen, J., *Pride and Prejudice*, P. Rogers, (ed.) (Cambridge: Cambridge University Press, 2006).

Austen, J., *Sense and Sensibility* (Harmondsworth: Penguin, 2007).

Babbitt, I., *Literature and the American College* (Houghton: Mifflin, 1908).

Badia, J. and Phegler, J. (eds) *Reading Women: Literary Figures and Cultural Icons from the Victorian Age to the Present* (Toronto: Toronto University Press, 2005).

Barber, N., 'Becoming Jane', *The Independent* (11 March 2007).

Barnard, J., 'Introduction', in *George Etherege: The Man of Mode* (London: A & C Black, 2007).

Baron, S.A., Lindquist, E., and Shevlin, E. (eds.) *Agent of Change: Print Culture Studies and the Legacy of Eisenstein* (Amherst: University of Massachusetts, 2007).

Barthes, R., *The Pleasure of the Text*, trans. R. Miller. (New York: Hill and Wang, 1975 [1973]).

Barthes, R., 'Upon Leaving the Movie Theater', in *The Rustle of Language* (New York: Hill and Wang, 1990), pp. 345–6.

Batchelor, J. (ed.) *The Art of Literary Biography* (Oxford: Clarendon Press, 1995).

Bate, J., *The Genius of Shakespeare* (New York and Oxford: Oxford University Press, 1998).

Bazin, A., 'Adaptation, or the Cinema as Digest', first published in French in 1948. In J. Naremore (ed.) *Film Adaptation* (London: The Athlone Press, 2000), pp. 19–27.

Bazin, A., *What is Cinema?* Vols 1 and 2, trans. Hugh Gray (Berkeley: University of California Press, 1967–1971).

Beal, P., 'Notions in Garrison: The Seventeenth-Century Commonplace Book', in W. Speed Hill (ed.) *New Ways of Looking at Old Texts: Papers of the Renaissance English Text Society, 1985–1991* (Medieval & Renaissance Texts and Studies, 1993).

Beevers, R., *The Byronic Image: The Poet Portrayed* (Abingdon: Olivia Press, 2005).

Benedictus, L., 'Calamity Jane?' *Guardian Unlimited* (2 March, 2007), at: http://www.guardian.co.uk/film/2007/mar/02/3

Benjamin, W., *Understanding Brecht* trans. A. Bostock (London: Verso, 1998).

Bentley, G.E., *The Profession of the Dramatist in Shakespeare's Time, 1590–1642* (Princeton: Princeton University Press, 1971).

Benton, M., *Literary Biography: An Introduction* (Chichester: John Wiley & Sons, 2009).

Bernanos, G., *The Diary of a Country Priest* trans. P. Morris (New York: Carroll and Graf, 1983).

Bingham, D., *Whose Lives Are They Anyway?: The Biopic as Contemporary Film Genre* (New Brunswick, NJ: Rutgers University Press, 2010).

Blanchard, G., 'Le Scriptovisuel ou Cinémato-Graphe', in *L'Espace et la lettre: Écritures, typographies* (Paris: Union Générale d'Editions, 1977).

Bluestone, G., *Novels into Film: The Metamorphoses of Fiction into Cinema* (Berkeley and Los Angeles: University of California Press, 1957).

Bolter, J.D. and Grusin, R., *Remediation: Understanding New Media* (Cambridge: The MIT Press, 2000).

Boozer, J. (ed.) *Authorship in Film Adaptation* (Austin: University of Texas Press, 2008).

Bornstein, G. 'Introduction', in G. Bornstein and R.G. Williams (eds.) *Palimpsest: Editorial Theory in the Humanities* (Ann Arbor: The University of Michigan Press, 1993), pp. 1–6.

Bornstein, G. and Williams, R.G. (eds.) *Palimpsest: Editorial Theory in the Humanities* (Ann Arbor: The University of Michigan Press, 1993).

Bradshaw P., 'Review: The Edge of Love' *The Guardian* (20 June 2008), at: http://www.guardian.co.uk/culture/2008/jun/20/filmandmusic1.filmandmusic9

Braudy, L., *The Frenzy of Renown: Fame and its History* (Oxford and New York: Oxford University Press, 1986).

Bresson, R., *Notes sur le cinématographe* (Paris: Editions Gallimard 1975).

Bronte, C., *Jane Eyre* (Harmondsworth: Penguin, 1994).

Brosh, L., 'Consuming Women: *Pride and Prejudice* and *Wuthering Heights*', in *Screening Novel Women: From British Domestic Fiction to Film* (Basingstoke: Palgrave, 2008).

Brosh, L., *Screening Novel Women: From British Domestic Fiction to Film* (Basingstoke: Palgrave, 2008).

Browne, N., 'Film Form/Voice-Over: Bresson's *Diary of a Country Priest*', in J. Quandt (ed.) *Robert Bresson* (Ontario: Cinematheque Ontario, 1998).

Buchanan, J. *Shakespeare on Film* (Harlow: Longman-Pearson, 2005).

Buchanan, J. *Shakespeare on Silent Film: An Excellent Dumb Discourse* (Cambridge: Cambridge University Press, 2009).

Buchanan, J. 'Literary Adaptation in the Silent Era', in D. Cartmell (ed.) *A Companion to Literature, Film and Adaptation* (Oxford: Wiley-Blackwell, 2012).

Buckland, W. (ed.) *Puzzle Films: Complex Storytelling in Contemporary Cinema* (Chichester, UK: Wiley-Blackwell, 2009).

Bulman, J. (ed.) *Shakespeare, Theory and Performance* (London: Routledge, 1996).

Burke, S., *Authorship: From Plato to the Postmodern* (Edinburgh: Edinburgh University Press, 1995).

Burnett, M.T. and Wray. R. (eds.) *Shakespeare, Film, Fin de Siècle* (Basingstoke: Palgrave, 2000).

Burr, T., 'Review: The Edge of Love', *The Boston Globe* (3 April 2009), at: http://www.boston.com/ae/movies/articles/2009/04/03/the_edge_of_love/ (accessed 14 December 2012).

Burt, R., *Medieval and Early Modern Film and Media* (New York: Palgrave, 2008; rev. 2010).

Burt, R., 'Shakespeare in Love and the End of History', in M.T. Burnett and R. Wray (eds.) *Shakespeare, Film, Fin de Siècle* (Houndmills: Palgrave, 2000), pp. 203–31.

Campion, J., 'In Search of Janet Frame', *The Guardian* (19 January 2008), at: http://www.guardian.co.uk/books/2008/jan/19/fiction5 (accessed 14 December 2012).

Campion, J., Interview with Nick James, *Sight and Sound*, 19(12) (December, 2009).

Carringer, R.L., 'Collaboration and Concepts of Authorship', *Publications of the Modern Language Association of America*, 116(2), (March, 2001).

Carter, H., 'Gillian Armstrong', *Senses of Cinema*, 22 (4 October 2002).

Cartmell, D., and Whelehan, I. (eds.) *The Cambridge Companion to Literature on Screen* (Cambridge: Cambridge University Press, 2007).

Cartmell, D., '"A more gentle sensation towards the original": Pride and Prejudice as concealed autobiography', in D. Cartmell, *Screen Adaptations: Jane Austen's 'Pride and Prejudice'* (London: Methuen, 2010).

Cartmell, D., *Screen Adaptations: Jane Austen's 'Pride and Prejudice'* (London: Methuen, 2010).

Cartmell, D., (ed.) *A Companion to Literature, Film and Adaptation* (Oxford: Wiley-Blackwell, 2012).

Caughie, J. (ed.) *Theories of Authorship: A Reader* (London: Routledge, 1981, 2001).

Cavell, S., *Contesting Tears: The Hollywood Melodrama of the Unknown Woman* (Chicago and London: University of Chicago Press, 1997).

Champion, E., 'The Perils of Literary Biography', *The Chronicle of Higher Education*, The Chronicle Review (21 December, 2007), at: http://chronicle.com/article/The-Perils-of-Literary/10084/

Chion, M., *The Voice in Cinema* (New York: Columbia University Press, 1999).

Chion, M., *Film: A Sound Art* (New York: Columbia University Press, 2009).

Coleridge, S.T., 'Frost at Midnight' in *The Complete Poems of Samuel Taylor Coleridge*, (Harmondsworth: Penguin, 1997), pp. 231–2.

Coleridge, S.T., 'Kubla Khan', in T.F. Huntington (ed.) *Coleridge's Ancient Mariner, Kubla Khan and Christabel* (London: MacMillan and Co., Ltd, 1907), pp. 35–7.

Coleridge, S.T., 'The Rime of the Ancient Mariner', in T.F. Huntington (ed.) *Coleridge's Ancient Mariner, Kubla Khan and Christabel* (London: MacMillan and Co., Ltd, 1907), pp. 1–33.

Coleridge, S.T., 'Xanadu', in *The Complete Poems of Samuel Taylor Coleridge* (Harmondsworth: Penguin, 1997), pp. 249–51.

Conley T., *Film Hieroglyphs: Ruptures in Classical Cinema*, 2nd cdn (Minneapolis: University of Minnesota Press).

Connell, R.W., *Masculinities* (Cambridge: Polity Press, 1996).

Cooke P., *Representing East Germany since Unification* (Oxford: Berg, 2005).

Cooper, R., 'Daddy's Girl?', *Commonweal* 130(20), (2003): 17.

Cope, W., 'Triolet', in A. Goldrick-Jones and H, Rosengarten (eds.) *Broadview Anthology of Poetry*, 2nd edn (London: Broadview Press, 2008), p. 887.

Corrigan, T., *A Cinema Without Walls: Movies and Culture after Vietnam* (New Brunswick, NJ: Rutgers University Press, 1991).

Corrigan, T., 'Literature on Screen, A History: In the Gap', in D. Cartmell and I. Whelehan (eds.) *The Cambridge Companion to Literature on Screen* (Cambridge: Cambridge University Press, 2007), pp. 29–44.

Cowen Orlin, L., *Locating Privacy in Tudor London* (Oxford: Oxford University Press, 2007).

Cronenberg, D., 'Charlie Kaufman', *Interview Magazine* (November 2008), at: http://www.interviewmagazine.com/film/charlie-kaufman/

Crow, T., 'Regarding *Howards End*', *Los Angeles Village View* (17–23 April 1992).

Cumming, L., *A Face to the World: On Self-Portraits* (London: Harper Press, 2009).

Darwin, C., *On the Origin of Species by Means of Natural Selection* (London, 1859).

Davies, H., 'Jane Austen at 19: The Real Life Love Story', (6 April, 2006), at: http://www.telegraph.co.uk/news/uknews/1514932/Jane-Austen-at-19-the-real-life-love-story.html

Davis, T. and Womack, K., 'Reading (and Writing) the Ethics of Authorship: *Shakespeare in Love* as Postmodern Metanarrative', *Literature/Film Quarterly* 32(2), (2004): 153.

Day, J. *The Isle of Guls As it Hath been Often Played in the Blacke Fryars, by the Children of the Reuels* G.B. Harrison (ed.) (London: Oxford University Press, 1936).

De Waal, E., *The Hare with Amber Eyes: A Hidden Inheritance* (London: Chatto and Windus, 2010).

Deleuze, G., *Cinema 1. L'Image-mouvement* (Paris: Minuit, 1983).

Diamond, D., 'Empathy and Identification in von Donnersmarck's *The Lives of Others'*, *Journal of the American Psychoanalytic Association* 56 (2008): 811–32.

Doane, M.A., 'The Voice in Cinema: The Articulation of Body and Space', *Yale French Studies* 60 (1980): 33–50.

Dobie, M., 'Gender and the Heritage Genre', in S. Pucci and J. Thompson (eds.) *Jane Austen & Co: Remaking the Past in Contemporary Culture* (Albany: University of New York Press, 2003).

Dostoevsky, F., *Crime and Punishment* (Ware, UK: Wordsworth Editions, 2000).

Dzialo, C., 'The Screenplays of Charlie Kaufman', in W. Buckland (ed.) *Puzzle Films: Complex Storytelling in Contemporary Cinema* (Oxford: Wiley-Blackwell, 2009).

Eagleton, M., *Figuring the Woman Author in Contemporary Fiction* (New York: Palgrave Macmillan, 2005).

Edel, L., *Literary Biography* (New York: Anchor Books, 1959 [1957]).

Eisenberg, A., 'Holograms Deliver 3-D, Without the Goofy Glasses', *New York Times* (4 December, 2010).

Eisler, B., *Byron: Child of Passion, Fool of Fame* (London: Vintage, 2000).

Elle (December 2008) http://www.elleuk.com/elle-tv/red-carpet/parties-events/elle-in-association-with-the-edge-of-love

Elley, D., 'Quite a royal send-off', *Variety* (19–25 May 2003).

Ellmann, R., *Golden Codgers: Biographical Speculations* (London: Oxford University Press, 1973).

Ellmann, R., *Oscar Wilde* (London: Hamish Hamilton, 1987).

Etheredge, G., *George Etherege: The Man of Mode* (London: A&C Black, 2007).

Fielding, H., *The History of Tom Jones, A Foundling* (Rev edn. Oxford: Oxford Paperbacks, 2008 [1749]).

Flaubert, G., *Madame Bovary* trans. G. Wall (Rev edn. Harmondsworth: Penguin, 2003).

Fleishman, A., *Narrated Films: Storytelling Situations in Cinema History* (Baltimore: Johns Hopkins University Press, 2004 [1856 in French]).

Foster, R.F., *W.B. Yeats: A Life* (Oxford: Oxford University Press, 1997).

Foucault, M., 'What is an Author' (a 1969 lecture), in P. Rabinow (ed.) *The Foucault Reader: An Introduction to Foucault's Thought* (London: Penguin, 1991), pp. 101–20.

Franklin, M., *My Brilliant Career* (London: Virago Press, 1980).

French, P., 'Be-All and End-All for Triumph', *The Observer* (3 May 1992).

French, P., 'Review: The Edge of Love', *The Observer* (22 June 2008).

Fulbrook, M., *Anatomy of a Dictatorship* (Oxford: Oxford University Press, 1995).

Fullerton, J. and Olsson, J., *Allegories of Communication: Intermedial Concerns from Cinema to the Digital* (Rome: John Libbey, 2004).

Funder, A., 'Eyes Without a Face', *Sight and Sound* 7(5) (1 May 2007): 16–20.

Funder, A., 'Tyranny of Terror', film review of *The Lives of Others*, *The Guardian* (Saturday 5 May 2007), at: http://www.guardian.co.uk/books/2007/may/05/features reviews.guardianreview12

Gamwell, L. and Wells, R., *Sigmund Freud and Art: His Personal Collection of Antiquities* (London: Thames and Hudson, 1989).

Garcia, M., 'A Sweet Unrest: Jane Campion Recreates the Love Affair between Poet John Keats and Fanny Brawne' *Film Journal International*, CXII, 12 (September 2009), at: http://www.filmjournal.com/filmjournal/content_display/news-and-features/features/movies/e3ib9d44f33bad88c089200b320dd99e108

Garton Ash, T., *The File: A Personal History* (New York: Vintage Books, 1998).

Gaskell, E. *The Life of Charlotte Brontë*, E. Jay (ed.) (Harmondsworth: Penguin, 1997).

Genette, G., *Paratexts: Thresholds of Interpretation* trans. J. E. Lewin (Cambridge: Cambridge University Press, 1997).

Gershick, T. and Miller, A., 'Coming to Terms: Masculinity and Physical Disability', *American Sociological Association Annual Meeting* (Miami, 1993).

Gerstner, D. and Staiger, J., (eds) *Authorship and Film* (New York: Routledge, 2003).

Gilbert, S.M. and Gubar, S., *The Madwoman in the Attic* (New Haven: Yale University Press, 2000).

Glatzer, N.N., (ed.) *Franz Kafka: The Complete Stories* (New York: Schocken Books Inc., 1995).

Gleiberman, O., *Entertainment Weekly*, quoted in Miramax advertisement in *Screen International* (11 December 1998).

Godard, J.-L. and Delahaye, M., 'The Question', in *Cahiers du Cinéma in English* (London: British Film Institute, 1967).

Goldrick-Jones, A. and Rosengarten, H., (eds.) *Broadview Anthology of Poetry*, 2nd edn (London: Broadview Press, 2008).

Goodridge, M., 'Shakespeare in Love', *Screen International* (18 December 1998).

Gorki, M., *My Childhood* (Kessinger Publishing, 2005).

Grant, B.K., (ed.) *Auteurs and Authorship. A Film Reader* (Oxford: Blackwell Publishing, 2008).

Greenaway, P., *Prospero's Books: A Film of Shakespeare's 'The Tempest'* (London: Chatto & Windus, 1991).

Greenblatt, S., *Will in the World: How Shakespeare Became Shakespeare* (W.W. Norton & Company, 2005).

Greene, G., *Lord Rochester's Monkey: The Life of John Wilmot, Second Earl of Rochester* (London: Bodley Head, 1974).

Griffiths, A., *Shivers Down Your Spine: Cinema, Museums, and the Immersive View* (New York: Columbia University Press, 2008).

Gunning, T., 'Fritz Lang Calling: The Telephone and the Circuits of Modernity', in J. Fullerton and J. Olsson, *Allegories of Communication: Intermedial Concerns from Cinema to the Digital* (Rome: John Libbey, 2004), pp. 19–37.

Hackett, H., *Shakespeare and Elizabeth: The Meeting of Two Myths* (Princeton and Oxford: Princeton University Press, 2009).

Hall, E., *The Hidden Dimension* (New York: Doubleday, 1966).

Hamilton, I., *Keepers of the Flame: Literary Estates and the Rise of Biography* (Ann Arbor: University of Michigan University Press, 1992).

Hamilton Ball, R., *Shakespeare on Film: A Strange Eventful History* (New York: Theatre Arts Books, 1968).

Harman, C., *Jane's Fame: How Jane Austen Conquered the World* (Edinburgh: Canongate, 2009).

Harrison, G., *Shakespeare at Work 1592–1603* (London: George Routledge & Sons Ltd, 1933).

Hastings, C. Jones, B., and Plentl, S., 'Jane Austen to be the Latest Teenage Sensation', *The Sunday Telegraph* (4 February 2007).

Heidegger, M., *Poetry, Language, Thought* trans. A. Hofstadter (New York: HarperCollins Publishers, 2001).

Hellman, J., 'Bernanos, Drumont and the Rise of French Fascism', *The Review of Politics*, 52(3) (1990): 441–59.

Hellman, L., *Pentimento* (Canada: Penguin Group, 1973).

Hemingway, E., *Across the River and Into the Trees* (New York: Charles Scribner's Sons, 1950).

Hemingway, E., *A Farewell to Arms* (London: Arrow, 1994).

Hemingway, E., *A Movable Feast* (New York: Prentice Hall and IBD, 1971).

Hemingway, E., *Fiesta: The Sun Also Rises* (London: Arrow, 1994).

Hemingway, E., *For Whom the Bell Tolls* (London: Arrow, 1994).

Hemingway, E., *In Our Time* (Paris: Three Mountains Press, 1924).

Hemingway, E., *Islands in the Stream* (New York: Scribner, 1970).

Hemingway, E., *My Old Man* (Paris: Contact Publishing, 1923).

Hemingway, E., 'The End of Something', in E. Hemingway, *In Our Time* (Paris: Three Mountains Press, 1924).

Hemingway, E., *The Old Man and the Sea* (New York: Simon and Schuster, 2002).

Hemingway, E., 'The Short Happy Life of Francis Macomber', *Cosmopolitan Magazine*, (September 1936).

Hemingway, E., 'The Snows of Kilimanjaro', first published in *The Fifth Column and the First Forty-Nine Stories* (1938). Reprinted in *The Snows of Kilimanjaro and Other Stories* (1961).

Hemingway, E., *To Have and Have Not* (New York:. Simon and Schuster, 2006 [1944]).

Higgins, C. and Davies, C., 'A.S. Byatt says women who write intellectual books seen as unnatural', *The Guardian* (10 August 2010), at: http://www.guardian.co.uk/books/2010/aug/20/as-byatt-intellectual-women-strange

Higson, A., *English Heritage, English Cinema: Costume Drama since 1980* (Oxford: Oxford University Press, 2003).

Higson, A., 'English Heritage, English Literature, English Cinema: Selling Jane Austen to Movie Audiences in the 1990s', in E. Voigts-Virchow (ed.) *Janespotting and Beyond: British Heritage Retrovisions Since the Mid-1990s* (Tübingen: Gunter Narr Verlag, 2004).

Higson, A., *Film England: Culturally English Filmmaking since the 1990s* (London: I.B. Tauris, 2011).

Hill, W.S. (ed.) *New Ways of Looking at Old Texts: Papers of the Renaissance English Text Society, 1985–1991* (Binghampton, New York: Medieval & Renaissance Texts and Studies, 1993).

Hillis Miller, J., *Ariadne's Thread. Story Lines* (New Haven: Yale University Press, 1992).

Holderness, G., *Nine Lives of William Shakespeare* (London: Continuum, 2011).

Holmes, R., *Coleridge: Early Visions* (London: Hodder & Stoughton, 1989).

Holmes, R., *Footsteps: Adventures of a Romantic Biographer* (New York: Vintage, 1996 [1985]).

Holroyd, M., *Works on Paper: The Craft of Biography and Autobiography* (Washington DC: Counterpoint, 2002).

Hopkins, L., *Relocating Shakespeare and Austen on Screen* (Basingstoke: Palgrave, 2009).

Hotchner, A.E., *Papa Hemingway: A Personal Memoir* (New York: Random House, 1966).

Hotchner, A.E., *The Good Life According to Hemingway* (New York: Ecco, 2008).

Howlett, P., 'Film choice: Gosford Park', *The Guardian Guide* (21 March 2009).

Hunter, A. 'Becoming Jane' *Screendaily.com* (8 March, 2007), at: http://www.screen daily.com/becoming-jane/4031325.article (accessed by subscription).

Huntington, T.F. (ed.) *Coleridge's Ancient Mariner, Kubla Khan and Christabel* (London: Macmillan and Co., Ltd, 1907).

Ide, W., 'Breathing Passionate Life into the Nation's Favourite Spinster', *The Times* (8 March 2007), at: http://cma.staging-thetimes.co.uk/tto/arts/film/article2426 130.ece

Ioppolo, G., *Dramatists and their Manuscripts in the Age of Shakespeare, Jonson, Middleton and Heywood: Authorship, Authority and the Playhouse* (Abingdon: Routledge, 2006).

Jardine, L., *Erasmus Man of Letters: The Construction of Charisma in Print* (Princeton, NJ: Princeton University Press, 1993).

Jeffreys, S., *The Libertine* (London: Nick Hern Books,1994).

Johnson, S., 'Rochester', in R. Lonsdale (ed.) *The Lives of the Most Eminent English Poets: with Critical Observations on Their Works* (Oxford, Clarendon Press, 2009), pp. 198–207.

Jones, E., *Sigmund Freud: Life and Work*, vol 3: *The Last Phase 1919–1939* (London: Hogarth Press, 1957).

Jonson, B., *The Workes of Beniamin Ionson* (London, 1616).

Kafka, F., 'An Imperial Message', in N.N Glatzer (ed)., *Franz Kafka: The Complete Stories*. (New York: Schocken Books, 1995).

Kafka. F., *Letters to Milena* (New York: Schocken Books, 1990).

Kaplan, D., 'Mass Marketing *Jane Austen*: Men, Women and Courtship in Two Film Adaptations', in L. Troost and S. Greenfield (eds.) *Jane Austen in Hollywood* (Kentucky: The University Press of Kentucky, 2001), pp. 177–87.

Kaufman, C., *Being John Malkovich* (London: Faber and Faber, 2000).

Kaufman, C. and Kaufman, D., *Adaptation: The Shooting Script* (New York: Newmarket Press, 2002).

Kaufman, C., Interview with Marit Kapla. Göteburg International Film Festival (29 January 2011), at: http://www.youtube.com/watch?v=xpjgjJqayxI

Keats, J., *Endymion: A Poetic Romance* (London: Taylor and Hessey, 1818).

Keats, J., 'La Belle Dame Sans Merci', in J. Barnard (ed.) *John Keats: The Complete Poems*, 2nd edn (Harmondsworth: Penguin, 1977), pp. 334–5.

Keats, J., 'Ode to a Nightingale', in J. Barnard (ed.) *John Keats: The Complete Poems*, 2nd edn (Harmondsworth: Penguin, 1977), pp. 346–7.

Kenyon-Jones, C., *Byron: The Image of a Poet* (Newark: University of Delaware Press, 2008).

King, G., *Indiewood, USA* (London and New York: I.B. Tauris, 2009).

Kingsley-Smith, J., 'Shakespearean Authorship in Popular British Cinema', *Literature/ Film Quarterly* 30(3), (2002).

Kisonak, R., 'Adaptation', *Film Threat* (17 January 2003), at: http://www.filmthreat. com/reviews/4182/

Knapp, J., 'What is a Co-Author?' *Representations* 89 (Winter 2005).

Kohn, E., 'The Peculiarities of Soullessness: Sophie Barthes' *Cold Souls* (Sundance '09), at: http://www.indiewire.com/article/the_peculiarities_of_soullessness_sophie_ barthes_cold_souls_sundance_09

Kundera, M., *The Art of the Novel* (New York: HarperCollins, 2000).

Lanier, D., 'Drowning the Book: *Prospero's Books* and the Textual Shakespeare', in J. Bulman, (ed.) *Shakespeare, Theory and Performance* (London: Routledge, 1996), p.188.

Latour, B. and Weibel P. (eds.) *Iconoclash: Beyond the Image Wars in Science, Religion and Art* (London: MIT Press, 2002).

Lee, H., *Body Parts: Essays on Life Writing* (London: Chatto and Windus, 2005).

Lee, H., *Virginia Woolf* (London: Chatto and Windus, 1996).

Leff, L.J., *Hemingway and his Conspirators: Hollywood, Scribners, and the Making of American Celebrity Culture* (New York: Rowman & Littlefield, 1997).

Lonsdale, R. (ed.) *The Lives of the Most Eminent English Poets: with Critical Observations on Their Works* (Oxford, Clarendon Press, 2006).

López, M.C. '*Persuasion* Moves to Chicago: Rewriting Austen's Classic in *The Lake House*', *Persuasions On-Line* 29(1), (2008), at: http://www.jasna.org/persuasions/on-line/vol29no1/cano-lopez.html

López, M.C. and García-Periago, R.M., 'Becoming Shakespeare and Jane Austen in Love: An Intertextual Dialogue between Two Biopics', *Persuasions On-Line* 29(1), (2008) http://www.jasna.org/persuasions/on-line/vol29no1/cano-garcia.html

Lyons, J., NBC's *Reel Talk*. Quoted on the official DVD website, http://video.movies. go.com/becomingjane/ (no longer available).

Macaulay, T., 'Review of Moore's Life of Byron', *Edinburgh Review* 53 (June 1831).

Macherey P., 'A Theory of Literary Production' trans. G. Wall (London: Routledge, 2006).

Malvern, J., 'Austen's movie "a fanciful affair"', *TimesOnline* (18 March 2006).

Manovich, L., *The Language of New Media* (Cambridge, MA: MIT, 2002).

Margolis, H. (ed.) *Jane Campion's* 'The Piano' (Cambridge: Cambridge University Press, 2000).

Mariani P., 'Reassembling the Dust: Notes on the Art of the Biographer', in S.B. Oates (ed.) *Biography as High Adventure* (Amherst, MA: University of Massachusetts Press, 1986), pp. 104–23.

Marston, J., 'Antonio's Revenge' (1602) W. Reavley Gair, (ed.) (Manchester: Manchester University Press, 1999).

Masten, J., *Textual Intercourse: Collaboration, Authorship and Sexualities in Renaissance Drama* (Cambridge: Cambridge University Press, 1997).

Matejka, L. and Pomorska, K. (eds.) *Readings in Russian Poetics* (Cambridge, MA: MIT Press, 1971).

Mayne, Z., *Two Dissertations Concerning Sense and the Imagination with an Essay on Consciousness* (1728) York University Ebooks and Text Archive, at: http://www. archive.org/details/twodissertations00maynuoft (accessed 14 December 2012).

McHugh, K., *Jane Campion* (Urbana: University of Illinois Press, 2007).

McKee, R., 'Critical Commentary' in C. Kaufman and D. Kaufman (eds.) *Adaptation: The Shooting Script* (New York: Newmarket Press, 2002).

McLaren, D., *Looking for Enid: The Mysterious and Inventive Life of Enid Blyton* (London: Portabello Books Ltd., 2008).

McLean, C., '"Sexing up" Jane Austen', *The Daily Telegraph* (2 March 2007).

McMullan, G., *Shakespeare and the Idea of Late Writing: Authorship in the Proximity of Death* (Cambridge: Cambridge University Press, 2007).

Melville, H., *Bartleby the Scrivener* (London: Hesperus Press, 2007).

Melville, H., *Moby Dick* (London: Vintage Classics, 2007).

Mérigeau, P., *Mankiewicz* (Paris: Denoël, 1993).

Modleski, T., *Loving With a Vengeance* (London: Routledge, 1990).

Monod, R., 'Working with Bresson', *Sight and Sound* 26 (Summer 1957).

Moran, J., *Star Authors in America* (London: Pluto Press, 2000).

Motion, A., *Keats* (London: Faber and Faber, 1997).

Mottram, J., *The Sundance Kids: How the Mavericks Took Back Hollywood* (New York: Faber and Faber Inc., 2006).

Mowat, B., 'Prospero's Book', *Shakespeare Quarterly* 52(1), (Spring 2001): 1–33.

Mulvey, L., 'Visual Pleasure and Narrative Cinema', *Screen* 16(3), (Autumn 1975).

Naremore, J. (ed.) *Film Adaptation* (New Brunswick, New Jersey: Rutgers University Press, 2000 [1948 in French]).

Neale, S., *Genre and Hollywood* (London: Routledge, 2000).

Nokes, D., *Jane Austen* (London: Fourth Estate, 1998).

Norman, M. and Stoppard, T., 'Shakespeare in Love', *The Internet Movie Script Database*, at: http://www.imsdb.com/scripts/Shakespeare-in-Love.html

North, J., *The Domestication of Genius: Biography and the Romantic Poet* (Oxford: Oxford University Press, 2009).

Oates, S.B. (ed.) *Biography as High Adventure: Life-Writers Speak on their Art* (Amherst, MA: University of Massachusetts Press, 1986).

Parrill, S., *Jane Austen on Film and Television: A Critical Study of the Adaptations* (Jefferson and London: McFarland, 2002).

Peach, A., *Portraits of Byron* (London: The Walpole Society, 2000).

Perkins, V.F., 'Same Tune Again! Repetition and Framing in "Letter from an Unknown Woman"', *CineAction* 52 (2000): 40–8.

Perkins Wilder, L., *Shakespeare's Memory Theatre: Recollection, Properties and Character* (Cambridge: Cambridge University Press, 2010).

Phegley, J. and Badia, J., 'Introduction: Women Readers as Literary Figures and Cultural Icons', in J. Badia and J. Phegler (eds) *Reading Women: Literary Figures and Cultural Icons from the Victorian Age to the Present* (Toronto: Toronto University Press, 2005).

Phillips, G.D., *Hemingway and Film* (Ungar: University of Michigan, 1980).

Pierce, N., 'Becoming Jane', *Total Film* 126 (April 2007).

Plath, S., 'Daddy', in *Ariel* (London: Harper Collins, 1999).

Plath, S., *Ariel* (London: Harper Collins, 1999).

Plato, *Phaedrus* (Oxford: Oxford University Press, 2002).

Polan, D., 'Auteur Desire', *Screening the Past* 12 (March, 2001).

Polan, D., *Jane Campion* (London: British Film Institute, 2001).

Potter, S., interviewed by K. Widdicombe, , 'The Contemporary Auteur: An Interview with Sally Potter' (2003) www.bfi.org.uk/filmtvinfo/publications/16+/potter.html (no longer available).

Price, S., *The Screenplay: Authorship, Theory and Criticism* (New York: Palgrave Macmillan, 2010).

Pritchett, V.S., 'Rogue Poet', *The New York Review of Books* 21 (1974).

Proust, M., *In Search of Lost Time*, vol. 3 (London: Everyman, 2001).

Pucci, S. and Thompson, J. (eds.) *Jane Austen & Co: Remaking the Past in Contemporary Culture* (Albany: University of New York Press, 2003).

Quandt, J. (ed.) *Robert Bresson* (Ontario: Cinémathèque Ontario 1998).

Queenan, J., 'Without Rhyme or Reason', *The Guardian* (31 January 2004).

Radner, H., Fox, A., and Bessiere, I. (eds.) *Jane Campion: Cinema, Nation, Identity* (Detroit: Wayne State University Press, 2009).

Rancière, J., 'Aesthetics against Incarnation: an interview with Anne Marie Oliver', *Critical Inquiry* 35(1), (2008): 172–90.

Rancière, J., *The Future of the Image* (London: Verso 2007).

Raynal-Zougari, M., 'Bernanos-Bresson (*Journal d'un curé de campagne*): le spectateur du film/lecteur du journal, ou l'image des mots', *French Forum* 33(3), (2008): 105–21.

Reader, K., *Robert Bresson* (Manchester: Manchester University Press, 2000).

Reed, R., 'Grim Flicks Creep Out Toronto', *The New York Observer* (27 September 2004).

Reynolds, N., 'I Could Only Become Jane by Reading All her Letters, Admits Star', *Daily Telegraph* (7 March, 2007), at: http://www.telegraph.co.uk/news/uknews/1544587/I-could-only-become-Jane-by-reading-all-her-letters-admits-star.html (accessed 14 December 2012).

Rice, A., *Interview with the Vampire* (New York: Random House, 1997).

Roche, D., 'Books and Letters in Joe Wright's *Pride & Prejudice*: Anticipating the Spectator's Response through the Thematization of Film Adaptation', *Persuasions On-line* 27(2), (2007), at: http://www.jasna.org/persuasions/on-line/vol27no2/roche.htm (accessed 14 December 2012).

Roe, J., *Her Brilliant Career: The Life of Stella Miles Franklin* (Sydney: HarperCollins Publishers, 2008).

Roe, J.I., 'Franklin, Stella Maria Sarah Miles (1879–1954)' in *Australian Dictionary of Biography* (2006), at: www.adb.online.anu.edu.au/biogs/A080591b.htm (accessed 14 December 2012).

Rollins, H.E. (ed.) *The Letters of John Keats, 1814–21, 2 Vols* (Cambridge, MA: Harvard University Press, 1958).

Rooney, D., 'Stage Beauty' *Variety* (10–16 May 2004).

Ropars, M.-C., 'L'Oubli du Texte', *Cinémas* 4, 1 (Fall 1993), pp. 11–22.

Rosa, João Guimarães, 'Aletria e Hermenêutica', in *Tutaméia* (Terceiras Estórias) (Rio de Janeiro: Nova Fronteira, 1985).

Roth, P., *Portnoy's Complaint* (London: Vintage, 1995).

Russell, G., *Romantic Sociability: Social Networks and Literary Culture in Britain, 1770–1840* (Cambridge: Cambridge University Press, 2002).

Salamon, J., 'Film: Merchant Ivory's *Howards End*', *Wall St Journal* (12 March 1992).

Sanders, J., *Adaptation and Appropriation* (London: Routledge, 2006).

Sartre, J.-P., *What is Literature? And Other Essays* trans. B. Frechtman (Cambridge, MA: Harvard University Press, 1988).

Schatz, T., *The Genius of the System: Hollywood Filmmaking in the Studio Era* (London: Faber and Faber, 1988, 1998).

Schrader, P., 'Robert Bresson, Possibly', in J. Quandt (ed.) *Robert Bresson* (Ontario: Cinémathèque Ontario 1998).

Schrader, P., *Transcendental Style in Film: Ozu, Bresson, Dreyer* (Berkeley: University of California Press, 1972).

Sellors, C.P., *Film Authorship: Auteurs and Other Myths* (London: Wallflower Press, 2010).

Shakespeare, W., *As You Like It*, in B. Mowat and Paul Werstine (eds) (New York: Washington Square Press, 1992).

Shakespeare, W., *First Folio*, J. Heminge and H. Condell (eds) (London, 1623).

Shakespeare, W., *Hamlet*, A. Thompson and N. Taylor (eds) (London: Arden Shakespeare, 2006).

Shakespeare, W., *Romeo and Juliet*, in A. Thompson, D. Scott Kastan and R. Proudfoot (eds.) *Arden Shakespeare Complete Works* (London: A&C Black, 2001).

Shakespeare, W., *The Merchant of Venice*, in A. Thompson, D. Scott Kastan and R. Proudfoot (eds.) *Arden Shakespeare Complete Works* (London: A&C Black, 2001).

Shakespeare, W., *The Taming of the Shrew* in A. Thompson, D. Scott Kastan and R. Proudfoot (eds) *Arden Shakespeare Complete Works* (London: A&C Black, 2001).

Shakespeare, W., *The Tempest* in A. Thompson, D. Scott Kastan and R. Proudfoot (eds.) *Arden Shakespeare Complete Works* (London: A&C Black, 2001).

Shakespeare, W., *The Two Gentlemen of Verona*, W. Carroll, (ed.) (London: Arden Shakespeare, 2004).

Shakespeare, W., *Titus Andronicus* Jonathan Bate (ed.) (London: Arden Shakespeare, 2006).

Shakespeare, W., *Twelfth Night*, in A. Thompson, D. Scott Kastan and R. Proudfoot (eds.) *Arden Shakespeare Complete Works* (London: A&C Black, 2001).

Sherman, W.H., 'On the Threshold: Architecture, Paratext, and Early Print Culture', in S. A. Baron, E. Lindquist and E. Shevlin (eds.) *Agent of Change: Print Culture Studies and the Legacy of Eisenstein* (Amherst: Umiversity of Massachusetts, 2007), pp. 67–81.

Sherman, W.H., 'The Beginning of "The End": terminal paratext and the birth of print culture' in H. Smith (ed.) *Renaissance Paratexts* (Cambridge: Cambridge University Press, 2011), pp. 65–90.

Sinfield, A., *Faultlines: Cultural Materialism and the Politics of Dissident Reading* (Berkeley: University of California Press, 1992).

Sjogren, B., *Into the Vortex: Female Voice and Paradox in Film* (Chicago: University of Illinois Press, 2004).

Smallwood, I., *A Childhood at Green Hedges: A Fragment of Autobiography by Enid Blyton's Daughter* (London: Methuen, 1989).

Smith, H., *Renaissance Paratexts* (Cambridge: Cambridge University Press, 2011).

Smyth, A., *Autobiography in Early Modern England* (Cambridge: Cambridge University Press, 2010).

Sontag, S., 'Spiritual Style in the Films of Robert Bresson' in *Against Interpretation* (New York: Farrar, Strauss and Giroux, 1964).

Spence, J., *Becoming Jane Austen: A Life* (London: Continuum, 2003).

Stam, R., 'The Theory and Practice of Adaptation' in R. Stam and A. Raengo (eds.) *Literature and Film: A Guide to the Theory and Practice of Film Adaptation* (Oxford: Blackwell, 2005), pp. 1–52.

Stam, R. and Raengo, A. (eds.) *Literature and Film: A Guide to the Theory and Practice of Film Adaptation* (Oxford: Blackwell, 2005).

Stanitzek, G., 'Texts and Paratexts in Media' trans. Ellen Klein, *Critical Inquiry* 32(1), (Autumn 2005): 27–42.

Stein, A., *The Byronic Hero in Film, Fiction and Television* (Carbondale: Southern Illinois University Press, 2004).

Stern, T., *Making Shakespeare: From Stage to Page* (London: Routledge, 2004).

Stillinger, J., *Multiple Authorship and the Myth of Solitary Genius* (New York: Oxford University Press, 1991).

Stoney, B., *Enid Blyton: The Biography* (London: Hodder and Stoughton, 1974).

Storey, G. (ed.) *The Letters of Charles Dickens, 1820–1870* vol. 10 '1862–1864' (Oxford: Oxford University Press).

Storey, G. (ed.) *The Letters of Charles Dickens 1820–1870* vol. 12 '1868–1870', Last Will dated 12 May 1869 (Oxford: Oxford University Press).

Strachey, L., *Eminent Victorians* (London: Modern Library, 1918).

Sutherland, K., *Jane Austen's Textual Lives: From Aeschylus to Bollywood* (Oxford: Oxford University Press, 2005).

Tanz, J., 'Charlie Kaufman: Hollywood's Brainiest Screenwriter Pleases Crowds by Refusing to Please', *Wired* (October 2008).

Taymor, J., *The Tempest, Adapted From the Play by William Shakespeare* (New York: Abrams, 2010).

Tennant, E., *The Ballad of Sylvia and Ted* (Edinburgh: Mainstream Publishing, 2001).

Thomas, A., 'Italian audiences love *I Want You*', *Variety* (13 March 2007).

Thompson Scott, A., Kastan, D. and Proudfoot, R. (eds) *Arden Shakespeare Complete Works* (London: A&C Black, 2001).

Tomalin, C., *Thomas Hardy: the Time-Torn Man* (London: Viking, 2006).

Tomashevsky, B., 'Literature and Biography', in L. Matejka and K. Pomorska (eds.) *Readings in Russian Poetics* (Cambridge, MA: MIT Press, 1971), pp. 81–9.

Tomasulo, F.P., 'Adaptation as Adaptation: From Susan Orlean's *The Orchid Thief* to Charlie (and "Donald") Kaufman's Screenplay to Spike Jonze's Film', in J. Boozer (ed.) *Authorship in Film Adaptation* (Austin: University of Texas Press, 2008).

Tookey, C., 'Perfectly pleasant, but this Jane still falls short', *Daily Mail* (9 March, 2007), at: http://www.dailymail.co.uk/tvshowbiz/reviews/article-441197/Perfectly-pleasant-Jane-falls-short.html

Troost, L. and Greenfield, S. (eds.) *Jane Austen in Hollywood* (Lexington: University Press of Kentucky, 2001).

Troost, L. and Greenfield, S. 'Watching Ourselves Watching', in L. Troost and S. Greenfield, (eds.) *Jane Austen in Hollywood* (Lexington: University Press of Kentucky, 2001).

Verhoeven, D., *Jane Campion, Routledge Film Guides* (London: Routledge, 2009).

Vermeulen, T. and Van Den Akker, R., 'Notes on metamodernism', *Journal of Aesthetics and Culture* 2 (2010): 1–14.

Vernet, M., *Figures de l'absence: de l'invisible au cinéma* (Paris: Cahiers du Cinéma, 1988).

Vogue (September 2007), at: http://www.vogue.co.uk/magazine/archive/issue/2007/September/Page/1

Voigts-Virchow, E. (ed.) *Janespotting and Beyond: British Heritage Retrovisions Since the Mid-1990s* (Tübingen: Gunter Narr Verlag, 2004).

von Donnersmarck, F.H., *Das Leben der Anderen* (Frankfurt: Suhrkamp Verlag, 2006).

Wall, G., *Flaubert: A Life* (London: Faber, 2001).

West, W.E. and Curtis Pennington, E., 'Painting Lord Byron: An Account by William Edward West', *Archives of American Art Journal* 24(2) (1984).

Wexman, V.W. (ed.) *Jane Campion: Interviews* (Jackson MI: University Press of Mississippi, 1999).

Williams, S., 'Not so plain Jane', *Telegraph Magazine* (17 February 2007), at: http://www.telegraph.co.uk/culture/3663235/Not-so-plain-Jane.html

Wiltshire, J., *Recreating Jane Austen* (Cambridge: Cambridge University Press, 2001).

Witcher, R., *Grazia*. Qtd on Ecosse Films website, at: http://www.ecossefilms.com/film_becoming.aspx (no longer available).

Wolfson, S.J., *Romantic Interactions: Social Being and the Turns of Literary Action* (Baltimore: Johns Hopkins University Press, 2010).

Wood, R., *Sexual Politics and Narrative Film: Hollywood and Beyond* (New York: Columbia University Press, 1998).

Woolf, V. *A Room of One's Own* (London: Penguin Books, 2000 [1929]).

Woolf, V. 'Great Men's Houses' in *The London Scene* first pub. 1931 (London: Snowbooks, 1975).

Woolf, V. *Mrs Dalloway* (Rev edn Oxford: Oxford University Press, 2008 [1925]).

Woolf, V. *Orlando: A Biography*, B. Lyons (ed.) (London: Penguin, 1993).

Wordsworth, W., 'Tintern Abbey', in W. Wordsworth and S.T. Coleridge, *Lyrical Ballads* (London: Taylor and Francis, 2005).

Wordsworth, W. and Coleridge, S.T., *Lyrical Ballads* (London: Taylor and Francis, 2005).

Worthen, J., 'The Necessary Ignorance of a Biographer', in J. Batchelor (ed.) *The Art of Literary Biography* (Oxford: Clarendon Press, 1995), pp. 227–44.

Wright Wexman, V., *Film and Authorship* (Chapel Hill: Rutgers University Press, 2003).

Yates, F., *The Art of Memory* (London: Routledge & Kegan Paul, 1966).

Žižek, S., *Looking Awry: An Introduction to Jacques Lacan through Popular Culture* (Cambridge, MA: MIT Press, 1991).

Zweig, S., 'Letter from an Unknown Woman', repr. in *Selected Stories* (London: Pushkin Press, 2009).

Index

Note: page references to notes are in *italics*; page references to images are in **bold**. Individual films are given independent entries; literary works appear under the name of their author.

Ackroyd, Peter, biographer, novelist, critic   125, *133*

adaptation, theory and criticism   *31*, 46, 47, *48*, *49*, 51, 62, *63*, 76, *103*, 140, 157, 161, *162*, *163*, *176*, 206, 214

Adaptation, film (dir. Spike Jonze, 2002)   23, 27, 41–2, 164–5, 168–75, 169, *176*

Allen, Woody, film director   141, *150*; *see also Midnight in Paris*

Angel at My Table, An, film (dir. Jane Campion, 1990)   52, 60

animation   12, **13**, *31*, 44, 46, 178, 180–2, **181**, **188**, 187–90, **189**, *191*; *see also Howl*; illustration; *The Secret of Kells*; *Sleeping Beauty*

Anonymous, film (dir. Roland Emmerich, 2011)   19–20, **20**, *105*, 156

Armstrong, Gillian, film director   24, 51, 54, 55, 59, 69; *see also My Brilliant Career*

Arthur, Paul, film critic and historian   10, 27, *31*, *32*, 74, *76*, 93, 94, *103*

Asbury, Kelly, film director   19; *see also Gnomeo and Juliet*

Atonement, film (dir. Joe Wright, 2009)   23, 43

Attenborough, Richard, film director   52, 106; *see also Shadowlands*

Atwood, Margaret, writer   50, 62

Austen, Jane, novelist   114, *119*, 129, *133*
   adaptations/biography elided   112, **116**, 151–61
   novelist and film character   4, 5, 13, 14, 15, 17, 26, 27, 52, 53, 56, 57–8, 59, 61, *63*, 90, 93, 106, 107, 109, 110–18, **116**, *119*, 128, 129, 130, 151–60, 161, *161*, *162*, *163*;
   franchise   *63*, 110–11, *120*; literary works: *Emma*   161; *Mansfield Park*   58; *Northanger Abbey*   161; *Persuasion*   151, 158, 160, 161, *161*, *162*, *163*; *Pride and Prejudice*   57, 58, 61, *63*, 111, 114, 151, 152, 154, 156, 158, 160, 161, *161*, *162*; *Sense and Sensibility*   161
   see also biopics: *Becoming Jane*; *Lost in Austen*; *Miss Austen Regrets*;
   see also film/tv adaptations: *Mansfield Park*; *The Lake House*; *Northanger Abbey*; *Persuasion*; *Pride and Prejudice*; *Sense and Sensibility*

Auster, Paul, novelist and film director   38–40, 43, *48*; *see also Smoke*, film

auteur   25, 58, 78–81, 85, 86–7, 89, *90*, 91, 166, 167, *175*, 179, 182, 183, *215*

author-function   19, 223

autobiography   26, *31*, 54, 56, 60, 79, 86, 87, *104*, *133*, 137, 140, 141, 144, 146, 148, 152, 153, 154, *161*, *163*

Bacon, Francis, writer and philosopher *104*; *see also Master Shakespeare, Strolling Player*; *Master Will Shakespeare*

Barrett, Elizabeth, poet and film character   51; *see also The Barretts of Wimpole Street*

Barretts of Wimpole Street, The, film (dir. Sidney Franklin, 1934)   51–2

Barrie, J.M, writer   4, 106, 107, 109, 113; *see also Finding Neverland*

Barthes, Roland, theorist and critic   17–18, 19, 20, *31*, 106, 157, 191, 223

Barton Fink, film (dirs. Joel and Ethan
  Coen, 1991)   42, 126, 165
Bates, Kathy, film director   52; *see also
  Dash and Lilly*
Bazin, André, film theorist   51, 62, *63*,
  78, 157, 161, *162*, 213, 214, *217*
Becoming Jane, film (dir. Julian Jarrold,
  2007)   **2**, 5, 13–14, 15, 24, 27, 51,
  52, 53, 56, 57–60, 90, *103*, 106, 107,
  109, 110–18, **116**, *119*, *120*, 128,
  129–30, 153–7, **155**, 158, 159, 160,
  162
Being John Malkovich, film (dir. Spike
  Jonze, 1999)   164, 168, 170, 176
Bennett, Alan, playwright   175, *177*
Bentley, Thomas, film director and
  actor   36, *47–8*, 92, 97; *see also Old
  Bill Through the Ages*
Bernanos, Georges, writer   206, 208
Bernhardt, Curtis, film director   52;
  see also Devotion
biography, literary   4, 13, 15,18, 26,
  27, *30*, *31*, *32*, 46, 55, 57, *63*, 64,
  76, 77, 81–2, 84, *90*, *102*, *104*, 110,
  114, 121–33, *133*, 137–8, 141, *150*,
  151–2, 156, 161, *162*, 230, *234*,
  235; in film   27, 46, 52, 54, 65, 70,
  103, *104*, 110, 117, 142, 149, 154,
  157, 159, 220, 222, 224; *see also*
  autobiography; biopics
biopics   3–6, 13–14, 17, 22, 24, 25, 26,
  31, 47, 50, 51, 52–3, 54, 58, 62, *63*,
  65, 81, 86, 90, 93, 106–18, 121–33,
  151, 153–4, 155–8, *162*;
  see also examples: *An Angel at my
  Table*; *Anonymous*; *The Barretts of
  Wimpole Street*; *Barton Fink*; *Becoming
  Jane*; *Bright Star*; *Byron*; *Capote*;
  Carrington; *Cross Creek*; *Dash and
  Lilly*; *Devotion*; *The Edge of Love*;
  Enid; *Finding Neverland*; *Gothic*;
  Hedd Wyn; *The Hours*; *The Immortal
  Gentleman*; *Iris*; *Julia*; *The Libertine*;
  The Life of Shakespeare; *Master Will
  Shakespeare*; *Miss Austen Regrets*; *Miss
  Potter*; *Nora*; *Pandaemonium*; *The
  Passion of Ayn Rand*; *Pull My Daisy*;
  Quills; *Shadowlands*; *Shakespeare in
  Love*; *Stevie*; *Sylvia*; *Time Flies*; *Time
  Regained*; *Vigo, Passion for Life*; *Wilde*

Blyton, Enid, film character   10–12, **11**,
  13; writer   12, 31, 52; *see also Enid*
Bollywood   152, *163*
Bonham Carter, Helena, film actor:
  cover image   10–12, **11**, 13
Branagh, Kenneth, actor and film
  director: *see Mary Shelley's
  Frankenstein*
Brecht, Bertolt, playwright   121, *133*
Bresson, Robert, film director   5, 29,
  80–1, 206–15, *216*, *217*
Bride and Prejudice, film (dir. Gurinder
  Chadha, 2004)   111, 152–3
Bridget Jones's Diary, film (dir. Sharon
  Maguire, 2001)   111, 112, 119, 162
Bridget Jones: The Edge of Reason, film
  (dir. Beenan Kidron, 2004)   119,
  160
Bright Star, film (dir. Jane Campion,
  2009)   3, 5, 6, 14, 25, 53, 77–8,
  80–90, **83**, *91*, *103*, 106, 107, 109,
  128, 129–30, 154
British Broadcasting Corporation (BBC):
  see tv
Brontës, novelists   31, 52, 163;
  Charlotte Brontë   17, *32*, 160–1,
  163; *see also Jane Eyre*, novel;
  Devotion
Brooke, Arthur, poet   102
Browning, Robert, poet and film
  character   51; *see also The Barretts of
  Wimpole Street*
Buchanan, Judith   *30*, *47*, *97*, 100, *104*,
  185, 192
Burt, Richard   154, 162, 190
Byron, film (dir. Julian Farino, 2003)   53
Byron, Lord, poet   9, 15–16, 24, 64–5,
  66, 69, 72, 74, 75, *75*, *76*; images
  of   6, 9, *30*, *31*; and the Romantic
  poets   52, 77, 81; *see also Byron*;
  Gothic

Cage, Nicholas, film actor   41, 164,
  169, 171
Campion, Jane, film director   25,
  60, *63*, 78, 79–81, 85, 87, 89, 90,
  91,103; *see also An Angel at my
  Table*; *Bright Star*; *In the Cut*
Capote, film (dir. Bennett Miller,
  2007)   53

Capote, Truman, writer   4, 244; *see also Capote*, film

Carlyle, Thomas, Scottish essayist   26, *32*

Carrington, film (dir. Christopher Hampton, 1995)   107, 109

Cartmell, Deborah   111, 112, 119, 161, 163

co-authorship: *see* multiple authorship

Coen, Joel and Ethan, film directors   42, 126, 165; *see also Barton Fink*

Coleridge, Samuel, life   125, *133*; poetry, 88–9; and Romantic poets   77, 87; *see also Lyrical Ballads; Pandaemonium*

Confessions of a Dangerous Mind, film (dir. George Clooney, 2002)   170

Cornish, Abbie, film actor   14, 82, **83**; *see also Bright Star*

Craig, Daniel, film actor   14, 65, 67, **68**, 71

credit sequence: *see* title sequences

Cronenberg, David, film director   46, 167, 176; *see also Naked Lunch*

Cross Creek, film (dir. Martin Ritt, 1983)   52

Cumming, Laura, art critc   22, *31*

Daldry, Stephen, film director   52, *103*, 106, 126, 154; *see also The Hours*

Darwin, Charles, naturalist   4

Das Leben Der Anderen, film: *see The Lives of Others*

Dash and Lilly, film (dir. Kathy Bates, 1999); 14, 52

David Copperfield, film (dir. George Cukor, 1935)   36–7, *48*

Davis, Judy, film actor   54, 55

de Vere, Edward, 17th Earl of Oxford   4; *see also Anonymous*

Death of the Author, The, essay: *see* Barthes, Roland

Deleuze, Gilles, philosopher   194

DeMille, Cecil B, film director   *190*, 212, 214; *see also The Ten Commandments*

Depp, Johnny, film actor   113

desks   **2**, 4, 5, 7, **8**, 9, 17, 25, *31*, 36, 56, 92–102, 98, **99**, 128, 130, **155**, 159, 199, 200, 201, 211, 212, 218–19, **219**, 220 ; table-book (Early Modern)   93, 96, 102; *see also* writing implements; writing spaces

Devotion, film (dir. Curtis Bernhardt, 1946)   52

diaries   5, 29, 112, 154, 159, 206, 221; *see also* films: *Bridget Jones' Diary; Bridget Jones, The Edge of Reason; The End of the Affair; Journal d'un curé de campagne; Pickpocket*; and diarists: Frank, Anne; Garton Ash, Timothy; Pepys, Samuel

Diary of a Country Priest or *Journal d'un curé de campagne* (dir. Robert Bresson, 1951) film   5–6, 28–9, 206–15, *215–17*

Dickens, Charles, novelist   22, 23, *32*, 36–8, *47*, 48, 125, *133*, 138; *see also* films: *David Copperfield; Dickens' London; Great Expectations; Leaves from the Books of Charles Dicken; Oliver Twist; A Tale of Two Cities*

Dickens' London, film (dir. Frank Miller and Harry B. Parkinson, 1924)   36, *47*

digital, -age   121; 'digital turn', the   24, 121; -documents   24, 180; -filmmaking   24, 99, 178, 184, 187, *204, 234*; shift from analogue to   44, 187

Doctor Who, 'The Shakespeare Code', tv episode (dir. Charlie Palmer, 2007)   19, *31*

Donnersmarck, Florian Henckel von, film director   **2**, 5, 29, 218, **219**, 223, **225**, **228**, 233, *234*; *see also The Lives of Others*

Dostoevsky, Fyodor, novelist   206, *249*

Dunmore, Laurence, film director   53, 113, 131, 132, 133; *see also The Libertine*

Edge of Love, The, film (dir. John Maybury, 2008)   24, 64–7, 69–75, **76**, 107

Eisenstein, Sergei, film director and theorist   *191*

Eliot, T.S, poet   4, 107, 132; *see also Tom and Viv*

Emmerich, Roland, film director   19, *105*, 156; *see also Anonymous*

End of the Affair, The, film (dir. Neil
Jordan, 1999) 5
Enders, Robert, film director 53;
see also Stevie
Enid, film (dir. James Hawes, 2009) 6,
10–12, **11**, 13, 14, *31*, 52
Epstein, Rob, film director 2, 5, 6, 12,
13, 23, 44, 46; *see also Howl*
estates, literary 125, *133*
Eternal Sunshine of the Spotless Mind, film
(dir. Michael Gondry, 2004) 168,
170
Etherege, George, playwright 130, 131,
132, *133*
Eyre, Richard, theatre and film
director 61; *see also Iris*

Farewell to Arms, A, film (dir. Frank
Borzage, 1932) 142, 149; *see also*
Hemingway, Ernest
Farino, Julian, film director 53; *see also
Byron*, film
female audiences 26, 53, 56, 59, 68,
71, 85, 89, 106, 109
female authorship 24, 50–62, **54**,
62–63, 77, 84, 89–90, 114, 151, 183,
204, *256*
feminism 50–60, 62, 73, 80, 117, *204*
Fiennes, Joseph, film actor 5, 25, 101
Fiennes, Ralph, film actor 5
Fincher, David, film director 179, *191*;
see also Se7en
Finding Neverland, film (dir. Marc Forster,
2004) 53, 107, 113, 154
Fitzgerald, F. Scott, novelist 4, 146, *150*
Flaubert, Gustave, novelist 17, 128,
133
Fonda, Jane, film actor 2, 53–4, **54**
Fontaine, Joan, film actor 198
For Whom the Bell Tolls, film (dir. Sam
Wood, 1943) 141–2, 149
Forde, Walter, film director 92, 98; *see
also Time Flies*
Forster, Marc, film director 23, 42, 53,
113, 154; *see also Finding Neverland;
Stranger than Fiction*
Foucault, Michel, theorist 18, 19, *31*
Fox Film Corporation, film production
company:; *see* Twentieth Century
Fox Film Corporation

Frame, Janet, writer 60, *63*; *see also An
Angel at my Table*
Franco, James, film actor 2, 5, **13**, 44;
see also Howl
Frank, Anne, diarist 4
Frank, Robert, film director 45; *see also
Pull My Daisy*
Franklin, Sidney, film director 51;
see also The Barretts of Wimpole Street
Franklin, Stella Miles, writer and film
character 54–6, *63*; *see also My
Brilliant Career*
Freud, Sigmund 17, 124, 128, *133*
Friedman, Jeffrey, film director 2, 5, 6,
12, **13**, 23, 44, 46; *see also Howl*
Fukunaga, Cary, film director 160

Garton Ash, Timothy, historian 125,
133, 221–2, *234*
gender 24, 50–63, 64–76, 78, 81, 82,
85, 88–9, 106–7, 128, 160, 183;
see also femininity; masculinity
genre 6, 12, 14, 25, 26, *30*, 42, 51, 52,
56, 59, *63*, 79, 93, 106, 108, 109,
110, 114, 117, 118, *119*, 123, 124,
125, 126, 127, 130, 144, 154, 157,
165, 222; generic conventions and
expectations 6, 26, 51, 109, 110,
118, 124; literary biography 123,
125, 126, 127; *see also* biopics;
Bollywood
Gielgud, John, actor 2, 5, 25, 99, **99**,
104, 185, 186; *see also Prospero's
Books*
Gilbert, Brian, film director 53, 106,
108, 130; *see also Tom and Viv;
Wilde*
Ginsberg, Allen, poet and film
character 4, 5, 12, **13**, 14, 31,
44–5, 46, 47, *48*; *see also Howl; Pull
My Daisy*
Globe, The, playhouse 19–20, 96, 98
Gnomeo and Juliet, film (dir. Kelly
Asbury, 2011) 19
Gondry, Michael, film director 167,
168, 170; *see also Eternal Sunshine of
the Spotless Mind; Human Nature*
Gothic, film (dir. Ken Russell, 1986) 52
Graham-Wilcox Productions, film
production company *47*

Great Expectations, film (dir. David Lean, 1946) 36–8

Greenaway, Peter, film director **2**, 5, 25, 28, *30*, 92, **99**, 100, 101, *104*, 178, 182, 184, 185, **186**, **187**, 190, *191*, *192*; *see also Prospero's Books*

Griffith, D.W., film director 37; *see also Orphans of the Storm; Way Down East*

Growcott, Frank R., film director *104*; *see also The Life of William Shakespeare*

Gunning, Tom, film critic and historian 196, *204*

Hall, Edward, anthropologist 218

Hamlet, play: *see* Shakespeare, William

Hammett, Dashiell, writer 4; *see also Dash and Lilly*

Hampton, Christopher, writer and film director 43, 109; *see also Atonement; Carrington*

Hardy, Thomas, novelist and poet 125, *133*

Hannah, John, film actor 78

Hathaway, Anne, film actor 5, 13, 57, 58, 112–17, **116**, 128, 154–5, **155**, 160

Hawes, James, film director 6, 10, *31*, 52; *see also Enid*

Hedd Wyn, film (dir. Paul Turner, 1992) 107

Heidegger, Martin, philosopher 167, *176*,

Hellman, Lillian, writer 4, 53, **54**; *see also Julia; Dash and Lilly*

Hemingway, Ernest, writer 26, 27, 137, 138–9, 140–9, 145, *150*, 156; film character (implicitly) **145**; literary works: *Across the River and Into the Trees* 141; *The Breaking Point* 141; *The End of Something* 142; *A Farewell to Arms* 139, 140, 141, 142, 143, 149; *For Whom the Bell Tolls* 139, 143; *Islands in the Stream* 139, 148–9, *150*; *Movable Feast* 141, 150; *My Old Man* 147; *The Old Man and the Sea* 146, 148; *The Short Happy Life of Francis Macomber* 141; *The Snows of Kilimanjaro* 142–3, 143, 144, 146,

147, 150; *The Sun Also Rises* 140, 142, 143, 144; *Under my Skin* 141; *see also* films: *A Farewell to Arms*; *Islands in the Stream*; *Hemingway's Adventures of a Young Man*; *The Snows of Kilimanjaro*

Hemingway's Adventures of a Young Man, film (dir. Martin Ritt, 1962) 27, 142

Higson, Andrew *63*, *118*, *119*

Hobbes, Thomas, philosopher *103*

Hours, The, film (dir. Stephen Daldry, 2002) 52, 61, 103, 106, 107, 113, 126, 130, 154

Howl, film (dir. Rob Epstein and Jeffrey Friedman) **2**, 5, 6, 12–**13**, 14, 23–4, *31*, 44–47, *48*, *49*

Howl, poem: *see* Ginsberg, Allen

Hughes, Ted, poet 61, 65, 70, 72, 73, 74; *see also Sylvia*

Human Nature, film (dir. Michael Gondry, 2001) 168, 170

Ifans, Rhys, film actor 156

illustration 6, 12, **13**, 20–2, *21*, *31*, 36, 37, 44, *47*; *see also* animation; *Howl*; *Miss Potter*; Potter, Beatrix; portraiture, statuary

Immortal Gentleman, The, film (dir. Widgey R. Newman, 1935) 92, 94–5, 98

In The Cut, film (dir. Jane Campion, 2003) 80

intertextuality 59, *63*, 152, *162*

Iris, film (dir. Richard Eyre, 2001) 14, 24, 51, 52, 53, 61–62, *63*, 106, 107, 154

Islands in the Stream, film (dir. Franklin J. Schaffner, 1977) 27, 142, 148–50

Jane Eyre, film (dir. Cary Fukunaga, 2011) 160

Jane Eyre, novel 161, *163*; *see also* Brontës

Jarrold, Julian, film director **2**, 5, 24, 51, 52, 57, 90, *103*, 106, 114, 115, *119*, 128, 153, **155**; *see also Becoming Jane*

Jeffs, Christine, film director 14, 52, 65, **68**, 71, 72, 73, 90, 106, 130, 154; *see also Sylvia*

Johnson, Samuel, writer   130, 131, *133,*
134
Jonson, Ben, poet and playwright
20–2, **21,** 94, 95, *103,* 186;
film character   94; *see also*
films: *Anonymous; The Immortal*
Gentleman
Jonze, Spike, film director   170, 171;
see also Adaptation; Being John
Malkovich
Jordan, Neil, film director   5; *see also*
The End of the Affair
Journal d'un curé de campagne, film:
see Diary of a Country Priest
Joyce, James, writer and film character:
see Nora
Julia, film (dir. Fred Zinnemann,
1977)   **2,** 24, 52, 53–4, **54,** *63*

Kaufman, Charlie, screenwriter and
film director   4, 26, 27, 41–2,
164–5, 166–75, **169,** *176, 177*
(semi-)fictional character   27,
41–2, 164–5, 168–75, **169;**
'Kaufmanesque', The   *176; see also*
films: *Adaptation; Eternal Sunshine*
of the Spotless Mind; Synecdoche,
New York
Kaufman, Philip, film director   53;
see also Quills
Keats, John, poet   3, 4, 5, 14, 16,
24, 25, *31,* 77, 78, 80, 81–5, **83,**
88–90, *91,* 93, 107, 128, 129; film
character   3, 5, 14, 16, 78, 81–5,
83, 88–90, *91,* 128, 129; poetic
works: 'Endymion': 129; 'La Belle
Dame sans Merci': 129; 'Ode to a
Nightingale': 129; *see also Bright*
Star
Kerouac, Jack, novelist   45, 46
Kidman, Nicole, film actor   61, 113;
see also The Hours
Kidron, Beenan, film director   *119,*
160; *see also Bridget Jones: The Edge*
of Reason
King, Henry, film director   27, 142,
143, **145;** *see also* films: *The Snows of*
Kilimanjaro; The Sun Also Rises
Knightley, Keira, film actor   43, 65, 71,
72, 152, 153

Koch, Sebastian, film actor   5, 218, **219,**
225, 228
Kundera, Milan, novelist   137–8, *150*

Lacan, Jacques, theorist   *204*
Lake House, The, film (dir. Alejandro
Agresti, 2006)   160, *163*
Lang, Fritz, film director   *204*
Lean, David, film director   36, 37–8,
160; *see also Great Expectations;*
Oliver Twist
Leaves from the Books of Charles Dickens,
film (dir. unknown, 1912)   *47–8*
Les dames du Bois de Boulogne, film
(dir. Robert Bresson, 1945)   206
Leslie, Alfred, film director   45; *see also*
Pull My Daisy
Letter, The, film (dir. William Wyler,
1940)   *204*
Letter from an Unknown Woman, film
(dir. Max Ophüls, 1948)   28,
195–203
Letter from an unknown woman, novella;
see Zweig, Stefan
Letter to Three Wives, A, film (dir. Joseph
L. Mankiewicz, 1949)   28, 195–98,
201–2
letters, on screen   28, 42, 43, 58, 84–5,
128, 151, *161,* 193–203, *204,* 206,
213, 214, 224; real   *31, 32,* 58,
84–5, *91,* 114, *119,* 127, 129, 132,
151, 194, *204; see also* films: *The*
Letter; Letter from an Unknown
Woman; A Letter to Three Wives
Lewis, C.S, writer   4, 106, 107; *see also*
Shadowlands
Libertine, The, film (dir. Laurence
Dunmore, 2004)   53, 107, 113,
130–33, *134*
Life of Shakespeare, The, film (dir. Frank
Growcott and J.B. Macdowell,
1914)   *104*
Lives of Others, The, or *Das Leben Der*
Anderen, film (dir. Florian Henckel
von Donnersmarck, 2006)   **2,** 5, 17,
29, 218–33, **219, 225, 228,** *234*
Lloyd, Frank, film director   **2,** 227, **229;**
see also A Tale of Two Cities, film
Lost in Austen, tv mini-series (dir. Jeremy
Lovering, 2008)   158, 160, *162*

Lovering, Jeremy, film director 52, 59, 111, 130; *see also Miss Austen Regrets*

Luhrmann, Baz, film director 15, 170; *see also William Shakespeare's Romeo + Juliet; Moulin Rouge!*

Lyrical Ballads 88; *see also* Coleridge, Samuel; Wordsworth, William

Macdowell, J.B., film director *104*; *see also The Life of William Shakespeare*

Madden, John, film director 5, 25, 53, 58, 92, 101, *103*, 106, 126, 154, **156**; *see also Shakespeare in Love*

Maguire, Sharon, film director 112, *119*, *162*; *see also Bridget Jones' Diary*

Mamet, David, writer and film director 165; *see also State and Main*

Man of Mode, The, play: *see* Etherege, George

Mankiewicz, Joseph L., film director 28, 195, *204*; *see also A Letter to Three Wives*

Mansfield Park, film (dir. Patricia Rozema, 1999) 24, 51, 52, 58–59, 112, 113, 115, **116**, 157; film (dir. Iain B. MacDonald, 2007) 115, 244; *see also* Austen, Jane

manuscripts **20**, 28, 42, 44, 56, 74, 101, *103*, 129, 178, 185, 186–9, **186**, **187**, **189**, 200, 212, **229**

marketing 14–15, 20, 22, 24, 25, 26, 52–3, 56, 59, 61–2, *63*, 65, 71–2, 73, 79–80, 81, 89, 106, 107–9, 110, 111, 112, 113, 114, 117, 118, *119*, 123, 142, 154–5, 156, 158, 162, 226, 231–2; and *auterism* 79–80, 81; crossover audiences 109, 113; design 154; distribution 26, 79, 113; DVD 56, 61–2, *63*, *119*, *162*; film titles 14–15, 25, 52–3, 61, 65, 106–7, 110, 111, 142, 158; for female audiences 26, 56, 59, 71, 89, 106–7, 109; for 'middlebrow' audiences 26, 59, 107, 109, 110, 113, 114, 117; and literary authorship 112; 'literate film', the 107–9, 112, 113, 114,

117, 118, 154; posters 71–2, 73, *119*, 154–5, 156, 226, 231–2; taglines 52, 56, 59, 109, 113

Mary Shelley's Frankenstein, film (dir. Kenneth Branagh, 1994) 111

masculinity 15, 24, *63*, 64–75, *76*, 87

Master Shakespeare, Strolling Player, film (dir. Frederick Sullivan, 1916) *104*

Master Will Shakespeare, short film (dir. Jacques Tourneur, 1936) *103*

Maybury, John, film director 65, 71; *see also The Edge of Love*

McAvoy, James, film actor 43, 57, 114, **116**, 154–5

Méliès, Georges, early filmmaker 7–10, **8**, 23, 35, 92, 97; *see also Shakespeare Writing Julius Caesar* or *Shakespeare Écrivant La Mort de Jules César*

Méliès Star Film, film production company 35, 97

Melville, Herman, writer 197, 201

Menaul, Christopher, film director 52; *see also The Passion of Ayn Rand*

Metro-Goldwyn-Mayer (MGM), film production company *48*, 51, *103*

Midnight in Paris, film (dir. Woody Allen, 2010) 141, *150*

Miller, Bennett, film director 53; *see also Capote*

Miller, Frank, film director 36, *47*; *see also Dickens' London*

Milton, John, poet 130, 131

Minghella, Anthony, film director 71; *see also The Talented Mr. Ripley*

Miramax, film production company 57, 119, 133, **155**, **156**

Mirren, Helen, film actor 183

Miss Austen Regrets, tv film (dir. Jeremy Lovring, 2008) 24, 52, 53, 59–60, 111, 130, 151, 158

Miss Potter, film (dir. Chris Noonan, 2006) 5, 24, 51, 52, 53, 56–7, 90, 106, 107, 109, 113, 154

montage **11**, 86, 94, 101, 102, 184

Moore, Tomm, film director 28, 178, **188**; *see also The Secret of Kells*

Moulin Rouge!, film (dir. Baz Luhrmann, 2001) 170

Mühe, Ulrich, film actor **2**, **219**, 220, **225**; *see also The Lives of Others*

multiple authorship, co-authorship,
collaboration   27–8, *31*, 77, 79,
80, 84–5, 88, 90, *90*, *91*, 92, 93, 95,
98, *103*, 132–3, 141, 157, 165, 166,
167, 179, 183, 184, 230; collective
creativity   77, 79, 83–90, 97, 130,
166; *see also* The Romantic Poets
Murdoch, Iris, writer   4, 61, 107;
see also Iris
Murphy, Pat, film director   53, 130;
see also Nora
music   12–13, **13**, *31*, 43, 44, 45, 50, 61,
63, 74, 84, 86, 87, 121, 128, 132,
156, 170, 181–2, 183, *191*, 199, 210,
211; depicted graphically   12–13,
13, 44; film   43, 63, 74, 156,
181–82, 183, *191*, 210, 211; music
videos   86, 132
My Brilliant Career, film (dir. Gillian
Armstrong, 1979)   24, 51, 52,
54–56, 59, *63*

Naked Lunch, film (dir. David
Cronenberg, 1991)   46
Newman, Widgey R., film director   92,
94, 95; *see also The Immortal
Gentleman*
Noonan, Chris, film director   5, 24, 51,
52, 56, 90, 106; *see also Miss Potter*
Nora, film (dir. Pat Murphy, 2000)   53,
130
North, Julian   *90*
Northanger Abbey, film (dir. Jon Jones,
2007)   159; *see also* Austen, Jane.

O'Connor, Frances, film actor   58, 112,
113, **116**, 157
Old Bill Through the Ages, film (dir.
Thomas Bentley, 1924)   92, 97–8
Oliver Twist, film (dir. David Lean,
1948)   27
On the Road, novel; *see* Kerouac, Jack
One Day, film (dir. Lone Scherfig,
2011)   160
Ophüls, Max, film director   28, 195,
197, 198, 200, 203
Orphans of the Storm, film (dir.
D.W. Griffiths, 1921)   37
Out of Africa, film (dir. Sydney Pollack,
1985)   52

Paltrow, Gwyneth, film actor   65, **68**,
71, 113; *see also Shakespeare in Love*;
Sylvia
Pandaemonium, film (dir. Julien Temple,
2000)   25, 53, 77–8, 86–90, *91*,
107
Paramount Pictures, film studio   *217*
paratexts   28, 37, 137, *175*, 178–92,
190, *191*, *192*, *195*; *see also* title
sequences
Parker, Dorothy, writer   4
Parkinson, Harry B, film director   36,
47; *see also Dickens' London*
Passion of Ayn Rand, The, film
(dir. Christopher Menaul, 1999)   52
Pepys, Samuel, diarist   131; *see also
Stage Beauty*
Persuasion, film (dir. Roger Michell,
1995)   115, 158, 159; film
(dir. Adrian Shergold, 2007)   158,
159–60; *see also* Austen, Jane
Persuasion, novel: *see* Austen, Jane
Piper, Billie, film actor   115
Plath, Sylvia, poet and film
character   4, 61, 65, 70, 73, 74, 76,
107; *see also Sylvia*
poetry   3, 12, 14, 15–16, 20–1, **21**,
21–2, *31*, 44–7, *48*, *49*, 65, 68–9,
71–5, *76*, 81, 82, 84–5, 87, 88–9,
102, 129, 131–2, 144, 159, 166,
170, *176*, 185–6, **186**, 207; *see also*
Byron, Lord; Coleridge, Samuel
Taylor; Ginsberg, Allen; Hemingway,
Ernest; Hughes, Ted; Jonson, Ben;
Keats, John; Plath, Sylvia; Shelley,
Percy Bysshe; Thomas, Dylan;
Wilmot, John (Earl of Rochester);
Wordsworth, William
Pollack, Sydney, film director   52;
see also Out of Africa
PolyGram Filmed Entertainment, film
studio   *118*
portraiture, literary   6, 9, 15–16, 20–2,
21, *30*, *31*, *32*, 51, 96, 101, 123,
158; *see also* illustration; statuary
postmodernism   28, 52, *63*, 99, 101,
105, 164, 170, 207
Potter, Beatrix, writer and illustrator and
film character   4, 5, 56, 57, 106,
107, 109, 113; *see also Miss Potter*

Potter, Sally, film director   *91*
Price, Fanny, fictional character and
   authorial proxy   58–9, 112, 113,
   116, 157; *see also Mansfield Park,*
   film; Austen, Jane
Pride and Prejudice, BBC serialisation
   (dir. Simon Langton, 1995)   111,
   159; BBC mini-series (dir. Cyril
   Coke, 1980)   153; film (dir. Joe
   Wright, 2005)   71, 111, 152–3, 157,
   159, 160, *161, 162*; film (dir. Robert
   Z. Leonard, 1940)   152, 153;
   see also Austen, Jane
Pride and Prejudice, novel; *see* Austen,
   Jane
Pride and Prejudice: A Latter-Day Comedy,
   film (dir. Andrew-Black, 2003)   111,
   112
Prospero, Shakespearean character and
   authorial proxy   5, 25, 99, **99**,
   104, 185, 186; *see also* Gielgud,
   John; *Prospero's Books*; Shakespeare,
   William; *The Tempest*, film
Prospero's Books, film (dir. Peter
   Greenaway, 1991)   **2**, 5, 25, 27–8,
   30, 92, **99**, 99–102, *104*, 178,
   184–87, **186**, **187**, *191*, 192
Proust, Marcel, writer and film
   character   5, 166, *175*, 196–7, *204*,
   209, 221; *see also Time Regained*
publishing   18, 20–1, 44, 45, 56, 62, 95,
   122, 124, 125, 131, 132, 140, 144,
   148, 165–6, 172, 179, 180, 186, 198;
   in film   44, 56, 112, 224
Pull My Daisy, film (dir. Alfred Leslie and
   Robert Frank, 1959)   45
puzzle films   *176; see also* Kaufman,
   Charlie

Quills, film (dir. Philip Kaufman,
   2000)   53

Rand, Ayn, writer   4; *see also The
   Passion of Ayn Rand*
Rawlings, Marjorie Kinnan,
   novelist   52; *see also Cross Creek*
Renaissance, The   30, 98, 99, *103,
   104, 190; see also* Jonson, Ben;
   Shakespeare, William
Rhys, Matthew, film actor   65, 71

Ritt, Martin, film director   27, 52, 142;
   see also Cross Creek
Roache, Linus, film actor   78, 87
Romeo and Juliet, play: *see* Shakespeare,
   William
Roth, Philip, novelist   139–40
Rozema, Patricia, film director   58, 59;
   see also Mansfield Park, film
Ruiz, Raoul, film director   5; *see also
   Time Regained*
Russell, Ken, film director   52; *see also
   Gothic*

Scherfig, Lone, film director   160
screenwriting   4, 5, 27–8, 41–3, 56, 84,
   126, 132, 142–7, 150, 154, 164–76,
   179, 183, 185, 197
Se7en, film (dir. David Fincher, 1995)
   179, *191*
Secret of Kells, The, film (dir. Tom
   Moore)   28, 178, 187–90, **188**, **189**,
   191
Sense and Sensibility, film (dir. Ang Lee,
   1995)   58, 111, 162
Shadowlands, film (dir. Richard
   Attenborough, 1993)   52, 53, 106,
   107, 109
*Shakespeare Écrivant La Mort de Jules
   César*, film: *see Shakespeare Writing
   Julius Caesar*
Shakespeare in Love, film (dir. John
   Madden, 1998)   5, 14, 25, 53, 58,
   71, 92, 94, 98, 101–102, *103, 105*,
   106, 107, 108, 109, 110, 113, 117,
   119, 126, 130, 154–156, **156**, 158,
   162
Shakespeare, William, playwright   4, 6,
   7, 17, 19, 20, 21–3, 25, *31, 32*, 60,
   74, 92–6, 97, 98, 99, 100, 102, *103,
   104*, 106, 107, 109, 112, 154, 155–6,
   162, 170, *176*, 178, 182, 184–5, *191,
   192*;
   film character   4, 5, 7–10, **8**, 14,
   19–22, **20**, 23, 25, *30*, 35–6, *47*, 58,
   92–5, 97–102, **99**, *103, 104*, 107, 113,
   126, 130, 155, **156**, *162*, 184–6, *192*;
   First Folio   6, 20–22, **21**, 100, 184–6,
   186, *192*;
   on silent film   **2**, 7–10, **8**, 12, 23, *30,
   32*, 35–6, *47*, 92, 97–8, *104*;

Shakespeare, William,
  playwright – *continued*
  dramatic works: *As You Like It* 176;
    Hamlet 94, 96, *103*; *Henry V* 19;
    Love's Labours Lost 19; *The
    Merchant of Venice* 94; *Romeo
    and Juliet* 19, 94, 98, 102, 154;
    The Tempest 5, 99, *104*, 178,
    182, 184–5, 186, *191*, *192*; *Titus
    Andronicus 104*; *The Taming of
    the Shrew* 94; *Twelfth Night* 94,
    95, 154; *The Two Gentlemen of
    Verona* 96, *103*;
  see also films/tv: *Doctor Who: The
    Shakespeare Code*; *Gnomeo and
    Juliet*; *Prospero's Books*; *The Tempest*;
    William Shakespeare's Romeo + Juliet;
    Shakespeare in Love; *Shakespeare Writing
    Julius Caesar*; biopics: *Anonymous;
    The Immortal Gentleman; The Life of
    Shakespeare; Old Bill Through the Ages;
    Master Shakespeare, Strolling Player;
    Master Will Shakespeare; Shakespeare in
    Love; Shakespeare Writing Julius Caesar;
    Time Flies*
Shakespeare Writing Julius Caesar or
  *Shakespeare Écrivant La Mort de Jules
  César*, film (dir. Georges Méliès,
  1907) 7–10, **8**, 12, 23, *30*, 35–6,
  47, 92, 97
Shelley, Mary, writer 52, 111, 130;
  see also Mary Shelley's Frankenstein
Shelley, Percy Bysshe, poet 52, 77
Sherman, William H. 180, *190*
silent-era cinema **2**, 7–10, **8**, *30*, *32*,
  35–6, 38–9, *47*, 97–8, *104*, 227,
  229–30, **229**; *see also Dickens'
  London*; *Leaves from the Books
  of Charles Dickens*; *The Life of
  Shakespeare*; *Master Shakespeare,
  Strolling Player*; *Old Bill Through
  the Ages*; *Shakespeare Writing Julius
  Caesar*; *A Tale of Two Cities*
Sleeping Beauty, film (dir. Clyde
  Geronimi, 1959) 180–1, **181**, 189,
  192; *see also* animaation
Smoke, film (dir. Paul Auster and Wayne
  Wang, 1995) 40–1
smoking, as part of literary process 5,
  53, **54**, 126

Snows of Kilimanjaro, The, film
  (dir. Henry King, 1952) 27, 142,
  144–148, **145**
Spall, Rafe, film actor 20, **20**; *see also
  Anonymous*
Stage Beauty, film (dir. Richard Eyre,
  2004) 108, *118*
State and Main, film (dir. David Mamet,
  2000) 165
statuary 9, 17, 19, 22–3, *32*, 36, 97,
  128, 203
Stevie, film (dir. Robert Enders,
  1978) 53
Strachey, Lytton, writer 107, 124–5;
  see also Carrington
Stranger than Fiction, film (dir. Marc
  Forster, 2006) 23, 42
Stein, Gertrude, novelist 4, *150*
Stewart, Patrick, film actor 19
Stolen Kisses, film (dir. François Truffaut,
  1968) 28, 193–4
Streep, Meryl, film actor 41, 52, 165;
  see also Adaptation
studios, film production houses and
  commercial brands *90*, 143, 165,
  179, 182, *191*
study: *see* writing spaces
Sullivan, Frederick, film director *104*;
  *see also Master Shakespeare, Strolling
  Player*
Sun Also Rises, The, film (dir. Henry
  King, 1957) 143
Sunset Boulevard, film (dir. Billy Wilder,
  1950) 165
Sylvia, film (dir. Christine Jeffs,
  2003) 14, 24, 52, 53, 61, 64–75,
  68, 90, 106, 107, 130, 154
Synecdoche, New York, film (dir. Charlie
  Kaufman, 2009) 167, 168

table: *see* desks; writing spaces
table-book (Early Modern): *see* desks
Tale of Two Cities, A, film (dir. Frank
  Lloyd, 1917) **2**, 227–30, **229**
Talented Mr. Ripley, The, film (dir.
  Anthony Minghella, 1999) 71
Taymor, Julie, film director 28, 178,
  182–4, **183**, 190, *191*, *192*; as
  auteur 183, 184, *192*; *see also The
  Tempest*, film

television: *see* tv

Tempest, The, film (dir. Julie Taymor, 2010)   28, 178, 182–5, **183**, *191*

Tempest, The, play: *see* Shakespeare, William

Temple, Julien, film director   25, 53, 77, 88, *91;* as *auteur*   78, 86–7, 89, 90; *see also The Filth and the Fury*; *Pandaemonium*; *Vigo, Passion for Life*

Ten Commandments, The, film (dir. Cecil B. DeMille, 1956)   *190*

Thanhouser Film Corporation, film production company   *104*

Thomas, Dylan, poet and film character   4, 24, 65, 66–7, 69, 70–1, 72, 73–4, 75, 106, 107; *see also The Edge of Love*

Time Flies, film (dir. Walter Forde, 1944)   92, 98

Time Regained, film (dir. Raoul Ruiz, 1999)   5

title sequences   23, 28, 37, 41, 42, 43, 44, 58, 59, 89, 129, 178–90, **181**, **183**, **186**, **187**, **188**, **189**, *190*, *192*, 195, 210, 211, 214; *see also* paratexts

To Have and Have Not, film (dir. John Huston, 1944)   141, 149

Tom and Viv, film (dir. Brian Gilbert, 1994)   14, 106, 109, 130

Tom Jones, novel   130

Tourneur, Jacques, film director: *see Master Will Shakespeare*

Truffaut, François, film director   28, 78, 193, 194, 202; *see also Stolen Kisses*

tv   19, 52, 59, 61, 64, 67, 71, 86, 111, 115, 151, 153, 158–9, *162*, 187; British Broadcasting Corporation (BBC)   19, 52, 59, 61, 64, 67, 71, 86, 111, 115, 151, 153, 158–9, *162*, 187; Independent Television (ITV)   115; tv series   64, 111, 153, 158–9

Twentieth Century Fox Film Corporation, film production company   53, *63*, 142

typewriters: *see* writing implements

Universal Pictures, film production company   **156**, *191*

Vigo, Jean, film director   86; *see also Vigo, Passion for Life*

Vigo: Passion for Life, film (dir. Julien Temple, 1998)   86

voiceover   5, 36–7, 41–2, 44, 56, 74, 87, 146, 159, 164, 171, 180, *192*, 193, 195–6, 197, 200–1, *204*, 210, 211, 212, *217*

Wager, Tony, film actor   37

Warner Bros. Pictures, film production company   52

Way Down East, film (dir. D.W. Griffiths, 1920)   37

Whishaw, Ben, film actor   5, 14, 78, **83**, 128; *see also Bright Star*; *The Tempest*, film

Wilde, film (dir. Brian Gilbert, 1997)   53, 107, 108, 109, *119*

Wilde, Oscar, writer   106, 107, 108, 125, *133*; film character   107, 108; *see also Wilde* film

Wilder, Billy, film director   165; *see also Sunset Boulevard*

William Shakespeare's Romeo + Juliet, film (dir. Baz Luhrmann, 1995)   15

Williams, Olivia, film actor   59, 151

Wilmot, John (Earl of Rochester), poet   107, 130, 131–2, 133 *133*; film character   107, 130–3, *133*; *see also The Libertine*

Winslet, Kate, film actor   61

Wood, Sam, film director   140–41; *see also For Whom the Bell Tolls* film

Woolf, Virginia, writer   13, 16–17, 47, *49*, 50, 60, 61, *62*, 92, 93, 101, *102*, *103*, 125; film character   47, *49*; literary works: 'Great Men's Houses': 16–17, *31*; *Mrs Dalloway*   61; *Orlando*   92, 101, *102*, *103*; *A Room of One's Own*   50, 60, *62*, 93, *103*; *see also The Hours*

Wordsworth, William, poet   25, 77, 78, 81, 87–8, 107 film character   87–8 Works: 'Tintern Abbey': 88; *see also Lyrical Ballads*; *Pandaemonium*

Wright, Joe, film director   111, 152, 153, 154; *see also Pride and Prejudice* film

writer's block   7, 9, 42, 53, 147, 165,
   168
writing implements: computer   4, 5,
   43, 44, 122, 172, 187, 101, 155–6,
   186; pen   4, 5, 9, 28, *30*, 61, 92,
   94, 101, 155, 158, 159, 161, 210,
   211, 218; quill   **2**, 4, 5, **20**, 58,
   59, 100, 101, 155, 156, **156**, 186;
   typewriter   **2**, 4, 5, 10, 11, **11**,
   12, **13**, 23–4, 25, *30*, 40, 42–6, *48*,
   53, 126, **162**, 172, 218, **219**, 220,
   223, **228**
writing spaces   **2**, **8**, 9, 10, **11**, **13**, 25,
   35–6, 42, **54**, 58, 60, 93, 94–7, 98,
   99, **99**, 100–101, 102, 122, 128,

212, 218–20, **219**, 220, 227; *see also*
   desks; writing implements
Wyler, William, film director   *204*;
   see also The Letter, film

Yeats, W.B, poet   74, 125, *133*

Zeff, Dan, tv director   158; *see also*
   Lost in Austen
Zinnemann, Fred, film director   **2**, 52,
   53; *see also Julia*
Žižek, Slavoj, philosopher   198, *204*
Zweig, Stefan, writer   197, 198, 199,
   200; *Letter to an Unknown Woman*,
   novella   197–201

Printed and bound in Great Britain by
CPI Antony Rowe, Chippenham and Eastbourne